COLLECTIBLES

MARKET INDEX PRICE GUIDE

To Limited Edition Plates, Figurines, Bells, Graphics, Steins and Dolls

Edited by Susan K. Jones

Schiffer Publishing Ltd

Acknowledgments

The Collectors' Information Bureau would like to thank the following persons whose help and support have been instrumental in the creation of this book: Susan Bailen-Wittenbach, William E. Bales, Jr. of Collectors Mart, Sam Bauman of Plate World Magazine, Peter Canzone of American Artists/GBS, Louise Collins of American Bell Association, Susan K. Elliott of Plate Collector Magazine, Louise Goldstein of Globetrotter Incorporated, Jack Lowenstein of Stein Collectors International, Linda Olsen and Deborah McKinney of The Hamilton Collection, Eloise Parks of The National Association of Limited Edition Dealers, Arch Patterson of The Greenbook, Nick Procaccino and S. Michael Schnessel of The Exhumation, Carrie Reckert of The Bradford Exchange, Marge Rosenberg of Carol's Gift Shop, Peter Schiffer of Schiffer Publishing Limited and Diana Gordon Viktor.

The editor would also like to thank the following persons whose enthusiasm, dedication, hard work and encouragement have made this book possible: Catherine Bloom, Ralph Gadiel, John W. Graham, Ronald G. Gregory, Robert H. Kline, Brigitte Moore, Tom J. O'Meara, Heio W. Reich, Gene Ricks, and Paul Warden.

About the editor

Susan K. Jones has spent nearly a decade as a writer, observer, collector, and investment advisor for the limited edition collectibles field. Since 1980 she has been the owner of Susan K. Jones and Associates, a consulting and copywriting firm for direct marketers and limited edition marketers. Before that she spent more than three years as a Marketing Manager for The Hamilton Collection, and over three years as a copywriter for the advertising agency which handled writing and marketing assignments for The Bradford Exchange from 1973-75.

Today Ms. Jones serves a number of clients in the collectibles field and contributes to several collectibles publications. Since November, 1982 she has been Executive Director of COLLECTORS' INFORMATION BUREAU, and was a formative influence in the development of the organization.

Educated at Northwestern University, she holds a master's degree in advertising. She lives in East Grand Rapids, Michigan.

Library of Congress Catalog Number: 83–61660.

Designed by Ellen J. Taylor

Printed in the United States of America.
ISBN: 0-916838-85-4.
Published by Schiffer Publishing Ltd., Box E, Exton, Pennsylvania 19341

Table of contents

Acknowledgments ii
About the editor ii
Foreword 4
A word from the members of the Collectors' Information Bureau 5
Why do people collect...and what is collectible? 7
How to begin, develop and improve your collection 9
A brief survey of plate collecting: 1895 — Today 15
The market for limited edition figurines: An overview 33
An introduction to bells for limited edition collectors 35
An introduction to graphics for the collector 37
Classic German steins inspire contemporary collecting hobby 43
Limited edition marketers expand the popular market for collectible dolls 45
How to decorate with limited edition collectibles 51
Anna-Perenna captures the beauty of Europe's "Island of Flowers" on a collection of fine porcelain plates...The Flowers of Count Bernadotte 57
Porcelain and patinated bronze — a unique art concept from the Boehm Studios 60
Carmel Collection showcases top artists via collector plate medium 63
Yes, collectors, there is a Holly Hobbie® ! 65
America's finest equine artist wins praise from horse racing set...and limited edition collectors 67
The art of Sister M.I. Hummel charms generation after generation as figurines...and now as plates, bells, and dolls as well 71
Gorham offers limited edition works by America's most renowned artists 73
Sources worldwide bring Hamilton's collectors an international array of fine limited editions 77
Opa's Haus brings "new era" of German beer steins to American collectors 79
"America's favorite plate artist" faces the challenge of three-dimensional artwork with the McClelland's Endearing Porcelains 83
Rockwell admirer makes his dream come true: The story of Marshall Stoltz and The Norman Rockwell Museum 87
Frances Hook captures the simple charms of children in figurines, plates and prints 91
A fascinating story doll lovers will enjoy...creating the "Living Image" doll collection 95
Renowned German firm of Villeroy & Boch draws on its heritage to create today's limited editions 99
How to catalog, insure and care for your collection 101
About the secondary market 105
The collectors' club, convention and travel scene 107
National Association of Limited Edition Dealers 110
About the marketers and manufacturers of limited edition collectibles 115
About the artists 137
Book, magazines and newsletters for collectors 155
Glossary 157
Price Index 160

Foreword

By Heio W. Reich, President of COLLECTORS' INFORMATION BUREAU, and President of RECO International Corp., Port Washington, New York.

Dear Collector:

It is indeed a pleasure for me to introduce the first annual COLLECTIBLES MARKET INDEX PRICE GUIDE—1984. This book and its MARKET INDEX PRICE GUIDE to plates, figurines, bells, graphics, steins and dolls represent many months of enthusiastic cooperation and dedicated work by representatives of some of the world's finest manufacturers of limited edition collectibles.

For years our customers have asked for an authoritative source that would help them prepare for an enjoyable collecting hobby—and a MARKET INDEX PRICE GUIDE that was manageable in size and easy to use. As the limited edition market expands beyond plates...figurines, bells, and other items gain increasing prominence in the field...collectors seek new sources of information so that they may evaluate each of these new categories and make wise purchase decisions.

In this book you will find material of interest to you whether you're a novice collector or a veteran of many years with the hobby. What's more, you'll gain helpful tips on decorating with limited editions...keeping track of your collection...buying and selling...joining a collectors' club...and much more.

The COLLECTIBLES MARKET INDEX PRICE GUIDE—1984 is sponsored by COLLECTORS' INFORMATION BUREAU—A Business League which was formed to provide this service as well as a regular MARKET PRICE UPDATE to collectors all over the United States and beyond. We members of COLLECTORS' INFORMATION BUREAU invite you to enjoy this book, and to inquire about the products you see by writing to the manufacturers listed for them.

Cordially,

Heio W. Reich
Port Washington, New York
October, 1983

Heio Reich

A word from the members of the Collectors' Information Bureau

Just a decade or so ago, a collector could easily keep track of the limited edition market for plates, figurines, bells and other collectibles. There were no more than a handful of regular plate series, and a few large and long-established companies dominated the market for figurines and other limited edition categories.

But in recent years, expanding collector interest has inspired a great deal of growth not only in the plate and figurine market, but in bells, graphics, dolls and steins as well. And along with this growth comes an increasing desire for information on the part of collectors. To help serve this need, a group of limited edition manufacturers and marketers has formed the COLLECTORS' INFORMATION BUREAU: a not-for-profit Business League whose purpose is to provide facts and interesting feature material for collectors in the United States and beyond.

The address for the BUREAU is: COLLECTORS' INFORMATION BUREAU, 1860 Lake Drive S.E., East Grand Rapids, Michigan 49506

BUREAU members fit into two categories: MEMBERS, who market limited edition items of their own under one or more trade names, and ASSOCIATE MEMBERS, who provide materials and/or manufacturing facilities for limited edition marketers. Here is our membership roster for 1984:

CHARTER MEMBERS

AMERICAN ARTISTS/ GRAPHICS
BUYING SERVICE
225 West Hubbard, Fourth Floor
Chicago, Illinois 60610

ANNA-PERENNA PORCELAIN
32 Relyea Place
New Rochelle, New York 10801

THE BOEHM STUDIOS
25 Fairfacts
Trenton, New Jersey 08638

THE CARMEL COLLECTION
One Pebble Beach Plaza, P.O. Box 1030
Pebble Beach, California 93953

DESIGNERS COLLECTION
American Greetings
10500 American Road
Cleveland, Ohio 44144

GOEBEL
Division of Goebel Art Inc.
105 White Plains Road
Tarrytown, New York 10591

THE GORHAM COMPANY
333 Adelaide Avenue
Providence, Rhode Island 02907

THE HAMILTON COLLECTION
9550 Regency Square Blvd.
Jacksonville, Florida 32232

THE NORMAN ROCKWELL MUSEUM
2840 Maria Avenue
Northbrook, Illinois 60062

OPA'S HAUS, INC.
1600 River Road
New Braunfels, Texas 78130

RECO INTERNATIONAL CORP.
138-150 Haven Avenue
Port Washington, New York 11050

ROMAN, INC.
4850 N. Harlem Avenue
Harwood Heights, Illinois 60656

UNITED STATES HISTORICAL SOCIETY
First and Main Streets
Richmond, Virginia 23219

VILLEROY & BOCH
41 Madison Avenue
New York, New York 10010

CHARTER ASSOCIATE MEMBERS

BRYAN CHINA COMPANY
511 Samson Street
New Castle, Pennsylvania 16101

COMMERCIAL DECAL COMPANY
650 S. Columbus
Mt. Vernon, New York 10550

CUSTOM CHINA CREATIONS
13726 Seminole Drive
Chino, California 91710

EAST PALESTINE CHINA COMPANY
P.O. Box 108, 870 West Main
East Palestine, Ohio 44413

INSTAR SUPPLY COMPANY
11 East 26th Street
New York, New York 10010

MATTHEYPRINT CORPORATION
101 Great Valley Parkway
Malvern, Pennsylvania 19355

WOODMERE CHINA COMPANY
P.O. Box 5305
New Castle, Pennsylvania 16105

This new guide will cover six of the most active categories of today's limited edition collectibles market: plates, figurines, bells, graphics, steins and dolls.

Why do people collect...and what is collectible?

by Susan K. Jones
Executive Director, Collectors' Information Bureau

Most everyone collects something—whether it be license plates or limited edition collector plates...coins of the realm or custom-minted ingots. The urge to collect is universal, and it knows no boundary of age, income or personal background. The youngster who searches far and wide for the missing baseball card to complete his collection may well grow up to become a connoisseur of fine sculpture or antiques. The lady who buys a $25 china, child-subject plate because it reminds her of her granddaughter could be launching a rewarding hobby that will fill her walls with porcelain art over the years to come.

In recent years antiquing and collecting have multiplied over and over in popularity. The number of antique shows, flea markets, swap meets, collectors' shows and retail stores devoted to collectible items has skyrocketed in the last decade or so. As Ralph and Terry Kovel, pioneers in the reporting of trends in antiques and collectibles, told *Collector Editions* Magazine recently, "When we started collecting (30 years ago) there was one major antiques show in Cleveland, held twice a year. Now on any given weekend in Cleveland I can go to 10 antique shows."

The skyrocketing growth of the limited edition plate market—and with it a more recent growth in fields like figurines, bells, graphics, steins and dolls—is another example of this trend. *Plate Collector* Magazine debuted in 1972—a fledgling, almost "cult" publication that since has grown into a thriving, twice-monthly "must" for collectors, dealers and manufacturers in the limited edition field. Other publications like *Plate World* and *Dolls* have found important niches in the collecting marketplace since then, and more general magazines and newsletters such as *Collector Editions* and *Collectors Mart* devote more and more space to the dynamic world of limited edition collectibles.

The first International Plate Fair for collectors took place in South Bend, Indiana in July, 1975. Nine years later the fair is growing stronger every year, with charter flights bringing collectors from all over America and Canada, and even some from overseas, to learn what's new in plates, figurines, graphics, and other specialties. In 1983 a similar show premiered at Anaheim, California. With a reported 22,500 collectors in attendance the first year, the winter show at Anaheim is sure to become a strong annual event.

Why the Growth in Collecting?

The "boom" in collecting—especially in the limited edition realm—has roots in the changing lifestyle and interests of Americans. Time was, only the very rich could afford the luxury of collecting. Old Master paintings, sculptures, and other art objects commanded prices that most observers could hardly fathom, let alone pay.

Susan K. Jones

But several factors have combined over the past few decades to broaden the profile of the "typical collector." Surely there are still a number of wealthy individuals who pay tens of thousands of dollars for single items at auction houses like Sotheby Parke Bernet. But in addition, there is an exciting, affordable field of collecting for all Americans to enjoy.

More leisure time feeds the desire of these new collectors to enjoy stimulating and rewarding hobbies. The growing affluence of Americans has left many of us with more discretionary income, as well. Rising education levels encourage us to learn more about our hobbies—reading, attending shows and seminars, and forming clubs to share news and knowledge with like-minded collectors.

Many collectors also enjoy the excitement of tracking down an elusive plate or figurine—the perfect piece to round out a series or complete a home display. Some collectors are intrigued with the investment possibilities of limited editions, and study the market as they would the New York Stock Exchange, trying to establish trends that will help them make wise purchase decisions. Most, however, temper these urges with the all-important question, "Do I like it?" That way if a "sure thing" plate, bell or figurine never rises in market value, it will still bring personal pleasure with each and every viewing.

The decor aspects of limited edition collecting are important as well: few collecting categories offer as many fine possibilities for home display. A carefully-developed collection may serve as the theme for a room or an entire home—and it does wonders to add personality and appeal to an interior design.

What is "Collectible," and How Do I Start?

Some novice collectors jump right in and start purchasing items that appeal to them, and then slowly work at acquiring knowledge that will help them develop a well-rounded collection as time goes on. Other, more cautious or studious types, want to develop some background in the field before starting to buy. This book will be of help to both, as well as to the collector with some years of experience. To begin, then, let us establish the scope of our topic: the contemporary field of limited edition plates, figurines, bells, graphics, steins and dolls.

As many people know, the term "antique" generally refers to items which were made 100 years ago or more. In some fields, such as "antique" cars, the time frame is less stringent—25 years or so being considered enough time to make a car a "classic" if not an antique. In the area of furniture, some experts claim that a true "antique" must be 150 years old or more.

In general, then, items of significance, beauty, value or interest that are "too young" to be considered antiques, fall into the realm of "collectibles." But not all collectibles are limited editions, and many of them have been around for many decades: witness the popular turn-of-the-century posters, Art Deco and Art Nouveau items, Carnival and Depression glass, etc.

To limit the scope of our discussion in this volume, our topic is: *contemporary* limited editon plates, figurines, bells, graphics, steins and dolls. The oldest item listed in this book is the 1895 Bing & Grondahl Christmas plate—considered by many to be the first-ever limited edition collector's plate, and surely the "root" of today's plate collecting hobby. Most of the collectible items we'll discuss are products of the 1960's, 1970's and 1980's—recently-issued items which have generated interest in the contemporary limited edition market.

This book is not intended to be comprehensive, in and of itself. As an annual volume it will continue to provide more indepth information about limited edition collecting each year—as well as news about more different products with each volume and update. So whether you are a brand-new collector, or a veteran with scores of limited edition items adorning your home, we hope that this guide will provide stimulating and useful information which you can use—this year, and for many years to come.

In the past decade, a number of new publications devoted to limited edition collecting have entered the field. Some feature just one collecting category, such as Rockwells, dolls or plates, while others cover a wider range of items and news.

This is the plate that started plate collecting: The 1895 Bing & Grondahl Christmas issue, "Behind the Frozen Window." It premiered at just fifty cents and now brings **more than 8000 times** *that much at auction.*

How to begin, develop and improve your collection

Many collectors enjoy making a plan for their collections—combining education, stimulation and experimentation to develop a personal collecting style. And even those of us who reject the notion of "planned collecting" can refine our "selection skills" with some background information on the how-to's of collecting. So in this section, we consult with some of the leading experts in today's limited edition field to offer advice and guidance in the development of your own personal collection.

How Can I Learn More About Collecting?

More and more opportunities exist today for collectors to learn about the field. Our panel of experts suggests five main areas of collector education—many of which may be a great deal of fun, as well.

Read Up on Your Field of Interest. Collectors' magazines are one of the first and best means that a collector may use to learn more about the field. Don Hershleb of Commemorative Imports says: "New collectors should subscribe to a couple of different collectors' publications in order to obtain a good cross section of information and viewpoints." Most frequently mentioned publications were *Plate Collector* and *Plate World.* The addresses of these and a number of other fine, collectibles-related publications may be found in the "Books, Magazines and Newsletters" section of this book.

The experts were less impressed with the range of books currently available to collectors. "Not many books are available on collectibles," said David Henderson of Bing & Grondahl. He did point out that the books by Pat Owen on Bing & Grondahl and Royal Copenhagen plates were quite comprehensive and helpful to collectors with an interest in these producers.

Attend Conventions and Collectibles Shows. Brigitte Moore, vice-president for collectibles at Reco International Corp., strongly suggests a visit to Anaheim in March or South Bend in July for one of the major collectibles conventions. "I think that a collector would learn a great deal about collecting by attending these shows. There are two full days of seminars on a wide variety of subjects. There are a great many knowledgeable people to hear and talk to one-on-one. Subjects like artists, companies, decorating with collectibles or how to insure a collection would be covered. Obviously, these are extremely valuable opportunities." Addresses for more information about the South Bend and Anaheim shows are found in the "Club, Convention and Travel" section of this book.

For those who cannot travel to South Bend or Anaheim, there are a number of regional or local shows featuring one or more artists, manufacturers or product lines. News of these opportunities may be found in collector publications.

Join Collectors' Clubs. Many of our experts suggested that a collector find and join a local club for people who collect plates and other limited editions. Tom O'Meara, president of The Carmel Collection, explained: "I find that joining one or several clubs is extremely valuable. You learn many things from other club members . . . they are frequently eager to share their research, successful buys, and general information on collecting." Collector publications frequently list the location, date and time of plate clubs as a service to new collectors.

Collectors who have already narrowed their collecting horizons to the creations of a particular producer may want to join a club which focuses on this producer's work. A list of some of these organizations also may be found in the club section.

Learn from Dealers and Direct Marketers. The industry leaders we spoke to agreed that there is a great deal of stimulation and information available through both dealer and direct mail channels of distribution. As Don Herschleb asserted, "Collectors should establish a good relationship with a dealer that specializes in limited editions. They provide a number of brochures and background information which is invaluable to collectors. Dealers can also assist collectors in the selection of quality pieces which are within their price range." Many dealers also are happy to assist you in the acquisition of back issues to fill the gaps in your collection.

Direct mail literature can also be a source of guidance for collectors. Pat Owen of Viking Import House suggests that collectors keep their names on the mailing lists of all direct mail sellers they can find. Robert Kline, president of the United States Historical Society, says "The direct mail firms offer valuable information which should be read and noted for future reference."

Some collectors actually file all of their brochures and background material in case it should become useful in the future. John W. Graham, president of The Hamilton Collection, believes readers of direct mail literature can learn a great deal from the support pieces which many direct mailers supply. "As we at Hamilton present a new edition," he explains, "we try to place it in an historical perspective for our customers. Our literature explains the heritage of each piece and how it relates to other items already in the marketplace. I know that our articles are helping collectors to learn, because they often write in to discuss points we've made in the direct mail literature."

Direct mail literature may provide collectors with a great deal of background information on the plates, figurines, and other collectibles they're considering. In addition to selling literature, many such packages contain articles on how collectibles are made, the history of the field, artist biographies, and much more.

Should I Narrow My Collecting Horizons to a Particular Field?

Our panel of experts believes that each collector should decide for him/herself if he/she will "zero in" on a specific collecting area, or continue to buy appealing items of all types. Sam Bauman, editor of *Plate World* Magazine, explained that "Collecting is a very personal thing, and I think that the decision is up to the collector. Many people begin collecting things that have some personal significance for them. They start buying things with the lowest price and frequently accumulate so many things that they need a bigger house! At this point, they begin selling things to buy high quality pieces which they now know how to appreciate."

Susan Elliott, editor of *Plate Collector* Magazine, agrees that the narrowing of a collection is an evolutionary process. She says, "We have done a number of features on collecting and the thing that we seem to find is that collectors quite naturally begin to narrow the scope. People seem to collect along different levels—price is frequently a factor, the quality or value of an item, the subject matter, or the artist or manufacturer."

Ralph Gadiel, president of The Norman Rockwell Museum, defends an "open collection." "I'm not certain that it is desirable to limit a collection," he says. "If 70% of a collection is devoted to the things that the collector considers beautiful and wishes to display, it can be very effective. Don't try to manage a collection too tightly in the hope that it will be more valuable. Collect the things you like."

Other experts believe that some type of limitation is a natural part of an individual's selection process. Marge Rosenberg of Carol's Gift Shop explains: "If a collector buys only things that they like, the collection will be limited to a degree by their interests. However, I frequently will alert these collectors to other collectibles which would complement their current holdings. I like to at least make them aware of the many beautiful things which are available to them."

Klaus Vogt, president of Anna-Perenna, takes a similar stance. "Collection means group, and it is extremely important that good collectors limit the scope of their collection. First, select the things you like and you will quite naturally concentrate your attention on them and by selectively studying them become an expert on the subject of your collection. Mastering a subject may lead to a collection assembled around subject matter, the work of an artist or possibly around a company. As an example, think of the pleasure that has been derived by collectors of Wedgwood. When one becomes a master in the field, both the heart and mind find satisfaction."

Several of our respondents did believe that a wise collector will limit his or her activities to a specific area. Stafford Calvin of Calhoun's Collectors Society says, "I think that it is important and even desirable that collectors limit themselves to a certain theme, artist or manufacturer. A collector may have a collection of Bing & Grondahl Christmas plates which would provide more pleasure than a random sampling of plates with no theme. Other people enjoy collecting the work of Edna Hibel and their enjoyment grows as they learn more about the artist."

Robert Kline has a definite view about limiting a collection. "A collector should concentrate on one specific field, e.g. historical dolls or Shirley Temple dolls, pistols or figurines. It should be a field that the collector is personally interested in exploring. To achieve the most success, a collection should be studied in depth."

Several of our experts commented on the factor of personal taste and personality in the shaping of a collection. Don Herschleb said, "I think that the type of collection varies a great deal depending on the temperament of the collector. Some people are extremely well organized and this is reflected in their collections. These people are more apt to collect an entire series and frequently have very definite goals for their collection. Other collectors have a much more casual approach. It all boils down to the personality of the collector and the things that they enjoy."

Harriet Dalaskey of The Bradford Exchange agrees. "A collector's taste will be a major factor in limiting their collection," she says. The collector's taste may change and these changing preferences will be reflected in the art which they select."

Pat Owen gives a good, general rule for narrowing the collection—buy what you like. "It all depends on what a person derives pleasure and satisfaction from," she explains. "The first rule of collecting is, 'Enjoy your collection.' "

Where Should I Purchase My Limited Editions?

There are a number of ways in which a collector may locate and buy the limited edition collectibles he wishes to own. Giftware and limited edition dealers, direct mail or magazine ads, swap and sell programs, auctions, antique shops—even house sales may be fertile fields for the collector. In this book you will find names and addresses for the National Association of Limited Edition Dealers (NALED) member stores across the country. You'll also find addresses for a number of collectibles manufacturers and marketers—firms you may write to request information by mail, or to be placed on their regular mailing list. Swap and sells are held at many local collector's club meetings, and at major conventions such as the annual ones at South Bend in July and Anaheim in March. Watch local ads for auctions and antique shops which may offer contemporary limited editions as well as older items. As a house sale attendee, be on the lookout for back issue items—there are still many people who have no idea of the value of Aunt Sally's old blue-and-white "dishes," which may turn out to be early Bing & Grondahl or Royal Copenhagen plates worth a great deal of money. Here's more about some of these ways to purchase limited editions.

Limited Edition Dealers. Some dealers today offer only limited edition items, while others include giftware or a fuller line of merchandise in their shops. But whatever the merchandise make-up, what you will seek out is a pleasing selection, knowledgeable sales help, fair pricing, and a reasonable customer service policy.

As David Henderson of Bing & Grondahl says, "A retail dealer offers a collector one of the best ways to buy collectibles. They have first hand expertise in helping customers select pieces that they will enjoy."

Eloise Parks agrees. "I think customers receive the best service in the stores where they can see and touch the pieces. The selection and the fact that you can see several pieces before purchasing is very important."

Marge Rosenberg mentioned the advice factor in working with a dealer. "A good retail dealer can be extremely valuable to a collector in assisting him or her in the learning process. These dealers provide a good variety of merchandise from which the customer can make a choice, and a tradition and a continuity of service that a customer knows he can depend on."

Most experts agree with Mrs. Rosenberg that collectors seeking a dealer should look for a well-established firm. So-called "bedroom dealers" who sell collectibles as a hobby and may retreat from the business quite suddenly are not recommended. With a few exceptions, limited edition experts advise collectors to avoid discounters. Discounting dealers are less able in many cases to provide full-range services.

Mail Order Firms. The simplest and most obvious reason why a collector would buy by mail is that no limited edition collectibles dealer is available in close proximity to his home. Yet a great number of collectors choose to buy by mail for convenience or other reasons, even if they could purchase the same or similar merchandise in a local shop.

Mail order marketing is the "wave of the future," as people with busy lifestyles and two-career families find shopping time precious and very limited. And many collectors believe that the opportunity to sit back and consider an item without pressure—and to learn more about a given item and its history by means of well-written sales literature—is a pleasant way to make a buying decision. What's more, in buying by mail, the collector who wishes to purchase an entire series will have it delivered to his door—he need not make further efforts to visit a shop to secure later series issues.

Our experts emphasize the importance of checking the reputation of a mail order firm—perhaps by asking other collectors about their experiences or by ordering a small item to see how your order is handled. A fair returns policy is most often mentioned in evaluating a direct mail company.

Magazine and Newsletter Ads. There are two main types of ads from which you may purchase limited edition collectibles. The first type is an ad offering a new issue for sale, generally in a display ad format. The second type would more likely be a classified ad, placed by an individual or store to sell collectibles on the secondary market. Buying via ads—especially for secondary market items—can be a convenient way to "fill in" missing items in a collection, or to purchase quickly the items a collector knows he or she wants to own, without much explanatory literature or sales information.

Combination of Dealers and Direct Marketers. Many of our experts suggested a combined approach—purchasing both from the local collectibles dealer, and through direct mail channels. Collectors can obtain excellent service from both the direct mail companies and retail dealers. Because so many collectibles are currently being produced, very few stores in the country handle everything. Thus, collectors can supplement their available information by keeping up with what is available through direct mail and space advertising, and ordering intriguing items which are not readily available in stores.

Investment Potential versus "Buy What You Like"

Over and over, experts in the collectibles field advise collectors to let their own good taste be the number one guide in selecting items to purchase. "Buy What You Like" is heard again and again. As Susan Elliott of *Plate Collector* says, "Do not begin to collect solely for an investment. The enjoyment of collecting beautiful things should be the first consideration. With the rapid expansion of the field, it would be extremely difficult for a beginning collector to understand the psychology of the market well enough to select the few items which will eventually become valuable. With so many professionals involved in the field it would be extremely difficult for an individual collector to be able to be ahead of the market. Collecting should never be considered a short-term investment.

"While it is true that in the 1960's many plates appreciated in value almost overnight, today we have a totally different market. If 400 plates are produced each year, only a handful will become solid appreciation successes."

On the other hand, some experts believe that a collector can become a more intelligent consumer of limited edition items, and begin to select items that have an "edge" in the race for market appreciation. In addition to buying for beauty or for what they personally like, collectors might utilize certain checklists and guides. These criteria may be helpful in evaluating plates, figurines, bells, and many other collectibles categories. [*See checklist on page 12*].

William G. (Bill) Freudenberg of Hollywood Limited Editions, a pioneer in the collectibles world and observer in the antique and collectibles market for four decades, summed up the motivation to buy in this way: "Beauty is in the eye of the beholder. Many people buy for nostalgic reasons. They buy Rockwell because it reminds them of a time that they lived through when things were less complicated and values seemed truer. They enjoy children because they are thinking of their own children or grandchildren whom they love. Some people find madonnas, trains or skating appealing.

1. MAKER—Does the item's manufacturer have a reputation for quality and fine workmanship?

2. ARTISTRY—Is the plate art created by an artist of note? Is the subject one of broad, but not trite, appeal?

3. LIMITATION—Is the edition limited, yet not so limited that it cannot penetrate the market? If the edition is closed, are the dealers bidding in the secondary market?

4. COMMEMORATIVE IMPORTANCE—Does the plate commemorate a seasonal event or an historic event? If so, does it bring new insight to the event? Or is it an event in the history of the artists or of the maker?

5. MATERIAL—If the plate is made of ceramic, is it porcelain, bone china, or fine china? If it is made of some other material, is it a fine example of its type?

Collectors may also wish to become familiar with the five basic types of limited editions.

1. Limited by announced quantity, with each item numbered.
2. Limited by announced quantity, with items not numbered.
3. Limited by announced firing period, numbered or not numbered.
4. Limited by year of issue, restricting the quantity to the number produced during the year of issue.
5. Limited by an announced time period which may be more or less than one year.

Checklist

"Many people have the false impression that only editions that have small numbers of items produced will be valuable in the future. This is not always the case. There may be three to five million collectors and even if an item has a big run, it still may not get into the hands of every collector who wants it. Some plates can be forgotten when they were issued earlier (before the limited editions boom)—for example, some of Rockwell's earlier things."

Several of our experts made the point that if a collector buys for beauty, and with a good background of information to make him or her an informed consumer, that investment may follow as an added benefit. Ms. Dalaskey called investment "frosting on the cake" for the collector who buys what he or she likes. Brigitte Moore summed up by saying, "I feel that collectors should buy for enjoyment and beauty and if the item increases in value, that is an added bonus. If people go into collecting strictly for the investment, they will have a lot of disappointment. They may buy what they think is a 'hot item' only to have it remain relatively inactive."

Trends in the Market...What the Experts are Buying

With their hands-on perspective of the limited edition market, our panel of experts have definite views about today's collectible trends. Most often mentioned was a tendency toward more variety in types of items offered—branching off from plates into figurines, bells, and other areas. Several people also mentioned greater selectivity on the part of the collector. And our experts see a great potential in the area of limited edition dolls. Here are some of their specific comments, as well as notes on their own collecting preferences.

Variety/Branching Out. "Collectors, particularly plate collectors, are beginning to branch out into other forms," says Brigitte Moore. "They may complement their collections with fine prints or with figurines." Ralph Gadiel agrees. "I see a trend toward a wider variety of collectibles in the future. Collectors will buy more bells, figurines and other types of collectibles. While plates will continue to be important, the field will improve because of the newer, total collectible market." Mary Hugunin of Pemberton & Oakes had a more specific comment: "I think that different kinds of subjects will emerge. More modern art will be available. Figurines, limited edition prints, and bells will be collected more as well as dolls. By dolls I mean the high-quality, limited edition kind which have been produced during the last year."

For their own homes, both Ms. Moore and Ms. Hugunin find they treasure the plates and other collectibles created from the works of artists their firms promote—people like John McClelland and Sandra Kuck in Ms. Moore's case, and Donald Zolan for Ms. Hugunin. Ralph Gadiel especially enjoys porcelain products—figurines, birds and bells adorn his office and home.

Selectivity. Marge Rosenberg summed up this point well: "I believe that collectors will become much more sophisticated and more careful in their choices. A great many more things are being produced now, so collectors have more to choose from. Buyers should know what company or "brand name" produced the piece, the name of the artist, and how many were made. With so many things being produced, a collector can afford to be more discriminating." David Henderson of Bing & Grondahl made his point quite definitely. "There are too many new products on the market each year," he said. "I think that we will be seeing a sorting out of products. People are learning to be more selective about the things that they buy and more appreciative of quality workmanship."

When it comes to personal collecting, Mrs. Rosenberg enjoys her groupings of plates, bells, music boxes and unicorns. She began the latter collection with a tapestry, and it has expanded to other media with the unicorn theme. David Henderson says there is "no rhyme or reason" to his collecting. With his eclectic taste, he just keeps the things that he likes.

The Importance of Dolls. Klaus Vogt took this view of the doll market: "Collectible dolls may enjoy more interest in the future. However, dolls have always been important because we are very human, and we enjoy dolls because they evoke all the feelings of the human heart—when we think of a mother and child." Robert Kline agrees. "Dolls seem to be moving the fastest. Both the newer, high-quality and moderately-priced dolls as well as the antique dolls are being sought by collectors. People are beginning to appreciate the historical value of handcrafted items. There is a growing appreciation for individually produced items. Craftsmanship, hand-stitching, hand-painted figures all are things that collectors can see and touch. In the case of the dolls and finely-crafted figurines, people enjoy the three-dimensional quality."

For his own enjoyment, Klaus Vogt began collecting coins as a child. As an adult he has become a plate collector. He says, "While I collect for pleasure, I think

At collectibles conventions held annually in Anaheim and South Bend, both collectors and dealers learn the latest about trends in the market, manufacturing processes and artists at seminars chaired by expert speakers.

that most of us subliminally would like to think that 'we are smart,' and can select things that will be valuable." Robert Kline has an extensive collection including dolls, plates, swords and pistols. His collecting has a definite, historical flair.

Other Trends in the Market. Both Harriet Dalaskey of Bradford, and Klaus Vogt commented on the wider audience which collectibles will enjoy in the future. Ms. Dalaskey said, "One trend has been a shift from older collectors to a new breed of young collectors who can and do purchase collectibles and artwork that fits their lifestyle. Their taste will have a strong influence in the future." Vogt added, "I think that the field of collectibles will continue to grow. At the present time, many people enjoy art, but do not collect things like plates or figurines. This will change as people become more aware of the beauty to be found in porcelain. Man's art has developed on paper, wood, and canvas, and now people are beginning to realize that porcelain offers untried creative media. Artists with new techniques and new colors are sure to be appreciated by the collectors in the future."

John Graham of The Hamilton Collection detects a change in collectors' motivations. "Buyers are not simply hobby or investment-minded anymore," he explains. "Many people buy limited edition collectibles now as decor or gift items, and I see this trend growing."

Susan Elliott of *Plate Collector* sees more short series of plates coming up—no more than four at a time—to supplement the longer, open-ended series that initiated the hobby. She also agrees with Klaus Vogt about the expanding knowledge and range of interest of collectors. "As more and more collectors enter the field and form collectors' clubs, they become more knowledgeable and seem to be exerting more of an influence on the plates that are being produced. In 1978 only six plate clubs were listed in *Plate Collector* Magazine, and today 116 clubs are listed." As a by-product of this higher level of knowledge, Ms. Elliott predicts more sophistication in the products that appeal to most collectors. "People are gradually beginning to appreciate better art. We have gone through a stage of cutesy art, children, dogs, etc., but now I see a growing interest in finer art."

Several of our collectibles experts agreed that limited edition dolls are among the "hottest" items on today's market. Here, a recent issue from Shader China Dolls, Inc.: "Yola" from the Barbara Cartland series.

When decorating their own homes, Ms. Dalaskey and Ms. Elliott both thrive on variety in collecting. As Ms. Dalaskey says, "I have a personal preference for original oils, plates, bells, figurines and a few antiques. My modern prints blend with family antiques which have been handed down. I find it very liveable and it appeals to me. People who have Christmas plates will show them around the holidays, then in spring bring out the colorful and fresh designs. In the fall, they may again change the color or theme of the display. A few years ago, my father began an interesting tradition in our family. He began to give my mother annual plates in celebration of the birth of each of her grandchildren. He did this totally independent of me (it was before I had an interest in plate collecting) and it has become a beautiful family tradition." Ms. Elliott collects things such as restaurant menus, baskets, prints and tins in addition to individual, limited edition plates which appeal to her.

Although most people consider Bing & Grondahl's 1895 "Behind the Frozen Window" as the first collector's plate, this single-issue "Snow White" plate from Villeroy & Boch was introduced in 1890.

One of the most innovative of all limited edition collector plates, "Deux Oiseaux" was the first non-porcelain, non-blue-and-white, non-Christmas limited edition collector plate. It was introduced by Lalique of France in 1965.

The famed British firm of Wedgwood entered the limited edition plate market in 1969 with this bas-relief, jasperware issue. "Windsor Castle" premiered an annual series which continues active today.

A brief survey of plate collecting: 1895—Today

When Bing & Grondahl introduced its first dated and limited Christmas plate in 1895, few took notice beyond the several hundred people who purchased the plates as holiday gifts. But today—nearly a century later—"Behind the Frozen Window" begins nearly every discussion of the plate collecting hobby.

The fact is that Villeroy & Boch introduced a limited edition "Snow White and the Seven Dwarfs" plate in 1890, and it was made until 1905. But Heinrich Schlitt's "Snow White" was an individual issue—not the beginning of an open-ended series like the Bing & Grondahl Christmas plates—and thus the Danish procelain studio is generally considered to be the innovator in limited edition plates.

Harald Bing of Bing & Grondahl added a new "twist"—the limited edition concept—to a plate collecting hobby that was already underway in Europe. It is said that even in Ancient Egypt, people collected and displayed attractive plates made of decorated terra cotta. But the discovery of a formula for porcelain in Europe fed the interest in pretty plates which led to "Behind the Frozen Window."

In Denmark at Christmas, many people gave gifts of food and delicacies, and thus they needed a container for this purpose. Harald Bing had his artist, Frans August Hallin, design a plate with this use in mind, and date it 1895. After about 400 plates were sold, the molds were broken and this particular design in underglazed Copenhagen (Cobalt) blue never was made again. Bing & Grondahl continued the Christmas plate tradition each year thereafter, dating the plates on the front to mark the year of issue.

Other European Porcelain Houses Offer Christmas Plates

It was not long before other porcelain makers in Denmark and beyond began to experiment with their own Christmas plate concepts. Some, like the first efforts of Rorstrand of Sweden (1904—1925) and Rosenthal of Germany (1905—1909) lasted only a few years. Others, such as the work of Royal Copenhagen of Denmark (1908—present) inspired open-ended series which continue to this day.

In Holland, Blue Delft de Porceleyne Fles introduced its own Christmas series in 1915, and Rosenthal began a new collection in 1910 which issued annually until 1970. (Rosenthal premiered two Christmas series the next year—one by Bjorn Wiinblad, and one called "Traditional" Christmas.)

For years, the plate collecting hobby continued as a rather small-scale, holiday tradition. Limited edition plates were blue and white. They commemorated Christmas. They were issued annually. And beyond a small circle in Western Europe, they were largely unknown.

From time to time, when Danish immigrants came to America, they would bring their favorite blue-and-white Christmas plates along. These Danes fueled a small market for current and back-issues, and some few antique, gift and department stores began to carry a small stock of European Christmas issues. Prices of just a few dollars per plate were common, even on issues which today command hundreds or even thousands of dollars. But then, about 1965, the limited edition plate market in America began to grow, and finally to boom.

The Boom of the Late 1960's...The Shakeout of 1972-73

Several innovative plate issues helped lead to the "growth market" for collector plates in the early 1970's. The first was Lalique's 1965 first-issue annual plate, "Deux Oiseaux." This plate was the first non-Christmas, non-porcelain, non-blue-and-white offering to enter the marketplace, and market reaction was prompt. "Deux Oiseaux" rose from $25 issue to a level well over $1000 in months after the edition of 2000 closed. Today the plate stands at about $1650 on the secondary market.

The year 1969 saw the introduction of a first-issue Christmas plate from Wedgwood of England, as well as a second major innovation from Bing & Grondahl of Denmark: the first limited edition plate with a Mother's Day theme. And then in 1970 and 1971, the scope of the market suddenly widened greatly: Lenox introduced plates featuring the art of Edward Marshall Boehm; Pickard of Antioch, Illinois offered works on fine china from James Lockhart; the art of Sister M. Innocentia Hummel was introduced in plate form by Goebel; and Franklin Mint commissioned Norman Rockwell to create a bas-relief Christmas issue in precious metal.

These plates broadened the scope of the market tremendously, with the introduction of famous artists (Boehm, Lockhart, Hummel, Rockwell) and different materials (precious metal, bas-relief earthenware, jasper ware).

The excitement created by these new issues brought plate collecting to the attention of many people who had never before considered the hobby. But unfortunately, it also encouraged some speculators who bought plates as coin collectors sometimes do: hundreds at a time. At the time, very few guidelines were available for plate collectors: little was written to help them make wise buying decisions. And then a "glut" of precious metal plates entered the market by 1972.

One silver plate, issued by Lincoln Mint, became an object of special controversy over the way in which it was made. This problem helped bring on a shakeout of the market, sometimes called the "crash of 1972—73," during which speculators dumped the plates they had bought.

Today: A Well-Established, Growing Market

Ultimately, the "crash" did the plate collecting hobby good. It forced the less stable plate manufacturers out of the market, and weeded out the speculators who were looking only for a "quick dollar"—not for an enjoyable and rewarding hobby.

What's more, collectors began looking for more information and organization in the plate market: and they got it. In 1972 *Plate Collector* Magazine made its debut, and soon after, The Bradford Exhange of Niles, Illinois began to publish "The Bradford Exchange Current Quotations" list of 1000 of the most actively-traded plates. Other publications for plate collectors followed within a few years, and those which catered to limited edition collectors and antique buffs began to offer more information of interest to plate hobbyists.

In the last decade, plate collecting has become established as a major hobby in the United States and many other countries. There are "trends" as far as subject matter, of course. The art of Norman Rockwell continues to be a major force in the marketplace, and child-subject plates intrigue great numbers of collectors. There is a move toward plates inspired by favorite movies such as "The Black Stallion," "Annie," or "Gone With the Wind." Commemorative plates often score well, and many manufacturers still rely on annual Christmas and Mother's Day issues. Market observers, however, no longer consider plate collecting itself as a "fad" or even a "trend"—the hobby is now firmly entrenched, and as much a part of the United States collecting culture as stamps, coins or antiques.

The Pickard China Company of Antioch, Illinois impressed collectors in 1970 with this richly-decorated pair of wildlife plates by James Lockhart. "Woodcock" and "Grouse" feature a great deal of rich, gold trim.

Elegant collectibles inspired by Christmas and other religious subjects: The 1980 and 1981 Stained Glass Christmas plates from United States Historical Society; "The First Noel" Nativity grouping from The Boehm Studios; and "Holy Child of Prague" by Cybis.

Holiday issues–both whimsical and serious –have intrigued collectors for many decades. In the upper left corner is United States Historical's 1983 Christmas porcelain Christmas plate, and beside it are the 1983 "Christmas Keepsakes" limited edition bell and figurine from Designers Collection of American Greetings. The scene with Santa is "Christmas Delights" by Jerome Walczak for Carmel Collection. And the blue-and-white plate at left is a 1983 Royal Copenhagen issue which incorporates that firm's first-ever holiday motif, the 1908 **"Madonna and Child."**

Collectors love cats—and three of their favorite feline motifs include: "Kitty Love" (right) by Phyllis Hollands-Robinson for American Artists, and two plates by Thaddeus ("Uncle Tad") Krumeich—"Oliver's Birthday" (left), and "Pumpkin."

Animals and birds also "star" on the collectibles market: witness these issues from recent years. Top left and right are the "Boreal Owl" and "Canada Geese" first issues from The Boehm Studios. The "Pointers" plate at left is by the late Leo Jansen for Kern Collectibles. And the animal figurines below are by Herman and Neal Deaton for The Hamilton Collection: their titles are "Cougar" and "Jack Rabbit."

Equine art is represented by these three limited editions, among others. At top, "The Black Stallion" by Fred Stone for American Artists. Below, Kern's "Arabians" plate by Harland Young, and "The Lead Horse" Carousel figure by sculptor Peter Cozzolino for The Hamilton Collection.

Mother's Day
1983

Norman Rockwell

The many works of Norman Rockwell continue to win loyal admiration among collectors in America and around the world. Here, a sampling of the limited editions inspired by Rockwell's paintings. On the left page, the figurine at the top left is "Bedtime" from The Norman Rockwell Museum. Below that is Gorham's "Reminiscing" plate. "Add Two Cups and a Measure of Love" is the 1983 Mother's Day issue from Rockwell Society of America. Below is the delightful "Baby's First Step" figurine from The Norman Rockwell Museum. On the right page are three plates from Gorham: the 1983 "Christmas Dancers" issue above, and two of the 1983 "Four Seasons" plates below: "Endless Debate," and "Final Speech."

Collectors love children—or at least, they love child-subject art! These are some of their favorites. At left, Sandra Kuck created "Sunday Best" for Reco International. P. Buckley Moss did "Fiddlers Two" (lower left) for Anna-Perenna Porcelain. "Mary, Mary" from Reco International (lower right) was Plate of the Year in 1980—its creator is John McClelland. Right page, three issues by Thornton Utz for The Hamilton Collection and one by Donald Zolan for Pemberton & Oakes. Utz's "My Kitty" figurine and "Autumn Wanderer" plate are at top left and right, and his "A Friend in the Sky" plate is at lower right. Zolan's "Touching the Sky" is at lower left.

Ballet-subject plates and figurines have won many a collector's heart. Among these are: the "Darling Diana" plate from The Carmel Collection (upper left); three miniature figurines from Designers Collection of American Greetings (upper right); the "Nutcracker" plate from The Boehm Studios (lower left); and the "Clara and Nutcracker" plate and figurine by Shell Fisher for Viletta China Company.

Nature and outdoor themes make for vibrant collectible presentations. For instance, the "Lavender Fairy" figurine and "Willow Fairy" plate (upper left) from Villeroy & Boch. The plate at upper right is "Iris," first in a collection called **The Flowers of Count Bernadotte** *from Anna-Perenna. At right is Gorham's "Lewis and Clark in the Bitterroots" plate, first in a collection by John Clymer.*

Most steins in today's market are inspired by the classic models from Germany. On this page at top is a new piece of stein art by American artist Pat Ford, created for Opa's Haus. It is called "Explosion in the Marsh." This firm has worked with some of Germany's leading stein makers to create issues such as (from left below) Thewalt's "Beer Here" stein, Thewalt's "Bicycle" stein, and the Gerz "Four Seasons" stein. On the page at right, is the colorful "Hansel and Gretel" stein from Villeroy & Boch. Below, The Norman Rockwell Museum's "Looking Out to Sea" stein.

Norman
Rockwell

Designers Collection of American Greetings introduced several charming issues in 1983, including these: above right, the firm's fifth annual plate; above left, the 15th anniversary "Blue Girl" commemorative figurine; below left, the third annual bell; and below right, a matching plate and figurine titled "Recital."

Next page: Collectibles on all-American themes include these recent issues from various studios. The United States Historical Society's "Living Image" dolls (top) are inspired by historical figures including George Washington, Benjamin Franklin, Abigail Adams and Thomas Jefferson. New items from Roman, Inc. (center) include the "Freddie Trenkler" clown-on-ice plate and the "Balloons" figurine by Tom Rubel. Bottom left is Melanie Taylor Kent's "Macy's Thanksgiving Day Parade" plate from The Carmel Collection.

the world's largest store
macy's

Oriental collectibles intrigue American collectors because of their symbolic meanings and their ties to age-old art techniques. Some of the more recent Oriental items issued include: The Hamilton Collection's "Wisteria Maiden" Hakata doll figurine and "Pine and Crane" Chokin-style plate (top and left below); and The Boehm Studios' first-issue plate in a collection entitled "Life's Best Wishes."

The market for limited edition figurines: An overview

Since ancient times, man has expressed himself and his culture in the creation of three-dimensional artwork. Very often these sculptural works took on the form of the human figure: thus the term "figurine." But over the centuries, many sculptures have been inspired by animals and natural themes as well.

Just as the discovery of porcelain set the stage for the limited edition plate market, so did this remarkable material make great advances possible in the world of sculpture and figurines. Porcelain and other ceramics are perhaps the most frequently-used media for today's sculptural processes, although bronze and other metals, and wood carvings, also hold a place in the contemporary world of three-dimensional design.

Over the last few centuries, a number of superb porcelain studios in Europe developed—often due to the patronage of royalty or of governmental agencies. At the same time, firms such as Bing & Grondahl, Royal Copenhagen, Royal Doulton and others—noted for their fine tableware products—used their expertise in the field of porcelain to develop sculptural techniques as well.

The "roots" of today's limited edition figurine market are found in this European tradition of craftsmanship and quality, although many of the best-loved contemporary figurines now are made in the United States or in the Orient. A brief examination of the works of two firms, Goebel and Royal Doulton, will help explain this phenomenon.

Goebel Hummels and Royal Doultons Win Collector Approval

In 1935, Goebel of Germany introduced the first figurines inspired by the work of Sister M. Innocentia Hummel, a talented, Roman Catholic nun. At first available only in Europe, these hand-painted figures of children were exported to America before World War II, and then again after the war. Many American G.I.'s stationed in Europe found the "M.I. Hummels" attractive, and brought them home with them, fueling more interest in the United States for the Sister's work. As Americans began to travel more frequently in Europe, "M.I. Hummels" became a favorite souvenir. Eventually, a number of shops in the United States began to carry the figurines, and they became a collectible item with impressive secondary market action. The strength of Goebel Hummels also is borne out by the fact that Goebel Porzellanfabrik also has introduced a very successful limited edition collector plate series inspired by the Sister's work, and an annual series of bells as well. Today there are clubs, books, newsletters, columns and many other forms of communication and support for those who collect the pretty little "M.I. Hummels."

The Royal Doulton porcelain operation was begun in the early 19th century in England, but it was not until the early 20th century that the firm turned its attention seriously to figurines. Throughout the 20th century—except 1940 to 1949 due to World War II—this distinguished British firm produced figurines in various price ranges and subject areas. People, animals and the famous "Toby Jugs" (small mugs with sculptured facial expressions) became popular, and a number of collectors on both sides of the Atlantic had one or two Royal Doulton pieces as part of their decor. Then, in the early 1970's, collectors began to consider the concept of a Royal Doulton *collection*—and sought out early examples as well as contemporary pieces, some of which are limited editions.

New Makers and New Concepts Expand the Figurine Field

In the United States, several superb figurine makers developed their own collector following in the European tradition. Edward Marshall Boehm opened his studio a little more than 30 years ago, and within a couple of years had won a coveted spot in the permanent collection of the Metropolitan Museum of Art with his "Hereford Bull." Cybis and Burgues porcelain studios are two other important names in the American sculpture and figurine market.

The Boehm Studios particularly have become well known and respected among limited edition collectors, for in addition to this firm's exquisite sculptures of animals, birds and people which issue for $1000 and more, Boehm also offers elegant and beautifully-made limited edition figurines and sculptures in the affordable $100-$250 range.

The Plate/Figurine Connection

Perhaps the most important trend in today's limited edition figurine market has been the inter-relation of plates and figurines. In the case of Goebel Hummel, the firm's beloved figurines inspired the Goebel Hummel Annual plate collection. On the other hand, The Gorham Company was among the first to introduce figurines inspired by successful Rockwell-subject collector plates. The annual "Four Seasons" collections, for instance, premiered in the early 1970's. The first year, four related plates based on Rockwell art were offered. Then the next year, the same subject matter would provide inspiration for four hand-painted Rockwell figurines.

Another important aspect of today's figurine market is the advent of issues by well-known artists: some of whose works have never before been available in limited edition figurine form. Today, for instance, Calhoun's Collectors Society offers figurines by renowned artist Gunther Granget. Gorham, The Norman Rockwell Museum, Dave Grossman Designs and The Hamilton Collection all offer Norman Rockwell figurines, and Hamilton also has introduced the first-ever three-dimensional works by famed plate artist Thornton Utz. John McClelland, artist for the beloved "Mary, Mary" plate for Reco International, has created a group of figurines which display his special gift for capturing the innocent joy of childhood. And Designers Collection of American Greetings now offers the delightful Holly Hobbie® figurines in limited edition form.

Trading in the limited edition figurine market traditionally has taken place through antique "channels," auction houses, or on a dealer-to-collector or collector-to-collector basis. But today there is a strong movement in the field to establish secondary market trading for figurines along the lines of the current plate market: buy-sell opportunities via exchanges, swap and sell meets, etc. This trend can only help to increase demand for contemporary limited edition figurines, as it stimulates trading on earlier issues.

Edward Marshall Boehm is widely considered to have been America's finest porcelain artist. A look at his elegant "Song Sparrow" sculptures explains why: Boehm's mastery of detail in both bird and flower subjects is unsurpassed.

The collector plate/figurine connection is evidenced by these handsome, hand-painted offerings by John McClelland for Reco International Corp. The McClellands Endearing Porcelains *series includes youngsters at work and at play. McClelland's popularity as a plate artist is unsurpassed, so many of his admirers may be expected to purchase these three-dimensional works as well.*

The charming, child-subject figurines of Sister Maria Innocentia Hummel helped spark a growing interest in three-dimensional artwork both in Europe and in America. Here we see the current version of the "M.I. Hummel" figurine "Wash Day," on the right. On the left, an unreleased version of the figurine which is in the archives of the Goebel Company in West Germany.

An introduction to bells for limited edition collectors

Bells may well be the oldest collectible item — as old as recorded time, in fact. There is no way to tell when the first bell was made, but historians report that bells were part of the culture of most every ancient civilization.

In Persia, bronze bells were used as horse bells and harness ornaments. In ancient Egypt, a bell-rattle was part of the religious ceremony. Israel, Greece, Rome, and cultures in Central America, the Orient, India, Asia and Africa all used bells for worship, to warn of arrivals, as playthings or as decorative objects.

Once porcelain studios opened in Europe, bells of fine china became a part of the art scene. Meissen and Dresden were sites of the creation of many a collectible bell in the 18th century. Wedgwood in England and the various Delftware makers in Holland also made lovely bells using their traditional techniques.

Early Bells Foreshadow Today's Limited Edition Hobby

Although the collecting of series of limited edition bells is a rather recent phenomenon, some of the collectible bells of past eras foretold the popularity of this hobby. For instance, Royal Bayreuth of Germany introduced a set of "Sunbonnet Babies" bells at the turn of the century, as well as some charming nursery rhyme bells in a related grouping. Other makers offered flint glass bells — each with a different figure on the handle. Although as recently as 1960 these pieces commanded just a few dollars apiece in antique shops, today they may bring hundreds of dollars each, if they are in fine condition.

American commemorative bells have been collector's items for more than a century, with one early example being the reproduction of the Liberty Bell which was sold at the Centennial Exposition, 1876, in Philadelphia. Then in 1893 two different commemoratives were available at the Chicago World's Columbian Exposition. After this, there was at least one special bell offered at most every world's fair and major exposition in the United States.

Traditional Forms and Famous Artists Intrigue Bell Collectors

In recent years, a number of limited edition firms have offered series of bells — often inspired by traditional forms and subject matter. For instance, one classic of the bell world is the "figural" or "portrait" bell. These cast metal bells form the figure of a person — often a woman with a full skirt. In the late 1970's, The Gorham Company introduced a collection of such bells inspired by some of the world's most admired female historical subjects.

Gorham was well qualified for such a task, since this firm is widely considered to be America's premier bellmaker. For generations, Gorham has made bells of metal and fine china, and the firm's Victorian tea bells are still regarded as some of the finest American art objects of the late 19th century.

Another traditional bell form which Gorham has re-introduced is the classic "school bell." A graceful wooden handle tops a bell of fine china with a gold rim and colorful decoration. Using art by Norman Rockwell, Gorham's school bells have been offered in series to commemorate Christmas and many other subjects.

Rockwell bells have won the hearts of many collectors — series by firms including River Shore, The Danbury Mint, Dave Grossman Designs and others have debuted in the last decade or so.

Like figurines, often a bell or series of bells is offered to complement a popular limited edition collector plate. About five years ago, Goebel introduced its first Hummel bell, featuring the art of Sister M. Innocentia Hummel. "M.I. Hummels" already had become successful in the plate and figurine fields, and thus the transition to bells was an easy one for Goebel.

Bell Collectors Enjoy Association Membership

Long before plate collecting became popular here in the United States, a dedicated group of "bell lovers" formed the American Bell Association. Since 1940, thousands of bell hobbyists have met in local groups and enjoyed annual conventions—all planned to allow these enthusiasts to share the enjoyment of their collections.

At one time, such well-informed collectors were almost entirely inclined toward antique bells. But today, with increased demand and price escalation, and the small-but-growing variety of fine contemporary bell collections—these hobbyists have turned much of their attention toward new bell introductions.

Louise Collins, editor of the Association's "The Bell Tower" newsletter, cites uniqueness, historical significance, beauty, good tone and reasonable price as the main criteria for contemporary bell selection. She welcomes present bell collectors—and those who are interested in this hobby—to write for further information on the Association. (See the section on Clubs, Conventions and Travel in this book for the address of the ABA.) Members receive regular newsletters amounting to 300 pages of information per year. There are 47 regional chapters, and members also meet at the annual convention and during trips planned by the Association.

The "school bell" style is popular with collectors, as evidenced by this gold-rimmed, wooden-handled Hamilton Collection offering in a series called ***School Days Bells.*** *As with plates, figurines, and most every other area of collecting, the art of Norman Rockwell makes popular bell subject matter. This art originally appeared on the cover of the* ***Literary Digest*** *on Septermber 6, 1919.*

An introduction to graphics for the collector

by Diana Gordon Viktor

Throughout history, art has been accessible mainly to an elite few, who by virtue of wealth and stature could afford art—or cause art to be created. It has only been within the last 100 years or so that art collecting has been available to a more diverse audience.

One of the main forces behind this move toward universal art appreciation and ownership has been the recognition of "printmaking" as an art form. And today, printmaking ranks with painting, drawing and sculpture as one of the principal means of artistic expression.

A Brief History of Printmaking

The earliest printing process was engraving, done by the Sumerians, circa 3000 B.C. They used stone cylinder seals which were engraved and then rolled over soft clay tablets. The Chinese were said to have reproduced wood blocks on cloth in the 2nd Century A.D., and were using paper by the 9th Century. Printmaking itself dates back to the 14th Century in Japan, when the woodcut relief process was perfected.

The first Western (European) prints were woodcuts dating to 1418 A.D., at which time craftsmen were using woodcuts to decorate playing cards. These were the first large-volume printings. Soon after, finer woodcuts were used to mass-produce books.

Printmaking was not looked upon as a true art form until about 1440. At that time, goldsmiths who decorated armor, jewelry and silverware decided to produce engravings that were meant to be printing plates. They were the first to "pull" prints to see how far along they were in their work, and what corrections needed to be made. They looked upon engravings as a way to reproduce an image. These early engravings were said to have been produced for the upper class because of the high cost of materials and skilled craftsmen who produced them.

In the late 1700's, a German named Aloys Senefelder changed the direction of printmaking. He was in search of a way to reproduce sheet music and hoped to find a substitute for the tedious process of etching. His experimentation led to the discovery of "lithography." Lithography, a much freer form of printing, allowed many artists who were not yet printmakers to become quite proficient in the field.

The invention of photography, which became firmly established by 1850, caused a great deal of concern to those using other processes of printing. The photographic reproduction process seemed to threaten the very fiber of creativity, and artists were compelled to choose between remaining creative printmakers, or succumbing to the influence of this new commercial process. It has only been in the last 15 years or so that photographs have been looked upon as a collectible form of art.

Mass production in lithography began in France in 1890, when the French developed the first printing press which used large litho-stones. These stones could handle more than one image at a time, which greatly decreased the time and cost of production. It was quite a fad, between 1890-1900, to collect the many posters and color lithographs printed in this manner.

For the artist, printmaking has not changed much from the basic processes developed throughout history. But there is one major exception to this: "offset" printing. Advances in printmaking technology (the combination of computers, photographic techniques, inks, plates, and presses) have made printing available to all artists. Today, many artists who are not printmakers can have their original paintings or drawings reproduced in large quantities in this "photomechanical" process. The proliferation of this type of printing, as well as the other basic printmaking techniques, has brought many more people into the realm of print collecting.

Are All Graphics, or Prints, Alike?

In theory, prints are all alike. That is, all prints are made by pressing an inked "matrix," a printing surface made of wood, metal, stone or other material, against sheets of paper. Trying to define the word "print," or "graphic," is a subject of great concern in the art world today, mainly because of the many prejudices placed on the types of processes and methods currently used in the printing of artwork for collecting.

Traditionally, "prints" have been viewed as multiple images produced from a plate (or matrix). The plate is the hard, flat surface which contains the original design, picture or message. The surface receives the ink, and the ink is transferred to paper. The process can be repeated many times to produce nearly exact copies.

Webster has defined "print" as: "to make a copy by impressing paper against an inked positive surface; to impress with a design or pattern; to make (a positive picture) on a sensitized photographic surface from a negative or positive; a copy made by printing."

The art world seeks to make a distinction between "original prints" and "reproductions." This distinction is made mainly to protect the collector from the pitfalls of misrepresentation. None of us want to discover that our purchase is a fake, or sold to us under fraudulent representation. As a collector, you must learn to examine the prints you are interested in purchasing, and determine whether they are hand-made or reproductions.

"Original prints" are those in which the artist has created the original design directly on the matrix (plate, stone, screen, transfer paper, or film negative). Then he continues his involvement, either by actually doing the print or by overseeing the printing process. And finally, the artist approves each print by signing and numbering each piece.

"Reproductions" are prints made when an artist give an original work of art, a painting, or a drawing, to a printer. The printer uses a "photomechanical" process to reproduce the original work which is printed on an "offset" process. The artist has little to do with the printing process, but is usually the one to approve the edition for sale.

It is believed that "original prints" are of greater value than "reproductions," because of the greater degree of involvement the artist has in their production. But, as indicated over the last 15 years, "reproductions" have been so widely accepted as collectibles that there has been as much or more demand for them as for "original prints."

"Old prints" are both originals and reproductions which are in great demand by collectors. They may reflect an era, subject matter, or an artist's artistic development. Examples would be pretty ladies by Maxfield Parrish or Louis Icart, or fine etchings by Rembrandt or his peers, or fine lithographs by Picasso, Matisse or Miro. Collecting older editions can be extremely chancy because of the high level of fakes, forgeries and misrepresentations on the market today. You must be very well informed about that artist, his works, and your sources in order to protect yourself from making some very disappointing purchases.

The great joy in collecting "old prints" is that there are still some good buys from very famous artists. If you are willing to do your homework in this area, collecting "old prints" could be very rewarding.

The Four Basic Print Processes

Knowing what to look for is the most important factor in print collecting. Though prints come in many different forms, there are four basic printing processes a collector should be aware of: relief, intaglio, planographic, and stencil. These processes can be used individually or in combination. Artists sometimes alter or hand-color the final image to create a unique work of art. Here is more about each process.

Relief Printing

Relief prints are made by cutting into the matrix (surface) and gouging away the areas which are not part of the design. The raised portions left behind create the image, which is then inked and printed. This process can be as crude as a child's cutting pieces from a potato, or as exacting as the highly skilled Japanese artist using very sophisticated materials.

Woodcut is the ancient Japanese printmaking process which did not reach Europe until the 15th century, at which time some of the most exquisite prints ever made in the medium were produced by a German artist, Albrect Durer. In the 17th Century, woodcuts were of little interest to artists, and it was not until the 1890's when artists such as Paul Gauguin and Edvard Munch revived the process.

In this technique, the artist selects a block of even-grained wood to be carved using special woodcut tools. The tools range from chisels to knives, and all have straight wooden handles for easy maneuvering. The wood selected for this process must be very smooth and hard, in order to hold up under the pressure of printing. Apple, pear, beech and sycamore are the traditional hard-surfaced woods used in this process.

After selecting the proper piece of wood, the artist draws his design on the surface and carves away the areas of the block that **are not** part of the design. The completed woodcut is a raised design which is then inked and pressed against paper. An artist will often use the grains of the wood for part of the overall design, and the most distinctive feature of a woodcut is the appearance of a grained texture on the print.

Wood engraving is the same as a woodcut except that the artist uses an end cut of wood which has no grain pattern. There are various tools—**graver, tint tool,** and **scorper**—used to create the design. The artist removes the areas that are not part of the design, and the remaining raised areas are inked and printed. Because of their close, hard grain, boxwood and red maple are the best woods to use for engraving.

Linocut is a 20th-century refinement of the woodcut process. Linocuts begin with a sheet of linoleum mounted to a wood base. The soft linoleum is then carved with the same woodcutting tools used in other relief printing processes. Again, the non-image areas are carved away, leaving the image raised and ready for printing. The finished linocut is then inked and printed.

Intaglio Printing

Intaglio (pronounced, in-tal-yo) is an Italian word meaning **cut in.** There are five distinct intaglio printing processes (etching, drypoint, aquatint, engraving, and mezzotint. Though each of these has a different application, the same principal of "cutting into the surface" is used with all of them.

Etching was developed in Germany in the early 16th century, and is a process whereby the matrix (surface) is partially eaten away or "bitten into." By the middle of the 17th century, Rembrandt perfected this process and raised it to new artistic heights.

To produce an etching, an artist coats a metal plate (usually copper) with an acid-resistant ground (asphaltim varnish). He then draws the design through the coating to the surface of the plate with a steel etch needle, making sure not to scratch the surface of the plate. The plate is placed in an acid bath and the exposed areas or lines are "etched" or "bitten into."

The artist can control the depth of the etch and vary the lines to create different tonal effects. The deeper the etch, the darker the lines and vice-versa. Once the artist approves the depth of the etch, he removes the plate and cleans off the ground in preparation for inking. The ink is rolled over the entire surface of the etched plate, and settles into the etched grooves. The surface is then cleaned, leaving only the etched areas inked. The paper is dampened, to make it more flexible, and placed over the inked plate. The plate is then run through an etching press under great pressure. The force of the press pushes the paper into the etch which absorbs the ink. The print is then "pulled" from the plate and allowed to dry.

One of the distinct features of an etching is the obvious bend in the paper around the image. This is caused by the pressure of the press forcing the damp paper over the edges of the plate.

Drypoint technique of intaglio printing is accomplished by using a needle-like instrument to scratch and gouge a design directly on the surface of a metal plate (matrix). This groove will hold the ink much like an etch, however, the action of scraping the surface of the metal plate creates rough edges called "burrs." These burrs also fill with ink, and produce a soft, velvety tonal effect when printed.

This process is very delicate because the burrs wear down quickly under the pressures of printing. Seldom can more than 20 prints be produced, and the first prints in an edition are usually more sought-after than the later ones.

Aquatint was invented in the 18th century, and was used by artists to create a washed or shaded effect on etchings. To create this shaded effect, the artist dusts a rosin powder on the areas of the plate he wants to change. The plate is then heated which causes the particles to stick. This then causes a porous ground of acid-resistant dots. The artist then applies a layer of acid-resistant varnish to protect the other areas of the plate he doesn't want to change. The plate is then placed in an acid bath, which "bites" into the areas between the dot particles. The darkness or lightness of this tonal effect depends on the length of time the plate is etched. Often this process takes more than one time for an artist to achieve the desired effect.

Engraving, first used in the 15th century, was the earliest of the intaglio techniques, and it wasn't until the 17th century that artists were lured away from engraving to a much easier process of "etching." Engraving remained a freer and more expressive form of reproduction, however it never regained its previous popularity. Except for works by a few modern artists experimenting in this process, contemporary collectors will find it difficult to specialize in engraving. Engraving is a method similar to drypoint. It is the use of sharp tools to incise lines into the surfaces of a metal plate. However, the tonal areas are created by cross-hatching and varying the spaces between lines. The more cross-hatching or closer the lines, the darker the image will print. Also, by increasing the depth of the incised furrow, the lines will become darker.

Engraved plates are then inked, and because the pressure of a press usually destroys the artwork, there are only a small number of prints from each plate.

Mezzotint, invented in the 17th century, was used mostly for printing book illustrations. There were, however, many fine contemporary mezzotints produced in the 1950's and 1960's.

Mezzotint is a method of reverse engraving. The artist starts by roughening the surface of a copper plate with a spiked tool called a "rocker" or "cradle." This creates an overall "burr," which when printed is a velvety black. The artist burnishes or scrapes away the areas which are to be toned or white. Because of the delicate surface of the plate, mezzotint prints are usually few in number. It is also quite difficult to find mezzotints today.

Planograph Prints

The "planographic" process means "any image printed from a **flat** surface or plane." Before the invention of lithography in the 1700's, all printing was created from indented or relief areas of a surface.

Original Lithography is based on the principle that "oil and water do not mix." "Litho," a Greek word for **stone,** has both the image and non-image areas on the printing matrix (surface). The application of chemicals—which creates an attraction or repulsion to printing inks—makes this type of printing possible.

To produce a lithograph, the artist starts with a highly polished, thick slab of Bavarian limestone, or one of the more contemporary surfaces of zinc or aluminum plates. His design is drawn directly on the surface with a greasy crayon, or painted on with a greasy ink called "tusche" (pronounced "tooch"). The finished surface is then treated with an acid and gum arabic solution. This makes the image stick and the rest of the surface more receptive to water.

A thin film of water is then sponged over the surface, and a greasy lithographic ink is rolled over the entire surface. The greasy ink adheres to the image areas, and is repelled by the remaining watered non-image surface. Paper is then placed over the inked stone and run through a hand-operated lithography press. The stone must be inked after each printing, and if an artist wishes to use more than one color, he has to create a separate stone (surface) for each color.

The main difficulty in printing multi-color lithographs is the registration of the paper. This is the ability to place each sheet of paper in exactly the same place for each print. Often-times prints are destroyed because of improper registration.

Photo-Offset Lithography involves prints produced "photomechanically," and are often called "Collector Prints." These prints are based on the same lithographic principle of "oil and water don't mix," however, the artist does not create the original design on the matrix. He has an original painting or drawing reproduced by using an "offset" printing method.

After the artist selects the painting or drawing he wants to reproduce, he gives it to the printers. The work is photographed through color filters and a grid screen which results in negatives with "dot patterns." There is usually one negative for each of the four basic colors used in printing, but in some cases, a fine reproduction may have as many as 11 color negatives.

If corrections are needed in these "dot patterned" negatives, it is at this time that the "dot etchers" can manually alter the amount of color any area will eventually print. The approved negatives are then made into printing plates. Photosensitive printing plates, again one for each color, are exposed through the individual negatives which in turn, reflect the dot pattern of each negative.

The plates are mounted onto the cylinders of an "offset" printing press. The inks are mechanically applied, one color to each plate. The "offset" press has many rollers...one roller is a rubber pad called the "blanket" which, when rolled against the inked plate, picks up the image and transfers it to the paper. Thus, the printing is not direct but "offset."

Each time paper is fed through the press, the registry must be perfect or the layers of different-colored dots will cause the image to be soft or out of focus.

Photo-offset reproductions are normally created in edition sizes of 500 to 5,000; all of which are usually pencil signed by the artist upon his approval. Often you will also see a signature in the image which was part of the original painting or drawing.

"Kidnapped Mare" is a print by Fred Stone. It issued at $115.00 in an edition of 750.

Serigraphy, or more commonly called "silkscreen", printing has evolved from the ancient art of stencil. The Greek word "serikos" means "silk," and "graphos" means "writing" in Greek.

Early man used the "stencil" method on cave walls, and starting in the 17th century, stencils have been used to make wallpapers and decorative arts. It was not until the refinement of the process by the Japanese and Chinese that "silkscreen" became an important part of this printing method. In the United States around the 1930's, "silkscreens" were first promoted as an art form and called "serigraphy."

Serigraphy is a direct printing process whereby the artist designs, makes and prints his own stencils. A serigraph differs from other prints in that its images are created with paint films instead of printing inks. It is an extremely versatile technique which can often simulate the raised effects of an oil painting, the wash effects of a watercolor, or the soft effects of a pastel. There is a widely-held opinion that serigraphy is as much a painter's medium as a printmaker's medium.

For each color used in his design, the artist uses a silk (nylon or polyester) fabric stretched tightly over a wooden frame. A design is made by blocking out or plugging up the areas which the artist **does not** want to print. The design then is printed in this manner. Paper is placed under the prepared screen, and with a wood-and-rubber squeegee, the artist pulls the ink across the screen. This forces the ink through the open area onto the paper.

Each color has its own screen, and each must be dried after printing. The process is quite demanding, since some serigraphs have as many as 19 colors or more. Once an edition is finished, the screens are often damaged or reused for other prints. The artist approves each print by carefully checking for consistent quality. The prints are then signed and numbered by the artist in most cases.

Smart Print Collectors Learn What to Look For

In recent years, collectors have become more and more aware of the joys and advantages of owning and displaying fine prints in their homes. One reason is that, even if printmaking often demands more from an artist, a print usually is easier to acquire than a painting by the same artist. More collectors are able to display images created by their favorite artists, and prints have the mystique, as in any limited edition purchase, that "someday my investment may increase in value."

"Let the buyer beware" has always been the first rule when dealing in the art world, and prints are certainly not excluded. Make sure, as a collector, that you do your homework before any major purchases are consummated. It is up to you to learn as much as you can about a print you are intending to buy, and any reputable dealer should be able to provide you with the answers to most all of your questions. If you are not satisfied, have them call the publisher for the information.

There are three main guidelines in collecting fine prints that should not be overlooked. First, "know what you are purchasing." You must be able to recognize the different types of prints, and learn to recognize the artist's style and know about his background. This approach to selecting prints will help protect you from the many misrepresented prints on the market today.

Richard Zolan created "Christi's Kitty," which also inspired a limited edition plate. The 16x20" print premiered at $125 in an edition of 450.

Second, make sure you are buying a print because you like it, and not solely for investment. Prints are beautiful objects of art to display, but more often than not, a print will be difficult to resell. So you might be living with your purchase for quite awhile.

Third, you must learn to take care of your print collection. Prints, unlike most collectibles, are very fragile and will require special attention in storing, framing, and preserving.

Guidelines to safe and successful print collecting require you to recognize these important aspects of a print:

Artist's Reputation—his/her background and level of success.
Style—is the work currently fashionable, or a remnant of a passing fad?
Print Quality—is it the best representation of its printing technique, or is it of lesser quality?
Condition—is it in good shape with no tears, stains, mold, creases, fingerprints, etc.?
Rarity—the size of the edition versus the demand for it.
Subject—can you live with the subject depicted, and will it be a popular subject in the future?
Technique—what type of printing processes are used, and how involved in the process was the artist?
Price—is the price of fair market value, and what if any exchange or refund privileges come with the print?
Documentation—does the print come with the proper information, as explained below?

Proper documentation should come with every print you buy. Always find out the following information about a print you are intending to purchase:

Artist
Type of print
Number of impressions in the edition
How or if the edition is signed and numbered by the artist
Method of printing (by hand or machine)
Type and size of paper used
Master printer's name or publisher's workshop
Verification that the plate or matrix has been cancelled

The Care of Prints

Prints are very fragile and are easily damaged. Your investment declines rapidly once your print is damaged, so as a collector you must respond to the necessary steps to protect your prints.

Unframed prints should be stored flat, away from light and moisture, and between two sheets of good-quality, acid-free mat board. If you have a damaged print, **do not** attempt to correct it yourself. Instead, seek out the services of a paper restorer.

Framing is a fine way to protect your prints. The choice of a frame is up to you and your framer, but make sure you follow these rules in framing:

1. Never cut the margins of a print.
2. Never permanently mount your print on any surface. Japanese rice paper hinges and rice starch adhesives can attach your print safely to the backing.
3. Never back a print with anything but a 100% acid-free board, sometimes called "rag board."
4. Always frame your print under glass or acrylic.
5. Never allow your print to touch the glass. The methods of preventing this are called "floating," or "matting."
6. To prevent pollution from damaging your print, use a dust cover over the back of the frame, sealed by glue or an inert tape.

Print check-ups are a good way to assure that no damage has been done to your framed prints. Have your framer check every print within four to five years of framing. He should look for light damage, mold growth, insect damage and loose hinges, and correct any flaws in the original framing.

Terms for Print Collectors

Now that you are more familiar with printmaking processes, you will want to learn some of the terms used in connection with prints:

Edition—The total number of prints made from one design.

Edition Size—The actual number of prints in the edition. The value of a print often is determined by its rarity.

Cancelled Plates—Most artists cancel or mark up their plates to assure the end of an edition, and to prevent any unauthorized reprints from being produced.

Signed Copies—This is a relatively modern custom and it has nothing to do with the originality of the print. It establishes the artist's claim that the print is his work.

Artist's Proofs—A small number of prints of an edition which are usually reserved for the artist or his estate. They usually are marked with an "AP." These prints sometimes come into the market, and often are misrepresented as greater works than the rest of the edition. Remember, these prints are part of the original edition and differ only by the way they are marked.

Numbering—The numbering of prints appears in pencil in the lower left hand margin, or border. Example: 14/100 indicates the print is the 14th one approved by the artist in an edition of 100. The practice of numbering is to make an edition appear more unique. The order of the numbers are only to identify each print in an edition, and not to make one more valuable than another.

Remarqued Print—A print of any type which has been hand-colored, or somehow altered by the artist to make it "one of a kind." Example: an artist will sometimes draw or write in the margin and sign the print personally to the collector.

Restrikes—Most artists are careful to cancel their plates, however some artists keep them for additional printing if a print becomes popular with collectors. Restrikes are usually not of the same quality as the original edition, and most of them are unsigned by the artist.

Where and How to Find Prints

Here are a few sources of prints which will expand your knowledge and experience beyond this article:

Retail Dealers—Galleries that specialize in graphic arts.

Auctions—Special auction houses are heavily vested in prints.

Print Publishers—Going to the source is sometimes the only way to find the particular piece you want.

Public Galleries and Museums—Bookstores in these places often have many reproductions, and sometimes original prints.

Artists—They sometimes have editions available directly.

Other Collectors—Finding someone who has the same taste as you do in prints can help expand your knowledge and open the door to trading.

Antique Stores—They are not always aware of the true value of the prints they have available, and you can often find a real buy if you are willing to hunt for it.

Mail-Order Companies and Print Clubs—Though there are some risks in dealing through the mail with fragile prints, these sources can sometimes help you along with your collecting. You must be careful that the prints you are buying are properly represented.

Finding prints you like will most probably not be very difficult. Selecting the best print for the most reasonable price will be your biggest challenge. Best of luck to you, and "happy collecting."

DIANA GORDON VIKTOR has a wide and varied background in the field of fine arts and graphics. She is the former director of a Chicago art gallery, and has experience selling art to corporate representatives. She is the former director of The Bradford Museum of Collector Plates in Niles, Illinois. While at Bradford, she helped attract and develop artists for that firm's various plate programs. Ms. Viktor also is a former partner in Graphics Buying Service, a Chicago-based firm which sells limited edition prints created by noted collector plate artists. Today, Ms. Viktor is active as a seminar leader, teaching artists how to succeed in the business side of their profession. She resides in the Washington, D.C. area.

One of the most popular Fred Stone prints is "Man O War," which issued in an edition of 695 for $175.00.

"Flowers for Grandma" is a print by Donald Zolan. It issued at $135.00 in 1982, in an edition limited to 450.

Classic German steins inspire contemporary collecting hobby

In 19th-century Germany, heavy stoneware drinking vessels with hinged lids were extremely popular. These "steins," as they were called in the southwest region of Germany, had handles to make lifting easy and lids to keep the contents free from debris. They first were seen in Cologne during the 1500's, but they reached their peak of popularity and artistry some 300 years later.

Stoneware—in addition to the fact that it is considerably less expensive than porcelain—has an extra benefit to the beer drinker. This hard, dense material helps keep the beer fresh and cool.

Early steins were strictly functional—decorated with colored glazes which at first served mainly as protective coatings. But before long steinmaking developed into a high art: one which is celebrated even today by collectors in Germany, America, and many other countries.

Perhaps the best-known and most coveted of the 19th-century steins were those made in the Saar Valley at a town called Mettlach. There the family business called Villeroy & Boch created "cameo" and "chromolith" steins featuring artwork which told tales of battle, commemorated special occasions and places, or captured the characters of folk tales and legends.

Unfortunately, after World War I the Mettlach Studios discontinued stein production to concentrate on tableware and crystal. Some say that war destruction claimed the lives of too many trained craftspeople for Mettlach to continue with steins. Others claim the loss of machinery and molds was too great for Villeroy & Boch to sustain.

But whatever the reason for the end of their production, it seems that collector interest in the Mettlach steins—and those made by other fine firms like Simon Peter Gerz, Albert Jac. Thewalt, Reinhold Merkelbach and WickWerke—remained strong and even grew in some areas in the years following shut-down at Villeroy & Boch.

Here in America and elsewhere, a club called Stein Collectors International boasts thousands of members and scores of chapters. Numerous informational books and price guides are available to the stein collector who wants to be sure he acquires the finest specimens available for the funds he has to spend. (For the address of Stein Collectors International, see the section in this book on Clubs, Conventions and Travel.)

Steins which sold in Europe a century ago for fifty cents to $2.50 (two to 10 marks) now command as much as $1,500 to $2,500 on the American market. And novice collectors who attend art auctions may be floored by the intense bidding for what appears to be nothing more or less than an inlaid stoneware drinking vessel.

New Collectors Increase the Demand for Steins

According to Dr. Norman B. Medow, past president of Stein Collectors International and author of a fine two-part article called "Judging Mettlach Steins" (*Antique Journal,* June-July 1978), a number of new stein collectors have entered the market in recent years. Many are relatively inexperienced in the field and are searching for guidelines by which to evaluate the steins they may see at auction or in antique stores.

What's more, there has been an exciting new development in stein collecting: Villeroy & Boch, The Norman Rockwell Museum and Opa's Haus, among others, are creating steins inspired by the best in traditional stein design and workmanship, even though all of them are not German made.

Villeroy & Boch has introduced limited edition steins which are reminiscent of the well-loved chromolith and phanolith (cameo) steins of the 19th century. The Norman Rockwell Museum offers hand-painted, cast steins with relief motifs inspired by the works of Rockwell. And Opa's Haus contracts with some of Germany's best stein manufacturers to create original, limited editions for the American market.

What to Look for in Steins

The novice stein collector may find the following points of special interest, for they serve as a guide to the evaluation both of antique steins, and of newer items offered in limited edition form. Here are some things to consider in selecting a stein:

Weight and Size. Traditional steins are made of a heavy, clay stoneware which provides the "heft" necessary for a true stein body. Compare this to the light, thin-walled steins which may be presented to you as "traditional," and you will see the difference immediately. A solid pewter stein lid and decorative pewter lid hinge add to the weight as well.

Traditional steins come in many sizes—from novelty items holding 1/16 liter to huge 5-liter pieces. Half-liter sizes (holding approximately one pint) seem quite prevalent and popular among today's collectors.

Drinking Surface. Steins—even today's limited editions—were and are made for drinking. They are not simply decorative pieces. The inner surface, therefore, is finished most often with a white porcelainized glaze which prevents absorption.

Texture. Except for any incised, etched or cameo areas, most fine steins have an extremely smooth texture. Imitations may be quite gritty or coarse to the touch. Especially smooth are the Villeroy & Boch chromolith steins—this is a key to the technique.

Subject Matter. German beer steins tell stories, commemorate events and people, and focus on beloved legends. They are quite decorative and colorful. Artists who created steins are among the finest of their era—such as Heinrich Schlitt, a famous Villeroy & Boch artist who is also known for creating V&B's "Snow White and the Seven Dwarfs" plate.

Lids. It is the lid which makes a stein a stein—a drinking vessel with a handle but no lid is merely a mug. The reason for the lid was functional—a common sense precaution—for in the 15th or 16th century it was discovered that covering drinking vessels would prevent contamination effectively. Other attributes of lids include keeping liquids cool, preventing spillage, and providing an attractive finishing touch.

Pewter is the normal lid material, although the well-heeled stein buyer in Germany could opt for a custom lid of silver or another metal. Thumblifts, or hinges, are also crafted of pewter, and may be quite decorative. The steins with stoneware inserts in their lids are extremely popular with today's collectors, although some old steins have lids completely made of decorative pewter.

The firm of Albert Jac. Thewalt is one of the better-known creators of fine German beer steins. Here is a contemporary Thewalt stein from the "Oldie" series, called "Beer Here."

One of the first firms to offer limited edition steins to contemporary collectors was the studio of Simon Peter Gerz. Here, from left to right, are the Gerz annual limited edition steins for 1974, 1975, 1976, 1977, 1978, 1979, 1980, 1981, and 1982.

Limited edition marketers expand the popular market for collectible dolls

Doll collecting has been a top collecting hobby in the United States for decades. The first organized group of collectors surfaced in the late 1930's with the establishment of the National Doll and Toy Collectors Club, an organization that later spawned the United Federation of Doll Clubs and the Doll Collectors of America, Inc., as well as other organizations.

From these small groups has evolved an international body of hobbyists who are intensely interested in researching antique, collectible and modern dolls. The United Federation of Doll Clubs now numbers nearly 16,000 paid members.

Before the 1970's, doll collecting centered mainly on the antique varieties. But because demand was increasing faster than the supply of antique dolls, a contemporary market was opened, and prices for a wide range of dolls began to rise rapidly.

Some dolls—both old and more recent—have risen dramatically in value. For example, an Albert Marque doll sold in the late 1930's for $300; in the late 1970's these dolls were fetching $32,000 at auction; and in January, 1983 an Albert Marque sold at auction for $38,000.

While Albert Marque dolls are considered to be both rare and very fine, a similar experience on a smaller scale can be related about a relatively modern doll. The Barbie doll, created by Mattel in 1959, originally retailed for under $4; the current value of a mint-condition 1959 Barbie is many, many times that much. This escalation in value on the secondary market has influenced the value of collectible or special-edition dolls made especially for the collector market.

What to Look for in Contemporary Dolls

Just stroll through a department store or specialty shop that stocks a wide variety of dolls, and you will note the hundreds of choices offered to collectors. Antique doll prices have escalated to a level where many collectors have made the decision to buy more recently-made and affordable dolls, or new, limited-edition dolls that are still within financial reach.

The first consideration in selecting such dolls should be the collector's **personal preference.** He or she should only buy dolls that are especially appealing, and that can be displayed in the home among other antiques, collectibles and furnishings.

Next, collectors should consider the **popularity** of certain dolls—there are fads in doll collecting, just as there are in clothes, food and other aspects of life. If dolls are desirable and in great demand, collectors can

World Doll Company's porcelain Marilyn Monroe doll wearing a full-length white mink coat, sequin-decorated gown and diamond necklace and earrings retails for $6,500.

assume that those dolls will increase in value, making their purchase a good investment.

For instance, in recent years there has been a proliferation of celebrity dolls. Since this has been a recurring theme, potential collectors should take special note of it. Because of the special attention bestowed on celebrity dolls, they should prove to be an excellent area for investment. Well over 1,000 celebrity dolls have been made by doll manufacturers from 1900 to the present. A recent book, *The Encyclopedia of Celebrity Dolls,* by John Axe, illustrates over 1,100 such dolls and describes over 1,500 variations.

More Aspects to Consider

Another factor for collectors would be the **number** of dolls being produced. If inordinately high numbers are produced, then additional demand would have to be generated before a rise in value could occur.

One should also look at the **modeling and artistic aspects** of a doll. Because dolls are now considered an art form, collectors appreciate their beauty of design in sculpting as well as the designing of their clothes.

A good example of the craftsmanship among today's doll makers would be the United States Historical Society, which is currently creating a series of dolls known as *The Great Americans.* Their "Living Image" dolls, first released in 1982, now include Benjamin Franklin, George Washington, Thomas Jefferson and Abigail Adams. The sculptor of this limited edition series, Raymond Lamb, should be commended for the remarkable, life-like rendering his dolls exhibit.

"Mary," a porcelain doll, is the first in a planned edition of annual collectors' dolls by Bing & Grondahl.

Faith Wick's "Children's Costume Party" dolls are among the 1983 porcelain dolls from Dollspart.

1983 marked the inauguration of Effanbee's new series "The Presidents." The first two dolls were George Washington and Abraham Lincoln.

United States Historical Dolls Beautifully Dressed

Not only are the Lamb dolls finely sculptured, true-to-life portraits, but they are also authentically costumed. Benjamin Franklin, for instance, has 55 miniature reproduction pewter buttons sewn on his coat, and carries a precise miniature of his own cane—the original of which is now in The Smithsonian Institution collection.

George Washington's leather-covered scabbard holds a perfect pewter replica of his inaugural sword. Abigail Adams wears pretty silk-over-kid shoes. And Thomas Jefferson's greatcoat has a hand-stitched pocket to hold a replica of a Queen Anne pistol.

The **first doll** in any limited edition, such as those offered by the United States Historical Society, usually proves to be more desirable to collectors. This is evidenced by the first doll issued by the Effanbee Limited Edition Doll Club, which started in 1975. Their first doll, the 1975 "Precious Baby," originally sold for $35. It now realizes close to $400. In fact, one person who bought all eight dolls produced from 1975 to 1982—for a total investment of less than $300—recently sold them mint-in-box for $1,650!

Four of Gorham's porcelain edition of Holly Hobbie® dolls—Blue Girl, Heather, Little Amy and Robbie.

Original Boxes and Clothing Please Collectors

Collectors also put a high value on **"total originality."** This means that the doll must have its original box, as well as the dress, wig and accessories. If you wish to retain the value of your doll and realize a profit when you sell it, you must carefully store all parts and keep them in original condition.

Yet another important consideration would be the **workmanship** of the doll. Because doll making is still a process that involves handwork, the painting of the face, assembly and construction of the clothes can have variations of quality. Collectors should check all of these features very carefully when purchasing a doll, and always insist on top quality.

Another thing to keep in mind when buying a doll is its **availability.** That is, how difficult it is to find such a doll? With the ever-growing number of collectors, some dolls are in more demand than others, and supply often cannot keep up with demand. An excellent example of this is the current collection of dolls from the Alexander Doll Company. The demand for these dolls is so great that very few of them ever reach the shelves in many shops. Oftentimes, the shop will have a waiting list for the dolls long before they are delivered. It is not uncommon to see price tags on the second sale of these dolls double the manufacturer's suggested retail price—even within a few weeks or months after the original purchase.

Popular themes are still another consideration to be addressed by collectors. The Gorham Company recently entered the doll market and, in 1983, introduced a fascinating new series. The ever-popular Holly Hobbie® now will be made in porcelain by Gorham. The eight girls and one boy in this series are dressed in the country-casual style associated with Holly Hobbie.® The literary classic *Little Women* series—also being produced in porcelain by Gorham—includes 19-inch Meg, Jo, Beth, and Amy dolls. Bride dolls also are a perennial popular theme, as are some dolls representing royalty.

Clothing is very important to doll collectors, and should be given careful consideration before purchasing a doll. Make sure that the materials used in costuming the doll are of a scale that enhances, rather than detracts, from the doll's appearance. Also, carefully check the styling and be sure it is true to the period the doll represents.

Royal Doulton's *The Edwardian Social Season* series of dolls was designed to illustrate fine costumes worn by Edwardian ladies of fashion to special social events of the period. These dolls, with their opulent costumes, mirror a period in English history with an accuracy that does the manufacturer proud.

Some manufacturers use the same faces for their dolls and only change the costumes; this is rather prevalent nowadays. However, when a doll manufacturer goes to the trouble and expense of having individual dolls sculpted, collectors of the present and the future will always be appreciative.

Last Year Brings Important Doll Issues to the Market

Noteworthy porcelain dolls produced in 1983 bear such names as Bing & Grondahl, Dolls by Jerri, Avigail Brahams, Yolanda Bello, the *Here Comes the Brides* series by Dollsparts Doll Creations, dolls by Faith Wick, the Gerber Babies in porcelain, and the Shader China Dolls. The popularity of limited editions of bisque dolls is evidenced by the tremendous number of manufacturers entering this field. Some start in a garage and quickly blossom into full manufacturing complexes.

Limited productions of note in the vinyl doll line include: the Marilyn Monroe doll by World Doll Company; the Louis Nichole collection; Effanbee's *The Presidents,* Craftsman Corner and Legend series "Groucho Marx,"; Heidi Ott and Suzanne Gibson dolls—both distributed by Reeves International; and the reintroduction of the adorable "Kewpie" doll; the recreation of the original Lenci dolls; the *La Cheri* series from Mattel, and the dolls made by Sekiguchi Company, Inc.

Doll collectors may find price guides such as Jan Foulke's *Fifth Blue Book of Dolls and Values* very helpful.

There are several doll magazines currently being published, and most have merit. However, the magazine collectors have relied upon for years to provide in-depth coverage of antique, collectible, and limited-edition dolls is *Doll Reader* from Hobby House Press. The magazine often runs 200 pages per month or more, with articles written by a wide range of recognized authorities in the doll world. For more information, write *Doll Reader* in care of Hobby House Press, 900 Frederick Street, Cumberland, Maryland 21502.

Nursery Rhyme and Mother Goose Dolls by Suzanne Gibson include Jack and Jill, Mucy Locket, Little Bo-Peep and Mother Goose herself.

Dolls by Jerri for 1983 feature porcelain reproductions of Gainsborough's "Blue Boy" and Sr. Thomas Lawrence's "Pinky."

Royal Doulton's "The Edwardian Social Season" porcelain dolls.

*An etagere makes a fine display piece for plates, figurines and other collectibles. [Courtesy of **Plate Collector.**]*

*Collectors who specialize may want to group related items together—as did this collector of Delft items. [Courtesy of **Plate Collector.**]*

Bookcases are not just for books—as this grouping of Boehm figurines shows beautifully.

*Some collectors rotate their displays to fit the holidays—or add seasonal touches like these wreaths. [Courtesy of **Plate Collector.**]*

How to decorate with limited edition collectibles

by Catherine Bloom
Writer and Researcher, *Collectibles Market Index Price Guide*

A fresh and energetic spirit has transformed the art of collecting. And with it comes a new breed of collector—one who takes a new approach to displaying his or her treasures. Unwilling to hide that precious collection in a closet, he or she seeks new ways to make plates, figurines and other limited editions a part of everyday life. Unhampered by traditional rules, this collector brings a new perspective to displaying "the things they enjoy."

Susan Bailen-Wittenbach, an interior designer in Grand Rapids, Michigan, works frequently with collectors. She often finds that her first task is to assure her clients that they should trust their personal inclinations and select only things that they like personally.

People seem to need the encouragement and permission to "do their own thing" without fear, she believes.

The originality and personal taste of a collector are the most important factors in placing a personal imprint on his or her surroundings. By using a collection as a trademark or personal touch, a collector gains a number of advantages. Simply put, people are happier, and the world around them seems more interesting and challenging, when they are surrounded by beautiful things.

A collection also may become more valuable if it is well displayed. It is human nature to place more value on things that are exhibited properly.

"I tell clients not to be afraid to use what they have. With only a few basic elements of design, a collection can become the strength of a whole room," says Ms. Bailen-Wittenbach.

A number of experts in the collectibles field and several interior designers also were polled on this point. While their insights reflect their personal philosophies, most agreed on these basic guidelines.

Elements of Design: The Setting

Study the relationship between the living space and the collection you wish to display. A special chemistry is needed to bring together the artistry and theme of a collection, and a setting which complements it.

Both the individuality of the collection and the ambience of the space must be respected. This involves a delicate balancing act in which neither side is overpowered.

Experts agree that so many themes and styles of plate art are produced today that it is now possible to find a plate for every room of the house. Nevertheless, the appropriateness of each plate must be considered. What effect do you want to achieve with the collection? Will the grouping be the focal point of the room, or just a small, personal touch?

Many older homes are rich in architectural detail: mantles, lintels over the doors and windows, ledges, and plate rails—all of which can be turned into an advantage to the collector.

Today's homes, on the other hand, may be stark—without any architectural detailing. While they may lack inherent charm, these walls can serve as highly visible areas where collectibles can be displayed or stored with striking effects.

In rooms without a fireplace or other dominant architectural focus, the grouping can become the focal point. In these situations, Ms. Bailen-Wittenbach cautions that simplicity is the key. "Resist the temptation to overkill simply because you have many items available," she advises.

For the maximum dramatic effect, allow only one collection or area of emphasis in each room. More than one grouping dilutes the impact and may make the room appear disjointed or cluttered.

The Grouping

A grouping of items should be viewed as a unit. It may contain a variety of elements—plates, figurines, or lithographs. But like a formal English garden, each piece contributes its distinctive beauty within the well-planned dimensions of the garden. Whether it is a single figurine or an entire collection, there is a sense of order.

This order depends on a sense of balance. If a grouping is symmetrical or perfectly balanced, it can provide a sense of order and stability. The symmetry should be strong and dramatic to prevent the grouping from being monotonous.

An asymmetrical grouping is achieved by combining elements of different sizes and weights to achieve balance. There may be symmetrical elements within the grouping, but the sense of vitality and excitement comes from the skillful use of a variety of elements.

If a collection is large, many experts recommend selecting just enough pieces to determine the theme, and storing the rest—perhaps for rotation during the year. Like an iceberg, many of the best groupings are achieved with a limited number of pieces.

This advice is borne out by William Freudenberg of Hollywood Limited Editions: "As a general rule, if you want to present your collection as a work of art, it may be advisable to select only a few pieces for display, and rotate them several times a year. This tends to provide a freshness to the collection."

Plates, figurines and a handsome graphic make a harmonious display on an animal theme. [*Courtesy of* ***Plate Collector.***]

Planning a Grouping

Another expert in the field, Susan K. Elliott, editor of *Plate Collector,* believes: "The most important step in displaying collectibles is planning the display. Plates can be mixed with prints or figurines to create an attractive overall effect, but it takes planning."

Once the pieces are selected for the grouping, designers recommend placing them on the carpet in front of the wall where they will be displayed. There they can be re-arranged until the desired effect is achieved.

Then the grouping can be successfully transferred to the wall by cutting outlines in the shape of each piece and taping them on the wall to see if the pre-arranged grouping is as effective as it seems. It is much easier to make changes with paper and tape than with hammer and nails!

If two people work together during this phase, it is much easier. One can provide the perspective while the other person makes the necessary changes in the arrangement.

Focal Point

According to Susan Bailen-Wittenbach, the best method of designing a grouping is to begin with the piece that is to be the focal point of the grouping. Usually, it is the largest or most impressive piece and contains the colors, shapes or theme that will be echoed in other elements of the room.

A vibrant color or geometric pattern can be repeated with modifications in the carpet, draperies or fabrics to create a total environment for the room. It is this adaptation and repetition of the elements which can make collectibles such an important factor in the total design.

The focal point is placed at eye level. It is the first thing the eye makes contact with, and it provides a sense of familiarity and security. From this point the eye then explores the rest of the grouping.

As part of her "hands on" advice to collectors, Ms. Bailen-Wittenbach recommends groupings which contain an odd number of elements. For example, a grouping that contains five framed pieces or seven unframed is more interesting. The uneven numbers prevent the monotone, or repetitive feeling which may be present in an even-numbered grouping.

Establish at least one line—horizontal, vertical or diagonal—to provide a sense of order. A gentle curved or straight line provides a sense of unity and strength.

Consider the negative space (the space around and between each plate or work of art.) If there isn't enough negative space, a grouping will appear cramped or cluttered, so give it plenty of room to "breathe." Too much negative space results in a disconnected, floating effect which sends the attention outward instead of focusing it.

No grouping should be wider than the piece of furniture underneath it. If people will be seated in front of a collection, take into consideration the need for head space. If the grouping is to be viewed from a seated position, lower the focal point to a level in line with eye contact for a seated observer.

The color and surface of the wall on which a grouping is displayed is an important factor in its impact. Wallpaper with hibiscus blossoms or metallic

Playing up the "natural attributes" of a collectible piece can be a dramatic idea. Witness this display of glass or crystal plates where light can shine through. [*Courtesy of* ***Plate Collector.***]

stripes is a poor backdrop for a sensitively-styled lithograph or a delicately-painted porcelain.

The impact of the background is illustrated by placing a collection of blue-and-white plates against backgrounds of white, deep blue or soft apricot. If the collector is uncertain about background colors, a piece may be placed against fabrics of different colors and hues to determine the most effective background tone.

Frequently, one of the accent colors in the plate is used as the background color. Or in other cases, it will be repeated in other elements of the room to help integrate the collection into the room. It need not be bold or unusual to be effective.

Lighting

The proper use of lighting within a room can be an important factor in bringing out even the finest details and craftsmanship of a collection.

Track lighting, uplighting, or picture lighting can be used to illuminate an entire collection, or to highlight a favorite. Experiment with different colors of lighting. Technology has produced many subtle and attractive lighting systems. A soft white bulb can reveal beauty in an even more dramatic fashion than natural light. Cases and cabinets suitable for displaying collections may also be equipped with lighting for better display.

Frames and Mats

Dissimilar items may be pulled together and given a sense of unity and continuity by using color-coordinated mats and/or frames. The style of a frame and the color of the wood can play an important part in coordinating a collection with the decor. This topic will be covered under accessories, later in this article.

A corner cabinet becomes home for a collection of blue-and-white plates and various figurines. [*Courtesy of* ***Plate Collector***.]

Although Oriental-style artwork enhances most any decor, it can be especially appealing in a setting with Oriental touches. Here, a collection of Hakata doll figurines.

The "No Holds Barred" Collector

While guidelines and suggestions may be helpful for a collector interested in better displaying his or her collection, both Ms. Bailen-Wittenbach and Erli Gronberg, Chairman of the Interior Design Department of Kendall School of Design (Grand Rapids, Michigan) agree that there is another kind of collector.

This blithe spirit seemingly ignores all the rules. The collector seems charged with a sense of exuberance and fun, and it appears that his or her collection is displayed "everywhere."

The collector's eclectic taste provides an endless variety of contrasting shapes, colors and sizes. There is a feeling that something new and different will appear every day.

According to Gronberg, these are the collectors who enjoy the sheer fun of collecting. It represents a form of entertainment to them, with something new and different to see every time you look.

While they may be lightyears away from the serious collector/investor, these collectors are important in the scheme of things.

This is the person who has taken to heart Ms. Bailen-Wittenbach's advice: "It is important to have things you love around you. You know what you like—rely on your own taste.

"If it makes you feel good, then it is good for you. Don't be too concerned if the things that you enjoy change. That's all right. It's just part of the growing process. Just fill your space with the things you love."

Accessories for Displaying Collectibles

In response to the growth of the collectibles field, a number of companies now produce a wide variety of accessories for effectively displaying a full range of collectibles.

The price range varies from economical to moderately expensive. Collectors are advised to read the manufacturer's guarantee before deciding which product is most suitable for displaying their valuable collections. Here are some specifics on what is available for plates and a few other collectible categories.

Plates

Self-Hangers. Many collector plates have been designed and manufactured to assist the collector in display. Plates like the Bing & Grondahl Christmas and Mother's Day have two small holes in the foot rim on the back of the plate. A nylon cord threaded through these holes can then be formed into a loop for hanging.

These self-hangers are strong enough to bear the weight of the plate. The foot's rim is pierced before firing and usually glazed so there are no rough surfaces to scratch the plate or fray the cord.

Collectors are not encouraged to use wire to fashion the loop. In some climates, metal may rust and discolor the plate, or even lose strength and allow the plate to fall.

Glued Self-Hangers. Another type of hanger is the glued self-hanger. They have been used successfully by many collectors, but they do present an element of danger. One of the most common dangers is lack of longevity for the moisten-and-affix gum tab. It may give excellent service in hanging a poster or a small piece of craftwork. However, these tabs have a tendency to loosen and fall when subjected to humidity or drastic temperature changes.

Another type of hanger works on the same principle, but uses a glue that adheres to the porcelain. These are more reliable, according to expert reports. The glue used with these hangers dries by a chemical reaction rather than evaporation. Before hanging any valuable plate using this method, read the manufacturer's guarantee to see if there are provisions for breakage.

Wire Spring. Another popular plate hanger is the wire spring. These hangers grip the plate securely in four places. These grippers are attached to springs which hold the plate securely and have a hook for hanging.

Many are simply metal, while others have been coated with a plastic or rubber coating to prevent scratching the rim of the plate.

Plastic Plate Hangers. Increased technology in the plastics industry has also resulted in a number of plastic hangers. Some models grip the plate at three points and can be adjusted for use with various-sized plates. Another model has no metal or springs to mar a plate and is constructed with a safety rail receptacle which provides a safe, easy means of displaying plates.

In this model, the plate can easily be removed and replaced without adjustment. This hanger also provides non-skid stabilizers on the back to help lessen tilting.

Collectors who pursue a theme throughout their collections may also be able to find hangers to carry it through. Currently, hangers with nautical and patriotic themes are available.

Plate Stands. Plate stands continue among the most popular means of displaying plates. They provide a free-standing, safe way to exhibit the full face of the plate.

The mobility of the plate stand is one of its biggest advantages. No longer restricted to the wall, the stand enables collectors to place their plates wherever they wish. Collectors may use plate stands in the creation of settings on tabletops, mantles, and shelves of bookcases. Stands also are used in china cabinets and display cases because they present the plate so beautifully while adding an extra measure of protection.

Because they have been produced for a number of years, there is a wide variety of stands for collectors to choose from. For instance, there are stands of clear plastic which may be folded for easy storage. One manufacturer produces a sturdy stand of acrylic materials. It comes in a variety of colors and has non-skid stabilizers on the bottom.

Wood is one of the most popular materials used in plate stands. A number of different methods of construction are used, as well as a number of wood finishes. Some stands are designed to give the appearance of an easel. Produced in both brass and wood, they frequently are used to exhibit a plate as if it were a fine painting.

While plate stands are one of the most popular means of showing plate art, there are a number of limitations. Plate stands should not be used in open areas where small children or heavy traffic might lead to breakage. Because some stands have a tendency to creep a bit, the non-skid stabilizer may be a wise investment.

Frames. The single most important accessory developed for the plate industry is the plate frame. With the introduction of the frame, the plate took on a status

Careful placement yields an attractive arrangement of plates and graphic works. [*Courtesy of* ***Plate Collector.***]

similar to oil paintings, prints and other art items which are displayed in similar ways.

There are a number of excellent firms currently producing plate frames. One of these firms—Hamlin-Overton—entered the market with a shadowbox frame backed with Velcro. When Velcro strips are glued to the back of the plate, they can be secured to the inside of the shadowbox and then the box may be hung with dramatic results. A similar shadowbox has been designed to hold a plate and matching figurine.

This firm also produces a solid cherry "V.I.P. Plate Keep." This vertical wall hanger can hold four plates. While not a frame, the design and quality of the finished wood makes it an exceptional piece.

Frames are produced in a wide range of sizes, shapes, and woods. The wood used ranges in tone from light oak to warm maple hues. Finishes are equally varied and run from natural to gold leaf. Many frames have a gold stripe around the opening to highlight the gold in a plate's design.

The type of wood and the style of the frame can help coordinate a collection with the decor of the room. And the frame can have an interesting effect on the plate. Dark colors look darker against a light frame, and light colors look even lighter against a dark frame. If uncertain about the type of frame finish to select for a plate, try a neutral color like fruitwood.

Lon Ramsey is the president of Bard's—a firm which markets a wide variety of collectibles display materials. He offers these suggestions on framing.

"Don't over frame. If your attention is drawn to the frame and not the plate, then you have too much frame." And while most collectors are primarily interested in the aesthetics of exhibiting their collections, Ramsey reminds them: "It is extremely important that a display is constructed in a way that will not allow for scratching, breakage or wear to a collectible."

This collector enjoys both plates and bells, and displays them together with a pleasing effect. [Courtesy of ***Plate Collector.***]

In addition to wood frames, there are hand-crafted, molded polyester frames available. They are said to be stronger and more durable than wood, and they are available in simulated wood or a velvetized finish. The use of polyester eliminates problems of warping or mis-matched woodgrains. The Noble© division of House of Rynberk© creates these molded frames.

This firm constructs its frames with an anti-fall design. And there are no wires, springs, clips or metal parts to scratch or mar a plate. Non-skid stabilizers are used to prevent the "frame tilt" problem.

To make it easier for collectors to pick the correct size frame in the finish of their choice, House of Rynberk has developed charts of all currently traded plates, according to their size. Using this chart, the collector is assured of getting the frame that fits any plate.

Cupboards and Rails. The most nostalgic-looking way to display a plate collection is to return to the traditional groupings in cupboards and on shelves. With a renewed interest in the "Country Look," collectors will enjoy the more casual, relaxed style that plate rails and cupboard shelves provide.

There are a number of ways in which shelves and railings can be modified to handle a plate collection. An ordinary shelf can be improved by adding a batten or flexible strip of wood around the edge to make a lipped container. Or, you might place a strip of wood along the back one-third of the shelf to act as a plate stop. A dado groove can also be cut in a shelf or rail to help anchor the plate within the groove.

Many of the older cupboard shelves used for displaying plates were narrower and taller than most of our modern shelves. However, if the shelf is wide, many collectors use the space in front of the plates to store other collectibles or everyday china.

A number of hanging cupboards have also been designed for collectors. Equipped with one or two shelves and a smaller drawer underneath, they provide an attractive backdrop for a collection.

Dolls

The presence of a doll in any room adds an extra dimension. Human beings have always enjoyed dolls as a toy, or a nostalgic reminder of ourselves in bygone days.

Traditionally, collectors' dolls have been displayed on sideboards, mantles, or tables. However, interior designers tend towards more imaginative and safer methods of display.

One of the first considerations is the safety of the dolls. Experts caution that dolls should not be placed close to sources of heat that might crack or melt them. Placing them in front of windows is also discouraged—a breeze can knock over a doll and break it. Or the sunshine can fade the beauty of rich costume colors.

When an individual doll is to be featured, many experts recommend the use of a glass cover or dome. Many have wooden bases, which provide a stage for the doll. Dolls also are frequently displayed in china cabinets or display cases, many of which provide special lighting systems and protection from dust and handling.

When dolls are enclosed within domes or cases it is also wise to include a small bag or container of silica gel which can be inconspicuously concealed under a skirt. These crystals absorb moisture from the atmosphere which can be harmful to the dolls. Silica gel can be obtained from a pharmacy or camera shop.

If you rotate the dolls you display, and periodically store them, simple precautions should be taken. Wrap each doll in a cotton cloth, taking care to support the clothes and prevent wrinkles. Dolls can also be stored using acid-free tissue.

An imaginative use of dolls as part of the room's decor can create a special ambience within a room. Consider displaying dolls with a lithograph or a dried flower arrangement, perhaps using coordinated colors. A patriotic figure can be combined with historic memorabilia or antique furniture.

An attractive period display might feature a porcelain doll, dressed in baby cap and christening robe in an antique baby buggy. With it, a related lithograph or photo and antique baby clothing might be arranged to complement the dolls. Dolls are also frequently combined in groupings with toys and antique furniture.

Steins

Steins are frequently stereotyped as belonging in the beer halls of yesterday. But their bright, jewel-like colors and intricate designs have endeared them to collectors for centuries.

One collector with an extensive grouping displays them on specially-constructed shelves of roughcut lumber which has been stained a deep shade of brown. Backgrounds of this kind seem to be especially effective in highlighting the shapes and colors of the steins.

Other collectors prefer to display their steins on the mantle or on shelves built behind the bar in the family recreation room.

A number of restaurants and bars also have extensive collections of steins and pitchers. In these establishments, the collection is secured in locked glass cases to prevent breakage or theft.

A limited number of steins have been produced of porcelain or glass with inscriptions or hidden patterns which appear only when the stein is held up to the light. Collectibles with these properties can be effectively displayed only in cases with back lighting.

About the Author—Catherine Bloom

Catherine Bloom is a free lance writer who works primarily in education, small business, and the arts.

She attended Loretto Heights College, Denver, Colorado, and graduated from Creighton University in Omaha, Nebraska. She earned a bachelor's degree with a major in English and Radio and Television Communications. She also has done graduate work through The University of Michigan.

Ms. Bloom worked for stations KFAB and WOW in Omaha; WTOM in Lansing, Michigan, and Kendall School of Design, Grand Rapids, Michigan.

About the Design Consultant—Susan Bailen-Wittenbach

Susan Bailen-Wittenbach has been a free lance interior designer for the past six years.

A native of East Grand Rapids, Michigan, she attended The University of Colorado and earned a bachelor's degree with a major in Fine Art-Interior Design.

Ms. Bailen-Wittenbach worked for Zenith Radio in Chicago in the cabinet design department under Winsor White, a noted furniture designer. After returning to Grand Rapids, she worked for the Stanford Research Institute.

She is married and the mother of two children.

Susan Bailen-Wittenbach

Anna-Perenna captures the beauty of Europe's "Island of Flowers" on a collection of fine porcelain plates...The Flowers of Count Bernadotte

Once upon a time, a handsome young man—heir to the throne of Sweden—abandoned his succession to the crown to marry a commoner—the woman he loved. This "black sheep prince" took the title of Count Bernadotte, and moved with his beloved wife to an overgrown island in the heart of Europe. There he lovingly tended and nurtured the island into a sub-tropical paradise...and lived happily ever after!

This story may seem farfetched, even for a fairy tale. But it is the true-life saga of Count Lennart Bernadotte, ruler of Europe's "Island of Flowers," Mainau.

The Isle of Mainau is a very unique place nestled in Lake Constance—near Germany, Austria and Switzerland, and owned by a Swedish Count.

In 1930, the father of Count Bernadotte inherited the Isle of Mainau, which had been unattended for three decades. The young count eagerly took on the challenge presented by the overgrown island, and embarked on the agricultural and forestry studies necessary to undertake its "Renaissance."

As he says, "From the outset I realized the island's potential as a unique beauty spot in the midst of Europe. I decided to make this goal my life's work: to create an oasis where visitors could experience a serene, inspirational time among flowers and plants of every description."

A Garden is to be Enjoyed...and Shared

In the early 1930's, when Count Lennart Bernadotte became ruler of the Isle of Mainau, ecology was an unknown word. Yet the Count was an early spokesman for the preservation of the beauties of nature—"Gardening for the Sake of Mankind," as he put it.

On his island, the Count put his beliefs into practice by planting lovely, tranquil gardens everywhere. Always, the comfort and enjoyment of visitors was his main concern, and he has been most generous in sharing the beauty of his flowers and trees with people from all over the world.

As he puts it, "Anyone faced with the problems of *maintaining* a park like this has to deal with the concept of *sharing* it. What I really believe is that there would be no point in having gardens like these if no one were ever walking around in them. So here in Mainau, people are the most important consideration, both in the way we lay out our gardens and in everything else the island has to offer."

An Eight-Month "Floral Year"

The "floral year" at Mainau offers a panorama of vibrancy and beauty which lasts almost all year long. First comes a display of orchids at the end of March. Then in April and May, over a million magnificent bulbs are in bloom, including more than 800 varieties of tulips, narcissi and hyacinths. There are 200,000 pansies, forget-me-nots, and primroses to see in the spring, as well.

Roses are the highlight of June, and as the summer develops, the many trees and exotic plants come into their full flower. There are banana, lemon, orange and palm trees, and nearly 400,000 summer flowers to be enjoyed. Fall weather in September and October brings on a display of dahlias—20,000 plants in 200 different varieties.

The Count must take special care of some of the more delicate specimens to help them through the winter. Once the "official" floral season ends in October, protective houses are built around the tropical plants and trees to shield them from the cold. And of course, in the fall many thousands of bulbs are planted each year to insure a fine display the following season.

A Visiting Place for Renowned and Accomplished International Guests

In the outside world, the Count is just as active in ecological and humanitarian causes as he is on the Isle of Mainau. During World War II he worked tirelessly in the defense of war victims, having turned his back on the German regime in 1939. The isle of flowers at Mainau was an oasis of beauty in the rubble and ruins of post-war Germany, and the Count organized a number of Recreational Projects for youth at that time, making sure all who visited him were properly sheltered and fed.

Today Count Bernadotte also shares his floral paradise once a year with a group of scientists, politicians and philosophers at the famed Mainau Talks. Also, Nobel Prize winners convene here each year for the final session of their conference. And this year, the Count will offer the Nobel laureates a special and personal gift—*The Flowers of Count Bernadotte* Plate Collection from ANNA-PERENNA. The first plate of the first edition, however, had a very special destination: the Count has presented it to King Carl Gustaf of Sweden.

The Count Captures Floral Specimens with "Macro Photography"

In addition to his monumental responsibilities as caretaker of his island of flowers, the Count enjoys the hobby of photography, for which he has a highly artistic and professional talent. He says that he has had a lifelong "love affair" with cameras, and that his proudest achievement in the field is the 'macro-photography' technique which allows him to capture the finest floral specimens of Mainau at the peak of their beauty.

Some of his "macro," or close-up, photos inspired the Count to select the noted floral artist Garie Von Schunck to create a number of elegant paintings. The best of these paintings have now been transformed by ANNA-PERENNA onto gleaming white porcelain in *The Flowers of Count Bernadotte* Plate Collection.

ANNA-PERENNA Collection Wins Collector Praise and Interest

For a number of reasons, collectors have taken this new plate collection immediately to heart. To begin, it commemorates an important historical event: the 50th anniversary of the Renaissance of Mainau under Count Lennart Bernadotte. And second, there is the charisma of the Count himself—a romantic, idealistic, colorful figure whose photography inspired this exciting new plate collection.

Third, there is the exceptional work of Garie Von Schunck, who combined the Bernadotte floral photographs into eight lovely floral arrangements for this handsome plate series. Ms. Von Schunck is well known for her paintings on horticultural subjects, and she is the personal choice of Count Bernadotte for this plate collection.

Fourth, there is the beauty of the flowers themselves: the world's most vibrant floral specimens, portrayed at the height of their glory, and selected from among literally thousands of blooms of each type in the gardens of Mainau.

And finally there is the reputation of ANNA-PERENNA Porcelain—a well-known plate firm which truly has outdone itself with this vibrant presentation of Count Bernadotte's harmonious floral displays.

Issue price is $75.00 per plate, and the edition limit is 17,800. Dealer orders may be taken through ANNA-PERENNA Inc., 32 Relyea Place, New Rochelle, New York 10801.

*The photographs on these pages depict the splendor of the gardens of Mainau, inspiration for **The Flowers of Count Bernadotte** Plate Collection.*

"Iris" is the first issue in ***The Flowers of Count Bernadotte*** *Plate Collection. Like the other plates in the series, it carries an issue price of $75.00.*

Porcelain and patinated bronze—a unique art concept from the Boehm Studios

The Boehm Studios have joined two regal and ancient art media to create an art work combining the strength and nobility of bronze with the delicacy and realism of porcelain. The delicate flowers and petals can only be formed by hand from the finest quality bone china to assure the most translucent, realistic porcelain flowers possible. And the intricate bronze branches, stems, and leaves, with every authentic detail captured through the lost wax process, provide a strong yet delicate setting for the jewel-like porcelain flowers. Each unique process required both artistry and craftsmanship mastered at The Boehm Studios.

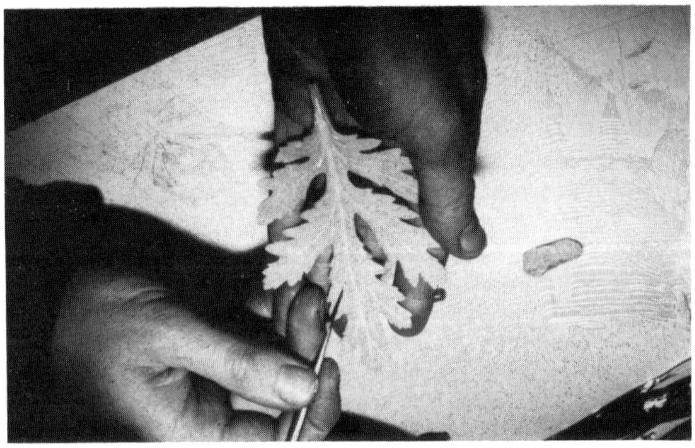

The Bronze Process

In order to create by hand one of the leaves used in the formation of the bronze base, a lump of plastiline (modeling clay) is molded to form the structure. The artist next applies the detail entirely by hand. The plastiline leaf must then be transferred into carvable metal which is accomplished by a "waste" mold. Extra fine detail is added skillfully to the soft metal.

The refined metal leaf is surrounded by thin layers of pure natural rubber, carefully packed around the leaf in a stainless steel frame. The natural rubber is heated to a temperature of approximately 570° F, when it becomes a vulcanized mold. The opening of the mold to remove the soft metal leaf and to leave behind a perfect negative cavity without nicking or spoiling this cavity is a delicate operation. A surgeon's instrument must be used with extreme skill and care.

The vulcanized rubber mold is encased in stainless steel plates, clamped tightly together. A small aperture is drilled into one end so the mold can receive an injection of hot wax under pressure. When the wax impression has set, the mold is opened and the wax model leaf, which has replaced both original plastiline and soft metal leaf, is removed and inspected.

A central rod called a "wax tree" is used to support the wax leaves. Heated knife blades are used to slightly melt areas where the wax leaves will be attached to the tree. The wax tree, with its leaf appendages, is then surrounded by a metal flask which will contain the coming plaster slurry, called the "investment." It will remain liquid for about eight minutes during which time all air is removed by vacuum. The investment slurry, after setting totally, has surrounded the wax tree and all of its attachments.

The flask next is placed into a special kiln which is fired at temperatures ranging from 480° F to 1200° F for a period of 16 to 24 hours depending on the size of the casting and thickness of the investment. During the firing, the melted wax tree and wax leaves escape from the flask and drop into a bottom tray. This is where the process called the "Lost Wax Casting" got its name. Absolutely no wax is left or is attached to the investment; a complete separation of properties, like water and oil.

The flask is removed from the kiln. Temperature at this time is critical. If it's too hot, the investment surrounding the negative cavities would break. The flask is placed into a vacuum casting machine. Pure bronze melted at a temperature of 1800° F is poured into the surface pouring holes of the investment. Vacuum created in the machine insures that the molten bronze fills all the cavities left behind by the disappearance of the lost wax, even the smallest crevices.

The hot flask is plunged into icy cold water. As the hot investment contacts the cold water, it crumbles and disintegrates leaving the rough bronze castings intact. An aqua blasting machine is used to clean the bronze parts. They are assembled and soldered together by hand. The final base structure can take up to more than 20 individual parts to assemble.

The patina on pure bronze is achieved by dipping the assembled casting into a solution of oxidizing agents. After oxidizing, the bronze is immersed into boiling water to permanently seal the patina. For special highlights, the bronze is polished on wire wheels and brushes. Finally the base structure is inspected and the Boehm hallmark is engraved into it.

The Flowermaking Process

The artists and craftsmen of Boehm work with the fragile, delicate medium of bone china. It is a highly fired, vitrified, translucent porcelain, composed of earth materials (kaolin, flint, etc.) and calcined bone ash; hence, the expression of bone china. The creation of the porcelain flower begins concurrent with the bronze-making process. Each petal is pressed and formed entirely by hand. On a bed of spun alumina the petals are carefully fitted and melded together, forming the first generation of the several generations of petals in a full grown bloom. The petals are bonded with liquid clay, a natural adhesive when mixed with sodium chloride.

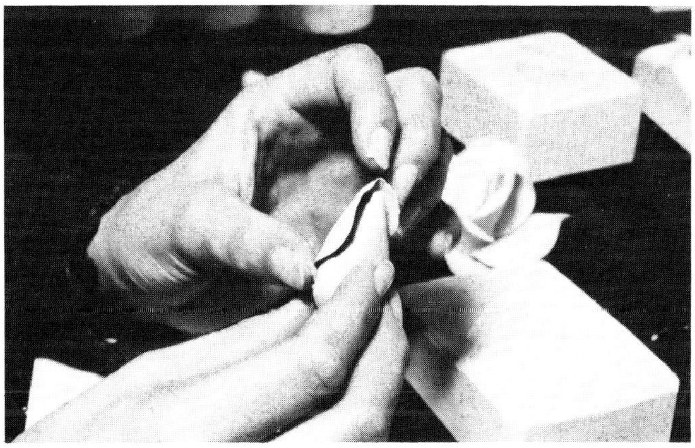

To fire the flowers successfully while retaining natural curls and spacings not only between the generations of petal groups but between individual petals as well, spun alumina, a cotton-like material which does not melt at high temperatures, must be used. It is carefully placed around and between petals and later will be removed when firings are completed. The blooms are placed on a fired porcelain plaque covered with powdered alumina (to prevent sticking), then into the bisque kiln and fired at a temperature of approximately 2100° F.

After the first firing each bloom is sprayed with a liquid glaze in preparation for the second gloss firing. The glaze further seals and strengthens the bone china.

Colors are hand applied to each bloom using powdered oxides and minerals mixed individually by each artist. The blooms are fired in a decorating kiln to permanently anneal the vibrant colors with the porcelain.

Finally, a decal or lithograped hallmark is transferred to the base of the porcelain bloom, which is fired once again to insure permanency of the important Boehm identification.

The blooms and their companion bronze base are joined permanently by use of a special epoxy. After final inspection and careful packaging, the completed sculpture is ready for Boehm collectors around the world to enjoy.

Carmel Collection showcases top artists via collector plate medium

The seaside town of Carmel, California is home to many renowned artists...and this famed art capital inspired the name of The Carmel Collection. This young-and-growing firm is a division of Pebble Beach Enterprises—a distributor and marketer of limited editions and giftware which is located in nearby Pebble Beach, California.

Tom J. O'Meara, well-known in the world of limited editions for the past decade, is the driving force behind The Carmel Collection. And today he has selected three superb American artists—each an established name in his or her own field of endeavor—to create a wide range of limited edition collector plates.

MELANIE TAYLOR KENT: SHE LOVES A PARADE

Melanie Taylor Kent is a California-based artist with a nationwide reputation for her colorful, naive-style paintings and murals. She is fascinated by the pageantry of life around her—especially complex and exciting events like parades. And thus she selected *Famous Parades* as the subject matter for her first limited edition collector plate series. The first-issue plate is "Macy's Thanksgiving Day Parade," inspired by the annual spectacle of the Macy's Parade in New York City.

Here is what Ms. Kent has to say about her own work:

"It is the intent of my work to capture those special times and places that portray and commemorate the passing American Panorama. I seek to chronicle yesterday's parade; to portray the glamour and excitement of the world's most famous boulevards and thorofares; or perhaps to present a vision of Hollywood's celluloid dreams come true.

"My paintings characterize the glitter, the extravagance, and the magic that is part of Americana. I seek to create a sense of joy and happiness that these times and places evoke by the application of brilliant colors which are more vibrant and dramatic than life itself.

"To recapture the spirit of a time at Christmas in New York City, I bring to the eye and mind a nostalgic glimpse of yuletide windows at Lord and Taylor; or I produce the images that recreate the Macy's Thanksgiving Day Parade!"

Ms. Kent's premiere plate, "Macy's Thanksgiving Day Parade," measures 10-1/4" in diameter with a 24K gold rim. It is made of fine Briggsmore china, and is limited to the year of issue. The issue price is $39.50.

THE FUND FOR ANIMALS OFFERS "CORKY'S DREAM"

The Carmel Collection has established a relationship with The Fund for Animals, an organization of Hollywood stars and other concerned people who work for the betterment of the animal kingdom. To benefit this worthy cause, Carmel offers a limited edition collector plate called "Corky's Dream."

Each purchase of "Corky's Dream," first issue in the *Help My Friends* series, will benefit the fine work of The Fund for Animals. The first-issue plate measures 8-1/2" in diameter with a 24K gold rim. Issue price is $35.00, and the china is from Briggsmore. The Carmel Collection also plans an additional, annual series of plates to benefit The Fund for Animals.

JEROME WALCZAK: A SELF-TAUGHT ARTIST WITH A SPECIAL TALENT

Some few artists are blessed with a natural talent which shines through even without formal training. Such is the case with Jerome Walczak, a young, California-based artist who recently introduced his first collector plate, "Christmas Delight," through The Carmel Collection.

Walczak says that his teachers, family and friends recognized his gift for art even when he was a tiny child. But after his years in prep school, he turned down the opportunity for an art scholarship to pursue his work on his own.

This versatile personality also excels in karate—he is an instructor with 15 years' experience. And he enjoys raising Irish Setters as show dogs. But his greatest talent is as a painter and portraitist.

Walczak is the winner of a number of juried shows in Southern California. Today he has turned his attention to the realm of limited edition collector plates, offering a first issue inspired by a baby's first visit to Santa Claus.

"Christmas Delight" premieres an annual collection entitled *The Joys of Christmas.* This Briggsmore fine china edition is limited to 19,500, and measures 8-1/2" in diameter with a 24K gold rim. The issue price is $39.50.

ELIZABETH MAXWELL: SHE ENJOYS THE FRESHNESS OF YOUTH

"I do love the freshness of youth," says Elizabeth Maxwell, creator of the new, first-issue plate "Darling

Diana." Mrs. Maxwell says that her own three children and five grandchildren offer a great deal of inspiration for her popular artwork. And children—from babies through adolescents—are her favorite subjects of all.

All through the years that her own youngsters were growing up, Mrs. Maxwell pursued her art, sketching daily, and landing commissions for portraits, book illustration and advertising work.

Then, once her children were grown, she pursued serious art study and expanded her knowledge of anatomy and draftsmanship. Her efforts have been rewarded in recent years as her work has been acquired for private collections from coast to coast.

"Every new subject or medium I try suggests another idea...and another," she says. "I'm now doing the type of art I really love—it's a great feeling. I can't wait for the next day!"

One of Ms. Maxwell's latest challenges has been her entrance into the collector plate field. Her "Darling Diana" plate is the premiere of a collection called *First Performances*—each plate will feature a youngster in his or her first recital or show. This $39.50 Carmel Collection issue is 8-1/2" in diameter with a 24K gold rim. The plate is limited to an edition of 19,500.

A young girl's first ballet performance inspired "Darling Diana," by Elizabeth Maxwell for The Carmel Collection. It is the first of a group of plates which will focus on the ***First Performances*** *of youngsters.*

"Macy's Thanksgiving Day Parade" by Melanie Taylor Kent captures the color and excitement of Macy's annual extravaganza in New York. The Carmel Collection first issue is on fine Briggsmore China, and it premieres a collection called ***Famous Parades.***

Jerome Walczak is the artist for "Christmas Delight," first in a holiday-theme collection from Carmel called ***The Joys of Christmas.*** *Plates will be issued annually.*

Yes, collectors, there is a Holly Hobbie® !

She's not just the sweet young girl in gingham and calico whose nostalgic appeal has endeared her to millions of fans around the world—she's also a charming woman with an abundance of talent: artist Holly Ulinskas Hobbie. She's the creator of a whole collection of winsome country children who evoke nostalgic feelings for a bygone era—a time when the simple things of life were dear to the heart and days were filled with homespun warmth and quiet pleasures.

In the late 1960's, while husband Doug was finishing his college education, Holly (who studied art education at Pratt Institute and painting at Boston University) heeded the suggestion of her brother-in-law and sent her portfolio to American Greetings—and thus began a career which has made her name a household word!

It's been a most successful association: Currently, Holly Hobbie products are a $100-million-per-year industry, including hundreds of licensed items in addition to those produced by the American Greetings family. And 1983 marked a very special milestone: Holly's 15th anniversary with the company.

The Holly Hobbie look made its first public appearance on a line of greeting cards, the success of which led to more products. In 1973 American Greetings introduced a new division, DESIGNERS COLLECTION, with a full line of collectibles and fine quality giftware featuring me-to-you sentiment. Among the items offered that first year were a series of six exquisitely-detailed Holly Hobbie figurines (including the first porcelain interpretation of Blue Girl) and a limited edition silver plate of 12-ounce sterling, also featuring Blue Girl. (Blue Girl has become the classic Holly Hobbie character. In her billowy bonnet and patchwork pinafore, she personifies the old-fashioned goodness, the warmth and innocence which make Holly Hobbie's world such a special place.)

Classic Collectibles

Collectors immediately took her into their hearts and homes—and Holly Hobbie has been a significant part of the DESIGNERS COLLECTION line ever since. Included have been collector plates, figurines, bells, and figurine bells in both limited and open editions, as well as a wide range of ceramic giftware featuring Holly Hobbie art—such items as trinket boxes, bud vases, photo frames, mugs, and decorator dishes.

The first Holly Hobbie seasonal collectibles were issued by DESIGNERS COLLECTION in 1976: figurines for Mother's Day and Christmas. Also notable among early commemoratives was a 6" high figurine, "I Love a Parade," issued in a limited edition of 2000 in observance of the United States Bicentennial.

The very popular Classics figurines series made its debut in 1979, and the Holly Hobbie Collector's Edition, a continuing series of companion-piece plates and figurines in limited editions of 2500 each, was inaugurated in 1981 with "On the Carousel." For 1983, a limited-edition Blue Girl figurine and two musical figurines commemorated Holly's 15th anniversary with the American Greetings family.

Collectors from Japan to South America have found Holly Hobbie irresistible. She is the magic of childhood remembered...the warmth of feelings shared...the joy of special times spent with friends...a charming reminder to "let love shine through in all you do."

Inspiration? She Lives It!

Where does her creator find inspiration? All around her! For Holly Hobbie the artist, inspiration begins at home—a 200-year-old colonial house (complete with herb garden) in scenic western Massachusetts, filled with antiques she and her writer-husband have collected over the years. The area itself is steeped in authentic Americana; its museums, antique shows, auctions, gardens, and handicrafts help contribute the detail which characterizes Holly Hobbie designs.

The artist attributes her fine eye for color and pattern to her mother, an accomplished quilter whose colorful materials were an endless source of fascination to this budding talent. Much of Holly's work reflects her memories of growing up in the peaceful, relaxed atmosphere of rural Connecticut: "I loved living on the farm, and I had special places where I would go to daydream and pretend. These are the places in my designs."

Children also have played an important part in her art. Though her own three (daughters Brett and Jocelyn and son Nathaniel) have often served as models, the art does not become a mirror image. "I have noticed, however, that my characters tend to grow up as my children grow," Holly relates, while explaining that children—what they are and what they do—are the greatest source of ideas to be found.

Timeless Appeal

In creating the character look which bears her name, Holly Hobbie has captured in rich detail the serenity and innocence of a long-ago world. Her designs possess a timeless appeal rooted in the homespun warmth and quiet pleasures of a simpler, gentler way of life. "While I have not deliberately tried to denote a specific time or person," the artist states, "my style and subjects bring back memories of a more tranquil and charming time period. They seem to evoke the 'good old days' captured in books or on film...a time beyond memory."

Is it any wonder, then, that Holly Hobbie has become a classic? She's more than just a character. She's a design look, a mood, a feeling, an enchantingly homespun world. She brings to life our American heritage—rocking chairs and patchwork quilts, warm gingerbread and cozy chats.

The sincerity and innocence of her bygone era tug nostaligically at our heartstrings. But perhaps her basic appeal lies in the fact that she brings a very precious bit of yesterday to today's world. In our age of confusion and change, Holly's values are unchanging, her world timeless—reassuringly stable and unquestionably good.

Aglow with old-fashioned goodness, Holly Hobbie's® portraits of Christmas have a timeless appeal. For 1983 her CHRISTMAS GREETINGS depicts the real message of the season: love. The offering includes the limited edition figurine and plate shown, plus a matching limited edition bell.

Holly Hobbie the artist.

Hand-painted fine porcelain Blue Girl figurine [center] and figurine musicals from DESIGNERS COLLECTION commemorate Holly Hobbie's® fifteenth anniversary.

America's finest equine artist wins praise from horse racing set...and limited edition collectors

Fred Stone has earned a coveted place in the art world with his superb equine artistry. Stone's paintings of horses are strikingly different from any of the horse racing paintings of the past. The rigid, traditional studies of the racing scene have been abandoned by Stone. Instead, his paintings give viewers an intimate, close-up view of thoroughbreds that is very unique.

Stone believes that the eyes of the horse have an expressiveness that most people never experience. To capture this beauty, he employs his sensitive approach.

The Evolution of the Artist

Born in St. Louis, Missouri in 1930, Fred Stone and his family moved to California when he was three. He grew up in Los Angeles with only two important interests: baseball and art.

His dreams of a baseball career were shattered by a sore arm. "I was heartbroken," he recalled. Then all of his energy was directed toward a career in art. In 1950, he graduated from the Art Center School in Los Angeles. After graduation he moved to Chicago, one of the main centers for commercial art and illustration. Although Stone enjoyed life as a magazine illustrator, he and his wife Norma missed the California lifestyle and their family, and they decided to return.

Stone did some free-lance work before entering the movie and television industry, painting background scenes for shows including "Gunsmoke," "Rawhide," and "Playhouse 90." These were large, sweeping landscapes that offered valuable training. But after three years, Stone was ready for something different.

A Varied Career Path

Television had dried up much of the illustration business, but there was a building boom in California. Stone and a partner established a successful business, creating murals for corporate headquarters of firms including Cessna Aircraft, Stauffer Chemical, and others.

In 1959, Stone began a 17-year hiatus from the world of art. He worked with his brother in the business world as a marketer and lobbyist. But by 1976 he was more than ready to leave corporate life and return to his art.

The first paintings he attempted were western landscapes. While they were technically good, Stone immediately realized two things. First, his work was not distinctive enough to make it the best western art, and second, the field already was saturated with a number of excellent artists.

It was his daughter, Laura, who kept trying to convince him that he should try a portrait of a horse.

Both Stone's wife and his daughter were avid horse fans, and have been involved with thoroughbred horses for over 12 years. Laura had ridden in horse shows and worked full-time at California's three major race tracks. When the Stones moved to the country in 1976, there was space for horses, and they became part of the family's daily life.

Horses and Horse Racing Intrigue the Artist

One day, while at the race track with his daughter, Stone decided to look into racing art. He discovered that the finest artist of horses had been Sir Alfred Munning, who had painted race horses in the early part of this century. Stone was fascinated by Munning's work. He also discovered what so many others knew: that horse racing has a delightful cast of colorful characters, and that horses themselves are a source of endless interest.

Stone started painting winners of races on speculation, and then going to the owner to show the finished work. This led to commissioned works, but before long Stone found such commissions too restrictive. Instead he began to paint only the horses of his choice.

It was his painting of Bill Shoemaker astride the great champion, Exceller, that was to be the turning point of his equine art career. Exceller was owned by Nelson Bunker Hunt, silver tycoon and billionaire horse breeder.

Hunt bought Stone's painting of Exceller and offered the artist an opportunity to exhibit his work at the sales pavilion at Hunt's yearling sale—held annually at Lexington, Kentucky. Stone sold all seven of his paintings in less than 30 minutes. He was also surprised to discover that every year the wealthiest people in the world gather in Kentucky to buy the finest thoroughbred yearlings.

Stone learned that these people were interested in his paintings, and were willing to pay $10,000 to $15,000 apiece for them. Personalities including Johnny Carson, George Steinbrenner, Nelson Bunker Hunt and Jack Klugman are among his clients today.

Stone's "Blue Chip" Clientele Grows

Triple-Crown winners and other top race horses soon became automatic subjects for Stone, considering his wealthy, new audience. Then, the following year, Stone was invited to the Kentucky Derby as the guest of Governor John Y. Brown and his wife, Phyllis George Brown. At the Governor's Breakfast, Stone's prints of

Kentucky Derby winner Seattle Slew were given as a special gift to the assembled guests.

Because of the amount of fine detailing involved in one of his watercolors, Stone can produce only about 10 paintings a year. Determined not to become trapped like so many gallery artists who are always under pressure to produce more paintings, Stone decided instead to begin producing fine prints of his work.

Stone's venture into the print field began in 1979. He wanted to introduce his work to people who could not afford to purchase his originals, but who were avid admirers of horses. Stone and his wife, Norma, handled all the details of producing his prints until he began distributing them through Graphics Buying Service.

Then before long, a Graphics Buying Service division, American Artists, introduced the first Fred Stone collector plates in association with Modern Masters. *The Horses of Fred Stone* plate series now has been followed by a second Stone series, with a first issue inspired by the popular MGM/United Artists film, "The Black Stallion."

Meanwhile, the audience for Stone prints is growing. All of his print issues sell out quickly, and many have increased in value six or seven times above their original prices.

Stone believes that his work will lead to a resurgence of painting in the horse field. And in spite of his success, he still is striving to equal the standards set by the great, turn-of-the-century horse race artist Sir Alfred Munnings.

"Power Horses" by Fred Stone.

The first Stone collector plate was "Patience," the premiere of the ***Horses of Fred Stone*** *series.*

"Man 'O War"—a Fred Stone print issued in an edition of 695 at $175.00.

The most recently-issued Fred Stone plate is "The Black Stallion." It is the first in a series of four, issued at $49.50.

"Contentment" is the final plate of four in Fred Stone's first plate series.

The "M.I. Hummel" figurine, "Stormy Weather."

The first-ever "M.I. Hummel" collector plate, "Heavenly Angel," issued in 1971 for $25. Recent quotes place its value in the $800 range.

Goebel's "M.I. Hummel" figurine, "Goose Girl."

The art of Sister M.I. Hummel charms generation after generation as figurines...and now as plates, bells, and dolls as well

In the world of limited editions, there are just a handful of artists whose work is so well loved that it is referred to by the artist's name alone. Surely "Rockwell" is in this category, and so is "M.I. Hummel"—the common name for the figurines and other limited editions inspired by the works of Sister M. Innocentia Hummel for Goebel of West Germany. Here is the story of this remarkable artist and her collectible works...

A little girl named Berta Hummel was born in Bavaria in 1909. She had a normal, happy childhood in a close, religious Roman Catholic family. But even as a youngster, it was apparent that Berta's special gift was in the realm of art and creativity.

It was highly unorthodox for a girl to leave home in those times, but Berta's father recognized her talent and arranged for her to attend the Munich Academy of Applied Arts. Berta stayed at the academy for four years, from age 18 to 22. Her teachers were thrilled with her natural gifts, and helped her to develop a personal style. They were most enthusiastic about her future in the world of art.

Imagine their surprise, then, when young Berta decided to enter a convent after graduation! The artist did not reach this decision lightly. She had considered this option for years—while living in Munich in a boarding house run by an order of the Roman Catholic Church.

There she befriended two nuns of the Franciscan Order from the Convent of Siessen in the state of Wurtternberg, near the Black Forest. The three had much in common, for the order placed a great deal of emphasis on the arts, and Berta's two friends were in Munich to further their training. She felt very much at home with them, and longed for the peace and security of convent life at a time when Germany's turmoil was increasing.

Sister M.I. Hummel Continues Her Art Career

At Siessen, Sister Maria Innocentia Hummel was encouraged to continue her art explorations. As always, her favorite subjects were rosy-cheeked children...children at work and at play, exploring the great, wide world around them. She painted, sketched and drew the youngsters who played in the convent garden, as well as those she could remember from her own childhood.

The Franciscan Order was a poor one, and so Sister Maria Innocentia asked for permission to sell some of her artwork to raise money for good works. Soon her charming postcards of children were "best sellers" in Germany. One of their admirers was Franz Goebel, fourth-generation owner and head of the company bearing his family name.

At the time, Goebel was looking for inspiration for a new line of figurines. The innocent purity of this artwork caught his attention, and he won permission from the Mother Superior and Sister Maria Innocentia to create the first "M.I. Hummel" figurines. Ultimately Goebel was licensed to translate into three-dimension, her two-dimensional art.

Hummel Figurines Make Their Debut

Although Sister Maria Innocentia worked only in two dimensions, Goebel had on his staff two master sculptors, Reinhold Unger and Arthur Moeller. They worked with the original two-dimensional art to create three-dimensional earthenware figurines which were hand-painted in accordance with the two-dimensional paintings.

The figurines were introduced in 1935 at the Leipzig Fair, then a major international show. They were an immediate success, and thus Sister Maria Innocentia Hummel continued to paint and to work with the Goebel factory to make sure that each new piece of art was faithfully rendered in three dimensions. (This procedure continues even today: representatives of the Goebel factory visit the convent with each new piece for approval at several stages of development.)

Worldwide Fame for "M.I. Hummel"

Unfortunately, World War II interrupted the blossoming international career of Sister Maria Innocentia. Although some of the "M.I. Hummel" figurines were exported before the war, it was not until after World War II that they and Sister Maria Innocentia achieved true international fame.

During the American occupation of Germany, many of the G.I.'s and their families fell in love with the pretty "Hummel" figurines and took them home as special gifts and mementos. Then as more Americans took pleasure tours to Europe, "Hummel" figurines became favorite gifts for the people back home. Soon the figurines were available at exclusive shops throughout the United States and other countries.

But the creator of the underlying art did not live to share in the excitement of this worldwide triumph: she died at 37 of tuberculosis, which had gone undiagnosed too long. In her time at the convent, however, she completed hundreds of individual pieces of artwork: a legacy which collectors continue to enjoy today.

Figurines...and Much More

Over the years, Goebel has carefully broadened the scope of its "M.I. Hummel" offerings. In 1971, the firm introduced the first "M.I. Hummel" annual plate, "Heavenly Angel." Limited to the year of issue, this charming, bas-relief porcelain plate delighted both those who had collected "M.I. Hummel" figurines, and those who collected limited edition plates. It was also the first hand-painted, bas-relief plate of its type. Thus, "Heavenly Angel" has become one of the most successful plates of all time, now commanding $800 to $900 in the secondary market. (Its issue price was $25.00.)

The plate series has continued each year since 1971, and there have been two anniversary plates as well—the 1975 "Stormy Weather," and the 1980 "Spring Dance." In addition, Goebel was inspired to offer limited edition "M.I. Hummel" bells beginning in 1978, and these also have appealed not only to "M.I. Hummel" collectors, but to those who specifically seek limited edition bells.

Doll collectors have enjoyed the attractive "M.I. Hummel" dolls, ranging from "Hansel and Gretel" to favorite "Hummel" characters like "Merry Wanderer" and "Goose Girl."

For all the many thousands of collectors who love Sister Maria Innocentia Hummel's work, a Goebel Collector's Club® has been formed. In addition to a number of other membership benefits, Club members have the opportunity to purchase collectibles which are exclusive—for the Club alone. To learn more about this very successful and active organization and its national and local chapters, write Joan N. Ostroff, the club's vice-president, at Goebel Collectors' Club, 105 White Plains Road, Tarrytown, New York 10591.

The famous "Apple Tree Girl" figurine.

Part of a line of handsome "M.I. Hummel" dolls. From left, they are: "On Secret Path," "Weary Wanderer," "Lost Stocking," and "Visiting an Invalid."

Gorham offers limited edition works by America's most renowned artists

The Gorham China Company of Providence, Rhode Island is one of only a handful of American tableware firms with a long and eventful history. From its founding by Jabez Gorham in 1831, this firm has excelled not only in works of fine metal, sterling flatware, bells, and figurines, but in fine china and crystal also—and most recently in reproduction dolls as well.

Jabez Gorham was a silversmith, and he prided himself on his firm's works in fine metal. At the turn of the century Gorham had earned the title of "America's premier bellmaker" for its superb bells in bronze and other bell metals. But although Gorham still makes some limited edition bells of fine metal, the firm is best known today for its china collector's plates, and its handsome, hand-painted figurines by renowned American artists like Norman Rockwell, John Clymer, Betty Felder, Irene Spencer and the late Ted DeGrazia.

Gorham Provides Affordable Art for Admirers of Top Artists

As collectors, many of us dream of owning an original Rockwell or Clymer—or the works of another superb artist with worldwide recognition. And Gorham was among the first companies to recognize this desire among collectors, and provide them with an alternative: the opportunity to own fine limited editions, inspired by the works of these celebrated artists, but at affordable issue prices.

And so in 1971, Gorham took its first "plunge" into the limited edition collector plate market with a first-issue annual set of Norman Rockwell "Four Seasons" plates. Issued at $50.00, the four 10-1/2" plates portrayed scenes entitled "A Boy and His Dog." Like many of the best-loved Gorham issues to come, these Rockwell offerings were generously sized—much larger than most plates created by American competitors. The full-sized plates provide an appropriate "canvas" for Rockwell's work, and collectors responded with great enthusiasm. "A Boy and His Dog" now commands at least $400 on the secondary market.

Fresh from this triumph, Gorham took another important step the next year with a matching set of hand-painted "A Boy and His Dog" figurines. And each year until 1980, Gorham introduced another set of four Rockwell plates—depicting the changing seasons in different motifs—with a matching group of figurines to follow the next year.

Another well-received Rockwell series from Gorham is still in annual production. The "Rockwell Christmas Series" debuted in 1974 with a "Tiny Tim" plate which issued at $12.50. This first issue has been quite active on the secondary market recently, and now brings about five times its issue price.

Gorham Plates Feature Works of Other Famed Artists

Perhaps not quite as well known to the American public as Norman Rockwell—but "household words" for seasoned plate collectors—are several other Gorham plate artists.

Irene Spencer is celebrated for her sensitive portrayals of mothers and children. And her unswerving attention to detail and quality are well respected among collectors and dealers. The first-issue "Spencer Annual" plate, called "Dear Child," was introduced in 1974 to immediate acclaim.

Ted DeGrazia, as well, was a specialist in the portrayal of children. His "Los Ninos" is something of a legend in the plate collecting world, for its rise on the market has been nothing short of phenomenal. Issued at $35.00 in 1976, the first-issue "Los Ninos" in the DeGrazia Children's Series commanded about $600 until the artist's death last year, and now may bring twice that figure or more!

Celebrated plate artist Leo Jansen also passed away recently, but his many charming collector plates will attest to his mastery for many generations to come. Not surprisingly, Jansen had two fine collector plate series created by Gorham—the "Sugar and Spice" plates and the "Prince Tatters" issues.

Two Recent "Coups" for Gorham: John Clymer and Betty Felder

Saturday Evening Post readers, of course, are well aware of the scores of *Post* covers created by Norman Rockwell. But those who were careful observers of that great magazine, particularly in the late 1940's and the 1950's, are just as familiar with John Clymer, a gifted illustrator and painter who specializes in the history of the American West.

Clymer has created two Gorham series of plates: one based on his collection of paintings of the Lewis and Clark Expedition, and another, more general series of western-subject plates. The *Lewis and Clark* plates have been offered by mail via The Hamilton Collection, and the Clymer *Encounter, Survival, Celebration* series is available through the regular retail distribution of Gorham.

Another new and exciting Gorham plate artist is Betty Felder, creator of the "When I Was a Child" plate for 1982 and a 1983 issue, "Gather the Children." This charming, southern artist is self-taught, yet her art has won the admiration of noted critics—and today her originals command as much as $10,000. So once again Gorham offers collectors the opportunity to own a limited edition created by a renowned artist whose one-of-a-kind originals have become prohibitively expensive.

A New Horizon for Gorham: Lovely, Beautifully-Dressed Dolls

Gorham introduced its elegant line of dolls in 1981. Since then their ranks have grown to 40 in all—each an individual personality with his or her own special attire and expression.

The Gorham dolls have bisque faces in the famous Bru and Jumeau styles. They wear typical Paris fashions of the mid-1800's—authentic in every detail. What's more, for a special touch, each doll has an 18-note musical movement which plays a tune to reflect his or her personality.

Like the other Gorham products, these dolls are hallmarked as exclusives of this fine Providence, Rhode Island firm. Collectors who wish to learn more about the dolls—or other Gorham products—should contact the Gorham retail store in their area. Or write Ed Purcell, The Gorham Company, 333 Adelaide Avenue, Providence, Rhode Island 02907, for the store nearest you.

The elegant "Cecile" is a third in Gorham's line of dolls.

Another Gorham musical doll, "Rosamond."

One of Gorham's annual Norman Rockwell Christmas plates, inspired by the story of Tiny Tim and Scrooge.

The 1972 Rockwell ***Four Seasons*** *figurine collection traces the story of a boy and his dog.*

"Christopher" from Gorham's collection of fine dolls.

*The Boehm Studios' **Romantic Moments** figurines brought praise from Hamilton collectors on both sides of the Atlantic. These were the first hand-painted ballet-subject figurines issued by Boehm in cooperation with Hamilton.*

*"Iris" premiered **The Flowers of Count Bernadotte,** a group of eight plates on fine German porcelain, offered jointly by Anna-Perenna and Hamilton to United States collectors.*

"Sweet Dreams" by Thornton Utz is one of The Hamilton Collection's sought-after plates of U.S. origin. It is the second issue in an annual collection by this renowned children's portraitist.

Sources worldwide bring Hamilton collectors an international array of fine limited editions

In today's limited edition field, some firms are characterized by their specialization: in the works of Rockwell, for instance, or in art objects made at one particular studio. But The Hamilton Collection has found its place in the collectibles field as a purveyor of fine limited editions from around the world. Hamilton offers collectors a diverse group of carefully-produced works of art from Great Britain, France, Germany, the Orient, and of course, the United States.

Hamilton is located in Jacksonville, Florida, but the firm's sources are international in scope. Not content merely to correspond with foreign studios and art houses, Hamilton's directors and artists take a "hands on" approach, and travel widely to make sure that their products fulfill high standards of uniqueness, fine taste, and quality.

American and British Art Studios Serve Hamilton Collectors

Some Hamilton products are created close to home: for instance, the firm works closely with The Boehm Studios of Trenton, New Jersey, on joint projects involving elegant, limited edition collector plates and figurines. Another U.S.-based associate of Hamilton's is The Gorham Company of Providence, Rhode Island—producer of John Clymer's impressive *Lewis and Clark* plates for Hamilton, as well as the sell-out Rockwell plate series called *Home of the Brave*. And Hamilton has worked extensively with Viletta China Company of Houston, Texas: makers of many plates by famed artists like Thornton Utz and Shell Fisher, which are offered exclusively to collectors through Hamilton.

In recent years The Hamilton Collection has developed an impressive list of British associates as well—partly due to the firm's establishment of a subsidiary in West Malvern, England.

For example, the famed Boehm Studios of Great Britain worked extensively with Hamilton to develop and offer a unique group of ballet-subject figurines that are painstakingly handpainted. All previous Boehm/-Hamilton ballet figurines had been created in pristine, white bisque porcelain, so the addition of color created quite a stir in the art collectibles world. What's more, the figures were sponsored by the renowned London Festival Ballet. Called *Romantic Moments,* these pieces were an immediate success on both sides of the Atlantic at the affordable issue price of $240 per figurine.

Another Hamilton colleague in Great Britain is the talented sculptor, Mark Jones. In cooperation with a fine English pewter casting studio, Tyler of Great Britain, Jones developed a group of 12 pewter, hand-painted figurines titled *The Alice in Wonderland Figurine Collection.* Offered exclusively through Hamilton both in the United States and in Great Britain, the figurines sold at $49.50 each.

French and German Works of Art are Recent Hamilton Offerings

Even in the early 1970's, The Hamilton Collection made important liasons in Europe for the creation of limited editions. For example, the firm was exclusive distributor of the Haviland-Parlon *Madonna* series of eight Christmas plates which debuted in 1972.

Recently Hamilton established a relationship with the renowned French firm of Porcelaine de Paris to design a collection of eight Limoges porcelain boxes with songbird motifs. Earlier, Porcelaine de Paris had created a series of plates by *naif*-style, or primitive artists from all over Europe, which told the story of Noah's Ark.

In addition, Hamilton has arranged with renowned German studios including Anna-Perenna Porcelain and Villeroy & Boch to offer their limited editions direct to United States collectors. Currently the firm offers *The Flowers of Count Bernadotte,* an Anna-Perenna Porcelain plate series inspired by the floral bounty of Europe's sub-tropical Isle of Mainau. And Hamilton has cooperated with Villeroy & Boch on several handsome series, including *The Fairy Tales of Boris Zvorykin,* two collections of steins, and a plate offering inspired by the works of famed French illustrator Edmund Dulac—entitled *The French Fairy Tales.*

Oriental Art Captures the Imagination of American Collectors

Perhaps the most unique aspect of The Hamilton Collection's international appeal has been the firm's dominant role in bringing fine Oriental limited editions to the American market. As prices for Oriental antiques and collectibles skyrocket, and United States collectors increase their awareness of the gentle beauty of Japanese and Chinese symbolic art, Hamilton has offered exclusive works such as fine Hakata dolls, and Satsuma and cloisonne plates.

For example, The Hamilton Collection commissioned a Japanese Hakata doll artist, Togo San, to recreate some of the most beloved characters of the Kabuki Theater in the form of limited-edition, hand-painted terra cotta dolls. Another elegant collection of these traditional Hakata dolls is titled *Mother and Child,* and was inspired by the National Treasure artwork of Japanese sculptor Goyo Hirata.

Just last year, The Hamilton Collection introduced the first-ever Satsuma ware limited-edition collector plate series, a group of 12 issues which depict the colorful beauty of the *Gardens of the Orient*. And a set of four symbolic plates of cloisonne enamel called *Treasures of the Chinese Mandarins* sold out in record time when Hamilton introduced them some months ago.

For the Future: Hamilton Continues on the International Scene

Hamilton Collection President John W. Graham has this to say about his firm's plans for future limited editions: "Our artists currently are developing some very exciting new products that will be announced to Hamilton's preferred collectors quite soon. Our goal is always this: to continue to bring United States collectors the very best in affordable limited editions from around the world.

"Those who would like to learn more about our products may do so by writing: Customer Service Department, The Hamilton Collection, 9550 Regency Square Blvd., Jacksonville, Florida 32232."

From the famed Limoges region of France came this delightful "Robin and Dogwood" box, created for The Hamilton Collection by Porcelaine de Paris.

"The White Rabbit" [foreground] is the first of 12 ***Alice in Wonderland*** *figurines created by British sculptor Mark Jones and cast and hand-painted at Tyler of Great Britain.*

"The Wisteria Maiden" is a hand-painted Hakata doll figurine—part of The Hamilton Collection's celebrated ***Art of Kabuki*** *collection.*

Opa's Haus brings "new era" of German beer steins to American collectors

"I firmly believe that a new golden era has dawned for the German beer stein. We are now seeing steins that, in quality and uniqueness of execution, were unimaginable outside of antique circles 10 years ago."

These are the words of Ken Armke, president and general manager of Opa's Haus, Inc. (OHI), a business which has been built around the importation and sale of German beer steins.

"In our early years of, say, 1969 — 1973, we were marketing new steins in what might now be called the traditional way — as gifts, as souvenirs, as decorator items, even as drinking vessels. For collectors, we were trying — with absolutely no success — to locate antique pieces in Germany."

Armke believes the turning point came in 1974. "In that year our major supplier, Gerz GmbzH, introduced two new steins. These were the first pieces in an annual limited edition series, and the Goetz stein featuring an ornate pewter lid. Each had great appeal to collectors. And by that time Albert Jac. Thewalt GmbH, another premier manufacturer, had begun dressing up some of his standard pieces with 'antiqued' lids and special markings in a successful effort to appeal to collectors.

"The earth didn't exactly shake, but it was a start. Every year since then, the offering for collectors has improved. In the last six years, particularly, we have seen experimentation by Gerz, Thewalt, and certain other manufacturers lead to new colors, new art executions, and new, dressy lids.

"It's been like a breath of fresh air to those of us who genuinely care about this art form. A number of the steins being produced right now in Germany compare very favorably in artistry with fine antique pieces. We couldn't say that a few years ago."

The steins which are OHI's best sellers today are products of this recent creativity; they weren't even available six years ago, according to Armke. He points to Thewalt's "oldie" series of limited editions and the firm's development of its "rustica" hand-painting process and to Gerz's figurine lid series, new colors, and certain new pieces such as the Four Seasons Stein.

"In my opinion," Armke says, "the Gerz Four Seasons Stein, designed by current master Edwin Breiden, has to be one of the most fantastic, truly original pieces of the past 60 years. Unfortunately, it was not produced as a limited edition and will likely not get all the recognition it deserves."

OHI Sparks Contemporary Production of Classic Steins

Opa's Haus itself has played a major role in the rejuvenated production of collector-quality steins in Germany.

"Among the manufacturers with whom we have some influence," Armke explains, "we have campaigned hard and repeatedly for more quality pieces and for more experimentation. Some of our 'suggestions' have been adopted and have been highly successful, such as the Gerz figurine lid series and Thewalt's recent offering of fancy pewter lids."

The theory of a new "golden era" for German steins was developed by Armke during the course of research he began five years ago for a still-uncompleted book on collecting steins.

"One of the things you quickly learn when you begin to delve deeply into the subject," he says, "is that steins are truly works of art, often involving several different art techniques to achieve one product. So it shouldn't come as a great surprise that this particular art form, like most others, has had great ups and downs. This is particularly true as it applies to stoneware, which is the source of the rich tradition and longstanding popularity of steins."

The first beer stein was made about 1550, but the first 300-plus years of steins — while fascinating from an historical perspective — are relatively unimportant to today's collector.

"These were largely 'pre-industry' pieces," Armke explains. Today, they are mostly housed in museums or in major private collections. Only scattered examples show up on the open market."

The "modern" stein industry in Germany began around 1880, and it was from then until about 1913 when most of the "antique" steins prized today were produced.

World War I Thwarts a Remarkable Industry

"This was the last golden era of the beer stein (1880 — 1913) — a truly remarkable period of artistry and inventiveness as symbolized by the much-admired products of Villeroy & Boch in Mettlach and other firms such as Gerz, Thewalt, Duemler & Breiden, Marzi & Remy, Reinhold Merkelbach, Girmscheid and others in the Westerwald," Armke says. "Most are still in business and, where stein production is concerned, their roots go back to this turn-of-the-century period."

Germany's involvement in World War I brought the era to an abrupt end.

"Art does not flourish during turmoil," Armke notes. "The recovery from World War I, the rampant inflation of the early 1920's, the depression of several years later, the Nazi period and build-up toward World War II...all of these served to thwart artistic development.

"This is particularly true when one considers that during the long interim between pre-World War I and post-World War II entire art processes, artists and workers themselves, and sometimes even the molds were lost. In short, the art continuity of the industry was virtually lost and had to be gradually re-built."

Mold Owners Shine in Current Market

A common misconception concerning beer steins, especially models done in relief (or bas-relief), concerns the origins of the artwork.

"The key to successful production of stoneware relief steins today," Armke says, "is ownership of old molds. It so happens that almost all of the surviving molds from the 16th through 19th centuries are in the hands of the few surviving manufacturers.

"It is these old molds, especially those of the late 19th century, that are the source of most of the stoneware relief steins seen today. The true rarity is a nicely executed new mold by a modern master, for there are barely a handful of these artists in the world today."

Opa's Haus: A Serious Commitment to Steins

Having made an early commitment to a collector approach with steins—the first in an annual series of limited edition festival mugs is dated 1972—Opa's Haus has worked as a pioneer in this mostly uncharted field.

Early efforts in this regard centered around the maintenance of a vast selection of German steins, usually in excess of 500 different designs, and in seeking out and offering the finest new steins Germany had to offer.

"Some of these pieces from a few years ago," Armke says, "have turned out to be desirable rarities. Unfortunately, these steins are now 'lost' in the hands of unknown private collectors and are not available in any secondary market form."

In early 1981, OHI sought to remedy this problem by instituting its own registration system for all limited edition pieces and other steins with high collector appeal.

"So far," Armke says, "our registration system has worked beautifully. Our dealers like it, and the collectors like it. I just wish we had started it sooner."

With the registration system, Armke explains, ownership of a collector-grade stein becomes a matter of record. The system will be used to issue value appraisals at appropriate times, but, more importantly, it offers the prospect of a real and valid secondary market.

"When a limited edition is sold out or another collector-grade piece is retired from production, we can survey all of the registered owners of the stein to determine, first, if they are willing to re-sell the piece and, second, at what specific price.

"In this way we will have a very true reflection of the secondary market value of every item surveyed. An important next step for us will be to educate our dealers

"The Festival Stein" is an Opa's Haus Inc. edition commissioned through Gerz.

The "Herring Stein" from Thewalt's Miscellaneous Reproductions.

in the secondary market process, because we consider their active involvement to be essential to the success of the program."

German and American Selling Philosophies Differ

Another collector-oriented problem faced by OHI is the difference in merchandising philosophy between Germany and the United States, Armke says.

"Probably because collecting is not as refined there as here," he explains, "the manufacturers there are hesitant about offering their collectibles with the extra 'frills' the American public has come to expect—things such as a standard issue price, individual numbering of limited edition pieces, certificates, special brochures, special boxing."

To partially overcome this problem, Opa's Haus in 1982 introduced an exclusive stein commissioned through and produced by Gerz in Germany.

"By having complete control over the Festival Stein," Armke says, "we were able to determine the edition limit (1000 pieces) and we handled the individual numbering, certification and, of course, the registration, ourselves."

Result was the fastest-selling stein in the entire OHI selection, one apparently headed for an early sell-out.

"We were able to prove something to ourselves with the success of the Festival Stein," Armke says. "We plan for our approach to be more and more along this line...commissioned pieces from the world's finest manufacturers which we will limit and market ourselves."

Indeed, in mid-1983 Opa's Haus introduced what Armke calls "our most ambitious and exciting project ever." This is a series of limited edition steins based on original paintings by noted wildlife artist Pat Ford. Three commissioned paintings have been completed thus far by Ms. Ford.

"The Pat Ford steins," Armke says, "are being marketed in much the same manner that collector plates are now marketed. We have an artist who, in our opinion, is unexcelled at what she does. We're going to do everything in our power to make these some of the most avidly sought collector steins of all time."

*The "Physician Stein" from the **Oldie** Series.*

*The **Oldie** Series "Railway Stein."*

Thewalt's Annual German Christmas plate is distributed through Opa's Haus Inc. It is made of bas-relief stoneware.

The Thewalt Commemorative Stein from the ***Oldie*** *Series.*

Opa's Haus Inc. commissioned Gerz to create these ***Lore of Germany*** *figurines. From left, top: "The Beer King"; "The Monk." From left, bottom: "The Dancing Couple," "The Cherub," "The Ibex."*

"America's favorite plate artist" faces the challenge of three-dimensional artwork with the McClelland's Endearing Porcelains

Even after being elected "America's Favorite Plate Artist" for the second year in a row, famed illustrator and painter John McClelland relishes the thought of a fresh challenge.

This desire to create something new and beautiful prompted him to agree to design a line of porcelain figurines, *The McClelland's Endearing Porcelains.*

According to Brigitte Moore, vice president of Reco International—maker of McClelland's well-loved plates and the McClelland's endearing porcelains—the first figurines premiered in 1981. They were affectionately named "John" and "Alice," after McClelland and his artist-wife.

Plate collectors were thrilled with the new, three-dimensional "McClellands," and the artist found a wider audience. Response prompted Reco to expand the line to 23 miniature figurines today—each an original, measuring three to four inches in height.

Rather than trying to copy popular plate art, both Reco and McClelland felt it was more important to create new art that would stand on its own merit. Figurines like "Quiet Moments," and "Smooth Sailing" capture children thoroughly immersed in their activities. But other McClelland figurines—"The Clown," "The Policeman," "Baker," "Fireman," "Chimney Sweep," or "Dressing Up"—provide glimpses into the wonderful world of make-believe.

How the "McClellands" Came to Be

When asked what new design challenges he faced in creating the figurines, John McClelland replied, "I had been working with only one view never concerning myself with how a subject looked in the back or from the side. At first it was a little bit difficult, thinking in the round.

"When I started to design figurines, I did a lot of different sketches from almost every angle. I gradually learned to do only a front and back sketch. I also sketch any special detailing that a figurine might demand," McClelland explained.

"For example, if a stack of books is part of the figurine, I might sketch out how the books are turned or one book may be a little thicker—this is just something that evolves naturally from doing portraits."

The Subjects Make the Magic for McClelland

It is McClelland's skill in painting children that has touched so many people. McClelland believes that the popularity of children in art, plates and figurines is due to the youngsters' own universal appeal.

"All families have children—we remember what it was like to be a child. Children are all around us and we enjoy watching them," he said.

For McClelland, part of the charm of children is that they are all different. He works with children as his models, but does not ask them to pose for long. It's difficult to get four and five-year-olds to sit still because of their short attention span. He brings them to his studio where he photographs them in black and white as he wants to create his own color combinations.

He involves the children in his artistry by asking them for suggestions. "A child frequently comes up with something that is more natural and more exciting," he explains.

Working from his photos, McClelland then begins sketching. Many experts note that he pays meticulous attention to details. According to McClelland, his skill at detailing is the result of his early training as an illustrator.

"If I'm painting a sleeve, I don't make it up. I like to have it in front of me. Something may happen and I might see a different and exciting new angle—it is easy to fall into a terrible rut by just painting because you know that is the way the object looks—you risk losing your freshness. I paint everything I see, and then later I may remove a line to simplify it."

The Making of an Artist

McClelland's career is a kaleidoscope of art-related experiences. Born in Stone Mountain, Georgia, he attended Auburn University and then went to New York to learn to be an illustrator.

Over the next few years, he worked for a printing company; the advertising department of Coca-Cola; the Air Force (where he illustrated manuals); an illustration studio; and finally he became a free-lance illustrator.

While he feels that sometimes it is a matter of being in the right place at the right time, he also follows the admonition of one of his instructors. "Just do everything you are asked to do. You never know where it will come in handy."

About the time that McClelland's success as an illustrator seemed assured, television came into its own and severely hurt general-interest publications, which were the biggest market for illustrations.

McClelland continued to do some ad illustrations, but gradually he began to do more commissioned portraits, gratefully acknowledging the influence of Jerry Farnsworth, the artist and instructor with whom he had studied after leaving the service.

John McClelland is "America's Favorite Plate Artist," according to a survey by a national magazine. This adorable "Johnny the Strongman" issue in his **Circus** *series for Reco helps explain why.*

A New Career as a Portraitist and Plate Artist

It was McClelland's painting of his daughter, Susan, that made everything click. An art director used the portrait for an ad in a trade magazine. It was seen by the people at Miles Kimball, a mail order house. This firm asked McClelland to do a cover for its Christmas catalog—the beginning of a long and successful association.

Brigitte Moore saw McClelland's work for Miles Kimball and brought it to the attention of Heio Reich, president of Reco International.

In 1977, McClelland's first limited edition plate, "Rainy Day Fun," was issued by Reco. It was the premiere of his *World of Children* series. In 1980 when the final plate was issued, the series had appreciated more than 60% in value. *World of Children* was followed by the *Mother Goose* and *The McClelland Children's Circus* series, also for Reco.

The affection and admiration which collectors have lavished on John McClelland was shown when they voted his "Little Boy Blue" the favorite plate of *Plate World* readers in 1980.

His "Mary, Mary," winner of the Bradex Plate of the Year Award, was selected by the National Association of Limited Edition Dealers (NALED) as the Best All-Around Collectible and Best Plate of 1980. That same year, NALED named McClelland the Best Artist of the Year.

A New Set of Challenges for McClelland

When asked about the gradual evolution of his career, McClelland admitted that as a young artist, eager to enter the business world, he wanted to be an illustrator. "I did it and I enjoyed it," he said. But once he knew that he could accomplish that goal, he wanted more of a challenge.

Designing and executing art, especially for plates and figurines, provided McClelland with a fascinating new opportunity. The first challenge he faced was the necessity of working in a circle.

While he noted that some plates have been produced from square paintings, original designs based on the circle may be better thought out. "I like things that flow around within the circle," he added.

Artists who designed the first multi-color plates were faced with a number of technical problems—brought on in part by the process of production. Colors, finishes and edges all had to be carefully considered. However, the technology has improved so much—even during the six years McClelland has been involved in plate-making—that many of these problems have been greatly reduced.

According to McClelland, figurines do not present the same technical problems. His figurines are hand-painted by skilled artists who pay close attention to color and detailing, after which they are fired again.

The Artist and His Admirers

McClelland is extremely conscious of the many collectors who enjoy his work. Meeting collectors at shows has proven to be a refreshing experience for him. "I have gotten to know the people who collect. They are enthusiastic and very helpful," he said.

McClelland feels that more and more people will turn to collectibles. "I've had many people tell me that they don't have the money for originals, but they can afford a figurine, a plate, or prints. They love artwork on the wall or somewhere in the room," he added.

"Chimney Sweep" and "Dressing Up" are limited editions of 10,000 each within the McClelland's **Endearing Porcelains** *series. They issued at $32.00 and $35.00 respectively.*

This new range of McClelland figurines focuses on children's occupations and pastimes including cowboy or cowgirl, doctor, lawyer, feeding chicks, or walking the baby.

"Little Bo Peep" is the most recent issue in McClelland's highly popular ***Mother Goose*** *series.*

The "John" and "Alice" figurines were named after their creator, John McClelland, and his wife.

Marshall Stoltz of The Norman Rockwell Museum presented this copy of his book about Norman Rockwell to the beloved American illustrator in the mid-1970's.

The Norman Rockwell Museum in Philadelphia, Pennsylvania.

An interior view of the museum, which holds thousands of pieces of classic Rockwell art and memorabilia.

Rockwell admirer makes his dream come true: The story of Marshall Stoltz and The Norman Rockwell Museum

Our childhood heroes—whether real or imagined—often shape our lives. For Marshall Stoltz and his brother, Donald, the hero was Norman Rockwell. They were fascinated by his seemingly endless parade of characters, marching across the American scene.

The Stoltz brothers' introduction to Rockwell's art was a Boy Scout calendar given to them by their father. The illustration showed a scout troop, leaving on a trip with their canoe on their shoulders. A younger boy sat forlorn and forgotten at the side of the road—the picture of desolation.

This became the first item in a growing Rockwell collection. Fortunately, the prolific Rockwell's art was easily accessible to the eager boys. As Boy Scouts, many of the Stoltz brothers' early acquisitions were scout-related. Rockwell created a calendar for the Boy Scouts of America nearly every year, and he also did scout-related work for *Boy's Life,* scouting awards, and hundreds of illustrations.

But Marshall and Donald soon moved beyond scouting art to other Rockwell horizons. As Marshall put it, "We collected anything and everything we could find." Over the years, they won a reputation as major Rockwell collectors.

The First Meeting With Rockwell...and Then the Museum

In 1971, Marshall wanted to plan a special birthday gift for his brother, Don. He made arrangements for Don to meet Rockwell in person, at the great illustrator's own studio. Instead of a five-minute courtesy call, which they expected, they were invited to spend over an hour talking with Rockwell and discussing his work. It was the beginning of a good friendship, and a close working relationship.

The collection—originally housed in the Stoltz home—had become so large, and such an attention-getter, that the brothers began to seek an appropriate site to display it. In 1976, Marshall Stoltz and Dr. Donald Stoltz opened The Norman Rockwell Museum on the first floor of the Curtis Publishing Building at 6th and Walnut Streets in Philadelphia. The building faced the tree-lined courtyard of Independence Hall. It was a fitting site, in view of the long and successful relationship between Rockwell and The *Saturday Evening Post,* which was published by Curtis.

Rockwell, sensing the gamble inherent in the venture, cautiously asked Marshall if he had carefully considered the consequences of leaving his job as a teacher to serve as Curator of The Norman Rockwell Museum. Stoltz assured Rockwell that he had considered it thoroughly, and was satisfied with his choice.

Rockwell's Public Enjoys the New Museum

The museum opened in time for the 1976 Bicentennial celebration, and soon it was filled with Rockwell's fans on a daily basis. Rockwell's "public" turned out to be the American family: people on vacation, who often looked as if they had just stepped out of one of the master illustrator's paintings. Old and young, they came to the museum to enjoy Rockwell's work.

There was another "public" that surprised the Stoltz brothers at first. A stream of foreign visitors made their way to the museum. They already were acquainted with Rockwell's work, and their presence was a constant reminder of the artist's universal appeal.

One of the highlights of the museum is a replica of Rockwell's studio at Stockbridge, with a life-sized figure of the artist seated at his easel. This gives visitors a sense of the atmosphere in which Rockwell worked.

Other contents of the museum are many and varied. For example, it features 324 Rockwell *Saturday Evening Post* covers as well as numerous other magazine covers which Rockwell produced during his career. Reproductions of the famed *American Family* series—commissioned by the Massachusetts Mutual Life Insurance Company—are on display, as well as more than 50 large canvas reproductions of Rockwell paintings.

The museum also displays a variety of lithographs, collotypes, prints, and sketches by Rockwell. And the museum is believed to have the most complete collection of Rockwell's work for the Boy Scouts of America. At one time or another, Rockwell created art for almost every major corporation in America. Scores of these ads for Ford, Chrysler, and even Jello are on display.

More Museum Attractions

The memorabilia created by Rockwell covers the spectrum of American life and almost defies description. Visitors to the museum also view a film and slide showing of Rockwell's life and work in the museum's theatre. The museum also houses a gift shop which offers one of the widest selections of Rockwell plates, figurines, bells, steins, prints and lithographs anywhere. The museum—determined to maintain the high standards of Rockwell's art—also produces high-quality Rockwell collectibles of its own.

When asked what pieces seem to be most popular with visitors, Stoltz replied, "The Little Spooner' is very popular. It features a young boy and girl sitting on a bench, with the boy's dog looking on with a forlorn and confused expression.

"Perhaps the most moving is the 'Golden Rule,' which depicts all races of the world with the golden triangle of humanity."

When asked why Rockwell's work is so popular today, Stoltz attributed it to two factors. The first is nostalgia. People long for the good old days when life was simpler and the human values seemed more attainable.

The other factor is that Norman Rockwell's work *never* lost its popularity. At the zenith of his career, when Rockwell was regularly doing covers for *The Saturday Evening Post,* Curtis Publishing discovered that if a magazine had a Rockwell cover they needed to increase the number of copies printed by 25%. The *average* number of *Post* readers was 25 million primary readers and 35 million pass-along readers!

Rockwell's Impact Continues After His Death

After Rockwell's death in 1978 at the age of 84, the demand for his work greatly increased. One evidence of this continued strength is the demand for Rockwell books offered by the Stoltz brothers in the past few years. Their first book, *Norman Rockwell and The Saturday Evening Post,* was well-received in 1976—but the second and third volumes were immediate sell-outs in 1979.

This year the latest Stoltz book, *The Advertising World of Norman Rockwell,* will be published. Stoltz noted that more than 100 American firms granted permission for their Rockwell illustrations and ads to be included.

Work is also underway on another book on the artistic value of Rockwell's work, Stoltz says.

When asked what impact his hero had on his life, Marshall Stoltz laughed and replied, "I had spent 18 years in the classroom, teaching math and science in the high school in Hatten Heights, New Jersey. I was a good teacher, and I liked it.

"Once the school bell rang in September, I knew where I would be every hour for the next 10 months. Last year I traveled 150,000 miles. I'm also a member of the National Speaker's Bureau, and I'm available for speaking engagements all over the nation, speaking primarily about Rockwell.

"I attend shows which have a Rockwell Day, and have a chance to meet and talk with people interested in Rockwell's work. It has given me an opportunity to meet some tremendous people."

More Plans for Rockwell Admirers to Enjoy

The search goes on at The Norman Rockwell Museum for more of Rockwell's art. A prolific artist, Rockwell gave many paintings away to people who enjoyed them and kept no record or catalog of his work.

Stoltz believes that there are still many valuable Rockwell paintings languishing in attics and basements, waiting to be discovered. And for the Stoltz brothers, this is part of the challenge.

In the future, they also have plans to produce more Norman Rockwell collectibles, especially plates and figurines. Stoltz summed it up when he added, "I couldn't be happier with my life—Rockwell still offers so many possibilities to be explored."

Some of the many collectible pieces created by The Norman Rockwell Museum in tribute to America's best-loved illustrator. They include four items from the ***Classic Figurine*** *series, Rockwell's "Freedom from Fear" from* ***The Four Freedoms*** *collection, and a stein called "Fishin' Pals."*

"Fishin' Pals"

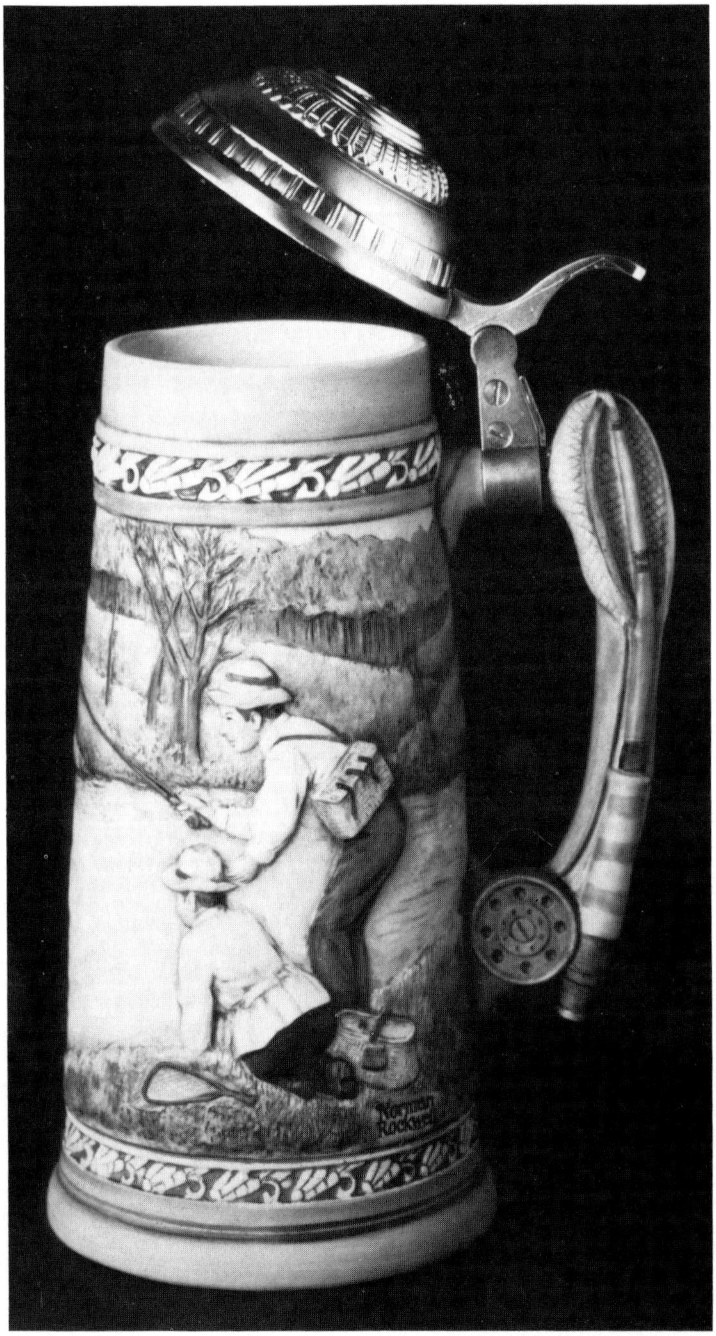

Four items from the Classic Figurine series.

"Freedom from Fear" from The Four Freedoms collection.

Frances Hook captures the simple charms of children in figurines, plates and prints

In a studio overlooking the rugged coastline of Maine, Frances Hook pre eminent artist of children creates the work for which she has become so famous.

There is a vitality in her art. But like the beach, it is scoured clean. All that remains are her warm and sensitive images of children: uniquely realistic, and fashioned in a style that belongs only to Frances Hook.

Even as a child, Frances liked to draw more than anything else. Born in Ambler, Pennsylvania, she took her first art classes in high school. Her work was good enough to merit a scholarship to the Pennsylvania Museum School of Art, where she studied under the famous illustrator, Harry Pitz.

While in school, she met her future husband, Richard Hook. Shortly after their graduation, they were married and began careers in commercial art. Richard was hired by an advertising agency, and Frances began as a free-lancer. Her first ad was a two-page spread in *The Saturday Evening Post*. She continued to produce work of this type for a number of major companies and publications.

The "Northern Children" are Hook Originals

Almost everyone recognizes those winsome children featured on the Northern Tissue packages of the mid-1960's, but few people realize that it was Frances Hook who created them. Not only did they appear on all the packages, but the prints were offered in a separate promotion.

However, for Mrs. Hook, work in the commercial art field grew more scarce as the television industry grew. In the years following her graduation from art school, a gradual evolution had taken place in her style. She had developed a soft, pastel look and the ability to capture the charm and wonder of childhood in a unique way.

In the past she had been too busy to accept many commissions, but companies in the inspirational field especially appreciated her talent and were eager to work with her. Mrs. Hook illustrated children's books, Bible stories, greeting cards and educational material.

At this time, she and her husband began collaborating. One of their most famous "joint ventures" was *The Living Bible* by Tyndale Publishers. Their work on this book was so successful that Tyndale thanked them with a trip to the Holy Land.

Mrs. Hook's Gift is in Relating to Children

In discussing her ability to capture the spontaneity of children, Frances Hook said, "Sometimes I spend days just being with the children who are my subjects. I study them at play as well as when they are very quiet. After a while they don't realize I'm there and I can capture their natural movements with my camera. In these moments, I am sometimes able to catch a special look, a smile, or a sweep of the hand."

Hook then returns to her studio and begins sketching from the photos she takes. She spends hours—sometimes even days—trying to capture with pencil, crayon and pastel the spontaneity that she remembers in her young subjects. From these sketches, her final artwork evolves.

The First Frances Hook Figurines

In 1979, Roman, Inc. approached Hook about doing figurines from her art. She hadn't done any sculpting since art school. She was apprehensive, but agreed to try. In no time, she "got the feel" for sculpture again.

The process of crafting a sculpture may take months from concept to completion. It begins with an original sculpture in clay. This is the most important step. Everything depends on that first model. Once it has been finalized, molds are then made. The creation of the first cast of the original is a critical step because there is always the danger that the original will be destroyed. Mr. Akira Hayakawa, master moldmaker at Ceramica Creativa in Piedras Negras, Mexico is in charge of this delicate operation.

Ceramica Creativa was chosen for its museum-quality porcelain and uncompromising standards. Their skilled artisans render porcelain to exacting specifications.

The original is then delicately cut apart so that the individual molds can be made for any part that cannot be cast as one piece. As many as 12 sets of molds are required for some figurines. When the master is approved from the sample mold, work on production and case molds begins. These molds can only be used about 30 times before they deteriorate to a level unsuitable for a limited edition.

Special mixers and grinders are used to assure a fine quality mix of the specially formulated porcelain. The molds are filled and after the material is set, the pieces are removed and assembled, and the mold marks removed.

The figures are then fired in sophisticated kilns to produce the porcelain white ware.

The Intricate Production Process Continues

Because the color will change in firing, Mrs. Hook must work with a master painter to achieve her special coloring technique. Once the proper colors are selected, the paints are mixed to match the master color sample. Each figure is then carefully painted by a team of artisans. As many as a dozen people may be involved in painting the eyes alone. The paint is then fired to the porcelain; in some cases, two separate firings are required.

In the last firing, each figurine is serially numbered to make it an official part of the limited edition.

A Child's World, Mrs. Hook's collection of hand-painted porcelain bisque figurines, is one of the most popular collections ever issued. The series, which contains 24 subjects, provided Hook with a fascinating challenge.

Hook's Varied Porcelain Art Offerings

Mrs. Hook's collectible art is not limited to figurines only. Her collector editions include porcelain busts of children, mounted on walnut bases. Her first limited edition plate, "Little Children, Come to Me," has enjoyed success in both the religious and collectible fields. It is an excellent example of Hook's Biblical art, which she developed especially for children. It was followed by the plate series, *A Child's Play,* and the larger *Frances Hook Collection.*

Child's Play features children playing outdoors, flying a kite surrounded by a warm summer field of flowers. The *Frances Hook Collection* also depicts children, but in this series only the head and shoulders are visible. Her newest series of plates is a 12-issue series based on the 12 months of the year.

Frances Hook also creates a number of limited edition prints for Roman, Inc. including "The Carpenter," a portrait of Jesus.

While many critics believe that Frances Hooks' porcelain figurines will be her most important work, that view is not shared by the artist. When asked what her favorite work was, she replied, "My next one!"

These delightful collector plates are part of The Frances Hook Collection *for Roman, Inc. Each is limited to 15,000. The diameter for each is 7½", and the issue price per plate is $24.95.*

Frances Hook works at her easel to create one of her beloved art masterworks.

The "Hug Me" figurine by Frances Hook emerges in stages. From original sculpture through final painting, the work is approved at every point by the artist herself.

The first four "Living Image" dolls within the United States Historical Society's collection make a handsome grouping. From left, they are Thomas Jefferson, Abigail Adams, Benjamin Franklin, and George Washington.

Tiny buttons are fastened with a delicate buttonhook.

A fascinating story doll lovers will enjoy...creating the "Living Image" doll collection

by Robert H. Kline, President, United States Historical Society

In all my years an an observer and participant in the limited edition collector's market, it strikes me that *very seldom* does a new offering have strong credentials both as a piece of fine art and as a product of serious historical research. As an historian myself, with a great appreciation for arts and crafts such as fine doll-making, I have done my best to "bridge the gap" and develop collector's items which are as true to history as they are beautiful and rewarding to own.

For many years, it has been our dream at the United States Historical Society to develop "Living Images" of some of America's best-loved patriotic figures. But little did we know when we set out to create the first four "Living Image" dolls that this would be the most challenging assignment in the Society's history. Let me explain why.

There are scores of books written about Benjamin Franklin, George Washington, Abigail Adams and Thomas Jefferson, but most of the material deals with the minds and deeds of these great Americans—not their hair colors, heights, physical appearances, postures or manners of dress. So even before we could think of designing the "Living Image" dolls, our researchers had to spend hundreds of hours researching for the tidbits of fact that would help us ascertain the necessary personal information about our subjects.

Questions About Ben Franklin

In researching Benjamin Franklin, for instance, we did not have the luxury of photographs or even much descriptive material. But we needed to know if Franklin wore a wig, or styled his own hair in the fashion of the day. We knew that his height was approximately 5'9", but we had to determine if his hands and feet were large or small...whether he truly had the "paunch" which history popularly declares...whether his legs were straight, knobby, heavily muscled or flabby...even the color of his eyes.

Franklin's clothing was a bit easier to plan, for he was known far and wide as the "fashion plate" of his day. There are many descriptions of the typical costume for a man of his rank and stature, and so we were able to proceed to the task of commissioning a special costume design for this first "Living Image" doll in our planned series. In time, with the help of a superb book called *Benjamin Franklin in Portraiture* (published by Yale University Press) we learned enough about Franklin's physical characteristics to begin work on his doll-body as well.

After some experimentation and consultation with top experts in the doll-making field, we determined that the sculptor Raymond Lamb was the only logical choice to create the Franklin figure. This celebrated artist joined enthusiastically into our project once he learned of our utter dedication to quality, and to fidelity to the historical truths we had uncovered. After intensive study of the Franklin sculpture by Houdon and the Franklin works by Duplesis, Sevres, Wilson, Peale, Suzanne and Trumbull, Lamb set to work on the Franklin figure.

The resulting 11" tall Benjamin Franklin "body" is a marvel of artistry and historic detail. Some of the things we discovered about Franklin—all of which are reflected in the Lamb sculpture—are that he had a high forehead; that his legs were well-formed but not bunched with muscles; and that he truly did have the paunch of a gourmet. Even a small mole on his left cheek is faithfully shown according to the most reliable Franklin portraits.

The head and elegant little hands are cast in the finest porcelain, kiln-fired and totally hand-painted. The body is an amalgam of porcelain and a unique, elastic material compounded especially to simulate human skin. The hair is of the same color and texture as Franklin's own. It is fashioned of the finest mohair—a material often used for antique dolls because real hair looks surprisingly "fake" on a miniature figure.

One of the many satisfactions in the work for this series has been the sculptor's reaction to the figurines of Franklin which have been created one by one from his original sculpture. "The mold makers are extremely competent," Lamb has declared, "and they have achieved marvelous details in their casting. It was very difficult for them to render Franklin's head, wrinkles and double chin. They had to pull the head out of the solid mold and leave the undercut."

Costuming Opens a New World of Doll Elegance

Once the creation of Benjamin Franklin's body was under control, we were able to turn our full attention to the making of his fine attire. We were extraordinarily fortunate to have noted lecturer and author on dolls Susan Sirkis as an advisor for the Society. And sculptor Ray Lamb worked hand-in-hand with Pauline Richardson, who used patterns generously supplied by the Smithsonian Institution for our inspiration and use. (The costumes for George Washington, Thomas Jefferson and Abigail Adams have been created by Ms. Sirkis and Nanette Atkinson, the master designer and seamstress.)

Lamb was as concerned as Ms. Sirkis and Ms. Richardson that Franklin's clothes be an exact and streamlined fit. After all, such a fashionable "look" would be expected of America's first "fashion plate." Franklin's portly build made the custom-tailoring an especially challenging undertaking.

Trial and error in pattern-making was the only answer. Once the patterns were perfected, we literally shopped in hundreds of stores searching for just the right fabric for historical accuracy and feasibility in sewing such tiny garments.

Eventually, velour was selected for Franklin's vest, and a fine batiste cotton was chosen for his tailored shirt. The top coat and breeches are fashioned of a very thin wool fabric which is capable of being turned and folded for a crisp, very life-like appearance.

I must confess that the footwear for Franklin never fails to bring a smile to my lips: his tiny, close-fitting socks are molded to his foot from infant sock material, and his buckled shoes feature real pewter buckles based on a small drawing in a rare book on Revolutionary War costumes. The shoes, of course, in keeping with our dedication to quality and detail, are modeled of real kid glove-leather.

Another favorite "touch" for Benjamin Franklin's costume is his set of sterling silver spectacles. Unlike many of his contemporaries, Franklin wore his spectacles almost constantly, and so we have created a pair for him in keeping with the style of the day. His sterling-silver-and-rosewood walking stick is a miniature, scale version of a favorite piece which Franklin used quite often. This particular stick was willed to George Washington and is now in the Smithsonian Institution.

And lest I forget one of the most painstaking of all operations in the evolution of each Franklin figure: the costume includes 55 miniature buttons of real pewter, each of which must be painted and sewn into place by hand.

Each "Living Image" Doll is Lovingly Researched and Hand-Crafted

The George Washington, Thomas Jefferson and Abigail Adams dolls have been just as carefully rendered as Benjamin Franklin.

Washington is based on the Houdon sculpture in the State Capitol in Richmond, and on paintings by Gilbert Stuart and Charles Willson Peale. He is shown as a man in his late 40's, as Commander-in-Chief of the Continental Army. Fortunately, we had access to his actual uniform now on display at the Smithsonian Institution.

Across Washington's chest is a blue ribbon, signifying his rank as Commander-in-Chief. The coat is rich navy blue wool; the lining, vest and pants are tan. His buttons are golden pewter. The boots are calfskin, black with tan flap. The spurs have tiny, moveable, star-pointed rowels.

The head of Thomas Jefferson is based on Houdon's from-life bust. Thus we know that this is indeed the man, not a fanciful interpretation. The other details have been drawn from personal descriptions of what Jefferson looked like when he received visitors, such as Lafayette, in his mountain home, Monticello. (You may be interested to know that the regents have elected to display the Jefferson Living Image Doll at Monticello.)

Jefferson's hair is auburn red, combed back to his neck and tied with a black ribbon. His eyes are green. His great coat is grey silk and his breeches are grey corduroy. Inside the great coat is a pocket that contains a miniature brass replica of Mr. Jefferson's pistol—the one he bought in London. The vest is paprika velveteen with simulated horn buttons. His shirt is cotton batiste with long, ruffled sleeves. He has a neckband with ruffles which attaches under his collar.

The shoes for Jefferson seem rather odd by the style of today, but they are authentic for his day. They are long and pointed with tapered heels and pewter buckles.

In his right hand, Jefferson holds a parchment facsimile (2-1/8" x 2-1/2") of The Declaration of Independence, which he wrote, and which you can actually read with a magnifying glass. The Jefferson doll stands 12-1/2" tall, the same as Washington. They were both 6'3" tall.

Abigail Adams was approximately 5'6" tall, with rather sharp features and an attractive, slender figure. She generally wore her hair tied in the back with a ribbon. Her elegant dress is of fine Chinese silk. Her silk chiffon sleeves extend from just below the elbow to the wrist. The quilted petticoat is also silk, decorated with 10 delicate, handmade roses.

In her right hand, Abigail is holding a fan typical of 18th century fashion. The blades, of man-made ivory, are connected by a pink ribbon. A real diamond is in the center. The pointed shoes are silk jacquard, over kid leather, with pewter buckles painted gold. The heel is of moderate height, tapered toward the toe.

The underclothes are just as authentic as the rest of the costumes. She has red ribbon garters over white stockings. She is wearing two cotton slips; her chemise extends just below the knee, and the other—her under-petticoat—to her ankles. Around her waist is a hand-laced corset with 36 eyelets, and cotton-filled bustles provide a shapely lift to the petticoat and dress.

Experts Unite in Praise for "Living Image" Dolls

Doll collecting experts and collectors have responded with great enthusiasm for the Benjamin Franklin doll, and for Washington, Mrs. Adams and Jefferson as well. As Rolf Ericson, Executive Director of the Doll Artisan Guild said: "These historical dolls—hand-made objects of art today and heirlooms of tomorrow—constitute one of the most important limited editions of dolls *ever* produced, and in my opinion, definitely *the* most exciting one."

And Gary Ruddell, publisher of *Doll Reader* Magazine, recently remarked, "It's too bad that every serious doll collector can't own them. They are spectacular."

Already two-thirds of the limited edition of 2500 Benjamin Franklin dolls have been "spoken for," and more orders arrive daily.

The original issue price for "Benjamin Franklin" and each of the first four dolls in the collection is $525, and convenient long-term payment plans are definitely available. We invite you to write for an illustrated brochure and description of the dolls, at no obligation of course. Simply drop a line to Mary Beth Gilman, U.S. Historical Society, First and Main Streets, Richmond, Virginia 23219.

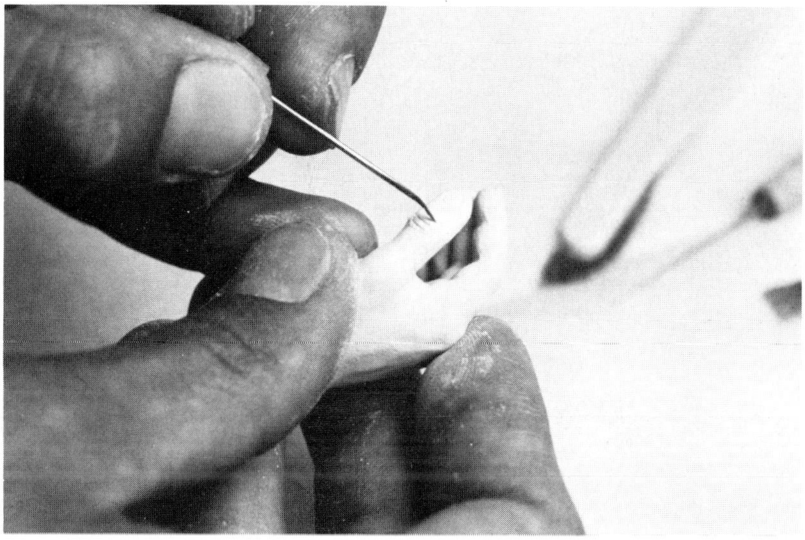

Each fine porcelain hand is individually crafted and painted. The United States Historical Society insists upon anatomical accuracy.

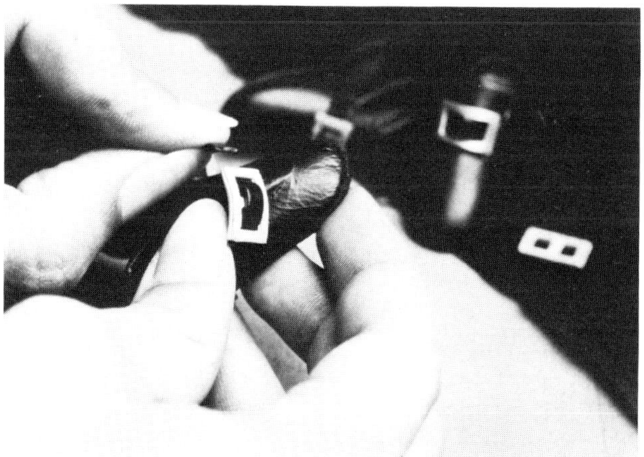

Real leather shoes are accented by pewter buckles.

A collector enjoys displaying her dolls on her mantelpiece.

The **World Wildlife Fund** *first-issue "Panda Bear" plate by Wolfgang Weber for Villeroy & Boch.*

Second-issue **World Wildlife Fund** *plate, entitled "Tiger."*

Renowned German firm of Villeroy & Boch draws on its heritage to create today's limited editions

For some collectors, an interest in the art forms of past eras develops when they begin learning about—and purchasing—contemporary limited editions. For others, the process is reversed: they become interested in the finest and most authentic of today's arts as a result of their study of elegant (and expensive) antiques.

In both cases, a look at the history and present-day activities of Villeroy & Boch makes for a number of interesting discoveries. You see, perhaps more than any other maker of limited editions today, V&B draws upon its art archives and its exclusive processes from the past to entice today's collectors with superb, limited edition artwork.

In recent years, Villeroy & Boch has drawn on its considerable art holdings to produce contemporary versions of its famed Chromolith and Phanolith steins.

Another contemporary success for Villeroy & Boch is its stunning *Russian Fairy Tales* collection of 12 plates. These vibrant plates are among the most intricate, highly-detailed presentations in the limited edition field.

The Story of Villeroy & Boch And its Mettlach and Heinrich Studios

The saga of this prolific firm dates back to 1748, in the quaint European village of Auden-le-Tiche. There Francois Boch opened his first pottery studio, and began the tradition of Villeroy & Boch. Today an eighth-generation descendant of Francois Boch sits as Managing Director of the firm.

The Villeroy family has been associated with clay and ceramic crafts for seven generations, and they joined forces with the Bochs in 1836. The merger fueled the creative fires of both families—for as they prospered artistically, they also became known as innovators in production techniques.

The potter's wheel at Mettlach was the first to be powered by water—this breakthrough occurred in 1813. In 1862 Villeroy & Boch developed a unique dry pressing process, and in 1901 they installed the first tunnel kiln. They were pioneers in what today is called "R&D" as well: their first testing and research department was established at Dresden in 1928.

Today Villeroy & Boch is internationally respected as a maker of superb dinnerware and elegant accessories as well as limited edition collector plates, plaques and steins. The firm now employs as many as 16,000 craftsmen at 18 locations throughout France, Luxembourg, Italy and Germany. But its headquarters still are located at Mettlach in an impressive, typically old-world setting of elegance and taste.

V&B Brings the Past to Life in Today's Limited Editions

Unlike some contemporary limited edition producers whose offerings are scorned by "serious" collectors, the works of Villeroy & Boch draw praise from experts for their fidelity to the originals.

Members and officers of Stein Collectors International, the most prominent group devoted to the study and collection of fine steins, have been actively involved as advisors during the creation of recent contemporary Mettlach steins.

Stein production at Mettlach stopped in 1927—due in part to the loss of trained craftspeople in World War I and in part to the loss of machinery and molds during the same war. So stein collectors—some of whom are no doubt weary of seeking out the relatively small numbers of surviving true Mettlach steins—are enthusiastic about such well-produced Chromolith (etched or incised) pieces as Villeroy & Boch's "Fairytale" and "Hero" editions.

There was also considerable interest in the firm's first contemporary stein offering—a set of four-seasons Phanolith (cameo) steins which appeared several years ago.

A Wide Range of Limited Edition Plates... and Now Figurines

Today Villeroy & Boch offers collector plates at various price levels—all of which are among the finest examples of their type. The Zvorykin "Fairy Tale" plates issued well under $100, but V&B recognizes that some collectors like to keep their purchases in the $30—$40 range.

Most offerings from the firm's Heinrich Studio at Selb fit this criterion—including a charming Unicef series based on children of many lands, and two series of "Flower Fairies" plates inspired by the well-loved art and poetry of Cicely Mary Barker, an Englishwoman.

Heinrich also has introduced a *Fairyland Lovers* collection of plates inspired by the works of famed turn-of-the-century illustrator Edmund Dulac. And the firm won the sponsorship of the World Wildlife Fund for a series of animal-subject plates by Wolfgang Weber. These plates feature a molded bas-relief effect which is quite striking and unique.

Following a trend toward figurines which match favorite plates, Villeroy & Boch recently premiered its first contemporary figurine limited edition, "The Lavender Fairy." This delicate, hand-painted piece is a tribute to the two-dimensional works of Cicely Mary Barker.

Marcia Richards Handles United States Collectibles Operations

Although Villeroy & Boch has offices in many major cities worldwide, one of the most active outposts for this German firm is at 41 Madison Avenue (New York, NY 10010). There Marcia Richards serves as vice president for collectibles, United States division.

Active at collectors' shows and open houses, Ms. Richards always is delighted to share her knowledge of Villeroy & Boch history and contemporary works. For more information about any of the products mentioned here, write her at the New York offices.

A handsome new stein from Villeroy & Boch: "Battle of Trafalgar," which premieres a series of six called ***Famous Sea Battles.***

Karin Blume's "Mexico" plate—sixth issue in a series called ***Children of the World*** *which benefits UNICEF.*

How to catalog, insure and care for your collection

Cataloging the Collection

Many collectors begin acquiring their limited editions one or two at a time, but before long they realize that they own a score or more of pieces—some of which may already have risen in market value. This is very gratifying and a fine source of enjoyment, but it also is cause for thought about record-keeping and insuring that growing and valuable collection.

The best advice we can give a new collector is to start a record-keeping system right away: and follow through as you add each new item to your collection or home display.

At least two publishers offer record books which you may find useful in documenting your collection. These are:

The Kovels' Organizer for Collectors by Ralph and Terry Kovel, published by Crown Publishers, One Park Avenue, New York, New York 10016.

The Antique Trader Weekly Antiques and Collectibles Record Book, published by The Babka Publishing Co., Dubuque, Iowa 52001.

Take time as soon as you obtain a new item to record all the details of purchase and price. If you do not, before long this information will escape you—and a prospective buyer or insurance appraiser may not take your word for a hazy memory of a $50 purchase price. It's a fine idea to photograph each of your collectibles—or to do so in small groups where each item may be easily identified. The books above each provide spaces for small photographs to be attached as a permanent record. For more on the "how-to" of a photo inventory, send 35 cents to Eastman Kodak Company, Consumer Markets Division, Rochester, New York 14650 and they will send you a helpful booklet.

In addition to the information you will record, also keep all written materials and certificates which you receive with your collectibles—receipts, flyers and stories, care and handling instructions, etc. They will help to document your collection for resale or replacement in the future.

There is some controversy among plate buyers and sellers as to the value of original boxes. Some experts believe it is essential to retain original plate boxes—even if they are only made of corrugated material. Others feel this pre-occupation with packaging is unfortunate. A possible compromise would be to save special or fancy packaging and discard inexpensive boxes which are obviously not "custom" for this limited edition. This decision is up to the individual collector.

Here are some of the specific points you will want to address in your records of each collectible item you own:

Manufacturer Name
Artist Name
Series Name
Item Name
Year of Issue
Edition Limit/Your Item's Number if Numbered
Size/Dimensions
Date of Purchase
Place of Purchase
Your Cost
Added Expenses (Shipping, Restoration, etc.)
Special Markings (Artist's Signature, etc.)
Secondary Market History (If Purchased on Secondary Market)
Location in Your Home (In Case of Burglary or Loss)
Insurance Company/Policy or Rider Number

Insuring the Collection

Your first step should be to check your present homeowner's or renter's policy to find out how extensively you are covered in case of fire, burglary or other risk. Some policies carry a fairly high maximum payment for items such as collectibles, while others offer very little of this type of protection.

Compare the amount of coverage you have to the value of your collection. Also ascertain whether you are covered for all eventualities—burglary, loss, damage, etc. It is essential as well that you determine how the value of your items would be assessed by your insurance company: on replacement value, purchase price, or some type of "depreciated value." Some insurance firms might well lump your precious collector plates in the same category with tableware dishes, for instance. It is up to you to point out the difference and make sure you have proper protection written into your coverage.

You are most likely to obtain the best price for additional coverage or riders on your collection if you can work with an insurance agent who already does business with you. Approaching an agent with a request for coverage *just* on your collection—unless it is very extensive and very valuable—is not likely to kindle a great deal of enthusiasm on his or her part.

If you are unable to gain cooperation from your regular insurance agent, then, you might consider shopping for another agent to handle all your insurance needs, and use that clout to obtain affordable coverage for your plates, figurines, bells, and other limited editions.

Other collectors in your area may well be a fine source of information on insurance protection. If you are able to join a local collecting club, ask fellow collectors how they insure their treasured items, and then investigate the firms and methods they suggest. You might even consider approaching insurance firms with a "group coverage" concept for your club—the volume of such a sale may win you a better price than any one collector could command alone.

Caring for the Collection

The care of your collection falls under two main headings: security, and cleaning/maintenance.

Where security is concerned, the usual common sense rules of home maintenance apply, of course. Avoid fire hazards, keep valuables out of the reach of children and pets, and "child proof" an adults—only house before the younger set comes to visit. Make sure you have sufficient smoke detectors in good working order. Collectors with extensive holdings may want to consider an electronic alarm system with sensors and electric eye equipment—especially if they live in a crime-sensitive area or if the home is well-known as one which contains many valuable items. Firms such as ADT, Radio Shack, Westinghouse and others sell custom or standard security systems, and they are listed in the Yellow Pages of your telephone book under "Security Control Equipment and Systems." Never discuss your collection in public, and avoid placing your valuables in areas where passersby can easily see and covet them through windows and doors.

If you have more collectibles than you can comfortably display, consider placing some of them in a secured vault or safe in a bank or other bonded area. Take steps yourself to secure your home better with dead-bolt locks, window locks, stronger doors, etc. Re-emphasize to yourself and your family the importance of keeping doors and windows locked—even in summer—when there is no one around to protect the territory. Tell the police and neighbors when you plan to be out of town, so they can watch your home. And stop deliveries of milk, newspapers, etc. when you travel so burglars won't have a tip-off that no one is home.

In terms of maintenance and cleaning of your collectibles, the proper advice depends upon the medium and the delicacy of the item involved. Many firms supply Care and Handling sheets with their products, and these should be kept for future reference. Write to the Customer Service Department of the manufacturer of an item if you are in doubt as to how to care for it. In general, it is good advice to keep hand-painted items out of direct sunlight to avoid fading. Hand-painted items of terra cotta, pewter and some other materials should not be handled any more than necessary, to avoid smudges or chipping.

If in doubt, don't put a collectible plate or other item in the dishwasher—many are not dishwasher safe. Most porcelain collector plates may be washed by hand with a mild soap, and spray-rinsed. Most porcelain figurines may be lightly dusted, or spray-washed and rinsed with mild soap and a gentle spray of water. To avoid problems with dust and dirt, many collectors favor frames and display cases with protective glass, especially for valuable or intricate items.

Keep a listing of your collectible items, including photos if possible.

Limited edition collectibles often come with certificates of authenticity and other documentation materials. Most experts advise collectors to keep these documents for the future. As for boxes, general advice is to keep those which obviously add to the value of the piece; discard plain corrugated boxes if you wish.

Some collectors with extensive holdings may wish to invest in security systems featuring electric eye monitoring or other means of spotting intruders. In this dining room, an electric eye device has been placed in the upper corner of the room to detect motion.

The Bradford Exchange serves as a "stock exchange"-type organization for collector plates only. Bradford also sells new plate issues created by its affiliated companies and other organizations.

How to Sell Your Plate:

1. **Bring your plates for registration and sale from 10:00 a.m. to 4:00 p.m. on Saturday, February 19, and from 8:00 a.m. to 1:00 p.m. on Sunday, February 20.**

2. **Fill out one sell form for each five plates offered.** (A volunteer from SCAPCC or a staff member at the registration area will be glad to help you).

3. **Take your form(s) and plates to the registration counter, pay a $2.00 registration fee for each plate you wish to sell.** This *fee is non-refundable, payable in advance,* and may be paid by cash or check only.

4. **If you are selling a complete set of plates** (i.e., a group of plates issued either at once or over a period of time, all of which are back issues) **list them as one plate for sale; they will be sold as a set only.** (They do, however, count as individual plates, adding to the 15-plate limit.)

5. **Set your asking price for each plate or set of plates.** (If you wish to change your asking price during the Swap'n'Sell, ask a staff member for assistance.)

6. **Upon registration, you will be given a receipt for your plates.** NOTE: RETAIN THIS RECEIPT. YOU MUST PRESENT IT TO CLAIM EITHER THE MONEY PAID FOR YOUR PLATES OR THE UNSOLD PLATES.

7. A Swap'n'Sell volunteer or staff member will take your plates to the appropriate display area, designated by category for your plate. For your reference, the display area will appear on your receipt.

8. All plates will be displayed, regardless of their asking prices.

9. **Check back periodically at the cashier's counter to see if your plates have been sold. Present your receipt to a cashier, and collect the money for your plate.**

10. **If your plate has not sold, and you wish to change your asking price, see a Swap'n'Sell Staff member for assistance. Do not change any prices without assistance of a staff member; this is for your protection!**

11. **If you wish to withdraw your plates from the Swap'n'Sell at any time, locate your plates in the designated area and bring them to the cashier's station. Staff members will provide you with the necessary receipts to allow you to leave the Swap'n'Sell room.**

12. **Remember to pick up your unsold plates when you are leaving the convention. *All plates must be claimed no later than 5:00 p.m. on Sunday, February 20, 1983.***

How to Buy or Bid:

1. **Browse the tables at all display areas.** Compare the asking prices that appear on the forms attached to each plate.

2. **Examine any plate carefully before you make your decision to buy it.** What you see is what you get.

3. **When you have decided you wish to buy the plate remove the plate, box and other accompanying papers from the display table and take it to a cashier.**

4. **A cashier will collect the asking price of the plate, and provide you with the necessary receipt to enable you to leave the Swap'n'Sell room.**

You may pay cash for your purchases, use a personal check or charge the purchase to your Visa or Mastercard.

"Swap and Sell" meets allow collectors to trade directly among themselves on an organized basis. Such an event is held yearly both at the Anaheim and South Bend conventions. Local collectors' clubs often sponsor similar events as well.

About the secondary market

Over and over again, collectors are advised to buy the limited edition items they like and let market appreciation take care of itself. But like fine jewelry, classic furniture, and even some items of clothing, many limited edition collectibles do develop a value beyond their original purchase price. And these assets may come in handy at some time to the collector who wishes to upgrade or change direction in his/her collection...or to liquidate it for cash. What's more, the new collector who has just discovered a series or type of collectible he/she truly enjoys may find it helpful to know of various ways to locate individuals and dealers willing to sell back issues.

The fact is that today, there are several well-structured ways for collectors of plates to buy and sell in the marketplace. Graphic works are actively traded in certain areas of the market. Less structure is apparent in the markets for figurines, bells, and contemporary, limited edition steins and dolls. However, with services like COLLECTORS' INFORMATION BUREAU and several others new to the marketplace or in their formative stages, collectors may expect much greater emphasis on these "quieter" secondary market areas in the very near future. As John Graham of The Hamilton Collection explains: "The limited edition plate 'boom' and the forum for buying and selling plates grew hand in hand during the 1970's. Now the firms which make other collectible items, and the dealers which sell them, recognize the need among collectors for a similar forum for figurines, bells, etc. A great deal of cooperative effort is in the works right now to provide such a forum, and collectors will benefit by it for many years to come."

Here then are the thoughts of some of the most knowledgeable spokespeople in the world of collectibles—first about the importance of the secondary market, and second on how a collector may use it to buy or sell.

The Importance of the Secondary Market

Industry leaders believe that the secondary market is important for several reasons: primarily to allow experienced collectors to upgrade their collections, to stimulate the market and encourage new collectors, and to provide a means for monetary appreciation. Here are some of their comments.

To Upgrade a Collection. Klaus Vogt of Anna-Perenna Porcelain suggests that "A collection should be carefully assembled of the most beautiful pieces which you can afford. If it is gathered in this fashion, a collector rarely disposes of his collection. However, as a collector matures he may wish to dispose of things that he no longer enjoys in order to have the capital to buy things which he enjoys more. The secondary market, when used in this fashion, is valuable to a collector." Marge Rosenberg of Carol's Gift Shop agrees. "As a dealer, I view the resale of a piece as just another step for a collector. If I buy back a plate from a collector and they are satisfied with that transaction, they will probably use the money to buy a plate which they enjoy more or will upgrade the collection." And Brigitte Moore of Reco stresses the budget factor: "Many of the people that we have contact with do not have a lot of money. One of the best ways that they have of improving their collections is to sell something and get something they like more. If the market is active, they can do this in a variety of ways. It is a given fact that a collector's taste changes, but what he is no longer interested in keeping is just what a new collector may be interested in acquiring. This trading stimulates new business and helps improve the art of collecting."

To stimulate the Market. "I see the secondary market as very important and growing stronger as the number of collectors increases," says Susan Elliott of *Plate Collector*. "Each year the market becomes more solid. It is an excellent way for new collectors to obtain some good quality pieces that have been traded in the past. They have an opportunity to learn the history of the hobby by owning some of the items that have been favorites in the past." Robert Kline of the United States Historical Society adds, "This market is also important because this is where collectors are likely to make their first purchase. They see something they like, and gradually become collectors." He mentioned auction houses, antique stores, estate sales and swap shows as examples. Mary Hugunin emphasized the enjoyment of tracking down an item in the secondary market. "Once the production of an item has stopped and all of the original issue has been sold, the secondary market is the only way to obtain these collectibles. It enhances the fun of collecting."

To Make Money—Or Enjoy the Thought of It. John Graham of The Hamilton Collection explains this theory: "Many a collector who would never consider selling his "Mary, Mary" plate or Boehm flower sculpture still enjoys pointing out the secondary market action of these favorite possessions. That quote price is a psychological 'lift' for the collector—it solidifies the collector's good judgment." Don Herschleb of Commemorative Imports agrees: "To see an item listed on a back issue list is very satisfying to a collector. They may not be interested in selling, but it does give a feeling of security just knowing there is an active market."

Other Considerations. In addition to the reasons listed above, Harriet Dalaskey of Bradford praises the organized secondary market as a means for collectors to "fill in" a missing item in a series or grouping. And Sam Bauman of *Plate World* believes the aftermarket serves as an "ultimate test" of an issue's worth. He says, "I define the secondary market as the sale of a collectible once it has been completely sold out at the retail level. The secondary market provides the real test of the value of a collectible and is the real secret in determining how valuable it is—in essence, the secondary market determines the value."

How to Buy and Sell

Experts offered several alternatives for the collector who wishes to buy or sell a collectible once it is sold out at the retail level. Most often mentioned were ads in collector publications, sales through a dealer, working with The Bradford Exchange (for plates), or attending collector club-sponsored swap meets or auctions. Here is more information about each of these means.

Ads in Collector Publications. Many experts advocate this method because it may allow the collector to set a price at or quite near the stated market value of the item. (If the collector sells through a dealer or exchange he/she may sacrifice some or all possible profits to the dealer's mark-up or exchange's brokerage fee.) On the other hand, the collector must weigh the factor of full market price against the cost of the ad or ads. A list of publications to consider for ads may be found in the "Books, Magazines and Newsletters" section of this book.

Robert Kline suggests, "Put an ad in collector magazines, trade publications or classified sections. Most purchases are made by collectors for their own personal collections so the sale of collectibles is steady throughout the whole year." Susan Elliott offers plate selling through *Plate Collector* Magazine: "If a collector is interested in obtaining the highest price for an item, selling to another collector may be the best option. They can use all of the traditional forms of advertising like classified ads, ads in collector magazines or maybe the new 'mail bid sale' service which is now being offered by *Plate Collector*. Under this new service, collectors pay $2 to have a plate listed. Bidders send their bids to *Plate Collector,* which determines the highest bidder. The bidder sends the money for the plate to *Plate Collector* which then notifies the seller that the plate has been sold and gives instructions for mailing to the new owner. At this point, the system seems to be operating successfully for all parties involved." Contact *Plate Collector* at P.O. Box 1729, San Marcos, Texas 78667.

Sales Through a Dealer. As mentioned above, generally the collector who sells his/her collectibles to a dealer will receive somewhat less than the quoted price, to allow the dealer a margin in the transaction. If the item is taken on consignment, a collector may be able to work out a less costly deal, but if he or she receives cash for the item, the dealer surely is entitled to some fair profit on the sale. The collector who buys back issues through a dealer may expect to pay quoted prices for them—considering that the dealer may have gone through a search to locate the item, or at least kept it in his/her inventory for a time.

Pat Owen of Viking Import House has this to say about sales through dealers, "Collectors who wish to sell pieces from their collections might contact a reputable dealer in their area to see if they are interested in purchasing them." Klaus Vogt of Anna-Perenna Porcelain points out that collectors may use dealers as resources for buy-sell ideas: "They are excellent resource people, and may have other possible suggestions."

The Bradford Exchange. Bradford offers its services only for limited edition collector plates, but some collectors may find this a very convenient way to sell plates, or to locate specific back issues. Harriet Dalaskey of Bradford explains: "Contact The Bradford Exchange for the purchase or sale of collector plates. The Exchange guarantees that the trader-seller will be paid. They buyer will get a plate in mint condition with proper certification. The Exchange stands in the middle to insure a trustworthy and fair transaction. There is no fee for listing a plate with the exchange, but a 30% fee will be subtracted from the sale price at the time the plate is sold. Through the use of computers, the Exchange maintains a constant monitoring of prices being paid by collectors. There is no risk for the collector: the Exchange assumes full responsibility for the sale and provides service to both the buyer and seller." For more information, contact Bradford and ask for the Trading Floor.

Swap Meets and Auctions. Many collector's clubs offer swap meets or auctions as a regular part of their activities. Major collectibles conventions usually feature such meets as well. These activities provide a forum for collectors to sell their extra items for a very modest registration fee. Thus buyers may obtain items reasonably as well.

A final note on the secondary market: if you have questions on how to buy or sell items created by one of the members of the COLLECTORS' INFORMATION BUREAU, contact that member directly. This policy may also be helpful with other collectibles firms, whose addresses are listed in the Company Summary section of this book.

The collectors' club, convention and travel scene

For many collectors, the enjoyment of their hobbies grows even richer when they can share it with others. Getting in touch with fellow collectors to learn...to socialize...and to admire each others' "finds" adds an extra dimension of pleasure to the collecting field.

In recent years, scores of local clubs for limited edition collectors have become active. Some are sponsored by a dealer, while others are completely collector-run and sponsored. In addition, a number of manufacturers sponsor clubs for people who enjoy collecting their products.

Local clubs meet once a month or perhaps every-other month, in most cases. Most charge modest dues in the area of \$5—\$10 per person or \$10—\$15 per couple annually. Programs may range from members' own presentations to celebrity appearances by top artists. Many manufacturers are producing films about their artists and creative processes, which are available to clubs at no charge or nominal charge for loan. Many clubs also serve refreshments, offer door prizes, monthly swap and sell programs, and other activities.

Manufacturers' clubs may or may not have local organizations with meetings. They usually offer exclusive products to members, as well as newsletters, "insider information," travel tours and other benefits. Some charge a yearly dues fee of \$10 to \$50, while others have purchase requirements which lead to membership.

Several times a year, national conventions attract collectors from all over the country to view the latest limited editions, meet favorite artists, swap and sell collectibles and enjoy each others' company.

And a new travel service allows collectors to journey in groups to American and European sites which have both tourist and collector appeal.

What's more, a number of museums, displays and tours offer collectors a chance to see fine collectibles and how they are made—or view the originals which inspired limited editions.

So take a look at these listings, and contact the local and national clubs and organizations you feel will enrich your collecting hobby. *Plate Collector* Magazine runs a regular listing of local clubs, locations and meeting times which you may want to consult.

NATIONAL AND INTERNATIONAL COLLECTOR, MANUFACTURER OR MARKETER-SPONSORED CLUBS

For specific information about dues, benefits, or how to join, please contact the club or clubs which interest you. And if you know of a club which has not been mentioned here, please contact COLLECTORS' INFORMATION BUREAU so that we may list it in our next update.

AMERICAN BELL ASSOCIATION
c/o Louise Collins
Alter Road, Box 386
Natrona Heights, Pennsylvania 15065

AMERICAN COLLECTOR CLUB
100 N. Edward Gary
P.O. Box 1729
San Marcos, Texas 78667

THE BELLEEK COLLECTORS' SOCIETY
1001 North U.S. Highway 1
P.O. Box 3179
Jupiter-Tequesta, Florida 33458-0287

THE BOEHM PORCELAIN GUILD
Edward Marshall Boehm, Inc.
P.O. Box 5051
Trenton, New Jersey 08638

CALHOUN'S COLLECTORS SOCIETY
Calhoun Center
Minneapolis, Minnesota 55435

CLUB ANRI
55 Pacella Park Drive
Randolph, Massachusetts 02368

DOWNS' COLLECTORS CLUB
2778 S. 35th Street
Milwaukee, Wisconsin 53215

THE FRANKLIN MINT COLLECTORS SOCIETY
The Franklin Mint
Franklin Center, Pennsylvania 19091

GOEBEL COLLECTORS' CLUB
Division of Goebel Art (GmbH) Inc.
105 White Plains Road
Tarrytown, New York 10591

GREENBOOK™ SOCIETY OF DEALERS AND COLLECTORS
348 Main Street
East Setauket, New York 11733

INTERNATIONAL PLATE COLLECTORS GUILD
c/o Mrs. Anita Smith
5581 Sandoval Avenue
Riverside, California 92509

MADAME ALEXANDER (DOLL) FAN CLUB
P.O. Box 146, New Lenox, Illinois 60451

THE NORMAN ROCKWELL MUSEUM COLLECTOR'S SOCIETY
2840 Maria Avenue
Northbrook, Illinois 60062

ORIGINAL PRINT COLLECTORS GROUP, LTD.
215 Lexington Avenue
New York, New York 10016

PRECIOUS MOMENTS COLLECTORS CLUB
2201 Arthur Avenue, P.O. Box 1466
Elk Grove Village, Illinois 60007

ROYAL DOULTON INTERNATIONAL COLLECTORS CLUB
USA Branch
Doulton & Co. Inc.
P.O. Box 1815
Somerset, New Jersey 08873

SEBASTIAN MINIATURE COLLECTORS SOCIETY
321 Central Street
Hudson, Massachusetts 01749

STEIN COLLECTORS INTERNATIONAL
c/o Jack Lowenstein
P.O. Box 463
Kingston, New Jersey 08528

THE WEDGWOOD COLLECTORS SOCIETY
41 Madison Avenue
New York, New York 10010

UNITED FEDERATION OF DOLL CLUBS
Mrs. Edward Buchholz, Membership Chairman
2814 Herron Lane
Glenshaw, Pennsylvania 15116

UNITED STATES HISTORICAL SOCIETY
First and Main Streets
Richmond, Virginia 23219

COLLECTORS' CONVENTIONS

The two conventions listed are known to be the largest annual gatherings in the limited editions field. A number of other regional and local shows are held either annually or on a periodic basis, and from time to time a manufacturer or dealer will sponsor an Artists' Fair or Festival. Dealers often schedule open houses with specific artists, too. To keep abreast of upcoming events, check the calendar column in publications such as *Plate Collector* Magazine.

PLATE COLLECTORS CONVENTION
Sponsored by the Southern California Association of Collector Clubs
Anaheim Convention Center, Anaheim, California
Annually in March
Write: SCAPCC
P.O. Box 8839
Anaheim, California 92802

INTERNATIONAL PLATE COLLECTORS' CONVENTION
Sponsored by Watson's Collectors Club and the National Association of Limited Edition Dealers
Century Center, South Bend, Indiana
Annually in July
Write: Joyce Zielinski
Watson's
135 E. Michigan
New Carlisle, Indiana 46552
Call: (219) 654-3695

TRAVEL SERVICE

Some national and international collectors' clubs sponsor trips to their factories and other points of interest—check the individual club to see if they offer this service. The source below specializes in international travel for the limited edition collector, with tours available to points in France, England, Germany, and other places of interest both to tourists and to collectors. For informational brochure about tours available, write:
Mrs. Louise Goldstein
GLOBETROTTER COLLECTORS' TOURS
2415 Ennalls Avenue
Wheaton, Maryland 20902
(301) 949-8500

MUSEUMS AND POINTS OF INTEREST

AMERICAN ROSE SOCIETY
(Plates and rose garden)
Shreveport, Louisiana

THE BOEHM STUDIOS
(Gallery and film)
Trenton, New Jersey

BRADFORD MUSEUM OF COLLECTOR'S PLATES
9333 N. Milwaukee Avenue
Niles, Illinois

COLLECTOR'S PLATE HALL OF FAME
Palm Beach Gardens Holiday Inn
PGA Boulevard at Interstate 95
Palm Beach Gardens, Florida

FRANKLIN MINT
(General tour)
Franklin Center, Pennsylvania

GOEBEL COLLECTORS' CLUB
(Gallery)
Tarrytown, New York

EDNA HIBEL MUSEUM
150 Royal Poinciana Plaza
Palm Beach, Florida 33480

THE NORMAN ROCKWELL MUSEUM
6th and Walnut Streets
Philadelphia, Pennsylvania

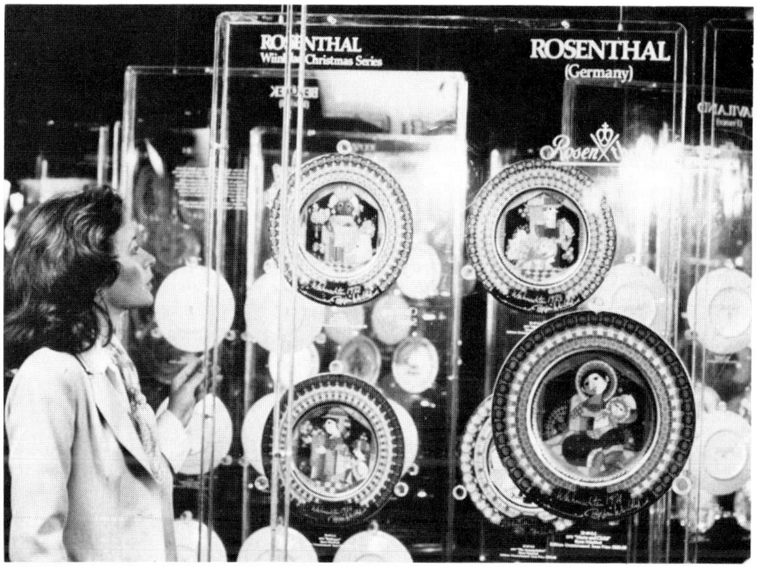

The Bradford Museum of Collector's Plates in Niles, Illinois is one of several points of interest collectors may visit in their travels. The museum features more than 1000 plates produced by 60 makers from 12 countries.

Collectors enjoy meeting with their favorite artists at dealers' open houses or club meetings. Here, Marge Rosenberg [left] of Carol's Gift Shop [Artesia, California] sports clown make-up in honor of John McClelland's visit in conjunction with the issuance of the "Tommy The Clown" plate.

Globetrotter Incorporated is a travel service by which collectors may visit points of interest in Europe and elsewhere, including tours of some of the world's most famous limited edition studios. Here, a group of collectors pause for a photo while visiting the Goebel factory in Rodental, Germany. Note the "M.I. Hummel" figure with umbrella at left.

National Association of Limited Edition Dealers

Here is the 1983 roster of the limited edition dealers who are members of NALED, a national group of retail and wholesale merchants who are in the specialized market of exchanging and selling limited edition plates, bells, figurines and other collectible items. The group was formed in 1976. This list will help collectors to locate limited edition dealers in various areas of the United States. The National Headquarters for NALED is located at P.O. Box 42135, Houston, Texas 77242. Telephone: (713) 981-1411.

ARIZONA

THE ARTISAN
Vicki Hobe
2330 East Southern Avenue
Tempe, AZ 85282
(602) 838-0147

FOX'S GIFTS AND COLLECTIBLES
Catherine Wilbern, Manager
Post Office Box 599
Scottsdale, AZ 85252
(602) 947-0560

GIFT HAUS - DORHAN ENTERPRISES
Doris and Henry Scheid
5708 W. Hayward
Glendale, AZ 85301
(602) 931-0858

CALIFORNIA

ARMSTRONG'S ENTERPRISES
David Armstrong
150 East Third Street
Pomona, CA 91766
(714) 623-6464

CAROL'S GIFT SHOP
Marge and Joe Rosenberg
17601 S. Popneer Blvd.
Artesia, CA 90701
(213) 924-6335

CECELIA'S COLLECTABLES
Maxine Anderson
9251 Magnolia Avenue
Riverside, CA 92503
(714) 359-5420

COPPOLA'S
D. Copeland and Louise Dosdourin
Box 1309 - 630A Grand Avenue
Carlsbad, CA 92008
(714) 729-0256

ERNST LIMITED EDITIONS
Ray Ernst
301 East Grand
Escondido, CA 92020
(714) 741-8700

EVA MARIE
Eva M. Simmons
1915 South Catalina
Redondo Beach, CA 90277
(213) 375-8422

FORTE OLIVIA
Olive J. Matthews
675 South Glendora Avenue
West Covina, CA 91790
(213) 962-2588

HANSON GALLERY
Marlene Bingham
2744 Macroni Avenue
Sacramento, CA 95821
(916) 484-1055

LEE'S
Lee Smith
Post Office Box 19133
Sacramento, CA 95819
(916) 457-4308

LENA'S LIMITED EDITIONS
Judy Lena
410 South Norfolk
San Mateo, CA 94401
(415) 342-1304

LYNN'S PLACE
Lynn E. Kennard
14464 Seventh Street
Victorville, CA 92392
(619) 245-5226

MT. WHITNEY COLLECTIBLES
Clarence and Margaret Streeter
335 Mt. View
Long Point, CA 93545
(714) 876]4269

NYBORG CASTLE
Bea Nyborg
Post Office Box 2388
Pleasant Hill, CA 94523
(415) 228]0334

NORTHERN LIGHTS, LTD.
Peter Clark
1560 Fourth Street
San Rafael, CA 94901
(415) 457-2884

OBJECTS OF MY AFFECTIONS
Carole Doolittle
15301 Ventura Blvd., Suite 260
Sherman Oaks, CA 91403
(213) 784]2377

THE OWL ANTIQUES, ETC.
Josephine K. Krause
216 N. Glendora Avenue
Glendora, CA 91740
(213) 963-5616

PARTYLAND
Harold Scott
122 S. Garfield Avenue
Alhambra, CA 91801
(213) 289-2828

PAT'S PLATES
Patricia Pettyjohn
11035 Ironwood Road
San Diego, CA 92131
(619) 271-8117

THE PLATE LADY
Jan Patterson
601 Van Ness Avenue
San Francisco, CA 94102
(415) 673-1491

RAE JEAN'S GALLERY
Rae Jean Manrique
415 Tennessee Street (V)
Redlands, CA 92373
(714) 793-6252

RAM ENTERPRISES
Lorraine S. Matthew
Post Office Box 468
Phelan, CA 92371
(714) 249-6039

RAVEN'S HALLMARK CARDS
Robert and Arlene Raven
3568 Tyler Mall
Riverside, CA 92503
(714) 688-2454

RUANN'S GIFT SHOP
Ann Bellock
2681 Orange Olive Road
Orange, CA 92665
(714) 997-7626

RUMMEL'S VILLAGE GUILD
Helene Rummel
2413 S. Garfield Avenue
Monterey Park, CA 91754
(213) 722-2691

RYSTAD'S LIMITED EDITIONS
Dean Rystad
1013 Lincoln Avenue
San Jose, CA 95125
(408) 279]1960

SHOWCASE LIMITED EDITIONS
W.H. Stephens and G.B. Helsley
5232½ Laurel Canyon Blvd.
North Hollywood, CA 91607
(213) 761-9992

COLORADO

ELEPHANT GIFTS
Kingston and Cornelia Minister
1912 West Colorado Avenue
Colorado Springs, CO 80904
(303) 636-2828

THE KENT COLLECTION
Reda Walsh
6460 East Yale Avenue
Denver, CO 80222
(303) 753-9600

PLATES, ETC.
Carol Hastie
8050 Chase Drive
Arvada, CO 80004
(303) 426-7785

CONNECTICUT

NASSER'S, INC.
Maurice Nasser
New London Shopping Center
New London, CT 06320
(203) 443-6523

FLORIDA

BE DAZZLED BY B.J.'S
Betty Jean Bass
751 Knowles Road
Brandon, FL 33511
(813) 689-2251

BONOVENTURE LIMITED EDITIONS
Mr. and Mrs. O.A. Griffis
4657 South U.S. Highway #1
Cocoa, FL 32922
(305) 632-0128

COBBS COLLECTIBLES-GIFTS-ART GALLERIES
Evelyn Cobb Parrish
404 Beach Drive N.E.
St. Petersburg, FL 33701
(813) 822-8288

THE GALLERY
Lorene McDonough
Roosevelt Mall
Jacksonville, FL 32210
(904) 384-2929

GLOMAR, LTD.
Gloria and Marshall Burns
9530 April Road
Miami, FL 33157
(305) 238-3884

GRANDMA'S GALLERY INC.
Fred and Rae Wakelin
12957 Gulf Blvd. E.
Madeira Beach, FL 33708
(813) 393-2777

HEIRLOOMS OF TOMORROW
Pearl Finkelstein
7124 Collins Avenue
Miami Beach, FL 33141
(305) 864-2782

THE HAMILTON COLLECTION
Ron Gregory
9550 Regency Square Blvd.
Post Office Box 2567
Jacksonville, FL 32232
(904) 723-6000

LOFT CANDY AND GIFT SHOPPE
Irene S. Boltz
7815 Seminole Mall
Seminole, FL 33542
(813) 392-8082

MCNAMARA'S
David McNamara
3556 North Ocean Blvd.
Ft. Lauderdale, FL 33308
(305) 561-0200

MCNAMARA'S
David McNamara
2200 Glades Road
Boca Raton, FL 33431
(305) 395-2343

NORDIC IMPORTS OF FLORIDA
Mitch Topeka and B. Padgett
5211 Hollywood Blvd.
Hollywood, FL 33021
(305) 981-5211

PAULINE'S COLLECTIBLES
Pauline Graham and Ralph Dawson
2445 Aloma Avenue - Crealde Mall
Winter Park, FL 32792
(305) 671-2665

PIPER COLLECTIBLES
Janet Diepenhorst
1301 South Tamiami Tr.
Sarasota, FL 33579
(813) 366-2225

PLATE WORLD
Heather Dean and Rita Geller
400 South Orlando Avenue
Winter Park, FL 32789
(305) 628-0637

VERO LIMITED EDITION DEALER
A.H. Samuels
906 Spyglass Lane
Vero Beach, FL 32960
(305) 231-5247

VIKING IMPORT HOUSE, INC.
Pat Owen
412 S.E. Sixth Street
Ft. Lauderdale, FL 33301
(305) 763-3388

VILLAGE PLATE COLLECTOR
Lois Epstein Felder
217 King Street
Cocoa, FL 32922
(305) 636-6914

GEORGIA

PLATES 'N THINGS
Paul Wasmer
2013 Carolyn Terrace
Valdosta, GA 31601
(912) 244-0777

ILLINOIS

AISLE FIVE EDITIONS LIMITED
Richard and Donna Sitarski
8215 Golf Road
Niles, IL 60648
(312) 966-0974

THE BRADFORD EXCHANGE
Karen Laakko
9301 Milwaukee Avenue
Niles, IL 60648
(312) 966-2770

CAPRICE FINE ARTS
Majorie Claussner
610 West Lunt Avenue
Schaumburg, IL 60193
(312) 293-1500

DARE TO BE DIFFERENT
Arnold and Alice Jensen
Route 6, Box 367
Lockport, IL 60441
(815) 838-8642

DORIS COLLECTIBLES
Doris J. Wallin
Main Street
St. Peter, IL 62880
(618) 349-6115

HOLLYWOOD LIMITED EDITIONS
Chip Freudenberg
6990 North Central Park Avenue
Lincolnwood, IL 60645
(312) 673-3250

KIEFER'S GALLERIES LTD.
Ray and Kitty Kiefer
2364 Plainfield Road
Crest Hill, IL 60435
(312) 354-1888

L E COLLECTOR CONNECTION
Mrs. E.M. Mangini
Post Office Box 23
Glen Ellyn, IL 60137
(312) 469-6516

MCHUGH'S GIFTS AND COLLECTIBLES
Don and Shirley Humes
3822 Fourteenth Street
Rock Island, IL 61201
(309) 788-9525

A.G. OLKER COLLECTIBLES
Alan G. Olker
2004 Lexington Drive
Palatine, IL 60067
(312) 991-2187

PIQUET LIMITED EDITIONS
Richard and Pat Kopinski
1015 Lunt Avenue
Schaumburg, IL 60172
(312) 529-4760

RUTH'S HALLMARK SHOPS
Mr. Robert Knill
217 Lakeshore
Bloomingdale, IL 60108
(312) 980-9717

THE SHOWCASE OF WHEELING NURSERY
Al Solomon
642 South Milwaukee
Wheeling, IL 60090
(312) 537-1111

STRAWBERRY HOUSE
Arlene M. Young
Post Office Box 491
Mundelein, IL 60060
(312) 566-8149

THE TOWER SHOP LTD.
Dolores R. Earle
17 East Burlington
Riverside, IL 60546
(312) 447-5258

WIKS POTTERY, INC.
Stephen and Robin Wikstrom
572 Orlando Square Mall
Orlando Park, IL 60462
(312) 349-2234

INDIANA

BEE-HIVE GIFTS, INC.
Richard and Elsie Bolinger
358 West North Boo Road
Burns Harbor, IN 46304
(219) 787-8745

SOUTHLAKE HOUSE OF SCHILLER
Jeffery G. Hirsch
2168 Southlake Mall
Merrillville, IN 46410
(219) 769-4545

WALTER'S COLLECTIBLES
William M. Walter
1647-E East Main Street
Plainfield, IN 46168
(317) 839-2954

WATSON'S
Winnie Watson
135 East Michigan Street
New Carlisle, IN 46552
(219) 654-3550

IOWA

FAMILY TREE GIFTIBLES
Ronald and Joyce Ford
799 Town Clock Plaza
Dubuque, IA 52001
(319) 557-7826

HICKORY HOUSE
Karl Wiltz
819 North Court
Ottumwa, IA 52501
(515) 682-8391

KANSAS

NOLES
Evelyn and Jack Noles
Post Office Box 8176
Wichita, KS 67208
(316) 682-3530

WACONDA ENTERPRISES
JoAnne Kieffer
209 Kansas Avenue Box 158
Glen Elder, KS 67446
(913) 545-3437

MARYLAND

JO JO'S COLLECTIBLES
J. Chamandy
Box 672
Rockville, MD 20851
(301) 949-1585

MARG'S MANIA
Margaret Norfolk
6900 Nashville Road
Lanham/Seabrook, MD 20706
(301) 552-2425

MY GRANDFATHER'S SHOP, LTD.
Martin Urban
2415 Ennalls Avenue
Wheaton, MD 20902
(301) 949-8500

STUDIO HAVEN
Mary E. Walker
8301 Dangerfield Road
Clinton, MD 20735
(301) 372-8455

TOMORROW'S TREASURES
Shirley and George Kraus
2456 Conowingo Road
Bel Air, MD 21014
(301) 836-9075

MASSACHUSETTS

BERNICE'S HOUSE OF PLATES
Frank and Bernice Reitter
7 Bellwood Way
Framingham, MA 01701
(617) 877-1828

DAN/FRAN
Daniel L. Needleman
56 Clearwater Road
Chestnut Hill, MA 02167
(617) 327-2066

SAM'S GLASS WORKS
Mr. and Mrs. Jeffery Cohen
1067 E. Columbus Avenue
Springfield, MA 01105
(413) 733-9492

MICHIGAN

BARAN COLLECTIBLES
Frances Baran and Pat Norton
108 N. Lafayette
South Lyon, MI 48178
(313) 437-1361

CRYSTAL FAIR
Mary C. Mamut
725 Adams Road
Birmingham, MI 48011
(313) 642-3660

FOXY LADY GALLERY OF COLLECTIBLES INC.
Eleanor Jackson
331 Main Street
Rochester, MI 48063
(313) 651-6686

GENNA'S
John and Kathy Genna
29092 Van Dyke
Waren, MI 48093
Warren, MI 48093
(313) 573-4542

HALL OF CARDS AND BOOKS, INC.
Robert Sones
2232 South Eleventh Street
Niles, MI 49120
(616) 684-5115

MIDWEST COLLECTIBLES, INC.
Douglas N. McFadden, Jr.
3021 Seneca
Flint, MI 48504
(313) 767-4871

P J ENTERPRISES
Patricia M. Watson
325 Court Street
Port Huron, MI 48060
(313) 984-4920

WE SEARCH THE WORLD TO SATISY
E.W. Hunt
Box 387
Bay City, MI 48707
(517) 892-3973

MINNESOTA

ANDREWS LIMITED EDITIONS
Mark and Pat Andrews
Box 20743, Garfield Avenue S.
Minneapolis, MN 55420
(612) 888-8511

BLUE BIRD GIFT SHOP
Alexis Bighley
138 Rosedale Center
St. Paul, MN 55113
(612) 631-2559

CALHOUN'S COLLECTORS SOCIETY, INC.
Stafford Calvin
7275 Bush Lake Road
Edina, MN 55435
(612) 835-0300

ODYSSEY
Basil and Linda Janavaras
1675 Mankato Mall
Mankato, MN 56001
(507) 388-2004

SEEFELDT LIMITED EDITIONS
Charles Seefeldt
900 Portland Avenue
St. Paul Park, MN 55071
(612) 459-2740

NEBRASKA

AUDREY'S GIFT SHOP
Audrey M. Beebe
7834 Dodge
Omaha, NB 68114
(402) 391-3662

COLLECTOR'S GALLERIA
Katherine B. Evans
3703 South Street
Lincoln, NB 68506
(402) 483-5620

MARIANNE K. FESTERSEN
Plates-Antiques
701 North 72nd Avenue
Omaha, NB 68114
(402) 393-4454

NEVADA

THE COLLECTOR'S GALLERY
Leona Bravin
5025 South Eastern Avenue
Las Vegas, NV 89119
(702) 736-7353

RAPHAEL GALLERIES, LTD.
Ralph Plotkin
3200 Las Vegas Blvd. South
Las Vegas, NV 89109
(702) 732-9523

NEW JERSEY

COLLECTORS' CONNECTION
Cynthia Schmid
42 Arcadia Way
Hillsdale, NJ 07675
(201) 391-5069

DELUCA'S GALLERY OF COLLECTIBLES
JoAnn DeLuca
Park Avenue and Front Street
Scotch Plains, NJ 07076
(201) 322-7750

FLOWERS BY FORD, INC.
Carl Ford, Jr.
256 North Virginia Drive
Penns Grove, NJ 08069
(609) 299-0200

NEEDLEWORKS COLLECTIBLES
Hermine and Arthur Weston
1140 Ocean Avenue
Elberon, NJ 07740
(201) 222-0292

OLD WAGON GIFTS
Don and Liz Peseux
30 Route 34 N., Box 238
Colts Neck, NJ 07722
(201) 780-6656

ZASLOW'S FINE COLLECTIBLES
Marlene and Irv Zaslow
Strathmore Shopping Center
Matawan, NJ 07747
(201) 583-1499

NEW MEXICO

LORRIE'S COLLECTIBLES
Lorrie Church
3107 Eubank N.E., Suite 32
Albuquerque, NM 87111
(505) 292-0020

NEW YORK

ART BIN GALLERY AND GIFTSHOP
Judi Schumacher
3 Main Street
Kings Park, NY 11754
(516) 269-5097

GEORGE BARKEN DISTRIBUTORS, INC.
George Barken
90 McLoughlin Street
Glen Cove, NY 11542
(516) 671-7451

CAESAR'S COLLECTIBLES LTD.
Victor and Jeanne Gerloven
1815 Broad Hollow Road
East Farmingdale, NY 11735
(516) 249-9669

CECILIA'S COLLECTIBLES
Cecilia G. Farrell
Post Office Box 342
Maspeth, NY 11378
(212) 457-4653

CERAMICA GIFT GALLERY, INC.
Shlomo Tsadko
1009 Sixth Avenue
New York, NY 10018
(212) 354-9216

THE COLLECTOR'S GALLERY
Florence Horowitz
26 Route 59
Suffern, NY 10901
(914) 357-4700

COLLECTOR'S PARADISE, INC.
Louis Mattola
3455 Merrick Road
Wantagh, NY 11793
(516) 783-8475

EAGLE QUALITY PRODUCTS, INC.
Illona and Steve Bloom
Box 54
Staten Island, NY 10312
(212) 948-1681

ELLIE'S ANTIQUES AND COLLECTIBLES
Eleanor Bilsky
35 Betty Ann Drive
South Setauket, NY 11720
(516) 981-9897

FRIVOLITE'
Sally Lee
520 Eighth Avenue N9
New York, NY 10018
(212) 736-4422

ISLAND TREASURES
Charles and Elizabeth Caggiano
2845 Richmond Avenue
Staten Island, NY 10314
(212) 698-1234

JOY'S LAMPLIGHT SHOPPE
Don Parker
5480 East Avon Road
Avon, NY 14414
(716) 226-3453

OREGON

ACCENT INTERIORS AND COLLECTIBLES
Rosalie Brown
12403 N.E. Glisan Street
Portland, OR 97230
(503) 253-0841

NORTHLAND GIFTS
Virginia Lowry
230 Valley River Center
Eugene, OR 97401
(503) 343-3514

WHITE'S COLLECTABLES
Garry White
104 South College Street
Newberg, OR 97132
(503) 538-7421

PENNSYLVANIA

DESIGN GALLERIES
Paul Stark
Wyoming Valley Mall
Wilkes Barre, PA 18702
(717) 822-6704

GILLESPIE JEWELERS
Inez Gillespie
1774 Main Street
North Hampton, PA 18067
(215) 262-2215

NAOMI'S-SOME PLATE SPECIAL
Naomi Patton
2605 Lutz Lane
Bethel Park, PA 15102
(412) 831-0500

OUR HOUSE
Lotta Veasey
1707-C Wilmington Road
New Castle, PA 16105
(412) 652-5848

SAVILLE'S LIMITED EDITIONS
Mayne Saville
4801 McKnight Road
Pittsburgh, PA 15237
(412) 366-5458

THE SIDE DOOR
Winfred Slack
366 South Washington Road
McMurray, PA 15317
(412) 941-3750

TENNESSEE

COLLECTOR'S SHOWCASE
Bob and Edna Johnson
Box 972
Paris, TN 38242
(901) 642-4995

TEXAS

COLLECTIBLES, LTD. (BY BETTY LEE'S)
Betty Farris
2204 Riverside
Harlingen, TX 78550
(512) 423-8234

COLLECTORS GALLERY
JoLynn Powell
7115 Blanco, Suite 105
San Antonio, TX 78216
(512) 341-7222

ELOISE'S COLLECTIBLES, INC.
Al and Eloise Parks
9140 Bellaire Blvd.
Houston, TX 77036
(713) 771-9329

IMM BE KAY'S
Marguerite McKune
8923 Altamont Drive
Houston, TX 77074
(713) 774-9148

K COINS AND COLLECTIBLES
Laverne Krugjohann
106 Main Street
Forney, TX 75126
(214) 552-1150

LADY BUG SHOPPE
Cathy and John Sweeney
785 Deer Park Avenue
N. Babylon, NY 11704
(516) 422-2977

THE LIMITED EDITION
Ruth Wolf
2170 Sunrise Highway
Merrick, NY 11566
(516) 623-4400

PAUL'S ECONOMY PHARMACY
Rhoda Turkowitz
169 Richmond Avenue
Staten Island, NY 10302
(212) 442-2924

THE PLATE COTTAGE
Frank and Margaret Welskopf
532 North Country Road
St. James, NY 11780
(516) 979-0847

TODAY'S PLEASURE TOMORROWS TREASURE
Mildred Long
New Turnpike
Cochecton, NY 12726
(914) 932-8308

TOMORROW'S CHERISHED TREASURES
Ann Castellano
53 Merrivale Drive
Hauppauge, NY 11787
(516) 368-8184

NORTH DAKOTA

BERGSTRAND'S GIFT SHOP
John L. Bergstrand
200 North Central Avenue
Valley City, ND 58072
(701) 845-4252

PRAIRE HILL PLATES
Wayne and Judith Heringer
Highway 83
Washburn, ND 58577
(701) 462-8344

OKLAHOMA

ALMA'S ANTIQUES AND COLLECTABLES
Alma L. Powell
311 South Klein No. 50
Oklahoma City, OK 73108
(405) 235-5110

ANN'S ANTIQUES
George and Wanda Godfrey
7312 East 59th Place
Tulsa, OK 74145
(918) 250-8764

SUZANNE'S COLLECTORS GALLERY
Suzanne Stoll
100 North Main Street
Miami, OK 74354
(918) 542-3808

OHIO

CAREN'S, LTD.
Karen Belich
2409 Cleveland-Massillon
Bath, OH 44210
(216) 666-7447

COLLECTOR'S PLATE GALLERY
Dolores Oblinger
422 Louisiana Avenue
Perrysburg, OH 43551
(419) 874-6537

RINGER IMPORT ENTERPRISES
John Ringer
606 Nakota Drive
Fairborn, OH 45324
(513) 878-6196

SUNSHINE HOUSE
Joan and Hirschel Parrish
914 18th Street
Plano, TX 75074
(214) 424-5015

UTAH

COLLECTORS WHOLESALE SUPPLY, INC.
Alan E. Mann
4636 South Highland Drive
Salt Lake City, UT 84117
(801) 272-9213

VIRGINIA

LIMITED EDITIONS OF SPRINGFIELD
Patricia Verzolini
6330 Springfield Plaza II
Springfield, VA 22150
(703) 569-8623

THE TINDER BOX
Dwight E. Chadbourn
244 New Market North
Hampton, VA 23605
(313) 827-0372

WASHINGTON

THE CHALET COLLECTORS GALLERY
Howard and Christine Hemmerling
7024 - 27th Street West
Tacoma, WA 98466
(206) 564-0326

THE GIFT HAUS, INC.
Loraine Gibson
601 West Wishkah Street
Aberdeen, WA 98520
(206) 532-8261

GRANDMOTHER'S CORNER GALLERY
Dana Swain
9685 Firdale Avenue
Edmonds, WA 98020
(206) 789-0747

WASHINGTON D.C.

THE COLUMBIA MINT, INC.
W.F. Krieg
905 Sixteenth Street N.W.
Washington, DC 20006
(202) 269-0259

WEST VIRGINIA

ARACOMA DRUG CO. GIFT GALLERIES
George Kostas
305 Stratton Street Box 507
Logan, WV 25601
(304) 752-3811

WISCONSIN

BOOK AND GIFT SHOP
Norbert and Violet Kustka
831 South Eighth Street
Manitowoc, WI 54220
(414) 684-4300

CELLAR ANTIQUES
Robert Sadoff
1611 Keith Street
Baraboo, WI 53913
(608) 356-5118

CENTURY COIN SERVICE
Earl G. Leach
2473 Sun Valley Court
Green Bay, WI 54304
(414) 494-2719

COLLECTIBLES ETC., INC.
Paul and Sandy Forgach
8326 North 49th Street
Brown Deer, WI 53223
(800) 558-5594

A COUNTRY MOUSE
Dorothy Smith
7940 West Layton Avenue
Milwaukee, WI 53220
(414) 281-4210

DOWNS' COLLECTORS SHOWCASE
William McKay
2778 South 35th Street
Milwaukee, WI 53215
(414) 643-7300

FAIRVIEW COLLECTIBLES
August Schuth
Fairview Mall 2100 E. Milwaukee
Janesville, MI 53545
(608) 755-1751

JACQUELINE'S OF SUSSEX
Marjorie Prag
W238 N6223 Park Court
Sussex, WI 53089
(414) 246-8436

RED CROSS PHARMACY, INC.
Kris Busch
146 Walnut
Spooner, WI 54801
(71 5) 635-2117

SUZANNE'S HALLMARK SHOP
Sue and James Beam
757 Main Street
Lake Geneva, WI 53147
(414) 248-9510

CANADA

ARCHIBALD GALLERIES LTD.
Sam Agronin
10154 - 103 Street
Edmonton, Alberta T5JOX7
(403) 422-5717

MAKKIR'S LIMITED EDITION
William R. Dabbs
Bay 10, 3200 14th Avenue N.E.
Calgary, Albcan T2A5K8
(403) 235-5060

About the marketers and manufacturers of limited edition collectibles

There are several hundred firms actively involved in today's world of limited edition collectibles, with bases of operation in the United States and in many other countries. Here you'll find some basic background information about some of the more prominent firms in the field. With each there is an address, and in many cases a contact person, which you may use to inquire about a firm's products and services. There is also a listing of the types of limited edition products each firm makes or markets.

AMERICAN ARTISTS/GRAPHICS BUYING SERVICE
c/o Peter Canzone
225 W. Hubbard Street, Fourth Floor
Chicago, Illinois 60610

PLATES, GRAPHICS

Graphics Buying Service (GBS) originated three years ago as a firm devoted to the commissioning and marketing of limited edition graphic art. The company was the first of its kind—offering quality, limited edition prints by top plate artists, at affordable prices.

GBS artists have included James Auckland, Irene Spencer, Frank Russell and Gertrude Barrer, Donald Zolan, Richard Zolan, Fred Stone, Dave Chapple and Mary Vickers. Each original edition is made into 150 to 500 prints, and each is signed and sequentially numbered by the artist. These editions are very limited—especially compared to the plate market—and thus they have made for some impressive secondary market gains in a short time period.

In 1981, GBS began a new division called American Artists, dedicated to the creation of the finest in limited edition collector plates by United States art masters. In cooperation with Modern Masters of Frankfort, Illinois, American Artists introduced a series of plates called *The Horses of Fred Stone,* with a first issue titled "Patience." Since then American Artists has offered two series by Richard Zolan in association with Modern Masters as well.

Today, American Artists/GBS continues in both the graphics field and the realm of limited edition plates. The firm recently introduced a plate titled "The Black Stallion," first of a collection of four by Fred Stone. Other current offerings include a series of cat plates by Phyllis Hollands-Robinson, and works by Donald Zolan.

"Kitty Love" by Phyllis Hollands-Robinson for American Artists, division of Graphics Buying Service.

ANNA-PERENNA PORCELAIN, INC.
c/o Ann Peters
32 Relyea Place
New Rochelle, NY 10801

PLATES, FIGURINES, GRAPHICS

Anna-Perenna Porcelain, Inc. is one of the few international firms specializing in fine art on limited edition collector plates only. Offerings of this firm are made of the finest hard-paste porcelain, created in a tradition dating back many generations.

The firm was founded on 7-7-77 by Klaus D. Vogt, former president of Rosenthal, U.S.A. Vogt was fascinated by the possibilities of fine art on fine porcelain, and left Rosenthal to pursue this new art medium with his own firm.

The name Anna-Perenna came from the Roman goddess of spring. From her name the English words for "annual" and "perennial" were derived. This international firm required a name which could be pronounced easily in English, German or French, and Anna-Perenna filled the bill. Even more appropriately, this goddess was also the protectorate of the arts.

Anna-Perenna Porcelain has commissioned some of the world's most celebrated and unique artists to create original artwork for collector plates. Each Anna-Perenna artist must submit paintings "in the round," and as near to the actual size of the plate as possible, as

"Jingle Bells" by Thaddeus Krumeich for Anna-Perenna.

Vogt stresses that this is the only way to achieve fidelity in the creation of multi-colored art transfers.

Anna-Perenna artists include: Thaddeus "Uncle Tad" Krumeich, creator of numerous charming cat-subject plates; Frank Russell and Gertrude Barrer, who introduced the triptych concept to the plate world; actress-turned-artist Elke Sommer; Mary Ellen Wehrli, artist for whimsical studies of bunnies; Margaret Kane, creator of the unique "Masquerade Fantasy" plates; Pat Buckley Moss, artist for "American Silhouettes," Canadian-Indian master artist Norval Morrisseau, cartoonist-turned-plate-artist Al Hirschfeld, and Nori Peters, a Canadian artist who paints Eskimos.

The 1982 ***Kalevala*** *series plate from Arabia of Finland.*

ANRI
c/o Helmar Narath
55 Pacella Park Drive
Randolph, Massachusetts 02368

PLATES, FIGURINES, BELLS

Anri is a firm which prides itself on its superb wood carvings, including several series of limited edition plates, and a wide range of hand-painted figurines.

This family firm was founded in 1916 by Anton Riffeser Sr. The operation is located in the Tyrolean Alps, where wood carving is a renowned art.

Many of Anri's products are created by means of a process called toriart. A wood material is used for molding, and then it is carved to establish the exceptional detail for which Anri is renowned. Hand-painting completes the effect.

ARABIA OF FINLAND
c/o Tankmar Horn
5603 Howard Street
Niles, Illinois 60648

PLATES

Arabia traces its lineage back to the Swedish firm of Rorstrand, the second oldest porcelain maker in Europe. Only Meissen is older. Rorstrand constructed its Finnish plant in 1873 on a meadow called Arabia on the outskirts of Helsinki. By the next year, Arabia was molding and producing pottery.

In 1976, Arabia fired the first of its annual plate series which featured central scenes from the Finnish national epic, the Kalevala. Following the story line of the Kalevala, each annual plate depicts a scene from the epic.

The fragments of the ancient epic were compiled by Elias Lonnrot in 1835 and the day of the Kalevala's initial publication, February 28, is celebrated as a Finnish national holiday.

Raija Uosikkinen, one of Finland's foremost artist-designers, presents the scenes with an economy of line and detail typical of Scandinavian folk art. The motif for the annual plate appears in the verse printed on the back of the plate.

ARTISTS OF THE WORLD
c/o James LaFond
2915 N. 67th Place
Scottsdale, Arizona 85251

PLATES

Artists of the World initially was organized as DeGrazia of Scottsdale. Founded by James LaFond, the company's primary purpose was to represent the works of artist Ted DeGrazia.

In 1977, the name was changed to Artists of the World, and the company enlarged to include a number of other artists. DeGrazia continued to make a major contribution with his *Holiday* and *Children* series.

The artistry of Don Ruffin in both the *Don Ruffin* and the *Children of Don Ruffin* series is a major achievement. In the *Children of Aberdeen* series, Kee Fung Ng depicts the children who live on boats anchored near Hong Kong.

Larry Toschik's *Prowlers of the Sky* series as well as works by Vel Miller and Anthony Sidoni are among the newest offerings of Artists of the World.

Artists of the World plates have been manufactured by both Fairmont and Pickard China Companies.

Ted DeGrazia's 1982 "Blue Boy" for Artists of the World.

B & J ART DESIGNS
c/o Bill and Jan Hagara
3910 Sequoia Trails West
Georgetown, Texas 78626

PLATES, GRAPHICS, DOLLS

B & J Art Designs was established in 1975 to produce and market reproductions of Jan Hagara's work. It is an independent, family business owned solely by Bill and Jan Hagara.

Their business began in Tempe, Arizona. At first they produced only cards and fine art prints which featured children with an "old-fashioned look" that became Jan's trademark.

In 1978 the first series of porcelain plates was introduced. It featured a series of *Yesterday's Children.* "Lisa and the Jumeau Doll" was the first in the series of four. Jan's work was featured in the *American Has Heart* and *Old-Fashioned Mother's Day* series for The Carson Mint. However, in the fall of 1983, B & J Art Designs issued two new series featuring Jan's work, a *Christmas* and a *Country* series.

B & J Art Designs is now located outside Georgetown, Texas. The firm manufactures and distributes Jan's work through both a wholesale and a retail operation. Bill and Jan Hagara take pride in supervising every step of the production.

BAREUTHER
c/o Walter Rautenberg
20101 West Eight Mile Road
Detroit, Michigan 48219

PLATES, BELLS

The Bareuther & Company porcelain factory of Germany began producing giftware, vases and dinnerware in 1867. Established by Johann Matthaeus Reis, the shop contained a porcelain kiln and an annular brick kiln.

The business later was sold to Oskar Bareuther, who continued to produce quality tableware.

To celebrate the 100th anniversary of Bareuther, the company began to issue limited edition Christmas plates, which are Cobalt blue. Their Father's Day series, which features many of the great German castles, was initiated in 1969. The firm now also issues Mother's Day and Thanksgiving plate series.

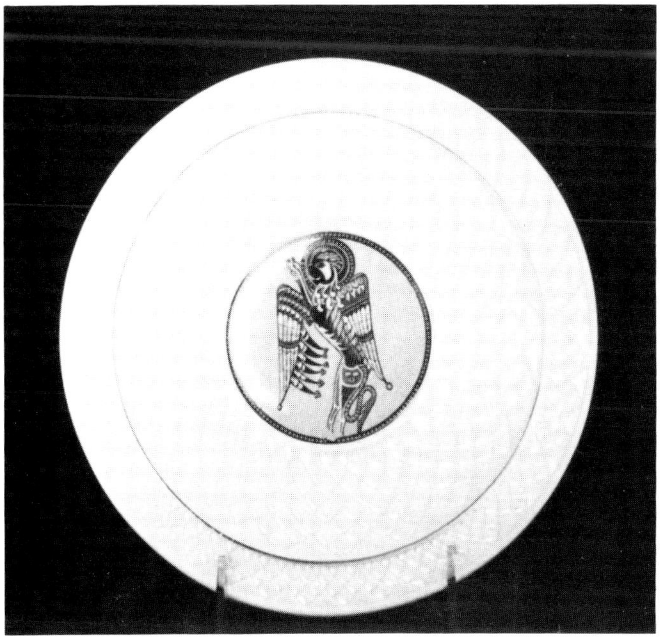

The "St. Luke" plate from Belleek.

BELLEEK IRELAND
15 E. 26th Street
New York, New York 10010

PLATES

In the wake of Ireland's "Great Famine" in 1849, John Caldwell Bloomfield inherited the estate which contained the village of Belleek. Concerned about the welfare of his tenants, he sought some means of finding them employment.

Bloomfield was interested in ceramics, and he was attracted to the brilliant whitewash of his workers' cottages. Further investigation revealed all the natural materials needed to produce china. Bloomfield sought capital from David McBirney and the artistic skills of an architect, Robert W. Armstrong. The firm of D. McBirney and Co. began production in 1857.

Armstrong was instrumental in bringing craftsmen from England, and he helped design many of the first pieces. The first metallic glazes were developed by Armstrong. However, the secret of the mother-of-pearl luster, for which Belleek is famous, was purchased by Armstrong from the French inventor, J.J.H. Brianchon.

In 1865, the unique iridescent quality of Belleek won its first Gold Medal in the Dublin International Exposition. Queen Victoria and her son, the Prince of

Wales, were among the first and most prestigious customers.

After the death of McBirney and Armstrong, a new company called Belleek was formed in 1884. Belleek Pottery Ltd. has produced a Christmas series of plates, a second Christmas collection inspired by Irish wildlife, an Apostle series and a Bicentennial plate for the United States celebration in 1976.

Bing & Grondahl's 1969 Mother's Day "Dog and Puppies"—the first-ever Mother's Day limited edition collector plate.

BING & GRONDAHL
111 N. Lawn Avenue
Elmsford, New York 10123

PLATES, FIGURINES, BELLS, DOLLS

This Danish firm is known as the "founder of plate collecting" for its 1895 Christmas plate, "Behind the Frozen Window." This first issue began a tradition which continues today with a new, annual, blue-and-white plate to mark each holiday season. Bing & Grondahl also offered the world's first porcelain Mother's Day plate, "Dog and Puppies," in 1969.

Bing & Grondahl was founded in 1853 by Frederick Vilhelm Grondahl and M.H. and J.H. Bing. The artist and sculptor was Grondahl, while the Bings provided business expertise. The firm's quality is internationally known, and Bing & Grondahl items are a part of the collections of many museums worldwide. The firm has won appointment to the courts of Denmark, Sweden and Great Britain.

In addition to collector plates and tableware, Bing & Grondahl makes a wide variety of figurines and other porcelain articles. In 1982 the firm introduced its first collectible doll, "Mary," which was inspired by a favorite Bing & Grondahl figurine by the same name.

THE BOEHM STUDIOS
c/o Larry Parks
25 Fairfacts
Trenton, New Jersey 08638

PLATES. FIGURINES

From its inception in 1950 The Boehm Studio has specialized in the art of birds, flowers and animals; and Boehm masterworks portraying these have been among the most treasured, highly valued and sought-after works of porcelain art in the world. Edward Marshall Boehm, who died in 1969, and Helen, his wife and studio partner, started a basement studio in Trenton, New Jersey, ceramic center of the United States since the middle of the last century. The studio was relocated in 1955 to its present location.

When the Boehms opened their studio, Edward Boehm, the naturalist-farmer, had only an innate talent as a sculptor and craftsman which was joined with an intense desire to excel in any endeavor he attempted. Helen Boehm was the perfect complement, a dynamic, energetic, brillian tactician whose inexperience often proved to be an asset; for she forged courageous new promotional and marketing concepts.

"The Peace Rose" from The Boehm Studios represents a recent innovation of this famed porcelain house: the delicate petals of the rose are porcelain, and the stems and leaves are crafted of bronze. A detailed description of this process may be found in the feature section of this book.

When Edward Boehm passed away it was assumed by many that the studio would not continue. What they did not know were the enormous skills of the art team Mr. Boehm had assembled and trained. One of his unique talents was an uncommon practice of sharing his knowledge and expertise with respected artists and craftsmen who joined him. Perhaps his greatest legacy was his unselfish desire to perpetuate what he had begun.

Leading the team now was his most dedicated student, Helen Boehm. Through the prior two decades of working together they had shared each new art concept. Helen had brought back ideas and needs from the vast market before them. Edward utilized the information when formulating and executing his designs. It was natural in 1969 for Helen Boehm to assume the design responsibility as well—not directly creating the porcelains, but energizing, motivating and orchestrating the "new" designs of the team her late husband had formed.

Today, Boehm porcelains are in more than 100 museums and institutions throughout the world, including the White House, the Metropolitan Museum of Art, the Smithsonian Institution, Buckingham Palace and the Vatican.

Traditionally Boehm artworks were marketed in selected art galleries, fine jewelers and noted retailers. 1970 saw the first entry of Boehm into the direct mail market in an association with the Lenox China Company, also headquartered in Trenton. Series of animal and bird plates were introduced and marketed broadly. In recent years Boehm has increased its direct mail activity. It associated itself with The Hamilton Collection of Jacksonville, Florida, for the marketing of fine plates, bisque sculpture, and recently introduced a unique combination of porcelain and bronze. Current activities also include programs with American Express, the Audubon Society and Boehm's own direct mail projects.

Male and female "Penguins" from Burgues Porcelain.

BURGUES PORCELAIN STUDIO
183 Spruce Street
Lakewood, New Jersey 08701

PLATES, FIGURINES

The Burgues Porcelain Studio was established in 1964. Dr. Irving Carl Burgues and his wife, Carol Werner Burgues, are the principal artists for this firm, which produces porcelain sculptures and hand-painted designer vases.

The Burgues' work was distributed by Spode for four years before Burgues became an independent marketer 12 years ago.

Works from the artists have been used extensively by United States Presidents and the State Department for Gifts of State to foreign dignitaries and European governments.

Irving Carl Burgues' sculptures are on display in museums including The Smithsonian Institution, and he has been commissioned to sculpt both public and private works. Burgues porcelains are on display throughout the country at prestigious jewelers and porcelain galleries.

In 1978 and 1979, both Burgues artists created limited edition collector plates which were offered through Anna-Perenna.

CALHOUN'S COLLECTORS SOCIETY
c/o Stafford Calvin
Calhoun Center
Minneapolis, Minnesota 55435

PLATES, FIGURINES, BELLS, GRAPHICS

Calhoun's is a family business which originated in 1928 under the leadership of Carl Calvin. His son, Stafford Calvin, today is the president of Calhoun's—one of the largest and most diverse marketers of limited edition collectibles in the United States.

Calhoun's seeks out sources all over the world for its collector plates, figurines and other limited edition items. The firm is a direct marketer, but it also sells through dealer channels by means of its distributor, Hummelwerk.

The firm is strictly a marketer of limited edition items—not a manufacturer. Plates are offered under the name of Royal Cornwall, and recent series include *Two Thousand Years of Sailing Ships* by artist Alan D'Estrehan, and *America's Golden Years* by Robert Pettes.

Calhoun's other offerings include thimbles and collectors' stamps, as well as a number of Oriental items and figurines inspired by the sculptures of Gunther Granget.

THE CARMEL COLLECTION
c/o Tom J. O'Meara
One Pebble Beach Plaza, P.O. Box 1030
Pebble Beach, California 93954

PLATES, FIGURINES

The Carmel Collection is a division of Pebble Beach Enterprises, a firm which Tom J. O'Meara began in November, 1982. Pebble Beach Enterprises includes: The Limited Edition Group, a distributor of limited edition items; The Carmel Collection, a marketer of limited edition plates and figurines; and a giftware marketing division.

The founder of the company, Tom O'Meara, is the veteran of nearly a decade in the field of limited editions and tableware. His new firm already has four different limited edition series underway, with several more on the drawing board.

Among these are: the "Macy's Thanksgiving Day Parade" plate by Melanie Taylor Kent, first issue in the *Famous Parades* series; the "Darling Diana" plate by Elizabeth Maxwell, premiere of the *First Performances* collection; the "Christmas Delight" plate by Jerome Walczak, first in an annual holiday series called *The Joys of Christmas,* and "Corky's Dream" plate, first of an annual series of plates to be created under the sponsorship of the Fund for Animals. All of these plates will be issued on fine Briggsmore china for The Carmel Collection.

THE CARSON MINT
c/o Sherry Marks
5525 Lamona Avenue
Fresno, California 93727

PLATES

In 1978, Leland McCarthy founded The Carson Mint at Carson City, Nevada. Administrative offices are in Fresno, California. McCarthy, a noted lover of the arts, is known for having opened his home to art shows honoring several artists in past years. He saw The Carson Mint as an opportunity to "showcase" some of America's promising artists by offering their works in the form of limited edition collectibles.

The Carson Mint's artists today include Jan Hagara, Don Price, and Susan Anderson. Jan Hagara has completed a series for the firm called *Old-Fashioned Mother's Day.* She also is the artist for an *America Has Heart* collection which benefitted the American Heart Association. Don Price is the artist for "Candice," first issue in The Carson Mint's *Nature's Children* collection. And Susan Anderson recently introduced "Teddy Bear Picnic," first in a collection of plates inspired by the fantasy antics of teddy bears.

CREATIVE WORLD
c/o Dick Gabbe
39 Westmoreland Avenue
White Plains, New York 10606

PLATES, FIGURINES, BELLS, STEINS

A ceramic liquor bottle in the shape of the car that won the 1911 Indianapolis Speedway Race was Dick Gabbe's introduction to the world of collectibles. Now president of Creative World, Gabbe was so pleased with the replica cars that he began selling them to collectors. It was also the premiere of his "Famous First" series.

A friend, Lee Benson, persuaded Gabbe that collectible plates would be the thing of the future. They formed Creative World and produced their first series, *The Antique Trader,* which featured Currier & Ives prints.

While in Italy, Benson came across a process, the "Veneto Flair technique," which was used to produce the firm's very successful "Madonna" plate, released in 1971. It was followed by a number of hand-made, hand-decorated Veneto Flair collections, including those for Christmas, Children's Christmas, Mother and Child Animals, and Valentine's Day. The original artist for Veneto Flair, Vincente Tiziano, retired in 1982. Franco Lamincia is the new artist.

In the realm of transfer-decorated porcelain plates, Creative World is known for its *Benji, The Prize,* and *Living Doll* series.

The cold-cast bronze formula was used by Creative World to produce an *Aesop's Fable* series of plates. This method combines bronze powder and acrylic, and it was also used in the wildlife series, *The Bronze Menagerie,* which is now distributed by Royal Doulton.

Creative World also produces a number of miniature plates with Norman Rockwell's "Looking Out to Sea" as one of the most popular. In addition to plates, Creative World offers steins, bells, cups and saucer sets, and Christmas ornaments.

CYBIS STUDIO
c/o Joseph W. Chorlton
65 Norman Avenue
Trenton, New Jersey 08618

FIGURINES

Cybis is America's oldest existing art porcelain studio. It was founded by Boleslaw Cybis, a professor at the Academy of Fine Art in Warsaw, Poland, and an internationally renowned artist.

Boleslaw Cybis and his wife, Marja, came to the United States in 1939 to paint murals commissioned by his government in the Hall of Honor at the New York World's Fair. Unable to return to their homeland after the outbreak of World War II, they chose to remain in this country, founding an artists' studio to create porcelain sculpture in the tradition of the ancient European studios.

The original Cybis Studio was in New York. It later was moved to Trenton, New Jersey, where it continues to flourish today. The Cybis artists create sculptures portraying a variety of themes ranging from the world of nature, to elegant historical figurines, to the realm of fantasy.

Cybis sculptures are in major collections throughout the world, including The Vatican, Buckingham Palace, the Moscow Museum and The Smithsonian Institution. During Queen Elizabeth's recent visit to the United States, she was presented with the "Mother Bear with Three Cubs," a Cybis porcelain.

Joseph W. Chorlton, current president of Cybis, is determined to carry on the firm's tradition for fine quality porcelains.

DESIGNERS COLLECTION OF AMERICAN GREETINGS
c/o Mary Lee Bowen
10500 American Road
Cleveland, Ohio 44144

PLATES, FIGURINES, BELLS

The exclusive house of Holly Hobbie® fine porcelains, DESIGNERS COLLECTION introduced its popular line of collectibles and quality giftware in 1973. Emphasizing creative leadership and fine craftsmanship, the company is known for its exclusive character looks combined with me-to-you sentiments that turn gifts into treasured keepsakes.

Indeed, the DESIGNERS COLLECTION line is gifted with character. In addition to Holly Hobbie, the company is the giftware source for such established consumer favorites as Ziggy™ and Strawberry Shortcake™ and such rising stars as Sherman On The Mount™. New to the line in 1983 were Care Bears™ and Cathy™, both growing rapidly in popularity.

DESIGNERS COLLECTION has developed an extensive line of collector figurines, plates, and bells, many in continuing series to enhance their collectibility. All of its limited editions are specified by number rather than firing period and feature a full complement of such accessories as registration cards, gift tags or presentation cards, and—more recently—certificates of authenticity.

In addition, the company markets a complete line of distinctive seasonal and everyday giftware, including decorative accessories, novelty gifts, and musicals.

DESIGNERS COLLECTION is a division of American Greetings, the world's largest publicly-owned manufacturer of greeting cards and related personal communications merchandise.

Holly Hobbie® , Strawberry Shortcake, and Care Bears are trademarks of American Greetings Corporation and its subsidiaries. Ziggy and Cathy are trademarks of Universal Press Syndicate. Sherman on the Mount is a trademark of Sharman, A Partnership.

D'ARCEAU-LIMOGES
c/o The Bradford Exchange
9333 Milwaukee Avenue
Niles, Illinois 60048

PLATES

The name of Henri D'Arceau Limoges et Fils is one of the most respected in Limoges, the famous French porcelain center. The firm adheres to the original "Grellet Standard" of 1768 for hand-craftsmanship.

D'Arceau-Limoges was commissioned by L'Association L'Esprit de Lafayette to produce a series of plates honoring the Marquis de Lafayette, in celebration of America's Bicentennial. *Le Patrimoine de Lafayette* was introduced in 1973. In English, the series name is *The Lafayette Legacy.*

This firm's Christmas series, *Noel Vitrail,* was inspired by the stained glass windows at Chartres. *Les Femmes du Siecle* (Women of the Century) is also sometimes referred to as "Ganeau's Women." This series, which had the recognition of the United Nations, depicted women's fashions over the past century.

Les Jeunes Filles des Saison (Girls of the Season) and *Les Tres Riches Heures* (The Book of Hours) — adapted from a 15th century illuminated manuscript — were both important plate series offerings from the firm. In 1980, the French Impressionist artist, Louis Dali, was responsible for *La Ville de Paris* (City of Paris) series.

Gerald Boyer, a descendant of the founder, is director of D'Arceau Limoges today. The firm's artists include the late Andre Restieau, Guy Cambier, Francois Ganeau, and Louis Dali.

"The Hunter's Reward" by Nori Peter for Ebeling & Reuss.

EBELING & REUSS
1041 West Valley Road
Devon, Pennsylvania 19333

PLATES, FIGURINES, BELLS

Ebeling & Reuss was founded in Philadelphia in 1886 when J.E. Zeh, Frederick Ebeling, and Theodore Reuss shook hands over a cup of coffee. Zeh soon retired and by 1932, the Ebeling interests were sole owners of the business.

When World War II eliminated the sources of supply and the public demand for German china, this firm began to obtain merchandise from Portugal, Mexico and Brazil. These lines were augmented with products from California factories.

In 1981, Ebeling & Reuss became a part of the Alco Standard Corporation.

Ebeling & Reuss has maintained its long-standing connections with the important European china and glass manufacturers. Much of the company's merchandise is produced by these firms, according to Ebeling & Reuss' specifications, and in many cases, their designs.

Currently, Ebeling & Reuss issues the *Little Men, People of the Midnight Sun, Little Clowns, Yesterday's World,* and the *Joan Walsh Anglund Christmas* collections.

Effanbee's "Groucho Marx" doll.

EFFANBEE DOLL COMPANY
200 Fifth Avenue
New York, New York 10010

DOLLS

Effanbee is one of the oldest and most respected American doll makers. The company was organized in 1910 and known as Fleischker and Baum, jobber and retailer of toys. In 1913 they formed Effanbee and began producing rag dolls and dolls of a crude, hard composition.

When the First World War cut off the supply of dolls from Europe, Effanbee accelerated production to fill the need.

Their first major success was "Patsy," introduced in 1924 and long regarded as a classic. It was followed in 1934 by the "DyDee" doll—the first doll to drink and wet. Today Effanbee continues to produce a full line of quality dolls.

In 1975, recognizing the need for collectibles dolls, Effanbee began to develop the first collectible series. These include the *Wonderful World of Effanbee* (11" collectors' series), the *Grande Dames, Send in the Clowns,* and *Craftsman's Corner* collections.

In 1980, the firm introduced the *Legend* series with a W.C. Field character doll. It was followed by character dolls of John Wayne, Mae West, and Groucho Marx. In addition to the *Legend* series, Effanbee also produces the *Presidents* and *Great Moments in Literature* collections.

Effanbee also sponsors a Limited Edition Doll Club, with special, limited edition issues for members only.

THE FRANKLIN MINT
Franklin Center, Pennsylvania 19091

PLATES, FIGURINES, BELLS, GRAPHICS, DOLLS

The Franklin Mint develops, produces and markets a broad range of collectible, luxury, jewelry, home decor and leisure products. Franklin is a world leader in Direct Response Marketing, selling primarily through direct mail and the print media.

Principal products include decorative porcelain plates and figurines; medals, coins and ingots; stamps and related philatelic products; collector records; jewelry; fine books; sculpture; decorative wall products; objets d'art; collector furniture; and items of home decor.

THE GHENT COLLECTION
Riverparke Building
Suite No. 103
1653 Merriman Road
Akron, Ohio 44313

PLATES, FIGURINES, GRAPHICS

The Ghent Collection, the limited edition collectibles division of NUMA, Ltd., has offered a variety of fine artwork to collectors over the past nine years. The direct mail firm began with a line of heraldic products displaying family crests, and has gone on to offer custom greeting cards, sculptures, medallics, limited edition lithographs and serigraphs, as well as an exclusive line of collector plates.

Master artists including Harry Moeller, Guy Tudor, Edward Bierly, Jay Matternes, Charles Frace, Dean Fausett and Alton Tobey have worked for Ghent Collection. This firm has produced pieces of historical interest such as the *Treasures of Tutankhamun* plate series, and the *American Bicentennial Wildlife Collection.*

A pioneer in new techniques in porcelain, Ghent works with manufacturers including Kaiser, Fairmont, Viletta, Lenox, Gorham, Woodmere, Caverswall, and Porcelaine Etienne.

Other notable issues include the Ghent Christmas and Mother's Day series, a collection called *From Sea to Shining Sea,* the official 1980 Olympic Summer Games plate, and Norman Rockwell's *April Fools Day* plates. Ghent's most recent contributions have been the *American Classics* series, *Lands of Fable, Hans Brinker Delft* plate collection, *Man's Dream of Flight,* and the annual *Memory* plates.

The president of Ghent Collection is Dennis B. Haslinger, and the vice president of operations is Garrett W. Curtis.

The Goebel Collectors' Society figurine, "Spring Dance".

GOEBEL COLLECTORS' CLUB®
Division of Goebel Art (GmbH) Inc.
c/o Joan N. Ostroff
105 White Plains Road
Tarrytown, NY 10591

PLATES, FIGURINES, BELLS, DOLLS

The Goebel Collectors' Club is an organization designed to serve and inform those who enjoy and collect works produced by the Goebel Company. In addition, the Club offers items exclusively for its members.

Goebel is known all over the world as a producer of fine collectibles and dinnerware. The firm's name is synonymous with the art of Sister Maria Innocentia Hummel, the talented Roman Catholic nun whose two-dimensional artworks have been produced in three-dimensional form by Goebel since 1935.

Franz Detleff Goebel and his son William founded the F. & W. Goebel Company in 1871 in the Coburg area of Bavaria. Originally the firm made slates, pencils, and marbles. Then eight years later the Duke of Saxe-Coburg granted permission for a kiln for porcelain-making to be built on the factory grounds.

The first porcelain pieces produced were those for everyday table use, but by the turn of the century figurines became part of the line. The beginning of a new era for Goebel came in 1926, when Max-Louis Goebel, the son of William, added earthenware to the line which had been exclusively porcelain. His daring during a time of economic crisis proved wise, for without his foresight, "M.I. Hummel" figurines—with their unique appearance and coloring—would not have been possible.

Max-Louis's son, Franz, took up the family banner of innovation in 1934, when he discovered the two-dimensional works of Sister M.I. Hummel and introduced them the next year in three-dimensional form. Today, in addition to the famed "M.I. Hummel" figurines, the Goebel firm offers "M.I. Hummel" plates, bells, dolls, and a number of other beautifully-made collectible items.

A Norman Rockwell "Four Seasons" stein from Gorham.

THE GORHAM COMPANY
c/o Edward J. Purcell
333 Adelaide Avenue
Providence, Rhode Island 02907

PLATES, FIGURINES, BELLS, STEINS, DOLLS

Jabez Gorham founded the company which bears his name in 1831. Gorham, a silversmith, soon branched into other areas and by the latter part of the 19th century his firm was known as "America's premier bellmaker."

Today Gorham is a multi-faceted firm, owned by Textron Inc. One of the most successful aspects of Gorham's business is in the realm of limited edition collectibles, including plates, figurines, bells, and dolls.

Gorham is the maker and marketer of a wide range of plates featuring art by Norman Rockwell. The firm introduced the "Four Seasons" plate concept—four related issues by Rockwell, telling a story for each season of the year—and then followed by matching figurines the following year. What's more, Gorham offers an annual Rockwell Christmas plate.

Gorham plate artists also include the renowned *Saturday Evening Post* illustrator and fine artist John Clymer; Betty Felder; Irene Spencer; and the late Ted DeGrazia.

In 1981, Gorham entered the growing market for beautifully-made, contemporary dolls with a line which has now expanded to include 40 different issues. These bisque-headed dolls are reminiscent of the famous Bru and Jumeau styles, and their clothing is typical of Paris fashions of the mid-1800's. Each doll has an 18-note musical movement which reflects his or her personality.

DAVE GROSSMAN DESIGNS, INC.
c/o Steven B. Weinreich
2383 Chaffee Drive
St. Louis, Missouri 63146

PLATES, FIGURINES, BELLS, GRAPHICS

Dave Grossman Designs Inc. began as the freelance venture of sculptor Dave Grossman. The metal sculptures he designed and built were so impressive that eventually he was commissioned to create pieces for Presidents Nixon and Johnson, and The Lincoln Center.

This led to statuary, and eventually to a line of figurines, the "Urchins," which were not limited editions.

Fascinated by the success of the "M.I. Hummel" figurines, Grossman was determined to produce figurines which were not "me-too" copies, but something uniquely American. Because Norman Rockwell had captured the spirit of America, Grossman negotiated with *The Saturday Evening Post* for the rights to many of Rockwell's covers.

In 1973, his first limited edition, the "Doctor and Doll" figurine, was issued. It was followed by the "Tom Sawyer" and "Huckleberry Finn" plate and figurine series. In 1979, Grossman introduced the first bas relief plate inspired from Rockwell art, titled "Leapfrog." He also produces limited edition ornaments and lithographs based on Rockwell's work.

The Grossman Designs/Norman Rockwell Club now offers collectors annual issues of limited editions. Most Grossman works are produced in Japan.

The Dave Grossman Designs figurine, "On The Ice".

THE HAMILTON COLLECTION
c/o Karen Stevens
9550 Regency Square Blvd., P.O. Box 2567
Jacksonville, Florida 32232

PLATES, FIGURINES, BELLS, STEINS

The Hamilton Collection is an international purveyor of fine limited editions including plates, figurines, bells, boxes, and vases. The firm originated in the Chicago area, but moved corporate headquarters to Jacksonville, Florida in the late 1970's. The firm is privately held by a group of investors headed by Chairman and Chief Executive Officer James P. Smith, Jr. and President and Chief Operating Officer John W. Graham.

In the early 1970's, the firm's Hamilton Mint division created a wide range of precious metal ingots, medallions, plates and jewelry.

In 1978 The Hamilton Collection made its first major move into the realm of marketing limited edition plates with a series called *The Nutcracker Ballet Plate Collection.* The first issue in that series, "Clara and Nutcracker," has multiplied several times in value since it was issued.

HACKETT AMERICAN
c/o James Hackett
5122 Bolsa Avenue
Huntington Beach, California 92649

PLATES

Hackett American Collectors Company was established in 1978 by Jim Hackett, President of the firm. The company is dedicated to bringing collectors the finest art available in the area of limited edition collector plates.

In addition to providing innovative designs, Hackett's policy is to sell only issues which guarantee both a pre-announced size of the edition, and price.

Hackett offers plates designed by notable artists like Violet Parkhurst, Chuck Oberstein, Sue Etem, Vincent Ozz Franca, and Sadako Mano. Promising new artists are Cassidy Alexander, Ivan Anderson, Irish McCalla, Christopher Paluso and William Selden.

Currently, one of Hackett's most popular offerings is a single issue of plates featuring professional baseball stars including Reggie Jackson and Steve Garvey.

"The Lead Horse," first issue in ***The Art of the Carousel*** *series from the Hamilton Collection.*

In 1979 Hamilton introduced its first collector plate by famed illustrator and child portraitist Thornton Utz. "A Friend in the Sky" was Utz's debut as the creator of a collector plate series, and since then he has offered a number of plates and figurines exclusively through Hamilton.

In the last few years The Hamilton Collection has expanded its product offerings from art studios all over the world. An ongoing association with The Boehm Studios of Trenton, N.J. and Malvern, England has yielded a number of superb collections of fine plates and figurines, which Hamilton offers to collectors in the United States and Great Britain.

Recently, The Hamilton Collection premiered the first-ever limited edition Satsuma ware collector plate series, as well as several groups of elegant Hakata doll figurines created by traditional craftsmen in the Hakata-city region of Japan. Other well known Hamilton products include plates and figurines sponsored by Ringling Bros. and Barnum & Bailey Circus, and *The Art of the Carousel* Figurine Collection.

HAVILAND & COMPANY
11 E. 26th Street
New York, New York 10010

PLATES

In 1839, a young American named David Haviland was in his china shop when a customer brought a cup in to be replaced. Haviland had no replacement, but the piece was so extraordinary that he immediately began to seek out its maker.

His search led him to Limoges, France, where he found the makers of this exceptional china. He immediately began to export it to America. But French and American tastes were different, and the French were unwilling to change their patterns and styles for export. So Haviland decided to move to France and build his own factory in Limoges. There was some resistance, but by 1842, Haviland was exporting his own products from France.

Haviland always has maintained the highest standards, but the company has also been willing to try new methods. Haviland was the first to engage famous artists to design decorations, and the first to introduce chromo-lithographic decoration.

The Haviland Company's ***Night Before Christmas*** *plate series.*

Haviland's Christmas series include *The Twelve Days of Christmas,* and the current series, *'Twas the Night Before Christmas*. To make this Christmas more joyous and memorable, Haviland presents its annual Christmas Angel. Created by the distinguished, contemporary American artist, Elissa Stone, the Haviland Christmas Angels captures the warmth and innocence of Christmas. The firm also has offered an American Bicentennial series and a French collection, among other limited editions.

HAVILAND PARLON
c/o Jacques Jugeat
225 Fifth Avenue
New York, New York 10010

PLATES

The origins of Haviland Parlon are tied to the story of Haviland & Company of Limoges, France. In 1853, Robert Haviland joined his brother, David, in Limoges to help build the Haviland & Company business. Then in 1870, Robert's son Charles established his own porcelain factory in the same region. This became Haviland Parlon.

Haviland Parlon entered the limited edition market in 1971 with the *Tapestry* series, inspired by the Metropolitan Museum's "Hunt of the Unicorn" tapestries. It was followed in 1972 by a Christmas series featuring Madonnas of renowned artists including Rafael, Murillo and Bellini.

A second *Tapestry* series was inspired by scenes from "The Lady and the Unicorn" tapestries which hang in the Cluny Museum in Paris, and a third, called *The Enchanted Forest,* debuted in 1983.

THE HIBEL STUDIO
c/o Bill Hibel
1530 West 53rd Street
Mangonia Park, Florida 33407

PLATES, GRAPHICS

Edna Hibel is among the foremost American women artists, and this firm offers her graphics, limited edition plates and other collectible items. Since 1935, museums and private collectors have recognized Ms. Hibel's special talent. A museum in Palm Beach, Florida is dedicated to her work.

HUTSCHENREUTHER PORCELAIN
100 Shaw Road
North Branford, Connecticut 06571

PLATES, FIGURES

Hutschenreuther is a famed German maker of fine porcelain items, located in the Selb region of Bavaria. A long-time leader in superb-quality figurines and other collector's items, as well as fine dinnerware, Hutschenreuther entered the limited edition plate market in 1973.

Since then, the firm has introduced several series of plates by the husband-and-wife team of Charlotte and William Hallett. In 1982, The Hamilton Collection offered Hutschenreuther's *The Roses of Redoute* collection of eight plates. Other artists whose works have graced the plates of Hutschenreuther include Ole Winther, Gunther Granget, Edna Hibel, Hans Achtziger and Dolores Valenza.

"Lancelot and Guinevere" from Incolay's ***Great Romances*** *collection.*

INCOLAY STUDIOS INC.
445 North Fox Street
P.O. Box 711
San Fernando, California 91340

PLATES

One of the most ancient forms of art was the detailed carvings of cameo from multi-layered gemstones. The white layers were used for the heads, figures and scenes, while the multi-colored layers formed the background.

The artisans of Incolay Studios Incorporated have revived this lost art by using a totally different medium, handcrafted Incolay Stone.

The Incolay Stone process is a closely guarded secret in which various colored minerals and coupling agents are combined in the stratified background to reproduce the same variegated formations and beauty of natural stone. The minerals include Carnelian, Sardonyx, Onyx, Smokey Topaz, Banded Agate, Sapphire Blue and Rhodochrosite.

In 1977 Incolay Studios entered the limited edition collectors plate market with the first issue in the "Romantic Poets" series. This plate, "She Walks in Beauty", became an immediate success and was named the "favorite collector plate" by the readers of *Plate Collector* Magazine.

In addition to the "Romantic Poets" series in Incolay Carnelian by Gayle Bright Appleby and Roger Akers, Incolay Studios released "The Great Romances of History" series in Incolay Smokey Topaz by Carl Romanelli.

A series entitled "Life's Interludes" has been sculpted by J.W. Roberts and produced in French Bronze and Incolay Ivory.

The newest series is the "Four Elements" Micro plate series. Reproductions of restored museum chalk impressions are incorporated in a 2 3/4 inch Incolay Banded Agate plate with a 24K gold-plated Grecian border.

KAISER PORCELAIN
c/o Viking Import House
412 S.E. 6th
Fort Lauderdale, Florida 33301

PLATES, FIGURINES, BELLS

In 1872, August Alboth, chief painter at the famous porcelain factory in Thuringia, Germany, decided to establish his own business. Alboth moved to Coburg, where he began to design and decorate porcelain in his workshop. Later, his son Ernest joined the father and the two moved the business to Kronach, Bavaria.

In 1922, Ernest's daughter Erma married Georg Kaiser, who became a partner in the firm. The company's trademark "Alka-Kunst" was created in 1925, combining the first two letters of Alboth and Kaiser, and Kunst, the German word for art.

The business was a success, and in 1938 the firm bought a well-known Bavarian firm, which had been cited by Ludwig II of Bavaria in 1882 for "magnificent application of Cobalt blue underglaze."

In 1953, a new, modern factory was built in Staffelstein, West Germany. The firm was also modernized by changing the trademark from "Alka" to "Kaiser Porcelain" in 1970. Kaiser Porcelain Company is famous for its elegant dinnerware, very fine gift porcelain, graceful figurines, and an exquisite line of collectors' limited editions. Hubert Kaiser is chief executive officer of this international firm, which is still a family-owned concern.

KERN COLLECTIBLES
c/o Matt Brummer
1987 Industrial Boulevard
Stillwater, Minnesota 55082

PLATES

Kern Collectibles of Stillwater, Minnesota has made an important contribution to the field of plate collecting since its inception in 1969. The firm was founded by Oscar L. "Bud" Kern under the name of Commemorative Imports, as a distributor of limited edition collectibles.

In 1972, Kern expanded the business with the establishment of Kern Collectibles. Kern Collectibles issues limited edition plates produced especially for the company by some of the world's finest china manufacturers.

While they are by no means the largest producer of limited editions, Kern Collectibles has earned a reputation for quality and integrity. Series like the ones from Royal Bayreuth and the many plates created by the late artist Leo Jansen have earned the firm its place in the industry. Other artists chosen to paint for Kern include Harland Young, Patti Canaris, Gregory Perillo, Marvin Nye and Edward Runci.

Today Kern is a division of Press On, Inc.

EDWIN M. KNOWLES CHINA COMPANY
P.O. Box 296
Newell, West Virginia 26050

PLATES

The firm of Edwin M. Knowles traces its history back to the early 19th century when Isaac Knowles, father of Edwin, established the family business—Knowles, Taylor and Knowles—in East Liverpool, Ohio. After apprenticing with his father, Edwin established his own company in Newell, West Virginia. At one time, Edwin Knowles was president of the United States Potters Association.

After Edwin Knowles' death, the firm ceased operations until entering into an affiliation with The Bradford Exchange to preserve this time-honored name. Since 1975, the Edwin M. Knowles name has appeared on issues certified by the Rockwell Society of America. The *Wizard of Oz* collection was the first proprietary series from Knowles. It was followed by the *Americana Holidays* and *Gone With the Wind* series. Knowles' latest series is the *Csatari Grandparent* collection which began in 1980.

Artists for Edwin M. Knowles include Raymond Kursar, James Auckland, Don Spaulding and Joseph Csatari, as well as Norman Rockwell. Kursar created *Gone With the Wind,* and he is well-known for his Broadway show posters. Auckland was the artist for *Wizard of Oz*. Spaulding, a Norman Rockwell protege, was selected to create the *Americana Holiday* series. Csatari, an award-winning illustrator, created the grandparents' series which bears his name.

KONIGSZELT BAYERN
c/o The Bradford Exchange
9333 Milwaukee Avenue
Niles, Illinois 60648

PLATES

The first porcelain bearing the hallmark of Konigszelt of Silesia of Prussia was issued more than a century ago. The likeness of Wilhelm I, king of Prussia and first sovereign of a united Germany, is incorporated into the hallmark of Konigszelt Bavaria. The hallmark is a tribute to the King's early patronage under which Bavarian porcelain became recognized as one of the finest porcelains in the world.

Konigszelt Bayern entered the limited edition market in 1979 with the first issue in a Christmas-theme series. The *Hedi Keller* series features holiday-theme works by this Bavarian-born Primitivist artist. Her work has been exhibited in major shows in Berlin, Munich and Dusseldorf.

The second series of plates from Konigszelt Bayern, *Grimm's Fairy Tales,* features the work of Charles Gehm.

LALIQUE
11, Rue Royale
8e Paris, France

PLATES

Lalique is a family-owned maker of exceptionally fine crystal products, including one of the most famous plates in the limited edition market: the first-issue, 1965 "Deux Oiseaux." This plate opened the way for a new variety in collectible issues: it was the first non-blue-and-white, non-Christmas, non-porcelain collector plate in the market.

The founder of the firm was Rene Lalique, a goldsmith and jeweler. He began his business late in the 19th century, and then purchased a small glassworks in 1902. Lalique built a reputation for fine, Art Deco-style items including perfume bottles, vases and figurines. After the death of Rene Lalique, his son Marc took over the presidency until his death in 1977. Then Marie-

Claude Lalique, Marc's daughter, stepped in to head the firm. She is also its chief designer, and she was the creator of the famous "Deux Oiseaux" and the other plates in the 12-year annual series.

One of Lenox's ***Butterflies and Flowers*** *plates.*

LENOX
c/o Rhea E. Goldman
Old Princeton Pike
Lawrenceville, New Jersey 08648

PLATES

Walter Scott Lenox and his partner, Jonathan Coxon Sr., established the Ceramic Art Company in Trenton, New Jersey in 1889. In 1895 Lenox assumed full control of the company that was later to be known as Lenox, Incorporated.

Lenox was determined to make American china the finest in the world. The company produced vases, bowls, and later tableware made of "American Belleek." It was similar to the creamy, ivory-colored china produced in Ireland. However, Lenox slowly developed his own formula and, after the turn of the century, he was making tableware comparable to the best in the world.

During World War I, Lenox was commissioned to supply President Wilson with a complete set of dinner service for the White House. Later, Presidents Franklin D. Roosevelt, Harry Truman and Ronald Reagan COMMISSIONED Lenox to make sets of dinnerware.

Lenox China, Incorporated continues to grow, while steadfastly maintaining a reputation for "old world quality" and value. In recent years, the firm has entered the limited edition collectibles market with plates on a variety of subjects.

OPA'S HAUS INC.
c/o Jim Brooks
1600 River Road
New Braunfels, Texas 78130

PLATES, STEINS

Opa's Haus, Inc. (OHI) is an import and marketing firm established in 1969. OHI prides itself on being a trend-setter in the marketing of contemporary German beer steins as collectibles.

Founded as a partnership specializing in steins, OHI was incorporated in 1976 and has experienced major annual growth ever since. European clocks, dolls, music boxes and other items have been added to the firm's offerings in recent years.

In addition to its import-wholesale program, OHI operates two retail locations—in New Braunfels and Fredericksburg, Texas—where many of the country's popular quality collectibles are featured. This retail experience has led to the development of collector-oriented programs which are novel to the realm of steins.

Opa's Haus presents the "Bicycle" stein from Thewalt's ***Oldie*** *series.*

Foremost among these is an ownership registration system developed by Opa's Haus for collector-quality German steins, and instituted in early 1981. With the system, it is possible to match potential buyers with potential sellers in the secondary market. The system will also be used to determine reliable and accurate secondary market values.

The company's first exclusive stein design was commissioned in 1976, and its first exclusive limited edition stein—the 1000-piece Festival Stein—was introduced in 1982. It was followed in 1983 by several other exclusive limited editions, including three steins that incorporate the commissioned artwork of renowned wildlife artist Pat Ford.

"Erik and Dandelion," the first plate presented by Pemberton & Oakes in 1978.

PEMBERTON & OAKES
c/o Mary Hugunin
113 E. Carrillo
Santa Barbara, California 93103

PLATES, FIGURINES, GRAPHICS

Pemberton & Oakes is most widely known in the limited edition field for its Donald Zolan collector plates on child subjects.

Beginning with Zolan's 1978 "Erik and Dandelion," the firm issued three Zolan series—the *Zolan's Children* Collection, the *Children at Christmas* Collection, and the *Wonder of Childhood* Collection. It also has issued figurines and limited-edition prints by Zolan.

In addition, the firm has issued the *Nutcracker Ballet II* Plate Collection by Shell Fisher, and the *Moments Alone* Collection by Robert Bentley.

The Pemberton & Oakes Gallery in Santa Barbara, California offers original works, and displays all the original paintings for the plates in the series named above.

The president of Pemberton & Oakes is John Hugunin, former president of The Bradford Exchange.

Pickard China Company's "A Girl with a Watering Can".

PICKARD CHINA COMPANY
c/o Lynn Walker
782 Corona
Antioch, Illinois 60002

PLATES

Pickard, Incorporated was founded in 1894 by Wilder A. Pickard. For some 40 years the Pickard China Studios, as the firm was then known, was a decorating company specializing in hand-painted art pieces and dessert and tea sets.

In 1937 the Studio moved from Chicago to Antioch, Illinois where Pickard's fine china formula was perfected.

The company produces dinnerware, giftware, fine china for the commercial field, and limited edition collector plates.

Pickard has been the recipient of several limited edition awards including "Best Manufacturer of Limited Editions" from several groups and publications.

The firm produces a wide spectrum of collector plates including a Christmas series which began with the famous "Alba Madonna," the *Wilderness* series by James Lockhart, *Children of Renoir, Mother's Love, Children of Mexico,* and *Symphony of Roses.*

The president of Pickard is Henry A. "Pete" Pickard. He is the third generation to enter the business, which is the only American china company still managed by its founding family.

RECO INTERNATIONAL CORP.
c/o Brigitte Moore
150 Haven Avenue, P.O. Box 951
Port Washington, New York 11050

PLATES, FIGURINES, BELLS, GRAPHICS

Reco International Corp. was founded in 1967 by Heio Reich, a native of Berlin, Germany. From its very inception, Reco has been dedicated to the world of limited editions, and particularly collector plates.

In its early years, Reco introduced innovative plates created in association with renowned European names including Fuerstenberg, Royale, Dresden, Royal Germania Crystal, King's and Moser. All of these series have been completed and now may be found only on the secondary market.

Then in 1977 Reco discovered John McClelland, a well-known illustrator and fine artist with a special flair for child-subject art. McClelland's first series, *The World of Children,* premiered in 1977 with "Rainy Day Fun," and concluded in 1980. McClelland also is the creator of a *Mother Goose* plate collection, and *The McClelland Children's Circus* series. Recently Reco introduced a line of hand-painted figurines, *The McClellands Endearing Porcelains.*

Another noted Reco artist is Sandra Kuck, creator of four different plate series including *Games Children Play, The Grandparent Collector's Plates, Little Professionals,* and the new *Days Gone By* series of nostalgic, child-subject plates.

Carol Greunke is a photographer by profession, and her photo stylings for the *Arabelle and Friends* collection have added a new dimension to the limited edition plate market. Ms. Greunke photographs classic dolls and toys—all specially costumed to create a scene of great charm and beauty.

In addition to collector plates and the McClelland figurines, Reco has introduced bells, lithographs and various giftware items in recent years.

"Little Jack Horner" from Reco International Corp.

THE NORMAN ROCKWELL MUSEUM
c/o Donna Benson
2840 Maria Avenue
Northbrook, Illinois 60062

PLATES, FIGURINES, BELLS, GRAPHICS, STEINS

The genius of Norman Rockwell is memorialized in The Norman Rockwell Museum in a wing of the first floor of the historic old Curtis Publishing Building in Independence Square, Philadelphia.

In the same building where *The Saturday Evening Post* was published for so many years, and where Norman Rockwell's works achieved their greatest acclaim, visitors are greeted by a 60-year panorama of the most famous works of America's best-known artist and illustrator. Appropriately, the Museum opened in 1976, America's Bicentennial year.

In 1978, the museum began manufacturing fine porcelain collectibles inspired by the immortal Norman Rockwell's works—many of which are on public view in the museum's galleries. Today, plates, steins, figurines, bells, mugs and other museum porcelains are sought-after by collectors worldwide. The creative work and marketing of museum products takes place at the firm's marketing headquarters in Northbrook, Illinois.

Directing the staff of The Norman Rockwell Museum is Curator Marshall Stoltz, a personal friend of Norman Rockwell, and widely acknowledged as the country's leading expert on Rockwell's life and art. A museum collectible is never issued, nor is the museum's Seal of Authenticity ever affixed to a collectible without the signature of the curator. Ralph Gadiel is President of the Museum, and he directs the firm's marketing operations.

In 1982, the Museum announced its two new divisions: Nostalgia Collectibles and John James Audubon Porcelains. Nostalgia Collectibles manufactures the popular *Shirley Temple Collection* of porcelain plates and figurines. John James Audubon Porcelains is well known to collectors for its famous *Birds of America Collection* of beautiful bird figurines.

ROMAN, INC.
c/o MaryAnn Wellander, Dept. 263
4850 North Harlem
Harwood Heights, Illinois 60656

PLATES, FIGURINES, BELLS, LITHOGRAPHS

When Ronald T. Jedlinski was a boy of six, his father opened a card and gift retail shop. In addition to the religious articles carried by the shop, they had one proprietary product: a painting on glass that was sold in the store and through other retailers as well. From his high school days on, Jedlinski sold for his father and had accumulated about 100 accounts by the time he graduated from college.

When he returned from the Navy, Jedlinski established his own organization as a jobber. Roman Religious Goods grew rapidly, and before long its owner was importing from Europe as well as working with domestic suppliers. By 1973 Roman was importing regularly from Italy, including many items from the famous Fontanini artisans of Tuscany.

In the mid-1970's Roman established the Ceramica Excelsis line of limited edition porcelains. These products—numbered and limited to 5000 each—were made at Ceramica Creativa in Piedras Negras, Mexico. Through this association the firm became associated with other porcelain manufacturers including House of Maruri in Japan.

Since the late 1970's, Roman has acquired a number of licenses under which it has brought distinctive limited

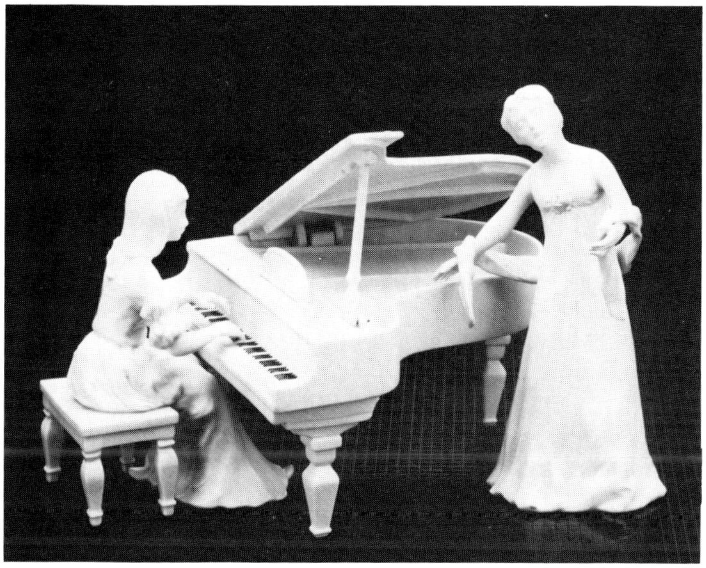

"Singer" and "Pianist and Piano" by Charles Andreoli for Roman, Inc.

editions and giftware to the market. These include the Dance Studio collection of bone china figurines, endorsed by The Joffrey Ballet. A line of collectible plates, figurines and accessories by Roman also has been endorsed by Ice Capades, Inc.

Frances Hook is surely the best-known Roman artist. Her collector plates, prints and figurines reflect the same sensitivity that endeared her to millions as creator of the original Northern Tissue children. Since 1980, Roman, Inc. has also signed contracts with a number of other artists. Charles Andreoli has created a line of limited edition figurines for Roman. Edward J. Rohn, best known to collectors for his clown busts, is creating several new limited editions for the firm. And Frances Hook's protege, Abigail Williams, has also joined the ranks of Roman artists, as well as Linda Cannon—whose artwork is distinguished by various distinctive characters.

RORSTRAND PORCELAIN
c/o Kosta Boda USA Ltd.
225 Fifth Avenue
New York, New York 10010

PLATES

Rorstrand Porcelain, founded in 1726, is the oldest porcelain factory in Sweden. Originally founded in Stockholm, it was moved inland to Lidkoping for safety during World War II.

The founding of Rorstrand is tied closely to the European search for the secret of porcelain, which was being imported from China in the early 18th century.

An "alchemist" named Bottger was employed by the king of Saxony to make gold—or another material that could bring profit—from the nation's national resources. In his prison cell in 1709, Bottger stumbled on a way to make porcelain from the clay of Saxony. The next year, the first porcelain factory was opened.

In 1726 Rorstrand was founded under governmental patronage. It has earned an international reputation for its original shapes and colors of dinnerware and decorative art in feldspar, porcelain, stoneware, and high-fired earthenware.

Rorstrand issued a Christmas plate series between 1904 and 1925. Then in 1968 they resumed the Christmas series with a square plate featuring "Nils," a boy from a Swedish literary classic. Gunnar Nylund, the artist responsible for this series, is widely known for his monumental ceramic reliefs and has exhibited at the Swedish National Museum.

ROSENTHAL U.S.A.
411 East 76th Street
New York, New York 10021

PLATES

Rosenthal was founded by Philip Rosenthal in 1879, in Selb, Bavaria. At first, Rosenthal bought white ware from other porcelain manufacturers and painted it with his own designs. Then in 1895, he established his own factory at Kronach, where he produced fine porcelain with his signature on the back.

The Rosenthal Christmas plate series began in 1910, and ended in 1974. These Cobalt blue plates were reissued in small quantities. The plates all bear a post-1957 backstamp. However, this practice was discontinued after 1971.

A second traditional Christmas series was introduced in the 1970's. This series of blue-and-white plates feature churchs and public buildings, and bear the Rosenthal Classic Rose Collection backstamp.

In 1971, Rosenthal issued the first of its Studio-Line Collections with the *Wiinblad Christmas* series. These plates bear intricate modern designs, partially hand-painted in as many as 18 colors, and embellished with platinum and 18K gold. A second series by Bjorn Wiinblad entitled *Fantasies and Fables* began in 1976 and contains two plates. In 1976, Wiinblad began a series of crystal Christmas plates for Rosenthal. Based on scenes from the traditional Christmas story, Wiinblad used the traditional Danish colors of blue and white in a unique manner.

Two series featuring the work of Edna Hibel, *The Nobility of Children,* and *Oriental Gold,* were introduced by Rosenthal in 1976.

Philip Rosenthal, son of the founder, is currently the president and chief executive officer of Rosenthal A.G. He holds citizenship in both England and Germany and is a member of the Bundestag, the German Congress.

ROYAL COPENHAGEN
225 Fifth Avenue
New York, New York 10010

PLATES, FIGURINES

The Royal Copenhagen Porcelain Manufactory Ltd. is Denmark's oldest porcelain maker. It was established in 1775 by Franz Henrich Muller, a pharmacist and chemist who was the first to duplicate porcelain in Denmark. He was supported by Denmark's dowager queen, Juliane Marie.

In 1779 "The Danish Porcelain Factory" came under royal control where it remained until 1867, when it was sold to a private owner. However, the firm still is a supplier to the royal court. The royal control is symbolized by a crown in the firm's trademark. The three wavy lines under the crown part of the trademark represent Denmark's three ancient waterways: the Sound, the Great Belt, and the Little Belt.

The first Royal Copenhagen commemorative plate was produced in 1888, but it was not until 1908 that Royal Copenhagen introduced its Christmas series, which annually depicts a religious motif or a winter scene. The first three plates were six inches in diameter, but after 1911 the size was changed to seven inches.

The Christmas plates were issued with the text in English, German, French, and Czechoslovakian until 1931 when Dutch was added. However, in 1933 the Dutch was dropped. The various foreign texts were available until 1945, when they were dropped.

The Royal Copenhagen Mother's Day series was added in 1971, and ended in 1972. In 1975 the *Historical* series was issued to celebrate the firm's 200th anniversary. Royal Copenhagen also offers a plate series called *National Parks of America.* A new *Motherhood* series by Svend Vestergard premiered in 1972.

The famous Danish underglazing technique, introduced by Arnold Krog in 1888, is Royal Copenhagen's most popular finish. Artist Kai Lange is regarded as the firm's top artist in this porcelain medium. His design was selected for the 1940 issue and since 1963 every Christmas plate has been a Kai Lange creation. Ib Spang Olsen is the artist for the Mother's Day series, and Sven Vestergaard creates the *National Parks* plates.

ROYAL DEVON
c/o The Gorham Company
333 Adelaide Avenue
Providence, Rhode Island 02907

PLATES

Royal Devon is a trademark owned by The Gorham Company, and used for several series of limited edition collectors plates including Norman Rockwell Christmas and Mother's Day series, and the Rockwell *Home of the Brave* Plate Collection. All three of these series were marketed by The Hamilton Collection and its sister company, Joy's Limited Editions.

ROYAL DOULTON
c/o David Bicho
700 Cottontail Lane
Somerset, New Jersey 08873

PLATES, FIGURINES

Royal Doulton, a firm with a fine reputation worldwide for excellence in dinnerware and in figurines, also has established itself as the creator of a wide range of limited edition collector plates.

Doulton & Company was founded in England in 1815. In 1901 the firm won its royal warrant, and the right to call itself "Royal Doulton."

The company's limited edition offerings began in 1972 with a Christmas series inspired by holiday traditions in many lands. The hand-cast plates were hand-painted on a bas-relief surface. In 1973 Royal Doulton introduced a *Mother and Child* series by Edna Hibel, and in 1974 the firm commissioned Leroy Neiman to create a *Commedia Dell' Arte* series. Other artists among the many renowned names Royal Doulton attracts include Hahn Vidal, Dong Kingman, Chen Chi and John Stobart.

In addition to its collector plates, Royal Doulton attracts collectors by means of its wide range of figurines, and its famous Character Jugs, which depict amusing characters in bas relief.

ROYAL ORLEANS
c/o Bill Uglow
4500 Tchoupitoulas Street
New Orleans, Louisiana 70115

PLATES, FIGURINES

Royal Orleans is one of the newest names on today's limited edition scene, but it is owned by a firm with a long history in the field of giftware, United China and Glass Company.

The company already has introduced a series of plates and figurines inspired by the life and films of Marilyn Monroe, and a collection of Christmas plates—hand-painted in bas-relief—inspired by the famous "Coca-Cola Santa Claus." Royal Orleans also markets a Pink Panther Christmas plate, licensed through MGM/United Artists.

ROYAL WORCESTER SPODE
26 Kennedy Boulevard
East Brunswick, New Jersey 08816

PLATES, FIGURINES

The Royal Worcester Porcelain Company, the oldest porcelain manufacturer in England today, was founded in 1751 at Worcester, England. Two of the original stockholders—Dr. John Wall, a physician and amateur artist, and William Davis, an apothecary—are credited with perfecting the formula used to make soft-paste porcelain, which was used until the introduction of bone china in the 19th century.

King George III gave the company permission to call itself "Manufacturers to their Majesties" in 1788. In 1862 it was reorganized as the Royal Worcester Porcelain Company, and in 1976 it was merged with Spode. However, each company still retains its own trademark.

Royal Worcester produces two kinds of collector plates: bone china and porcelain. The bone china is produced in England. For example, in 1972 Royal Worcester in England produced the *Doughty Birds* series, based on the porcelain sculptures of American birds by Dorothy Doughty, a prominent English sculptor of wildlife. This was followed by the *Currier & Ives* and *Fabulous Birds* series, the *Audubon Birds* pair, and a Christmas plate.

SCHMID
c/o Donna Rossetti
55 Pacella Park Drive
Randolph, Massachusetts 02368

PLATES, FIGURINES, BELLS, GRAPHICS

Schmid was founded in Boston during the 1930's. It has become a specialized importer of porcelain plates, bells and mugs. Limited edition plates are produced for Schmid by a respected maker of figurines and tableware.

In 1971, Schmid issued the first in a Christmas series and the following year added a Mother's Day series. Both featured the work of Berta Hummel, and many bear her signature as she signed the original artwork. Schmid-Germany also produced the *Ferrandiz Mother and Child* series and the *Jubilee* plates by Juan Ferrandiz.

The Charles Schulz *Peanuts Christmas* and *Peanuts Mother's Day* series began in 1972. The *Peanut's Valentine's Day* series followed in 1977. The *Disney Christmas* and *Disney Mother's Day* series feature cartoon characters from Disney's most popular productions. They were followed by the Raggedy Ann-subject Christmas, Mother's Day, Valentine and annual series. Schmid's latest personality is Paddington Bear, featured in *A Year With Paddington Bear* series.

Schmid's current artists include Lowell Davis, Don Polland, Jessica Zemsky, and Jack Hines.

SEBASTIAN MINIATURES
c/o Lance International
225 Fifth Avenue
New York, New York 10010

PLATES, FIGURINES

Sebastian Miniatures are the creation of Prescott Baston. He designed a pair of Shaker figurines for a friend's restaurant during the 1930's, and she was so pleased that she ordered more. Thus began his prolific career as a sculptor.

Baston began selling his figurines through a gift distributor in 1939, and devoted himself completely to the creation of "Baston figurines." The company was run by his wife during World War II. After the war, the firm moved to Marblehead, Massachusetts. Still working with the distributor, Carbone, Baston also signed with Schmid to create *Folks in Little* and the *Dickens Collection.* In the period between 1946 and 1950, Baston designed an astonishing 100 pieces for Carbone and Schmid collectors.

In 1951, Baston began to handle more commercial accounts. He designed figurines which were meant to be given away by companies to help identify and promote a product or service. They did work for Puritan Candy, Necco, Jello, Johnson & Johnson, and *The Saturday Evening Post.*

In 1968, Lance Corporation approached Baston's firm, called "Sebastian," with a proposal to produce high-quality pewter figurines based on his designs. These colonial sculptures and the Currier and Ives plates which followed were extremely successful.

With the renewed interest in collectibles and figurines in 1975-76, Lance took over the production and distribution of Sebastian Miniatures and successfully returned the company to the production of collectible figurines. In cooperation with Baston, the first Sebastian limited edition figurines were issued in 1976. Lance and Baston also established the Sebastian Collectors Society to assist collectors interested in their figurines.

SHADER'S CHINA DOLLS
c/o Kenneth B. Shader
625 Dawson Drive
Newark, Delaware 19713

It all began with a china doll. Ken and Stephanie Shader made the doll as a loving gift for their six-year-old daughter, Pam. It was 1976, and they were living in Iowa at the time. The little doll turned out so well that the Shaders soon were making dolls in their basement for family and friends. In 1978 they moved to Delaware, where they continued to make dolls, and to sell them through local toy and gift shops.

Business was so good that by early 1979, Ken Shader left his position with a major chemical company and the firm of Shader's China Doll was formed. Stephanie Shader has a unique talent for painting and costume design, while Ken's corporate business experience provides the needed management know-how.

An important factor in the firm's success has been its over-riding philosophy of quality. No matter how large the company becomes, the Shaders are determined that each doll will be made with the same attention to detail and quality that they once put into the dolls they made in the basement, one by one.

The production of the porcelain parts takes 18 steps and only the finest quality porcelain bisque is used. There are up to 16 parts in a fully-jointed doll, and the eyes are of German crystal.

Working only with the most delicate laces and the finest fabrics, experienced seamstresses produce each piece of costume by hand, from special designs created by Stephanie Shader. Each doll is signed and dated, and each seamstress has her own label to sew into the Shader dresses she completes.

Shader's China Dolls' "Gunther Gebel-Williams" from the Ringling Brothers series.

STUDIO DANTE DI VOLTERADICI
c/o The Bradford Exchange
9333 Milwaukee Avenue
Niles, Illinois 60048

PLATES

The Studio Dante di Volteradici is located near Volterra in Tuscany, Italy. In this center for the mining and carving of alabaster, Studio Dante di Volteradici continues the Italian tradition of sculptured alabaster.

Studio Dante's *Grand Opera* series was commissioned to commemorate the 200th anniversary of La Scala Opera House. The *Madonna Viventi* series is the firm's first proprietary series. It began in 1978, and represents the work of Ado Santine and Alberto Santangela.

Gino Ruggeri originated the *Grand Opera* series. He is a sculptor in the neo-classical tradition and is best known for his work, "The Crucifix," sculpted for the Casa Serene Institute of Cecina Mare and for his two "Memorials to the Fallen," sculptures which pay tribute to World War I victims. Now in his late 70's, Ruggeri's last complete work was the "Aida" plate.

His successor as designer of the *Grand Opera* series is Franco Ingargiola, whom Ruggeri personally tutored and who works in onyx and ceramics as well as alabaster. Alberto Santangela, current sculptor of the *Madonna Viventi* series, sculpts in the style of the Italian High Renaissance.

Svend Jensen's 1983 Mother's Day plate.

SVEND JENSEN OF DENMARK
1010 Boston Post Road
Rye, New York 10580

PLATES

Svend Jensen's creations are the culmination of the art heritage he learned from his father. This talent is evident in his works in glass, porcelain and metal. However, his greatest success was in his favorite art form—plates—where he collaborated with H.C. Torbol, a porcelain expert skilled in producing the "Old Copenhagen Blue."

The crowning moment for Jensen came after the introduction of his first limited edition plates in 1970. King Frederick IX of Denmark honored Jensen's work by presenting him with Denmark's coveted "Symbol of Growth" for his achievements.

That year Svend Jensen issued two limited-edition plates which were the premiere offerings in two annual collections. The Christmas collection is based on Hans Christian Andersen's tales. There is a Mother's Day collection as well.

Two artists are primarily associated with these works. Svend Otto is known for his spare, but vigorous, illustrations of the beloved Hans Christian Andersen stories. Copenhagen-born Mads Stage was trained at the Royal Danish Academy of Arts and has won numerous awards for his illustrations of Danish literary works. His simple, almost child-like style has brought him a wide following in both Denmark and the United States.

UNICOVER CORPORATION
c/o The Fleetwood Collection
One Unicover Center
Cheyenne, Wyoming 82008

PLATES, BELLS

Unicover Corporation comprises four main divisions, including The Fleetwood Collection: a designer and marketer of fine porcelain collectibles including collector plates, bells and thimbles.

The parent company, Unicover, also includes three other divisions: Fleetwood, United States First Day Cover Society, and China Stamp Agency in North America.

The Fleetwood division was acquired by Unicover about 15 years ago. This firm's basic product is the First Day Cover, first introduced by Fleetwood in 1929. This stamp-related product line is still the mainstay of Fleetwood's business. The First Day Cover Society was established in 1936 as an arm of Fleetwood.

The China Stamp Agency is the official agency of the People's Republic of China for the sale of its postage stamps and Philatelic products to dealers and individual collectors in North America.

*One of the **Pandas of Wu Zuoren** for Fleetwood Collection, a division of the Unicover Corporation.*

UNITED STATES HISTORICAL SOCIETY
c/o Emily Preston
25 East Main Street
Richmond, Virginia 23219

PLATES, GRAPHICS, DOLLS

The United States Historical Society is a private, non-governmental organization dedicated to historical research and the sponsorship of projects and issuance of objects which are artistically and historically significant. The Society works with museums, historic homes and other organizations to create objects for collection that have historic significance, artistic value, and a high level of craftsmanship. Virginius Dabney, the Pulitzer-prize winning historian, is chairman of the Society.

Organizations with which the Society has worked include the National Gallery of Art, the Smithsonian Institution, the National Park Service, the West Point Museum, the Morristown Museum, the Chase Manhattan Bank Collection, Monticello, Winterthur Museum, Eli Whitney Museum, the Buffalo Bill Historical Center, the Confederate Museum, the Wadsworth Atheneum, the Metropolitan Museum of Art, the University of Virginia, Canterbury Cathedral, Cathedral of St. John the Divine, the Washington Cathedral, St. Paul's of San Francisco, and the Los Angeles Cathedral. Trustees of the Society have included Samuel Eliot Morison, Buckminster Fuller, Alistair Cooke, Henry Steel Commager, Lester Cooke, and others.

Among the projects of the Society are the reproduction of George Washington's Flintlock Pistols and his Inaugural Sword, reproductions of Thomas Jefferson's Queen Anne Pistols and his telescope, reproductions of the Alexander Hamilton-Aaron Burr Dueling Pistols, and the issuance of the Young America of Winslow Homer Plates, the George Patton Sword, the Robert E. Lee Commemorative Pistol, and the Paul Revere Silver Tankards. The Society also is issuing a continuing series of to-scale Living Image portrait dolls of Great Americans and the annual Stained Glass and Pewter Christmas Plate.

Books the Society has sponsored include *The Patriots American Revolution, Generation of Genius, Morristown the War Years 1775-83,* and *The Great American Quilts.*

With the New York Council on the Arts, the Society sponsored the composing and presentation at the Kennedy Center of the American Symphony by Morton Gould.

"Flight Into Egypt" is a stained glass Christmas plate from United States Historical Society.

Viletta China Company's 1978 "Clara and Nutcracker".

VILETTA CHINA COMPANY
8000 Harwin, #150
Houston, Texas 77036

PLATES, FIGURINES, BELLS

Viletta China Company, founded in 1959, produces limited edition collectibles and fine china dinnerware. The Houston based company is one of the world's largest producers of limited edition collector plates and has developed a fine reputation for quality. Viletta recently expanded into Canada. The new company, Viletta China Canada, Ltd., is based in Toronto and distributes a full line of collectibles and the Viletta dinnerware line.

A number of limited edition collector plates are manufactured under the Viletta name. The official commemorative plate for the 1980 Olympics was produced by Viletta. *Clara and the Nutcracker* collection and *Precious Moments* series by Thornton Utz were made for The Hamilton Collection.

VILLEROY & BOCH
c/o Marcia Richards
41 Madison Avenue
New York, New York 10010

PLATES, FIGURINES, STEINS

Villeroy & Boch is a German firm with a long heritage of quality in tableware and art items. The firm was founded in 1748, when Francois Boch opened his first pottery studio at Auden-le-Tiche. The Villeroy fmily joined with the Bochs in 1836. Together the families became renowned for their innovations and artistic flair—and today an eighth-generation descendant of the Boch family sits as Managing Director of the firm.

Today Villeroy & Boch is an internationally-known maker of dinnerware and accessories in addition to collector plates, plaques, figurines and steins. The firm has as many as 16,000 employees in its 18 locations across France, Luxembourg, Italy and Germany. Headquarters are at Mettlach, West Germany.

Villeroy & Boch has a well-deserved reputation as the world's finest maker of steins. The firm developed both the Chromolith (etched or incised) process and the Phanolith (cameo) process. Although stein production stopped at Mettlach in 1927, the firm has offered several contemporary limited editions in recent years.

The Heinrich Studios in the Bavarian town of Selb create most of Villeroy & Boch's collector plates, including two "Flower Fairies" series, the elegant *Russian Fairy Tales,* and a current collection sponsored by the World Wildlife Fund.

One of Cicely Mary Barker's delightful "Flower Fairy" plates for Villeroy & Boch.

WEDGWOOD
c/o Jim Fulks
41 Madison Avenue
New York, New York 10010

PLATES, BELLS

Josiah Wedgwood, born in 1730, was a fourth-generation potter. He was apprenticed at the age of nine to his brother, and later became the partner of Thomas Whieldon, England's finest potter.

In 1759 young Josiah founded Wedgwood. A partner, Thomas Bentley, joined the firm in 1769. Bentley provided a knowledge of the arts and many social contacts for the fledgling firm. Josiah Wedgwood's greatest personal achievement was the development of a new and affordable dinnerware. This cream-colored earthenware with a rich glaze was quite popular with Queen Charlotte. By her command it was named "Queen's Ware." In 1774, Wedgwood received his most prestigious commission—a 952-piece set of "Queen's Ware" china for Empress Catherine II.

In addition to his "useful wares," Wedgwood experimented with a new black basalt which became one of the company's most popular products. His most famous invention was jasper, an unglazed, vitreous, fine stoneware which can be stained various colors such as blue, green, lilac, yellow or maroon. It provides a suitable background for white relief work on classic subjects, or portraits.

Wedgwood's policy was to hire leading artists of his time, including John Flaxman and George Stubbs. That tradition continues today, and in the past 30 years artists including Rex Whistler, Eric Ravilious, Edward Bawden, Arnold Machin, Richard Guyatt, Eduardo Paolozzi and David Gentleman have designed for Wedgwood.

Wedgwood has been extremely active in the collectibles field, producing Christmas plates, thimbles, bells, mugs, and eggs in their famous jasper. The firm also produces several plate series in fine bone china or earthenware, including *Child's Christmas, Peter Rabbit's Christmas, Children's Story,* and *The Blossoming of Suzanne* series.

The 1983 Wedgwood Mother's Day plate.

About the Artists

Limited edition artists are the object of a great deal of interest and admiration on the part of collectors. Some collectors will travel hundreds of miles to attend an open house or convention featuring that special artist or craftsman. Here is some brief biographical information about some of the best-known artists in today's world of limited editions. This listing is not comprehensive, but it will provide an introduction to a good number of the talented men and women whose work brings pleasure to collectors all over the world.

CHARLES ANDREOLI

Charles Andreoli's rich and diverse talents range from art restorer, set designer and commercial interior designer to lighting designer and porcelain sculptor.

Born in Kenosha, Wisconsin, Andreoli studied at the American Academy of Art and DePaul University. He enjoyed the tutelage of Alexander Zlatoff-Mierski, a renowned painter and authority on Russian art. During five years of study, Andreoli majored in philosophy and art history, and received an education in the Old Renaissance tradition.

Andreoli first worked in the motion picture industry as a set designer. Later, he returned to Chicago where he became a portraitist, earning critical praise for his works. During this period, he also produced a portrait of St. Augustine, an altar piece, a mosaic mural, and the interior design and mural for Cardinal Stritch's private chapel. Andreoli next turned to designing interiors for hotels and restaurants, which in some cases led to his personal execution of wood carvings—for interiors including the Mayan Room, Rockefeller Center and the Emerald Door in New Orleans. Since the 1960's, his career has focused more on the home furnishings industry, particularly the lamp and lighting design field.

In 1980, Andreoli turned to sculpting porcelain figurines. His Cotillion figurines helped propel him into the ranks of the most respected limited edition artists. Today he creates limited editions for Roman, Inc.

JOAN WALSH ANGLUND

Joan Walsh Anglund is the artist/writer of *A Friend is Someone Who Likes You,* which sold over 11,000,000 copies.

Anglund's parents were artists, and she studied at the Chicago Institute of Art and the American Academy of Art. She was a commercial artist before her marriage and children. Her first "fine art" drawings were of her own children while struggling with her feelings of loneliness in New York.

Anglund's button-eyed children are her trademark. Her drawings, books, cards and plates are enjoyed by all ages. Anglund plates are distributed through Ebeling & Reuss.

JOHN JAMES AUDUBON

The works of Audubon have inspired several contemporary collections of limited edition collectibles: most recently, the *Birds of America* figurines. Today, John James Audubon is considered by many as the father of wildlife conservation. His dramatic and realistic paintings touch almost everyone, and they are as timely today as when they were first painted nearly two centuries ago.

Audubon was born in Haiti in 1785. Reared in France, his artistic ability emerged early and he was sent to study with the prominent French painter, Jacques Louis David. Audubon's father sent him to America with a gift of money and land, but by the time he was 30, he found himself married, the father of two sons, and penniless. Farming was not his talent.

But in this new land, Audubon found a dream: to paint the birds—and eventually the animals—of North America. Although he faced poverty and left his family for months on end to tramp the woodlands and meadows in search of new species, he remained steadfast to that dream for nearly 20 years.

Finally Audubon amassed a portfolio of 435 watercolors depicting 1,000 birds. Frustrated in a vain attempt to find sponsorship in America, he set sail for England in 1826 in search of a publisher. Art patrons in London and Paris backed his project and eventually the Double Elephant Portfolio was published in an edition of 200 at $1,000 each. Today an original copy sells for about $400,000. Later Audubon added *Quadrupeds of North America* to his portfolio, and again won kudos from his contemporaries...and continued praise today from naturalists and art lovers.

DON BALKE

Don Balke, creator of The Fleetwood Collection's "Canada Geese" plate, has been painting the birds and animals of the countryside for over 25 years. He is recognized today as one of America's finest wildlife artists for his realistic portrayal of the drama and emotion of life in the woodlands.

The plate was issued for Mother's Day, 1983, and shows a Mother Goose with her gosling family.

CICELY MARY BARKER

Cicely Mary Barker, creator of the art and poetry which has inspired two "Flower Fairies" plate series and a collection of figurines from the Heinrich Studios of Villeroy & Boch, was born on June 28, 1895, at Croydon, England. Her father, Walter Thomas Barker, was a London merchant. Because of her ill health, Miss Barker was largely home educated, and self-taught in the arts except for a brief time as a student at Croydon School of Art.

From her earliest years, she had an ardent love of nature, and took long country walks, gathering knowledge about flowers and trees which is reflected in her "Flower Fairies."

Miss Barker's best-remembered works are the "Flower Fairy" books, first published in 1923 and re-discovered by generation after generation of children. She created each Flower Fairy character, and wrote a lilting verse for each—describing its flower or tree in detail.

Deeply religious and a regular churchgoer, Miss Barker created a stained glass window for St. Andrews Church in Croydon. She also illustrated many books and post cards. One of her paintings, "The Darling of the World is Come," is in the possession of the British royal household. This prolific artist and poetess died at Worthing, Sussex, on February 16, 1973.

PRESCOTT BASTON

Prescott Baston was born the son of a miniaturist who created models for an architectural firm. Forced by the Depression and the death of his father to seek work, the 20-year-old art student worked at a variety of jobs. A friend asked him to design a pair of figurines for a restaurant and people were so pleased with them that he decided to approach a wholesale gift dealer.

Carbone liked his line and agreed to handle his work. In 1939, Baston began working full-time in his figurine business. The war interrupted his work, but after he returned to the business he entered one of his most productive periods, designing figurines with strong historical and literary overtones for Carbone and Schmid.

He later turned to more commercial work, designing premium figurines for businesses. His association with Ray Kennedy of Lance Corporation led to a return to the high-quality figurines on which his reputation was established. Baston continues to work on a limited basis with the company he established.

ROBERT BENTLEY

Robert Bentley's paintings capture the beauty and vitality of people. A graduate of Yale University, this Chicago-area artist tried a business career, but gave it up to paint full-time.

Fascinated by people, he studied anatomy, the Old Masters, and the faces around him in an effort to capture that rare spark of life. His first plate collection, *Moments Alone,* is a successful display of his gift. *Moments Alone* is marketed by Pemberton & Oakes.

KARIN BLUME

Karin Blume is a resident of Dusseldorf, Germany, and an artist with a unique ability to see her subject with both the eye and the heart. She is the creator of a series of plates for Villeroy & Boch called *Children of the World.*

This plate collection was issued to benefit Unicef, and each depicts a child or children from various parts of the world. In her Unicef plate illustrations, Ms. Blume fully utilizes her expressionistic talents and flair for color.

EDWARD MARSHALL BOEHM

Edward Marshall Boehm, who died in 1969 at the age of fifty-five, was the first American to produce porcelain art objects equal to those of superior European and Asiatic craftsmen. His extraordinary lifelike figures of birds, animals and plants are in museums, galleries, and palaces, including the White House, Metropolitan Museum of Art, Smithsonian Institution, Buckingham Palace and the Vatican. One of the many remarkable aspects of his genius is that, nearly fifteen years after his death, Boehm porcelains are still being created in all the diversity and fidelity to nature of their originator.

Porcelain art, to the degree developed by Edward Boehm, required the unique combination in one man of the talents of a renaissance artist and a naturalist. To this we must add a thorough knowledge of ceramics and the subjects to which his creative efforts largely were directed.

Edward Boehm had no patronage or financial backing. But he had the unswerving faith in his genius of Helen, his wife and talented assistant. After his death she became his successor and has done much to spread his fame. Mr. Boehm was first in America to achieve international recognition by heads of state and leading connoisseurs for fine hard-paste porcelain of artistic and technical excellence.

When he started his studio in Trenton, New Jersey in 1950, Edward Boehm had only an innate talent as a sculptor and craftsman and the potential for versatility and excellence. In a relatively short period of time, this total craftsman started a studio, formulated a hard-paste porcelain, learned and mastered each step in a complicated process, produced sculpture that was artistically and technically desirable, and inspired other artisans with his techniques and standards of excellence. All this with no formal art education or even a prior basic knowledge of ceramics. Under the constant guidance of Helen, Edward Boehm's legacy continues today with every porcelain art work created in the Boehm studio.

GENE BOYER

Ever since he was a child, growing up in a small town in Illinois, Gene Boyer has enjoyed sketching the everyday scenes of life around him. He soon discovered—and began to develop—a profound talent for capturing life's most tender emotions on canvas.

Boyer first gained national attention when he placed second in a contest sponsored by *The Saturday Evening Post*. As a result of this success, the illustrious magazine offered him a permanent position, and the opportunity to join forces with notable artists including Norman Rockwell. Since that time, Boyer has created many acclaimed works of art, including "Mom's Apple Pie," the artwork for his first collector plate for The Fleetwood Collection.

CAROL WERNER BURGUES

Carol Werner Burgues was born and educated in Germany. She came to the United States in the mid-1950's, and in 1964 she became the protege of Dr. Irving Carl Burgues, already a noted porcelain sculptor. Later she married her mentor.

In addition to designing some of the Burgues porcelain sculptures, she introduced a porcelain vase series. This fine gift line is produced in hard, high-fired porcelain, and painted entirely by hand.

Mrs. Burgues also has designed a Nature Series of mushrooms and flowers in pewter, and a group of prestigious collector plates for Anna-Perenna. Her paintings have won numerous awards, and are noted for their great detail and individuality.

DR. IRVING BURGUES

Dr. Irving Carl Burgues was born in Austria. He earned an M.A. in fine arts from the Academy of Vienna, and later he studied at the Academy of Fine Arts in Vienna, and with Molet in Paris.

In search of artistic perfection, he has fashioned intricate jewelry and has worked in bronze, pewter, marble and wood. His sculptures are found in the White House, the President's mansion in Jerusalem, the Vatican Palace, Palaces of England and Belgium, and the Foreign Embassies of Spain and Austria. His work may be found in numerous museums including The Smithsonian Institution, which acquired his horse sculpture, "Spirit of Freedom."

Many of Burgues' works reflect his love of nature. He is also a lecturing conservationist. His "American Wild Goat" was commissioned by the State of Montana for the 1976 Bicentennial, to focus awareness on the conservation of this unique animal.

Dr. Burgues is an active member of the United World Colleges and has been knighted into the order of Knights Hospitallers of St. John.

PATTI CANARIS

Patti Canaris is recognized as one of today's most popular bird and wildlife artists. She grew up on a ranch near Billings, Montana, where she developed a keen eye for the beauty of nature. As an artist, she now seeks to communicate this beauty through her paintings. Her work reflects a sense of serenity and peace.

Ms. Canaris made her debut in the field of limited editions in 1980, with her award-winning '*Songbird* series, made by Haviland-Parlon for Kern Collectibles. In her second series, the *Butterfly* collection, she offers her public four of the world's most beautiful butterflies in the fine china medium.

Linda Cannon's love of children and art led her to a major in art education at John Herron School of Art at Indiana/Purdue University in Indianapolis, Indiana. Her high level of academic achievement is reflected in her professional career: she was selected as one of 12 artists to create the first Indiana Postcard series. Her work also has been featured in several "one woman" shows.

Cannon's work has been published in "Health and Wholeness" publications and "Growing Child." Active in children's art education, she is responsible for summer art, private classes and "Children's Day In" programs around her native Indianapolis.

Ms. Cannon frequently is commissioned to create illustrations and portraits. Frequently, she works with faded photos. She explains that painting memories "helps people deal with painful things."

A favorite technique for revealing character is Ms. Cannon's montage of poses. This approach, combined with the special characters she has created, distinguish the limited editions which Ms. Cannon now renders for Roman, Inc.

LINDA CANNON

WILLIAM CHAMBERS

William Chambers already was a well-known illustrator and portraitist when he was selected by Columbia Pictures and the Edwin M. Knowles China Company to design the *Annie* collector plate series.

Chambers is a native of Chicago. He graduated from Northeastern Illinois University and the American Academy of Art, Chicago. His paintings are displayed in numerous galleries, and he is represented by Portraits, Inc. of New York.

He has received top awards in the American Society of Illustrators' Annual New York Show, and first prize in the John Howard Sanden portrait competition in Chicago.

JOHN CLYMER

John Clymer is today's most historically accurate and gifted artist of the American West. His mural-style paintings appear in some of the nation's finest museums, including the Whitney Gallery of Western Art, the National Cowboy Hall of Fame, and many others.

After an early correspondence course in drawing, the young Clymer won the attention of a famed Vancouver, B.C. illustrator, George Southwell. This experienced artist gave the boy lessons, and for a time Clymer combined art school, apprenticeship to Southwell, and a full-time job. Eventually Clymer took a job on a paddle wheeler on the Yukon River. There he soaked up the atmosphere of nature and adventure that would inspire his later works.

Clymer later returned to Vancouver and then to Toronto, where he worked as an illustrator. As a young husband and father he found himself in Westport, Connecticut, the "mecca" for illustrators of the day. After World War II, Clymer began painting regularly for *The Saturday Evening Post,* eventually completing more than 90 covers.

But always the call of the West was with him, and as soon as he was able, Clymer abandoned his flourishing career as an illustrator and became a fine artist, specializing in Western themes. His success is almost unparallelled: the owner of one of his Lewis & Clark-theme paintings, "Sacajawea at the Big Water," recently turned down $250,000 for it.

To date, John Clymer has completed two series of collector plates for Gorham. One collection, inspired by Clymer's monumental body of work tracing the journey of Lewis & Clark, was introduced in association with The Hamilton Collection in 1981. The other, currently being distributed, is *Encounter, Survival, and Celebrations,* a six-plate series, each limited to 7,500.

PETER N. COZZOLINO

Peter Cozzolino is a sculptor of considerable fame and achievement. He is the executive director of the Old Church Cultural Center and School of Art, in Demarest, New Jersey, which he founded in 1974. Cozzolino is a master of sculpture in a wide variety of media, including bronze, clay, plaster, cement, wood and marble.

His schooling included a Bachelor of Fine Arts degree from the School of Fine and Applied Arts, Boston University, followed by a two-year course of study at the School of Medical Illustration, Massachusetts General Hospital, and then two years of independent study in

Italy. From 1965-1968, he attended the National Academy School of Fine Arts, where he studied with noted masters Carl Schmitz, Michael Lantz, Mitchell Fields, and Granville Carter.

With more than 30 exhibitions and shows to his credit, Cozzolino has had occasion to earn a number of awards for his work. He was the recipient of a National Academy of Design Merit Award in 1977, and the coveted John Gregory Memorial Prize in 1979 from the National Sculpture Society. This latter award indicated work which most displayed originality, imagination, and expert craftsmanship.

For The Hamilton Collection, Cozzolino has created two collections of fine, hand-painted figurines: *The Art of the Carousel,* and *The Ringling Bros. and Barnun & Bailey Circus Animal Figurine Collection.*

JOSEPH CSATARI

Joseph Csatari was a long-time friend and protege of Norman Rockwell. He studied at the Academy of Art, Newark, New Jersey, and Pratt Institute in Brooklyn, New York.

Csatari was the recipient of the Gold Medal award from the Society of Illustrators. For a decade, he collaborated with Rockwell on the annual Boy Scouts of America calendar.

In 1979 he was commissioned by the Postal Service to design a commemorative stamp honoring Seeing Eye, Inc. Csatari's first collector plate, "Bedtime Story," was issued in 1980. It premiered his *Grandparents* series for the Edwin M. Knowles China Company.

BOLESLAW CYBIS

Boleslaw Cybis was born in 1895, in Wilno, Lithuania. The son of a respected architect, he studied at the St. Petersburg Academy of Fine Arts until he was forced to flee to Istanbul during the Russian Revolution.

By 1923, Cybis was able to return to Warsaw where he enrolled in the Academy of Fine Arts. It was here that he helped form the Brotherhood of St. Luke, an artists' group dedicated to studying the techniques of the Old Masters.

He traveled extensively until he was appointed a professor at the Warsaw Academy in 1937. In 1938, Cybis and his wife, Marja, were commissioned to paint a mural in the Hall of Fame at the New York World's Fair. Prevented from returning to Poland because of World War II, they settled in New York. Later, the Cybis Studio was moved to Trenton, New Jersey.

Boleslaw Cybis died in 1957, and his wife died the following year, but they left a group of personally-trained, skilled artists to carry on their work.

NORMAN N. AND HERMAN DEATON

Norman N. (Neal) Deaton and his brother Herman are two of the most talented sculptors of animals living in the world today. Even as youngsters, they were fascinated by the opportunity to observe, study—and model in clay—the small wild creatures of their native Iowa.

The Deatons are especially noted for their famous hand-painted animal sculptures for The National Wildlife Federation. Their works are exhibited at such prominent museums as The Smithsonian Institution in Washington, D.C., and The National Museum of Canada in Ottawa. And Deaton works are held in many important private collections—including those of such notables as United States Senators Morris Udall and Frank Church.

In all of their works, the Deatons combine an eye for natural beauty with a passion for authenticity—qualities that distinguish the two groups of hand-painted, cold-cast bronze figurines they have created for The Hamilton Collection.

Titled *The Audubon Bronzes* and *An American Wildlife Bronze Collection,* each comprises six figurines inspired by the works of famed wildlife historian and painter John James Audubon.

ETTORE "TED" DE GRAZIA

Ted DeGrazia, one-time apprentice to the great Mexican muralist Diego Rivera, took great pride in describing himself as "a working artist." From his early life in a copper mining town to his final years as one of America's most distinctive and popular artists, he lived primarily for his art.

DeGrazia gained international attention in 1960 when his "Los Ninos" was selected as the Unicef Christmas Card.

Collectors prized his plate by the same name, and others in his *Children* and *Holiday* series. DeGrazia mini-plates and collector bells are also in great demand.

DeGrazia died in 1982. He will be best remembered for his paintings of round-faced Indian children. "I paint what I know," he said.

EDMUND DULAC

Around the turn of the century in England, a "Golden Age" of illustration for children's books was led by an artist named Edmund Dulac. A talented artist from childhood, the Frenchman Dulac emmigrated to England and began a varied career which included designing postage stamps, stage costumes and furniture, composing music, drafting and watercolor painting.

Works of Dulac hang in such fine collections as The British Museum, The Department of Coins and Medals, The Imperial War Museum, The Victoria and Albert

Museum, The London Museum, The Wallace Collection, The National Postal Museum, and others.

Americans knew Dulac for his association with the *American Weekly* Magazine from 1924 until 1951, just two years before his death. The artist created more than 100 covers for this publication. Among these were eight "Fairyland Lovers," which have inspired a collection of plates by the Heinrich Studios of Villeroy & Boch. The plates, and another Heinrich series by Dulac, *French Fairy Tales,* mark the 100th anniversary of this talented artist's birth.

RENEE FAURE

An accomplished artist and illustrator, Renee Faure has a successful career in two normally exclusive areas—those of commercial art and painting. Already known to limited edition collectors for her plate art, Ms. Faure is also the creator of fairy tale paintings for Villeroy & Boch's steins inspired by the stories of "Peter Pan," "Hansel and Gretel," "The Pied Piper," and "Pinnochio."

Born in New York, a third-generation artist, she follows in the footsteps of her grandfather, Impressionist Edmund Graecen and her mother, a successful painter named Nan Graecen. Renee began studying art at an early age, and graduated from Mary Wheeler School in Long Island. She also studied at the Art Students League in New York, the National Academy of Design, and the Boston Museum of Fine Art. She also was a student of philosophy.

In the early 1970's, Ms. Faure moved to Jacksonville, Florida and soon was commissioned for two murals—one in a hospital and the other at the State Senate Building.

Ms. Faure has won a number of awards, and has exhibited with the American Watercolor Society and the National Society of Illustrators. She is frequently published in professional art publications.

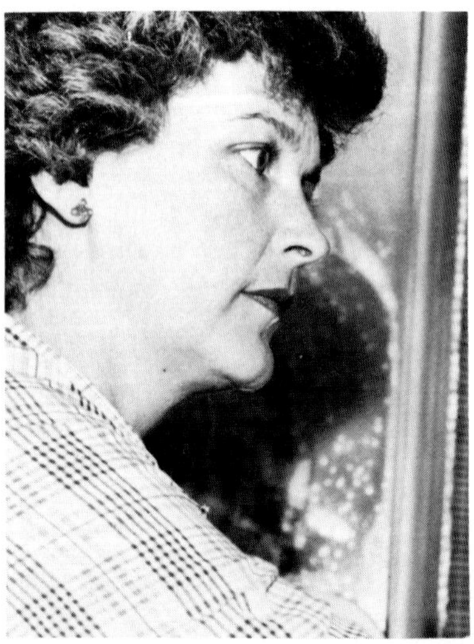

BETTIE FELDER

Bettie Felder's paintings are reminiscent of the warmth and charm of the Tennessee Smoky Mountains of her childhood. A self-taught artist, she did not begin to paint seriously until her second child was born. Felder's first paintings were sold at sidewalk shows, but she was spotted by a prestigious Dallas gallery, which handled her first show.

Bettie and her husband, Bob, have formed their own publishing company, Marinatha Press, which issues both limited and unlimited prints. Much of the profit from her enterprises is donated to charitable organizations. Devoutly religious, Ms. Felder begins each day with an hour of prayer.

Bettie Felder's debut in the limited edition plate field is the *Pastoral Symphony* series, produced by Gorham.

SHELL FISHER

Shell Fisher is a skilled portraitist who has painted scores of notables, including Queen Elizabeth of England. Originally from the Chicago area, he now lives and works in Pebble Beach, California and operates a gallery in the artist's colony of Carmel.

Fisher is a graduate of the Chicago Art Institute, and later went on to study at the University of Illinois and the American Academy of Art. In addition to his fine art paintings—which now command $10,000 and more—Fisher has created a number of illustrations for many magazines, including *Playboy.*

His first collector plate series was *The Nutcracker Ballet,* which premiered in 1978 with "Clara and Nutcracker." After that six-plate series was complete, Fisher began an annual *Nutcracker II* series, which features a new plate each holiday season, inspired by the world's best-loved ballet. In association with Pemberton & Oakes, Fisher recently introduced a third ballet-inspired series called *Swan Lake,* which will comprise five plates.

PAT FORD

Wildlife artist Pat Ford sees this as the ultimate goal of her labors: "...that the great-great-grandchildren of those who buy my paintings will know that this is really what the animal or bird looked like." Wife of an outdoorsman, she spends countless hours in wildlife refuges or just walking the woods, armed with a camera and slide film to gain reference material.

A native of Oklahoma, Pat Ford has been drawing and painting as long as she can remember. She credits early growth and development to an outstanding art program in the Tulsa schools. After receiving a scholarship for her skills, she earned an art degree from the University of Tulsa. After college, she sought a degree in advertising art, and later met and married Jack Ford. They moved to the Lower Rio Grande Valley of Texas, acquired some land, and began raising a family.

Meanwhile she continued to perfect her art, and to help Ducks Unlimited with donated art to the Houston chapter. One of her paintings financed a program for youth, and others raised $1,000,000 for DU within four years' time.

Today Pat Ford lives outside of Houston, nurtured by her number-one fan, husband Jack. She continues to earn glowing tributes—now for a new medium: that of limited edition steins. Her wildlife art is the feature of a new collection from Opa's Haus of New Braunfels, Texas.

CAROL GREUNKE

The dolls and teddy bears which her mother collected inspired Carol Greunke toward her successful career as a collector plate photographer/stylist.

Born in Westport, Connecticut, Ms. Greunke grew up in a home filled with her mother's treasured collection of dolls and toys. She studied art history at Finch College in New York, and worked at the Museum of Modern Art while going to school. For her, one of the most important classes the college offered was a photography course that brought famous photographers like W. Eugene Smith and Max Waldman into the classroom.

Greunke continued her studies at the University of London and later completed her education at Barnard College. Greunke later met Waldman again, and this

ballet and theatre photographer offered her a job at his studio. She apprenticed and learned the exacting art of studio photography by working with Waldman for five years.

It was he who suggested that she photograph her mother's antique doll collection for greeting cards. "Arabelle," a 32" Bru doll, became the star along with two Jumeau dolls and assorted toys. With the help of her grandmother, who worked on the costumes and props, Greunke carefully arranged and photographed the dolls.

It was her grandmother's plate collection which sparked Greunke's interest in photographing the dolls for a plate series. In "Ice Delight," the first plate in the series, the dolls as well as a teddy bear and "Uncle Max"—a 1930 ventriloquist doll—are posed in a snowy skating scene complete with tiny ice skates. The 2nd plate shows "Arabelle" in "First Love" enjoying a beautiful day in the park with her friends.

JAN HAGARA

Jan Hagara was born in Sand Springs, Oklahoma. Her talent for producing exquisite images of yesterday's children can be traced in part to her mother's love of antiques, and her father's artistic ability.

An award-winning, self-taught artist, she has combined her love of antique dolls and costumes with the sober, angelic look of carefully-selected children to create her unique paintings. Her models are photographed in her studio, and from these images she creates her watercolors.

Over 60 of these watercolors have been transformed into prints and cards since 1975. In 1978, her designs also were transferred to porcelain plates for the *Yesterday's Children* series. It was followed by the *America Has Heart* collection and an *Old Fashioned Mother's Day* series.

Because of her love of antique dolls, Ms. Hagara has also agreed to design a series of dolls for Effanbee. The Royal Orleans Company is planning to introduce a series of nine figurines and a porcelain doll based on Hagara designs. Her art will be translated into needlework designs in the near future as well.

Ms. Hagara's work will appear on two new plate series: one with a Christmas theme, and the other called *Country*. Both will be produced by B&J Designs.

AL HIRSCHFELD

Al Hirschfeld has had a love affair with "lines" for more than 50 years. What began as amusing sketches of the French actor, Sacha Guitry, eventually led to his incisive sketches in the Sunday Art & Leisure section of the *New York Times*.

Born in St. Louis in 1903, Hirschfeld enjoyed drawing even as a child. When his family moved to New York, he studied drawing, painting, sculpture, and lithography at the National Academy of Art and Design, the Art Students League, and later at County Council in London, and Julienne's in Paris.

He left his job as an art director at Selznick Pictures in 1924 to study in Paris, North Africa, and the Far East. He had his first show at the Newhouse Galleries in New York in 1925.

While in the Far East, he learned that the sun bleached out color and left only lines. It was this discovery which led to his dramatic use of the simple line—most recently in a series of limited edition collector plates for ANNA-PERENNA.

Through the years, Hirschfeld has played a whimsical game with the *New York Times* readers. Concealed somewhere within his drawings is his daughter's name, Nina. "Nina Watching" has become a Sunday pastime for many. Her presence is marked only by a tiny number beside his signature which indicates the number of times she appears.

HOLLY HOBBIE®

Although many collectors believe that Holly Hobbie is the name of a beloved character rather than an artist, actually Holly is both. Holly Ulinskas Hobbie, who resides in western Massachusetts in a 200-year-old colonial home, has been creating her nostalgic children for American Greetings (and its Designers Collection subsidiary) since the late 1960's.

Holly Hobbie says that she finds her inspiration all around her—the area of Massachusetts where she lives is rich in traditional Americana with many museums, antique shows, auctions, gardens and handicraft fairs. what's more, her three children often model for Holly, although she never uses them as "mirror images." She says, "I have noticed, however, that my characters tend to grow up as my children grow."

Holly Hobbie's goal is to bring back the serenity and innocence of a long-ago world. As she says, "While I have not deliberately tried to denote a specific time or person, my style and subjects bring back memories of a more tranquil and charming time period. They seem to

evoke the 'good old days' captured in books or on film...a time beyond memory."

Today collectors may purchase plates, figurines, bells and a wide range of giftware items featuring the art of the prolific Holly Hobbie.

Holly Hobbie® is a trademark of American Greetings Corporation and its subsidiaries.

PHYLLIS HOLLANDS-ROBINSON

Phyllis Holland-Robinson is an internationally-known artist whose entrance into the world of limited editions adds yet another aspect to a varied and fascinating career.

Born in Chicago, she was the only child of a prominent North Shore physician and his wife, a talented artist. Educated at Evanston's Roycemore School and New Trier High School in Winnetka, Illinois, she "painted her way through school" and later studied at the Chicago Academy of Fine Arts and the Academie de la Grande Chaumiere and other ateliers in Paris.

During the past few years, she has had more than 40 one-woman shows in galleries from Paris, London, New York and Chicago to Palm Beach, New Orleans, Denver, San Francisco, Milwaukee and Nantucket. Her paintings hang in private collections in the United States, Canada, and Europe including those of Mrs. Eunice Kennedy Shriver, M. and Mme. Pierre Bertrand, and Fred Astaire.

Although she travels extensively, Ms. Hollands-Robinson enjoys England most, and returns there time and again. She also loves France, and some of her finest works depict scenes from the French countryside.

A versatile artist who paints landscapes, animals and people with equal facility, Ms. Hollands-Robinson chose cats as the subject matter for her first limited edition plate. "Kitty Love" depicts the close relationship of a mother cat with her kitten. This plate and more in a series from this prolific artist will be marketed by the American Artists division of Graphics Buying Service.

FRANCES HOOK

From the moment she could put pencil to paper, Frances Hook knew that she liked drawing more than anything else. Born in Ambler, Pennsylvania, she took art lessons while in high school. This led to a scholarship at the Pennsylvania Museum School of Art, where she studied under illustrator Harry Pitz. She developed a pastel style and a unique way of capturing children.

While in school, Ms. Hook met her husband-to-be. After graduation, they married, and each began a career in commercial art. Her first ad was a two-page spread in *The Saturday Evening Post.*

It became increasingly clear over the years that Ms. Hook's talent lay in her sensitive portrayals of children. She had the ability to capture youngsters in their natural settings. The now-famous Northern Tissue children of the mid-1960's were drawn by Frances Hook. When television reduced the demand for commercial art, Ms. Hook turned to illustrating childrens' books. In collaboration with her husband, she illustrated *The Living Bible,* by Tyndale Publishing.

In 1979, Roman, Inc. approached Frances Hook and asked her to design a collection of porcelain figurines. Soon she produced a "Little Children Come to Me" plate and "The Carpenter," her print of Jesus. Hook has produced several limited edition plate series for Roman, as well as figurines and prints. *A Child's World* is her best-known figurine series.

BERTA HUMMEL

Berta Hummel received extensive training at the art academies in Simbach and Munich, where she developed her distinctive style. Her drawings are of children—frequently with a religious theme.

The works of the young girl, Berta Hummel, are featured on the limited edition collectibles by Schmid—prints, figurines, cards, plates, bells and other gift items.

The drawings featured on these Schmid collectibles were completed before Berta Hummel entered the Franciscan order at Siessen in 1934 and took the name of Sister Maria Innocentia Hummel.

SISTER MARIA INNOCENTIA HUMMEL

Sister Maria Innocentia Hummel was the creator of hundreds of colorful and charming sketches, drawings and paintings of children. Her work has inspired scores of appealing, hand-painted fine earthenware figurines, as well as limited edition plates and bells, created and offered exclusively by W. Goebel Porzellanfabrik of West Germany.

She was born Berta Hummel in Bavaria in 1909. Her father had inclinations toward art, and so did Berta, from earliest youth. She was graduated from the Munich Academy of Applied Art, meanwhile devoting much of her energies toward her religion as well.

Much to the dismay of her art teachers, Berta Hummel entered a convent upon her graduation, taking the name Sister Maria Innocentia. Because her convent, a teaching order, was quite poor, she gained permission to raise money by selling some of her artwork for postcards. In 1934 Franz Goebel, the fourth-generation head of the porcelain-producing firm bearing the family name, discovered her art at a time when he was searching for inspiration for a new line of figurines.

The first "M.I. Hummel" figurines debuted at the Leipzig Fair in 1935, and since then have been popular with collectors around the world. Sadly, their creator, Sister M.I. Hummel, died much too soon after her triumph as an artist. She succumbed to tuberculosis in 1946, at the age of 37.

LEO JANSEN

One of the most important artists in the field of limited edition plates is the late Leo Jansen. Jansen, a Dutch-born artist, excelled at capturing the essence of his subjects.

This brilliant portrait artist was introduced to collectors in 1974 through his interpretation of a black mother and child in the Royal Bayreuth series. This success was followed by *Prince Tatters* and the *Sugar and Spice* series. His *Leaders of Tomorrow* series in 1980 was followed by *My Favorite Pets* the next year.

Public demand resulted in the creation of Leo Jansen porcelain figurines featuring some of his best-loved work in three-dimensional form.

While a large number of Leo Jansen originals is not available for future reproduction, Kern Collectibles hopes to produce the remaining pieces as a memorial to this fine artist.

MARK JONES

Mark Jones is the creator of *The Alice in Wonderland Figurine Collection,* a group of 12 pewter, hand-painted figurines offered exclusively by The Hamilton Collection. A graduate of Birmingham College of Art & Design, he began his career as a restorer of classic European masterworks. Soon he developed an interest in historical characters and period costumes, which he pursued during studies in Rome during the early 1970's.

Later Jones was privileged to spend a year in the Alps, studying with one of Italy's finest sculptors. There he advanced his work in the sculptural medium.

On his return to Great Britain, Jones found that collectors were very much interested in his figurines. An early exhibit at Stratford-on-Avon was a fine success, as were subsequent gallery appearances and shows.

Jones was well suited to the Hamilton commission for *Alice in Wonderland,* as he specializes in whimsical and satirical portrayals of historic subjects. His *Alice* figurines are the product of Tyler of Great Britain, a leading caster and hand-painter.

MARGARET KANE

There were gifted artists on both sides of Margaret Kane's family, so her bent toward art seemed natural, and was encouraged. Ms. Kane loved art and her father taught her to paint when she was quite young.

Born and raised in England, Ms. Kane won her first art award at the age of 10. At 15 she won a scholarship to the London School of Art.

At 18 she came to the United States, where she was immediately recognized as an accomplished artist. This resulted in commissioned works which included a portrait of Clara Clemens, the daughter of Mark Twain.

Three of Kane's watercolors are in the permanent collection of the Toky Museum. Her works also are found in the Guggenheim Collection. Her lithographs and paintings are in permanent collections and galleries throughout Europe, Israel and the United States. She also sculpts, does portrait work, and loves to paint children.

Her art is fantastically complex, yet spontaneous. And though her work is a joyful fantasy, there also is an awareness of life's sorrows. Margaret Kane's limited edition plates are created by Anna-Perenna Porcelain.

MURRAY KARN

Murray Karn mastered his craft after years of studying in Europe, the Far East, and Africa. It was in this jungle land that his talent for painting animals was born.

A prize-winning artist, Karn is known for his innovative illustrations—many done under commission from Fortune 500 companies.

Painting animals is extremely difficult and demanding. Karn is able to successfully capture on canvas the charm and beauty of his subjects, including his latest, "Benji" and "Benji and Tiffany" for Creative World.

MELANIE TAYLOR KENT

Melanie Taylor Kent says, "It is my intent to capture America in the 1980's, its special places, people and events. I strive to portray the subject matter as we would want to remember it. In years to come my work will be a chronicle of America, whimsically depicted in a fantasy of time, place and color."

The works of Ms. Kent are in the "naive" style, combining a brilliant array of colors with whimsical imagery. This California artist won her first National Art Competition at the age of 12, and subsequently studied with several celebrated artists. She graduated from the UCLA School of Art, and has been a teacher and mural painter—creating and supervising the Los

Angeles Community Mural Printing Program. Her work has been acclaimed in newspaper and national magazine articles, and has been featured on two television "specials."

The works of Melanie Taylor Kent are found in art galleries throughout the United States and Europe. Her originals and serigraphs have been exhibited at: UCLA Art Gallery, USC Art Museum, Los Angeles County Museum of Art, Dorothy Chandler Pavilion—Los Angeles Music Center, Los Angeles Museum of Science and Industry, Pierce College Teaching Artist's Exhibit, Los Angeles Art Exposition 1980, San Francisco Art Exhibition 1981, and New York Art Exposition 1981, 1982 and 1983.

Melanie Taylor Kent is the creator of "Macy's Thanksgiving Day Parade," first issue in a plate collection called *Famous Parades,* which is being issued by The Carmel Collection.

THADDEUS KRUMEICH

Artist Thaddeus Krumeich was born in New York City in 1930. He attended New York University on a scholarship and completed his graduate studies at Columbia University in 1966. He taught art and design at the New York University at Farmingdale and at Columbia University. During this time, he developed a new and award-winning teaching concept which he outlined at the National Arts Convention.

In 1968, he entered the field of illustration, working for major publishers and for such magazines as *Family Circle, Woman's Day, Time/Life* and *Reader's Digest.*

Five of his paintings were chosen by UNICEF for their celebrated greeting cards, which showcase some of the world's finest artists. He has exhibited in major galleries from New York to California, and his paintings are on display in a number of collections.

Krumeich has been described as a "super realist." His paintings—which seem deceptively primitive—are bathed in jewel-like colors, creating a warm, cheerful ambience.

His genuine love for felines and other animals is reflected in his touching artwork, which is enjoyed both by animal lovers and by collectors. The meticulous care he has invested in his oil paintings can also be found in his *Uncle Tad's Cats* and other plate series, and in his art prints. His limited editions are available through Anna-Perenna Porcelain.

SANDRA KUCK

In Sandra Kuck's paintings of children, she displays a rare gift for capturing the true spirit of childhood. The creator of four series of plates for Reco International, Ms. Kuck lives in Long Island, New York.

She was educated at U.C.L.A., where she discovered that she loved to paint and draw. She moved to New York and entered the Art Students League where she learned to do portraiture and figure drawing. She disliked drawing and painting inanimate objects and soon discovered that people and in particular children, interested her most. Within a year, she began to win commissions from galleries for portraits and paintings.

Ms. Kuck's fascination with children as subjects began when she was pregnant with her first child. She began sketching children at play in the park, and eventually her own daughter became her best model.

Before long Ms. Kuck's child-subject paintings were on display in many New York-area galleries: she has sold more than 1200 original paintings. In a Long Island gallery, Reco International president Heio Reich spotted her work and approached her to create a series of plates, *Games Children Play.* Soon she added *The Grandparent Collector's Plates* series and one entitled *Little Professionals.* Ms. Kuck's latest collection, *Days Gone By,* is being offered by Reco and through The Hamilton Collection.

A.M. KURKIN

Born in the Russian city of Rolstov, A.M. Kurkin became fascinated with the artwork of the Palekh Masters at an early age. After completing his formal art studies he left Rolstov to live in Palekh. His goal was to dedicate his talents to the artwork unique to this tiny village.

After 10 years of study and practice, Kurkin at last produced his first Palekh work. Since then, he has excelled in his specialty and is now recognized as a master of Palekh Art.

In "The Tsarevich's Bride," Kurkin's first limited edition collection plate, Kurkin brings to life his favorite folk tale by means of his Palekh Art. The plate is the product of The Fleetwood Collection.

RAYMOND KURSAR

Raymond Kursar is well known for his movie art and Broadway posters. Thus he was an obvious choice to create the *Gone With the Wind* collector plate series for Edwin M. Knowles China Company.

Kursar studied at the School of Advertising Art and the Museum of Modern Art, both in Oregon. He has done theatrical posters for plays including "Hello, Dolly" and "Evita," and his illustrations have appeared in *Better Homes & Gardens* and *Good Housekeeping.* He researched the *Gone With the Wind* series at the MGM Photo Archives in New York.

CHARLES LUNDGREN

Charles Lundgren takes as his subject the great sailing ships of the world. His paintings are coveted by private collectors and museum curators throughout the world, and they hang in the National Gallery of Art in Washington, the Philadelphia Maritime Museum, and many other prestigious institutions.

Lundgren has studied at some of the finest art schools in the United States and Europe, but his most influential teacher has always been the sea itself. He sailed his first craft at the age of 11, and his years of ocean racing give him an intimate knowledge of the sea.

In the series of paintings he has created for The Fleetwood Collection's *Golden Age of Sail,* he has attempted to bring to life the proud era when the sailing ships of America were the rulers of the sea. This is his first collection of limited edition plates.

JOHN McCLELLAND

The life-sized portrait of his daughter, Susan, which John McClelland created some years back may well have been the major turning point of his career. An art director used the portrait for an ad in a trade magazine, and Miles Kimball, the mail order company, spotted it and asked John McClelland to do a Christmas cover for their catalog. That was the beginning of an association which continues today.

Brigitte Moore of Reco International saw McClelland's Miles Kimball art in the mid-1970's, and Reco arranged for the artist to create limited edition plates. McClelland today is one of the field's most celebrated artists, with numerous "Plate of the Year" and "Artist of the Year" awards to his credit. He also is the creator of a

[*Photograph courtesy of* Plate World *Magazine.*]

line of figurines and a number of limited edition lithographs pulled from 8 - 14 individual plates.

A native of Georgia, McClelland pursued his art career in New York after a hitch in the service. He met and married Alice Stephenson, a fashion artist, and they moved to Connecticut, where they still reside. In addition to his many limited edition offerings and his Miles Kimball work, McClelland is a portraitist with a large following. He also has created scores of illustrations for publications including *The Saturday Evening Post, Redbook, American,* and *Reader's Digest.*

McClelland has written two "how-to" books for artists: one on painting flowers and the other on portrait painting. He also has taught both intermediate and advanced classes in portrait painting.

JEFFERY MATTHEWS

Jeffery Matthews enjoys an international reputation and is a longtime favorite artist of the British Royal Family. He designed the official British stamps honoring "The Twenty-Fifth Anniversary of the Queen's Coronation," "The Royal Wedding of Princess Anne," and "The Queen Mother's Birthday."

In 1981, Matthews' exceptional talent was displayed in the stamp design for "The Royal Wedding of Prince Charles and Lady Diana Spencer." "The Royal Wedding Plate" is this British artist's first limited edition collector plate, created for The Fleetwood Collection.

ELIZABETH MAXWELL

Elizabeth Maxwell takes inspiration for her collector plate art from her own three children and five grandchildren. She says that she loves the freshness of youth, and enjoys painting babies through adolescents best of all.

This California artist sketched and painted all during the time her children were growing up, and did work as a book illustrator, portraitist and advertising artist.

After her children "left the nest," she became even more serious about her art, and studied under Manuel DeLeon and other noted masters.

Today her work is featured in private collections from coast to coast. She is the recipient of a number of art show awards, and her work is shown in galleries including Ira Roberts in Beverly Hills, California, B&Q in Long Beach, California, and others in Palm Springs and Las Vegas.

Ms. Maxwell is the creator of "Darling Diana," first issue in a series of plates for The Carmel Collection called *First Performances.* It depicts a young ballerina preparing for her first recital.

FRANKLIN MOODY

Franklin Moody is a remarkable artist with a life-long love for the pageantry of the circus and all its attractions. He is the creator of two circus-related plate series sponsored by Ringling Bros. and Barnum & Bailey Circus, and offered exclusively by The Hamilton Collection.

Moody found his research for *The Greatest Show on Earth* and the *Ringling Bros. and Barnum & Bailey* collections a pure joy: a fine opportunity to spend time in the circus world he loves so much.

A Florida native, Franklin Moody was educated at Florida Southern College and the University of Florida, earning bachelor's and master's degrees respectively. His teaching career has included positions with the University of North Carolina at Greensboro, the University of Tampa, and the University of Delaware. He has also directed and owned fine art galleries, including The Moody Gallery in New York and The Professional Artists Gallery in Miami Beach.

NORVAL MORRISSEAU

It is the destiny of Canadian artist Norval Morrisseau to break with the ancient traditions and taboos of his people, and record on canvas the mystical images of the Ojibway Indians. Morrisseau was born in Thunder Bay. Educated as a Roman Catholic, he left school after the fourth grade. Raised by his grandparents, he learned the ancient rituals and stories of the Ojibway Indians from his grandfather. As a young man he was given the sacred name of "Copper Thunderbird."

Although he received no formal art education, by 26 he was convinced that his divine calling was to record the ancient legends and ritual of his people through his paintings. In the tradition of the "Shamans," he believed it was his sacred duty to transmit the spiritual forces through physical objects and symbols of the world. His work is no longer limited to the scrolls and rock paintings of the Indians, but now includes the Christian, Aztec and Byzantine symbolism as well.

His success was not achieved without a struggle. During his early years as an artist, he lived with only the bare necessities in a shack in Beardmore, Northern Ontario. During this time he worked in a mine while perfecting his art and trying to attract patrons.

Morrisseau has had a number of one-man shows in Canada, the United States, and Europe. The Woodland Indian School of Art was founded by Morrisseau to provide an education for art students in Canada. His designs for fine porcelain—created for Anna-Perenna Porcelain—are a far cry from his early work done on brown paper and birch bark.

P. BUCKLEY MOSS

P. Buckley Moss is a prolific artist with her own gallery in the Georgetown section of Washington, D.C. Moss grew up during the depression in a close-knit family on Staten Island, New York. Her father was a stockbroker, her mother a dress designer.

She attended a special high school for artistic students, commuting daily to Manhattan. A scholarship to Cooper Union in New York provided her college education in art before she married and started raising her famiy of six children.

Painting at night, her work captured the simplicity of the Mennonites she saw at farm auctions. She exhibited her first works when her children ranged in age from one to eight. A friend had persuaded Ms. Moss to enter a local art show, which brought her prizes and an offer of a one-woman show.

Ms. Moss, who prefers to work in watercolor, continues to draw her inspiration from the Mennonite people. A woman with her baby, children at play, and the young bearded men in buggies are the subjects of her paintings. She has a clean, energetic style which reduces things to their simplest elements—a pristine combination of realism and the abstract. Her collector plate series for Anna-Perenna Porcelain is *American Silhouettes,* which contains three series: *Valley Life, The Children,* and *The Family.* All depict various scenes from Mennonite life.

NORI PETER

Nori Peter has created a number of limited-edition plates and figurines, and recently signed an exclusive agreement with Anna-Perenna Porcelain. She was born in Hungary, a member of an artistic family. After study at the College of Fine Art and the Hungarian Academy of Fine Arts in Budapest, she immigrated to Canada in 1957.

Ms. Peter took a number of trips to learn more about the cultures she would depict in her work. She was especially intrigued by the Ojibway Indian and Eskimo peoples, and she visited them time and again, sketching them and their activities for use in her paintings and sculptures.

This artist's work is characterized by attention to detail in both her two and three-dimensional works. Her art is on display in galleries in cities including Collingwood, Montreal, Ottawa, Toronto, and Winnipeg, Canada.

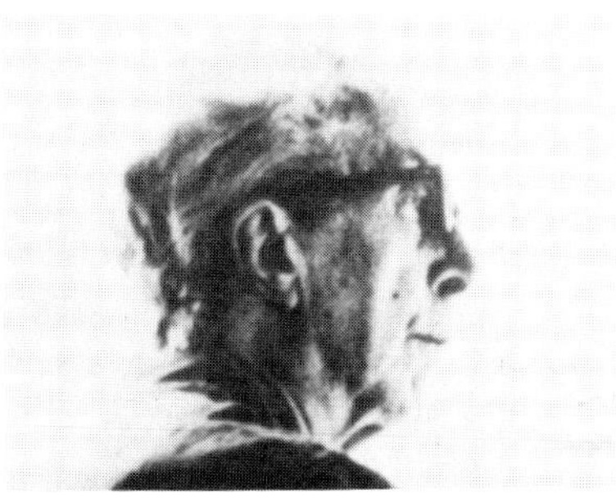

NORMAN ROCKWELL

"I paint life as I would like it to be," Norman Rockwell once said. "If there was a sadness in this creative world of mine, it was a pleasant sadness. If there were problems, they were humorous problems."

In his thousands of works, Norman Rockwell created a pictorial history of his times and illuminated the lives of his fellow Americans with gifted warmth and insight. Rockwell gained national prominence as an illustrator for *The Saturday Evening Post, Life, Look, Boy's Life,* Boy Scout calendars and major advertisers, all of which brought him close to the hearts of people the world over.

The man who was to become the 20th century's most popular American artist and illustrator was born in a brownstone in New York on February 3, 1894. He began drawing at five, and attended the Chase School of Fine and Applied Arts and the National Academy of Design. He sold his first *Post* cover in 1916, and by 1920 he was the *Post's* top cover illustrator.

One of his most distinguished projects was a series of more than 70 sketches depicting the American Family for the Massachusetts Mutual Life Insurance Company, a collection which is now on display at The Norman Rockwell Museum. During World War II, Rockwell's "Four Freedoms" art helped raise more than $130 million in war bond money. Beginning in the early 1970's, Rockwell's works became some of the most highly-sought subjects for limited edition collectibles. Today Rockwell limited editions are marketed by firms including The Norman Rockwell Museum, The Gorham Company, Dave Grossman Designs, and The Hamilton Collection.

Norman Rockwell continued his productive life as an artist and illustrator in his Stockbridge, Massachusetts studio until his death on November 9, 1978.

ED ROHN

Ed Rohn abandoned his career as a sales manager to return to his true profession: that of a sculptor. In the 13 years since he moved his family to a Chicago suburb and established his own porcelain studio, he has gone from an amateur to a skilled professional.

His busts of Harry Truman, Norman Rockwell, "The Tramp" and various clowns have become prized collectibles. They are exhibited in top galleries nationwide. He enjoys working with his hands, and feels comfortable with the three-dimensional medium.

In recent years, Rohn has entered the field of limited edition plates as well, with issues inspired by his three-dimensional clown busts. Most recently he has made an agreement with Roman, Inc. to create limited edition items.

FRANK RUSSELL AND GERTRUDE BARRER

The American team of artists—Frank Russell and Gertrude Barrer—brought a totally new dimension to plate collecting with the introduction of the triptych form—a set of three plates with a frame. This work for Anna-Perenna Porcelain was representative of their rich experience in the arts—with a total of over 70 years of combined craftsmanship.

This husband-and-wife team attended the Art Students League in Manhattan, a training ground in classical, historical, technical and modern art movements. Both came from families with a musical tradition. Barrer attended Julliard School of Music before entering the League.

Russell's first showing was in the landmark "Painters of Brooklyn" exhibit (1935) and Barrer's first exhibition was at Kenneth Laurence Beaudoin's Galerie Neuf (1947).

The two were married after World War II. While Barrer worked as a commercial artist, Russell was an electronics designer and interior photographer—and both painted at night. Barrer was one of the first abstract expressionists, and examples of her style may be found in several childrens' books which she illustrated.

In the 1940's, the two began collaborating on ceramic tile murals. It was this experience that eventually encouraged them to create ceramic plates. They have continued their commission work as well as printmaking, painting, book illustration and photography.

Their work has included 17 fresco triptychs. The tradition of the triptychs is rooted in the Christian and pre-Christian Byzantium iconography and religious art. The *Byzantine Triptych,* a set of three plates with their portable frames, is a major achievement. And now *The Jerusalem Triptych* also has been issued.

The latest Russell-Barrer series is *Romantic Love.* These plates offer a rich and colorful depiction of the loves of "Romeo and Juliet," "Lancelot and Guinevere," "Helen and Paris," and the "Lovers of the Taj Mahal."

DAVID SMITON

David Smiton is a scholarship graduate of the famed Parsons School of Design. He works simultaneously in commercial and fine art, never neglecting one for the other. While working in New York as an advertising art director, Smiton was commissioned to sketch the events of the Lt. Calley trial. He also was the trial artist for the Clifford Irving and Jean Harris trials. Smiton's fine art has been awarded the prestigious Grumbacher Award.

ELKE SOMMER

Elke Sommer was born in Berlin, Germany during World War II, the only daughter of a Lutheran minister. The family fled the devastation of Berlin. In her teens—determined to make her living as an interpreter—Ms. Sommer worked for a family in

London for $7 a week while learning the English language.

In 1958, she and her mother took a vacation in Viareggio, Italy. After winning the title of Miss Viareggio, Ms. Sommer was offered a part in a Vittorio de Sico movie. She is now an international film star, and lives in Hollywood, California.

As a young child, Ms. Sommer escaped her desolate, wartime surroundings and created her own fantasy world by writing and illustrating her own fairy tales and poetry. She has continued to draw and paint, and prefers to be thought of as an artist who acts rather than an actress who paints. Her most recent limited edition plate creations are *The Happy Village Collection* of four seasonal plates for Anna-Perenna.

IRENE SPENCER

Irene Spencer is a native of Chicago. She entered the Chicago Institute of Art at the age of nine, and later attended the American Academy of Art.

At age 20, desperate for a job, she and a friend joined the circus. She toured the country for two years as an apprentice elephant trainer, drawing the circus people and animals in her spare time.

After leaving the Big Top, she worked as a commercial artist for 22 years. This provided valuable experience in that Ms. Spencer created whatever the client required. She enjoyed a flexible schedule, so she could spend time with her children.

Finally, in 1964, she began to paint full-time for herself and within two years she was making a living doing commissions for galleries.

The Franklin Mint approached Ms. Spencer in 1972 to do an original design for the sterling silver Mother's Day plate. The silver series ended in 1976, but it was followed by an *Irene Spencer Annual* series on porcelain.

Today, Spencer lives in California and is affiliated with Pickard China in the production of limited edition plates. The oval-shaped *Mother's Love* series for Pickard is acclaimed by both collectors and dealers. Her newest plate, "Wild Irish Rose," could well become her most successful of all.

In addition to plates, Ms. Spencer's artwork can be found on plaques, lithographs, jewelry and porcelain figurines.

FRED STONE

Fred Stone is recognized as America's leading painter of horses. His paintings are unique because of their extreme close-up angles. Stone wants his audience to study the horse's eyes in great detail—for he believes that the eyes hold the key to a horse's life and personality.

Stone has painted many of the world's most famous horses, and his paintings hang in the homes of such noted personalities as Bert Firestone, Charlie Whittingham, Nelson Bunker Hunt, and Kentucky Governor John Y. Brown.

The creator of a number of highly-acclaimed lithographics and other graphics works, Stone has a reputation for prompt sellouts and impressive market appreciation—sometimes as much as 500% in just one year's time.

Fred Stone creates limited edition graphics and collector plates for American Artists and Graphics Buying Service. In association with Modern Masters, American Artists introduced the first Fred Stone collector plate, "Patience," in 1981. The artist's most recent plate offering is "The Black Stallion," first of a series of four.

Stone, a native Californian, lives there now with his wife, Norma, and daughter, Laura.

VINCENTE TIZIANO

Vicente Tiziano, a fine Italian artist, has revived the ancient Etruscan technique of ceramic production. His "Veneto Flair" technique was used to produce the famed "Bellini" Madonna plate, the *Last Supper* and *Mosaic* series, and series of dog and Christmas card plates among others.

Tiziano's plates are distributed by Creative World. They are completely hand-made, and thus are issued in extremely limited editions. Many boast rich touches of gold as well as hand-painting.

Tiziano was the recipient of the Amerigo Longhi Award for his contribution to the arts in Italy and abroad. He retired in 1982.

LORRAINE TRESTER

Lorraine Trester, artist for Kaiser limited edition plates and other collectibles, was born and raised in rural Ohio. There she enjoyed the beauties of nature. Even today, she nurtures this relationship to the great outdoors by living in a quiet farm area of Sheboygan, Wisconsin, and by frequent visits to the countrysides of Europe.

Ms. Trester's vision of the world is romantic and nostaligic, and she believes in the beauty of life around her. Her work is on display in major art centers and galleries in the United States and many other countries.

RAIJA UOSIKKINEN

One of the leading Finnish practitioners of ceramic art and design is Raija Uosikkinen, a member of the Arabia of Finland design staff since 1947.

She received her early training at the Institute of Industrial Arts in Helsinki, and later was the recipient of a grant-scholarship for study in Germany. She has taken additional study trips to Australia, England, Indonesia, and Turkey.

Ms. Uosikkinen had a one-woman exhibition of her work in Helsinki, as well as exhibitions abroad in Brussels, Milan, and in Sacramento, where she was awarded the Gold Medal. She has also taught at the Institute of Industrial Arts.

Born in Hollola, Ms. Uosikkinen, like most Finns, grew up knowing the stories of the Kalevala. And she brings to her *Kalevala* collector plate series her great talents as a designer, as well as a great pride in her homeland and its legends.

THORNTON UTZ

The limited edition field has added an exciting new dimension to the many-faceted career of portraitist, fine art painter, illustrator and sculptor Thornton Utz.

Along with Norman Rockwell, Utz provided scores of cover paintings for *The Saturday Evening Post.* His career as an illustrator spanned several decades and included work for nearly every major magazine in the United States.

And during the past 10 years or so, Thornton Utz has become known for his portraits and fine art paintings. Utz's appealing style that combines an impressionistic,

free-flowing background and a very realistic facial expression has won him international praise.

His list of famous portrait subjects includes the late Princess Grace of Monaco, Astronaut Alan Shepherd, Rosalyn and Amy Carter and other members of the Carter family.

In 1979, Utz introduced the first issue in his first series of limited edition plates—a piece called "A Friend in the Sky." The plate won the title of "Top First Issue of 1979" in a poll of dealers and collectors.

Later Utz plate offerings include an annual child-subject series, which began in 1981, the *Carefree Days* series of boy subjects, which premiered in 1982, a commemorative plate titled "Princess Grace," and a 1983 Mother's Day issue, "A Gift of Love."

Also in 1983 Utz introduced his first limited-edition figurine, "Snow Bunny," as the premiere of a series of eight. All of these Utz limited editions have been available exclusively through The Hamilton Collection.

JEROME WALCZAK

Jerome Walczak, artist for The Carmel Collection, is a native of California and presently resides in Cerritos. He attended private schools as a youngster, but never studied art—he is completely self-taught. But since first grade his teachers recognized his talent, and encouraged his efforts.

Walczak has won many juried art shows in Southern California for his portraits of people and animals. These include exhibitions at Knott's Berry Farm and the San Gabriel Art Association.

In addition to his artwork, Walczak enjoys karate and is an instructor with 15 years' experience.

WOLFGANG WEBER

Wolfgang Weber is an artist struggling for the preservation of nature. Early in life, he developed a deep feeling for nature, and especially for animals. While an

art student he regularly did unpaid jobs at the zoo in Frankfurt, Germany.

The veteran of a great deal of travel, Weber is currently a free-lance artist. He lives most of the time in East Africa, away from "tourist paths," where he can draw inspiration for his nature-oriented paintings.

Weber has been influenced in his watercolor paintings by the O. Kokoshka "School of Observation." His watercolors, as well as drawings, wood engravings and other graphics have been exhibited in Frankfurt, Berlin, Nairobi and Hanover. He has also illustrated books, and his watercolor calendar paintings are published annually at Weisbecker Verlag.

This Villeroy & Boch *World Wildlife Fund* artist has an unusual range of styles, from very free painting to extremely accurate and detail-oriented work. The theme which unites his art is the preservation of nature in a great range of floral and wildlife paintings.

FLAVIA WEEDN

Flavia Weedn has a special appreciation of life. She shares its beauty and simplicity through her Cottage Street figurines for Roman, Inc.

Flavia's respect for life is the common thread that is woven through every piece of work. "People see their own reflection in what I do," she explained. "That is the tie." People from the Cottage Street of Flavia's childhood inspired these figurines and the philosophies which accompany them.

Ms. Weedn first gained attention for her whimsical cards and stationery, and now has branched into various areas of collectibles and giftware, including fine figurines for Roman.

The California artist also has made prints, fabric designs, paintings and sculptured figurines. She has done design work for I.Magnin, Hallmark and American Heart Association. Roserich is her own company, which produces posters, cards, stationery and prints from her designs.

MARY ELLEN WEHRLI

Mary Ellen Wehrli, the gifted California artist, is fondly known as the "Rabbit Lady." Ms. Wehrli, who is a seventh-generation Californian, was born in San Francisco. She studied art at California State University. Her art education began at San Mateo High School and continued at San Jose College as well as the College of San Mateo.

She has exhibited in juried shows throughout California and has won dozens of awards including many first prizes. She is a skilled artist, working in a number of media and subjects, including figures, acrylics, chromatics, textural abstracts, and even paste modelings. Animals and water lilies are her best subjects. Her work appears on greeting cards, note paper, and puzzles as well as limited edition collector plates for Anna-Perenna Porcelain.

Wehrli's hobby is raising rabbits. She has become well-known for her realistic paintings of rabbits and kittens. Her fascination with rabbits is due in part to the fact that she finds rabbits funny, prolific, and perfect to portray urban living situations. Many of these are satires, straight from the pages of the daily paper.

Her collector plate series entitled *Bashful Bunnies* realistically demonstrates Wehrli's skill in capturing the lovable beauty of her favorite animals.

ABBIE WILLIAMS

Early in the 1900's, Abbie Williams' great-grandparents honeymooned in East Boothbay, Maine. This established a family tradition, and each summer for generations the artist's family returned to the small coast town.

Ms. Williams was born in northern New Jersey, and went to Moore College of Fine Arts in Philadelphia where she studied illustration. Early in the 1970's, she moved to the Boothbay area permanently. Here she met Frances Hook, who was to have a profound influence on her art. The kinship between the two artists was so strong that Ms. Williams became Mrs. Hook's protege. Under Mrs. Hook's direction, her technique was refined and matured. Through Mrs. Hook, she also obtained

valuable illustration and portrait commissions which enabled her to exhibit her talent.

Mrs. Hook also introduced her protege to Roman, Inc. Currently, Ms. Williams is creating a new line of collectibles and giftware for Roman.

JACK WOODSON

American artist Jack Woodson is a native of Richmond, Virginia, and he makes his home there—in the heart of Colonial and Civil War Americana. A prolific and versatile artist, Woodson is best known in limited edition circles for his work for United States Historical Society. This includes a series of plates inspired by Buffalo Bill and the Wild West, a 1983 Christmas plate, a child-subject plate series, and prints inspired by the Battle of Yorktown.

Woodson finds his inspiration in American history—he is equally well versed in the sagas of the west and of the south. He keeps a vast store of costumes and props in his studio so that he can dress models in authentic attire for photography and sketching sessions.

Woodson says he has been greatly influenced by the old masters, but he also has praise and admiration for American illustrators in the Howard Pyle "school" of illustration, and for Norman Rockwell.

The artist has created works for the Smithsonian Institution, National Geographic, the Maritime Museum, and was recently commissioned to create the official paintings for the Presidents Reagan and Mitterrand for the 200th anniversary of the American victory at Yorktown. His works are on display at museums and in private collections throughout the United States and abroad.

HARLAND YOUNG

For years, Harland Young has been recognized as one of the finest Old West and horse artists of our time.

He grew up on a ranch in California, where horses were the family trade. After serving in the armed forces, he received an art education and became an illustrator.

However, for quite some time now he has been devoted to the challenge of capturing the excitement of the West and the fine arts.

Harland's first limited edition plate was the award-winning "Arabian" in 1980. It was part of the *Great Achievements in Art* series. His *Adventures of the Old West* series, which contained "Grizzly Ambush" and the "Train Robbers," was equally well received.

In 1982 he opened his second series, *The Horses of Harland Young,* with his "Quarterhorses" plate. Young works with Kern Collectibles as marketer for his limited edition items.

REN YU

Ren Yu is a master floral artist in China. A student of classical Chinese painting, including the floral artists of the Sung dynasty, she depicts each flower exactly as it would appear in a Chinese garden.

Her medium is a fine, pointed brush and rainbow colors of ink. By this means she captures the likeness of each blossom she paints—as she puts it—both "in shape and spirit." Her first plate collection is called *The Blossoms of China,* and it was created for The Fleetwood Collection.

DONALD ZOLAN

Donald Zolan is a native of Chicago and a fifth-generation artist in a family of multi-talented individuals. At age 9, Zolan painted his first oil, and at 10 he was awarded a scholarship to the Art Institute of Chicago. He also earned a scholarship to the American Academy of Art in Chicago, where he met William Mosby, an instructor who taught him the skill of "seeing."

Zolan worked as a photo editor of *Playboy* before becoming a full-time artist. Because of his extensive research and meticulous attention to detail, Zolan is in great demand as a portrait artist.

His works hang in numerous galleries and corporate headquarters in the United States, and in private collections in Australia, Colombia, France, Italy, Mexico, and South Korea.

Zolan's first limited edition plate, "Erik and Dandelion," was issued in 1978 for Pemberton & Oakes. It was followed by "Sabina in the Grass." These plates featured Zolan's son and daughter, and brought him an entirely new audience.

His first series of plates, *Zolan's Children,* earned him major recognition in the limited edition field for his sensitive portrayal of children. It is his philosophy that life is good, and joy is all around us—and that is what is appealing to collectors.

Zolan's art is also available in the form of limited edition graphics through Graphics Buying Service of Chicago.

RICHARD ZOLAN

The paintings of Richard Zolan—tender and warm—are said to come from the heart. A native of the Chicago area, and a descendant of a long line of artists, Zolan graduated from the American Academy of Art in Chicago and attended the Art Students League in New York. He studied with William Mosby and Boris Anisfelt.

Strongly influenced by the Old Masters' technique of layered painting, Zolan spent two years in Europe perfecting his style and touring museums. Today his works have been exhibited throughout the United States.

His painting, "Cora's Recital," became an award-winning limited edition plate. It was selected as one of three to receive an award from a field of 5,000.

Zolan's first gallery was in Nantucket, and today his gallery is in Palm Desert, California. His limited edition collector plates and lithographs are distributed via the American Artists division of Graphics Buying Service. Zolan also is the author of a book on painting children in oils.

BORIS ZVORYKIN

Boris Zvorykin was born in Russia in 1872. As a young artist in his native land, he was engaged to paint the murals in the Cathedral of Simferopol. After a triumphant success at this endeavor, he won commission after commission from the Russian Imperial Court. Known as a master of color and form, Zvorykin's work is characterized by vibrancy and intricate detail.

Along with fine art greats including Chagall, Kandinksy, Stravinsky and others, Zvorykin fled Russia at the time of the Revolution. He established a studio in Paris, and soon was immersed in a new subject matter: ballet classics such as "The Snow Maiden" and "The Firebird." These beloved Russian fairy tales now were celebrated as popular ballets, and Zvorykin's artwork won a large and enthusiastic audience.

Unfortunately, Zvorykin's great talent has been nearly forgotten in recent years, but a book of his illustrations for Russian fairy tales—edited by Jacqueline Kennedy Onassis—rekindled interest on both sides of the Atlantic in 1979.

The Heinrich Studios of Villeroy & Boch introduced a 12-plate collection called *Russian Fairy Tales* in 1980.

Books, magazines and newsletters for collectors

Whether your special area of interest is plates, figurines, bells, graphics, dolls or steins—or some combination of these collecting media—you'll find a great deal of material available to you in collectibles books and periodicals. The books listed here are some of the most prominent in the limited edition collectibles field—there are many more available. To find more books in your area of interest, check *"Books in Print"* by subject at your local library, or contact a book seller that specializes in limited editions such as Lamplighter Books of Leon, Iowa 50144, or Collector Books, P.O. Box 3009, Paducah, Kentucky 42001.

The Bradford Book of Collector's Plates, edited by the staff of The Bradford Exchange, Ltd., Niles Chicago, Illinois 60648.

Collectibles: A Compendium by Marian Klamkin. Published by Dolphin Books, Doubleday & Company Inc., Garden City, New York.

Collector Plates: The Official Price Guide edited by Thomas Hudgeons, III. Published by The House of Collectibles, Inc., Orlando, Florida 32809.

Collector Prints: The Official Price Guide by Ruth M. Pollard. Published by The House of Collectibles, Inc., Orlando, Florida 32809.

Collector's Guide to Limited Edition Collecting, edited by Frances Knight. Published by Collector's Media, Inc., 100 N. Edward Gary, P.O. Box 1729, San Marcos, Texas 78667

Developing Your Doll Collection by Loretta Holz. Available from Doll Classics, Acquire Publishing Company, Inc., 170 Fifth Avenue, New York, New York 10010.

The Encyclopedia of Collectibles. Published by Time-Life Books, Time & Life Building, Chicago, Illinois 60611.

Figurine Collecting Guide by Linda Ellis Fishbeck. Published by Collector's Media, Inc., 100 N. Edward Gary, P.O. Box 1729, San Marcos, Texas 78667.

The Greenbook compiled by Arch Patterson. Published by Greenbook Society of Dealers and Collectors ™, 348 Main Street, East Setauket, New York 11733.

Guidebook of Franklin Mint Issues by Chester L. Krause. Published by Krause Publications, Iola, Wisconsin.

Hummel Figurines and Plates edited by Thomas Hudgeons, III. Published by The House of Collectibles, Inc., Orlando, Florida 32809.

The Kovels' Collector's Guide to Limited Editions by Ralph and Terry Kovel. Published by Crown Publishers, One Park Avenue, New York, New York 10016.

The Kovels' Illustrated Price Guide to Royal Doulton by Ralph and Terry Kovel. Published by Crown Publishers, One Park Avenue, New York, New York 10016.

Norman Rockwell Art and Collectibles by Carl F. Lucky. Published by Books Americana Inc., Florence, Alabama 35630.

Norman Rockwell Collectibles Value Guide by Mary Moline. Published by Rumblescat Press, Inc., San Francisco, California 94123.

The No. 1 Price Guide to M.I. Hummel® by Robert L. Miller. Published by Portfolio Press, Huntington, New York 11743.

Plate Collecting by Eleanor Clark. Published by Citadel Press, Secaucus, New Jersey 07094.

Price Guide to Twentieth Century Dolls Series by Carol Gast Glassmire. Published by Wallace-Homestead Book Company, 1912 Grand Avenue, Des Moines, Iowa 50305.

Wallace-Homestead Price Guide to Dolls by Robert W. Miller. Published by Wallace-Homestead Book Company, 1912 Grand Avenue, Des Moines, Iowa 50305.

Wonderful World of Plates by Louise Schaub Witt. Published by K&L Publications, Box 38, Shawnee Mission, Kansas 66201.

Magazines and newsletters about limited edition collectibles

The following are independent publications about the limited editions field. Many firms also publish newsletters and magazines which they provide free or at nominal cost to their collectors or preferred customers. For subscription information on these publications, write them directly.

THE ANTIQUE TRADER
P.O. Box 1050
Dubuque, Iowa 52001
(319) 588-2073

COLLECTIBLES ILLUSTRATED
Yankee Publishing Inc.
Dublin, New Hampshire 03444
(613) 563-8111

COLLECTOR EDITIONS
170 Fifth Avenue
New York, New York 10010
(212) 989-8700

COLLECTORS MART
15100 West Kellogg
Wichita, Kansas 67235
(316) 722-9650

COLLECTORS NEWS
P.O. Box 156
Grundy Center, Iowa 50638
(319) 824-5456

COLLECTORS' SHOWCASE
P.O. Box 6929
San Diego, California 92106

THE DOLL INVESTMENT NEWSLETTER
P.O. Box 1982
Centerville, Massachusetts 02632

DOLLS MAGAZINE
170 Fifth Avenue
New York, New York 10010

THE DOLL READER
4701 Queensbury Road
Riverdale, Maryland 29840

DOLL NEWS
732 W. Lakeshore Drive
Lincoln, Nebraska 68528

HOBBIES
1006 S. Michigan
Chicago, Illinois

KOVELS ON ANTIQUES AND COLLECTIBLES
P.O. Box 22200
Beachwood, Ohio 44122

PLATE COLLECTOR
100 N. Edward Gary, P.O. Box 1729
San Marcos, Texas 78667
(512) 396-1888

PLATE WORLD
6054 West Touhy Avenue
Chicago, Illinois 60648
(312) 763-7773

RARITIES
17337 Ventura Boulevard
Encino, California 91316
(213) 788-7080

ROCKWELL SOCIETY NEWS
P.O. Box BE
Stony Brook, New York 11790

SPINNING WHEEL
Hanover, Pennsylvania 17331

Glossary

Here you'll find some of the many terms and "buzz words" used by collectors and dealers to describe limited edition collectibles. This list is not all-inclusive, but it will provide a good starting point for approaching the collectibles field. And when a term that you don't understand is used, chances are you can find it here. If not, write the COLLECTORS' INFORMATION BUREAU and we'll do our best to define the term for you—and add it to next year's list!

ABBREVIATIONS

FE—First edition
FI—First issue
LE—Limited edition
M.I.B.—In mint condition, and in original box
MIN—Miniature
NR—Norman Rockwell
VAL—Valentine's Day
X—Xmas, or Christmas

GLOSSARY

ALABASTER. A compact, fine-textured gypsum which is usually white and translucent. Some collector plates are made of a material called *ivory* alabaster, which is not translucent, but has the look and patina of old ivory.

ALLOTMENT. The number within a limited edition which a manufacturer allows to a given dealer, direct marketer or collector.

ANNUAL. The term commonly used to describe a plate or other limited edition which is issued yearly, i.e. the Goebel Hummel *annual* plate. Many annual plates commemorate holidays or anniversaries, but they are commonly named by that special date, i.e. the Bing & Grondahl *Christmas* plate, issued annually to commemorate Christmas.

ARTIST PROOF. Originally, the first few in an edition of lithographs or prints created for the artist's approval. Now, many editions contain a small number of prints which are marked A/P instead of numbering—basically as a means of increasing the number in the edition.

BABY DOLL. A doll with the proportions of a baby, with lips parted to take a nipple, and chubby, short-limbed body.

BACKSTAMP. The information on the back of a plate or other limited edition, which serves to document it as part of its limited edition. This information may be hand-painted onto the plate, or it may be incised, or applied by means of a transfer (decal). Typical information which may appear on the backstamp includes the name of the series, name of the item, year of issue, some information about the subject, the artist's name and/or signature, the edition limit, the item's number within that edition, initials of firing master or other production supervisor, etc.

BAND. Also known as a rim, as in "24K gold banded, or rimmed." A typical method of finishing or decorating a plate, bell or stein is to band it in gold, platinum or silver. The firing process allows the precious material to adhere to the piece.

BAS-RELIEF. A technique in which the collectible has a raised design. This design may be achieved by pouring liquid material into a mold before firing, or by applying material to the flat surface of a plate, figurine, stein or other "blank" piece.

BAVARIA. A section of Germany known as one of the world's richest sources of kaolin clay—an essential component for fine porcelain production. Bavaria is home to a number of renowned porcelain factories.

BEDROOM DEALER. Slang term for an individual who functions as a small-scale seller of limited edition collectibles, usually from his or her home. Often unable to purchase at wholesale direct from manufacturers, these dealers may buy items at a discount from a larger dealer and then resell at a small profit.

BISQUE OR BISCUIT. A fired ware which has neither a glaze nor enamel applied to it. Bisque may be white or colored. It gets its name from its biscuit-like, matte texture.

BLUE CHIP. Slang for a well-established series that some believe represents a safe and sound collectibles investment. An interesting play on words in that many of the plate series that fall into this category are Copenhagen or Cobalt blue.

BODY. The basic form of a plate, figurine, bell or other item, or its component materials.

BONE ASH. By means of heat, animal bones are reduced to powder as an ingredient for bone china or porcelain. The name of the resulting powder is calcium phosphate, or bone ash.

BONE CHINA/BONE PORCELAIN. Bone porcelain is similar to hard porcelain in its ingredients, except that calcined bone ash comprises a large percentage of the mix and is the primary contributor to the vitrification and translucency. Bone clay is more malleable than hard porcelain clay, and it allows for extreme thinness without the sacrifice of strength and durability.

BOTTOMSTAMP. Same idea as the backstamp, but usually refers to documentation material which appears on the bottom of a figurine or stein. On a bell, such information may appear on the inside.

BYE-LO BABY. Grace Storey Putnam copyrighted this life-sized baby (three days old) in 1922. This style of baby doll is much in fashion today among limited edition collectors.

CAMEO. Relief decoration with a flat surface around it, similar to the look of a jeweler's cameo. A technique used by Wedgwood, Incolay and Avondale among others.

CAST. When liquid clay, or slip, is poured into a mold and hardened. Most often used for figurines, bells, and many other forms.

CERAMIC. The generic term for a piece which is made of some form of clay and finished by firing at high temperatures.

CERTIFICATE/CERTIFICATE OF AUTHENTICITY. A document which accompanies a limited edition item to establish its place within the limited edition. Such a certificate may include information such as the series name, item title, artist's name and/or signature, brief description of the item and its subject, signatures of sponsoring and marketing organization representatives, and other documentation material along with the item's individual number or a statement of the edition limit.

CHARACTER DOLLS. Usually made of bisque or composition, these dolls are created to resemble a real person, usually an actor or other celebrity.

CHINA. Originally "china" referred to all wares which came from China. Now this term means products which are fired at a high temperature. China usually is comprised of varying percentages of kaolin clay, feldspar and quartz. Also known as "porcelain."

CHRISTMAS SERIES. Plates, figurines, bells, and other collectible items which are issued to commemorate this yearly holiday, but which normally are sold and displayed all year around.

CINNABAR. A red mineral found in volcanic regions, and a principal ingredient in mercury. This material is frequently used to create collectors' items, and cinnabar-look plates and other collectibles are popular in some circles.

CIRE PERDUE. See lost wax.

CLAY. A general term for the materials used to make ceramic items. Malleable when moist, clay becomes hard and strong when fired. It may be composed of any number of earthen materials.

CLOISONNE. An enameling process in which thin metal strips are soldered in place on a base to create a pattern, and then enamel is poured in to provide the color.

CLOSED-END SERIES. A group of limited edition plates, figurines or other collectibles which comprise a specific number—be it 2, 4, 6, 8, 12 or more. This number normally is disclosed when the series begins.

COBALT BLUE. Also known as Copenhagen blue, this rich color is a favorite of ceramicists because it can withstand high firing temperatures. Cobalt oxide is a black powder when applied, but fires to a deep blue.

COLD CAST. A metal powder and a binder are forced into a mold or die under high pressure, and thus a forging process occurs. Allows for exceptional detail and creates pieces which take well to hand-painting.

COLLECTOR PLATE. A limited edition plate which is created with the expressed intent that it be collected.

COMMEMORATIVE. An item created to mark a special date, holiday or event.

DEALER. The individual or store from whom a collector purchases plates, bells, and other items at retail.

DECAL. Also known as a transfer, this is a lithographic or silkscreen rendering of a piece of artwork, which is applied to a ceramic, metal, glass or other material and then fired on to fuse it to the surface.

DELFTWARE. Heavy earthenware with a tin glaze. First developed in Delft, Holland in the 16th century.

DISTRIBUTOR. A person in the collectibles market who buys from a manufacturer and sells to dealers, who in turn sell to individual collectors.

EARTHENWARE. A non-vitrified ceramic, composed of ball clay, kaolin, and pegmatite. Most often glazed and fired.

EDITION. The term which refers to the number of items created with the same name and decoration.

FAIENÇE. Named after an Italian town called Faenza, faience is similar to Delftware in that it is a tin-glazed earthenware. Also similar to Majolica.

FELDSPAR. When decomposed, this mineral becomes kaolin, which is the essential ingredient in china and porcelain. When left in its undecomposed form, feldspar adds hardness to a ware.

FIRE. To heat, and thus harden, a ceramic ware in a kiln.

FIRING PERIOD. A time limit—usually 10 to 100 days—which serves to limit an edition, usually of plates. The number of items made is limited to the capacity of the manufacturer over that 10-to-100-day period.

FIRST ISSUE. The premiere item in a series, whether closed-ended or open-ended.

GLAZE. The liquid material which is applied to a ware to serve various purposes: cosmetically, it provides shine and decorative value. It also makes the item more durable. Decorations may be applied before or after glaze is applied.

GRAPHICS, PRINTS, LITHOGRAPHS. See article by Diana Gordon Viktor in this book.

HALLMARK. The mark or logo of the manufacturer of an item.

HARD PASTE PORCELAIN. The hardest porcelain made, this material uses feldspar to enhance vitrification and translucency, and is fired at about 3000 degrees farenheit.

INCISED. Writing or design which is cut into the piece—may provide a backstamp or a decorative purpose.

INCOLAY STONE. A man-made material combining minerals including carnelian and crystal quartz. Used to make cameo-style plates by Incolay Studios.

INLAY. To fill an etched or incised design with another material such as enamel, metal or jewels.

ISSUE. As a verb, to introduce. As a noun, this term means an item within a series or edition.

ISSUE PRICE. The original price upon introduction of a limited edition, established by its manufacturer or principle marketer.

JASPER WARE. Josiah Wedgwood's unglazed stoneware material, first introduced in the 1770's. Although Jasper is white in its original form, it can be stained throughout in various colors. Wedgwood typically offers Jasper in the medium blue called "Wedgwood Blue," as well as a darker blue, black, green, lilac, pink, yellow, tan and maroon. Colored Wedgwood "bodies" often are decorated with white bas-relief, or vice-versa.

KAOLIN. The essential ingredient in china and porcelain, this special clay is found in quantity at several spots throughout the world—and it is there that many famous porcelain houses have developed. These areas include Bavaria in Germany, and the Limoges region of France.

LEAD CRYSTAL. Lead oxide gives this glass its weight and brilliance, as well as its clear ring. "Full" lead crystal means the glass has at least 24% lead content.

LIMITED EDITION. An item produced only in a certain quantity or only during a certain time period. The typical ways in which collectibles editions are limited include: limited by number; limited by year; limited by specific time period; limited by firing period.

LIMOGES. A town in France which boasts a large deposit of kaolin clay, the essential ingredient in china and porcelain. Home of a number of top porcelain manufacturers.

LITHOGRAPHS, GRAPHICS, PRINTS. See article by Diana Gordon Viktor in this book.

LOST WAX. A wax "positive" is created by a sculptor, and used to create a ceramic "negative" shell. Then the ceramic shell becomes the original mold—basis for working molds used in the creation of an edition. A classic method of creating three-dimensional pieces.

MAJOLICA. Similar to Delftware and Faience, this is a glazed earthenware first made on the Spanish island, Majorca.

MARKET. The buy-sell medium for collectibles.

MARKET PRICE. The current average price at which an item will sell—may be higher or lower than its original issue price.

MARKS OR MARKINGS. The logo or insignia which certifies that an item is made by a particular firm.

MINT CONDITION. A term originally related to the coin collecting hobby, this means that a limited edition item is still in its original, like-new condition, with all accompanying documents.

MOLD. The form which supplies the shape for a plate, figurine, bell, doll, or other item.

OPEN-ENDED SERIES. A collection of plates or other limited editions which appear at intervals, usually annually, with no limit as to the number of years in which they will be produced. As an example, the Bing & Grondahl Christmas series has been produced annually since 1895, with no end in sight.

OVERGLAZE. A decoration which is applied to an item after its original glazing and firing.

PASTE. The raw material of porcelain before shaping and firing.

PEWTER. A material composed of 80% tin and 20% antimony and brass or copper (fine pewter) or lesser amounts of copper and antimony (pewter).

PORCELAIN. Made of kaolin, quartz and feldspar, porcelain is fired at up to 1450 degrees Centigrade. Porcelain is noted for its translucency and its true ring. Also called "china."

POTTERY. Ceramic ware, more specifically that which is earthenware or non-vitrified. Also a term for the manufacturing plant where such objects are made and fired.

PRIMARY MARKET. The buy-sell arrangement whereby individuals purchase collectibles direct from their manufacturer, or through a dealer, at issue price.

PRINTS, GRAPHICS, LITHOGRAPHS. See article by Diana Gordon Viktor in this book.

QUEEN'S WARE. Cream-colored earthenware developed by Josiah Wedgwood, now used as a generic term for similar materials.

QUOTE. The average selling price of a collectible at any given time—may be at issue, or above or below.

RELIEF. A raised design in various levels above a background.

REMARQUE. French term meaning a little sketch in the border of a picture by its artist—normally done in pencil.

SECOND. An item which is not first quality, and should not be included in the limited edition. Normally such items should be destroyed or at least marked on the backstamp or bottomstamp to indicate that they are not first quality.

SECONDARY MARKET. Once the original edition has been sold out, the buying and selling among collectors, through dealers or exchanges, takes place on the "secondary" market.

SERIGRAPH. See article by Diana Gordon Viktor in this book.

TERRA COTTA. A reddish earthenware, or a general term for any fired clay.

TIN GLAZE. The glaze used on Delftware, Faience or Majolica, this material allows for a heavy, white and opaque surface after firing.

TRANSFER. See Decal.

TRANSLUCENCY. Allowing light to shine through a non-transparent object. A positive quality of fine porcelain or china.

TRIPTYCH. A three-panel art piece, often of religious significance.

UNDERGLAZE. A decoration which is applied before the final glazing and firing of a plate or other item. Most often, such a decoration is painted by hand.

VITRIFICATION. At temperatures of 1250 to 1450 degrees Centigrade, the materials of the china body fuse in such a manner that they become compressed after cooling, and all hollow spaces are filled with glassy material of liquefied quartz. Thus the body becomes wholly vitrified.

FRONT COVER: Limited edition collectibles add personality and interest to any decor. Here, a collector displays figurines, plates, and steins.
BACK COVER: This montage of collectibles represents the various categories discussed in this volume. They are, from left front: Reco International's "Little Bo Peep" plate by John McClelland; United States Historical Society's "Benjamin Franklin" doll; Gorham's "The Marriage License" Rockwell figurine; Reco International's "Chimney Sweep" figurine; an M.I. Hummel bell from Goebel Collectors' Club; and one of Villeroy & Boch's "Famous Sea Battles" steins. Left rear is Fred Stone's "One, Two, Three" lithograph for Graphics Buying Service, and the two-plate series, "Hickory and Dickory" by Thaddeus Krumeich for Anna-Perenna (with display case).

Collectors' Information Bureau

PRICE INDEX

To Limited Edition Plates, Figurines, Bells, Graphics, Steins and Dolls

1984

This Index includes several thousand of the most widely-traded limited editions in today's collectibles market. It is based upon interviews with more than a score of the most experienced and well-informed limited edition dealers in the United States, as well as several independent market advisors.

If you should find that a specific, contemporary limited edition plate, figurine, bell, graphic, stein or doll in which you are interested is not included in the Index, write the Collectors' Information Bureau. We will do our best to provide a current quote. The address is: 1860 Lake Drive S. E., East Grand Rapids, MI 49506.

HOW TO USE THIS INDEX

Listings are set up using the following format:

Company	Series	Artist	Edition Limit
Company Name	Series Name	First Initial Last Name	Number or Time Period
Number*	Name	Issue Price	Quote
See Below	Item Name	In U.S. Dollars	Average of Input

Number

Each item in the index has been assigned an individual number for ease of access on computer. Here is how to interpret these numbers: Sample Number: 80-P-HC-5-005

Interpretation:

- 80 = 1980 (year of issue)
- P = Plate (category) – others are F for Figurine, B for Bell, G for Graphic, S for Stein, D for Doll.
- HC = Maker, Hamilton Collection. Each firm is assigned a two-letter code.
- 5 = Series number for Hamilton Collection plates. Each series within a category has a series number, but they are not necessarily chronological.
- 005 = Item number within series 5 of Hamilton Collection plates. Each item has a subsequent number within its series.

Category: Plates

Company	Series	Artist	Edition limit
Number	**Name**	**Issue Price**	**Quote**
American Artists -Modern Masters	The Horses of Fred Stone	F. Stone	9,500
81-P-AA-1-001	Patience	55.00	80.00
82-P-AA-1-002	Arabian Mare & Foal	55.00	55.00
82-P-AA-1-003	Safe & Sound	55.00	55.00
83-P-AA-1-004	Contentment	55.00	55.00
American Artists -Modern Masters	Family Treasures	R. Zolan	18,500
81-P-AA-2-001	Cora's Recital	39.50	45.00
82-P-AA-2-002	Cora's Tea Party	39.50	39.50
83-P-AA-2-003	Cora's Garden Party	39.50	39.50
American Artists -Modern Masters	A Child's Best Friend	R. Zolan	15 Day
82-P-AA-3-001	Christi's Kitty	29.50	29.50
83-P-AA-3-002	Patrick's Puppy	29.50	29.50
American Artists	Mother & Child Cats	P. Hollands-Robinson	19,500
83-P-AA-4-001	Kitty Love	29.50	29.50
American Artists	The Famous Stallions	F. Stone	19,500
83-P-AA-5-001	Black Stallion	49.50	49.50
American Rose Society	All-American Rose		9,800
75-P-AO-1-001	Oregold	39.00	105.00
75-P-AO-1-002	Arizona	39.00	105.00
75-P-AO-1-003	Rose Parade	39.00	105.00
76-P-AO-1-004	Yankee Doodle	39.00	105.00
76-P-AO-1-005	America	39.00	105.00
76-P-AO-1-006	Cathedral	39.00	105.00
76-P-AO-1-007	Seashell	39.00	105.00
77-P-AO-1-008	Double Delight	39.00	95.00
77-P-AO-1-009	Prominent	39.00	95.00
77-P-AO-1-010	First Edition	39.00	95.00
78-P-AO-1-011	Color Magic	39.00	73.00
78-P-AO-1-012	Charisma	39.00	73.00
79-P-AO-1-013	Paradise	39.00	65.00
79-P-AO-1-014	Sundowner	39.00	60.00
79-P-AO-1-015	Friendship	39.00	60.00
80-P-AO-1-016	Love	49.00	55.00
80-P-AO-1-017	Honor	49.00	55.00
80-P-AO-1-018	Cherish	49.00	55.00
81-P-AO-1-019	Bing Crosby	49.00	49.00
81-P-AO-1-020	White Lightnin'	49.00	49.00
81-P-AO-1-021	Marina	49.00	49.00
82-P-AO-1-022	Shreveport	49.00	49.00
82-P-AO-1-023	French Lace	49.00	49.00
82-P-AO-1-024	Brandy	49.00	49.00
82-P-AO-1-025	Mon Chere	49.00	49.00
Anna-Perenna	Carol Burgues	C. Burgues	5,000
78-P-AP-1-001	June Dream	75.00	75.00
79-P-AP-1-002	Summer Day	95.00	95.00
Anna-Perenna	Floral Fantasies	C. Burgues	5,000
78-P-AP-2-001	Empress Gold	110.00	110.00
Anna-Perenna	Dr. Irving Burgues	I. Burgues	5,000
78-P-AP-3-001	Chun Li	110.00	110.00
79-P-AP-3-002	Ming Tao	110.00	110.00
Anna-Perenna	Birds of Fancy	I. Burgues	5,000
78-P-AP-4-001	Firebird	110.00	110.00
Anna-Perenna	Uncle Tad's Cats	T. Krumeich	5,000
79-P-AP-5-001	Oliver's Birthday	75.00	170.00
80-P-AP-5-002	Peaches & Cream	75.00	80.00
81-P-AP-5-003	Princess Aurora	80.00	80.00
81-P-AP-5-004	Walter's Window	85.00	85.00
Anna-Perenna	Triptych Series	Russell-Barrer	5,000
78-P-AP-6-001	Byzantine Triptych	325.00	350.00
80-P-AP-6-002	Jerusalem Triptych	350.00	350.00
Anna-Perenna	Romantic Loves	Russell-Barker	7,500
79-P-AP-7-001	Romeo & Juliet	95.00	130.00
80-P-AP-7-002	Lancelot & Guinevere	95.00	100.00
81-P-AP-7-003	Helen & Paris	95.00	95.00
82-P-AP-7-004	Lovers of the Taj Mahal	95.00	95.00
Anna-Perenna	Capricious Clowns	M. Kane	9,800
81-P-AP=8-001	Clowns & Unicorns	95.00	95.00
81-P-AP=8-002	Masquerade Party	95.00	95.00
Anna-Perenna	Bashful Bunnies	H. Wehrli	15,000
81-P-AP-9-001	Spring's Surprise	62.50	62.50
82-P-AP-9-002	Summer's Sunshine	62.50	62.50
82-P-AP-9-003	Fall's Frolic	62.50	62.50
82-P-AP-9-004	Winter's Wonder	62.50	62.50
Anna-Perenna	American Silhouettes Collection I-The Children	P. Moss	5,000
81-P-AP-10-001	Fiddlers Two	75.00	75.00
82-P-AP-10-002	Mary with the Lambs	75.00	75.00
Anna-Perenna	American Silhouettes Collection II-The Family	P. Moss	5,000
82-P-AP-11-001	Family Outing	75.00	75.00
83-P-AP-11-002	John & Mary	75.00	75.00
Anna-Perenna	American Silhouettes Collection III-Valley Life	P. Moss	5,000
82-P-AP-12-001	Frosty Frolic	75.00	75.00
82-P-AP-12-002	Hayride	75.00	75.00
Anna-Perenna	Uncle Tad's Holiday Cats	T. Krumeich	9,800
82-P-AP-13-001	Jingle Bells	75.00	75.00
82-P-AP-13-002	Pollyanna	75.00	75.00
Anna-Perenna	Children of Mother Earth	N. Morriseau	2,500
82-P-AP-14-001	Spring	250.00	250.00
82-P-AP-14-002	Winter	250.00	250.00
82-P-AP-14-003	Autumn	250.00	250.00
82-P-AP-14-004	Summer	250.00	250.00

Company	Series	Artist	Edition limit
Number	**Name**	**Issue Price**	**Quote**
Anna-Perenna	Flowers of Count Bernadotte	Bernadotte	17,800
82-P-AP-15-001	The Iris	75.00	75.00
83-P-AP-15-002	Carnation	75.00	75.00
83-P-AP-15-003	Freesia	75.00	75.00
83-P-AP-15-004	Lily	75.00	75.00
83-P-AP-15-005	Orchid	75.00	75.00
Anna-Perenna	Uncle Tad's Tick Tock Clock	T. Krumeich	5,000
83-P-AP-16-001	Hickory-Dickory w/frame(2 plates)	150.00	150.00
Anna-Perenna	The Happy Village	E. Sommer	5,000
83-P-AP-17-001	Spring-Spring Picnic	55.00	55.00
83-P-AP-17-002	Summer-On the Pond	55.00	55.00
83-P-AP-17-003	Autumn-Harvest Dance	55.00	55.00
83-P-AP-17-004	Winter-Snow Kids	55.00	55.00
Anna-Perenna	Rhythm & Dance	A. Hirschfeld	5,000
83-P-AP-18-001	Ballroom	29.50	29.50
83-P-AP-18-002	Pas De Deux	29.50	29.50
83-P-AP-18-003	Swing	29.50	29.50
83-P-AP-18-004	Strut	29.50	29.50
83-P-AP-18-005	Jazz	29.50	29.50
83-P-AP-18-006	Aerobics	29.50	29.50
83-P-AP-18-007	Cake Walk	29.50	29.50
83-P-AP-18-008	Charleston	29.50	29.50
Anri	Christmas	J. Malfertheiner	10,000
71-P-AN-1-001	St. Jakob in Groden	37.50	110.00
72-P-AN-1-002	Pipers at Alberobello	45.00	140.00
73-P-AN-1-003	Alpine Horn	45.00	490.00
74-P-AN-1-004	Young Man & Girl	50.00	110.00
75-P-AN-1-005	Christmas in Ireland	60.00	90.00
76-P-AN-1-006	Alpine Christmas	65.00	220.00
Anri	Christmas	J. Malfertheiner	6,000
77-P-AN-1-007	Legend of Heiligenblut	65.00	150.00
78-P-AN-1-008	Klockler Singers	80.00	110.00
Anri	Christmas	Undiscl.	6,000
79-P-AN-1-009	Moss Gathers	135.00	135.00
80-P-AN-1-010	Wintry Church-Going	165.00	165.00
81-P-AN-1-011	Santa Claus in Tyrol	165.00	168.00
82-P-AN-1-012	The Star Singers	165.00	165.00
Anri	Ferrandiz Christmas	J. Ferrandiz	Annual
72-P-AN-2-001	Christ in the Manger	30.00	175.00
72-P-AN-2-002	Finishing Cradle Fe	35.00	235.00
73-P-AN-2-003	Christmas	30.00	225.00
73-P-AN-2-004	Shepherd & Sheep	40.00	165.00
74-P-AN-2-005	Holy Night	50.00	135.00
75-P-AN-2-006	Flight into Egypt	60.00	120.00
76-P-AN-2-007	Mary & Joseph	60.00	100.00
Anri	Ferrandiz Christmas	J. Ferrandiz	4,000
77-P-AN-2-008	Girl with Flowers	65.00	100.00
78-P-AN-2-009	Leading the Way	77.50	95.00
79-P-AN-2-010	The Drummer	120.00	120.00
80-P-AN-2-011	Rejoice	150.00	170.00
81-P-AN-2-012	Spreading the Word	150.00	150.00
82-P-AN-2-013	The Sheperd Family	150.00	150.00
Anri	Mother's Day	J. Ferrandiz	Annual
72-P-AN-3-001	Children Play House	35.00	140.00
73-P-AN-3-002	Mother & Child	40.00	120.00
74-P-AN-3-003	Mother Holding child	50.00	130.00
75-P-AN-3-004	Mother & Dove	60.00	110.00
76-P-AN-3-005	Mother & Child	60.00	100.00
77-P-AN-3-006	Girl & Flowers	65.00	115.00
Anri	Mother's Day	J. Ferrandiz	3,000
78-P-AN-3-007	The Beginning	77.50	85.00
79-P-AN-3-008	All Hearts	120.00	120.00
80-P-AN-3-009	Spring Arrivals	150.00	150.00
81-P-AN-3-010	Harmony	150.00	150.00
82-P-AN-3-011	With Love	150.00	150.00
Anri	Mother's Day	J. Ferrandiz	Annual
72-P-AN-4-001	Alpine Mother & Children	35.00	50.00
73-P-AN-4-002	Alpine Mother & Children	45.00	55.00
74-P-AN-4-003	Alpine Mother & Children	50.00	55.00
75-P-AN-4-004	Alpine Stroll	60.00	65.00
76-P-AN-4-005	Knitting	60.00	65.00
Anri	Father's Day		Annual
74-P-AN-5-001	Alpine Father & Children	35.00	85.00
75-P-AN-5-002	Alpine Father & Children	45.00	85.00
76-P-AN-5-003	Sailing	50.00	90.00
77-P-AN-5-004	Cliff Gazing	50.00	90.00
Arabia Annual	Kalevala	R.Vosikkinen	
76-P-AR-1-001	Vaninamoinen's Sowing	30.00	54.00
77-P-AR-1-002	Aino's Fate	30.00	51.00
78-P-AR-1-003	Lemminkainen's Chase	39.00	51.00
79-P-AR-1-004	Kullervo's Revenge	39.50	40.00
80-P-AR-1-005	Vainamoinen's Rescue	45.00	65.00
81-P-AR-1-006	Raija Vosikkinen	49.50	61.00
82-P-AR-1-007	Joukahainen Shods Horse	55.50	56.00
Artist of the World	Holiday	De Grazia	9,500
76-P-AW-1-001	Festival of Lights	45.00	270.00
77-P-AW-1-002	Bell of Hope	45.00	200.00
78-P-AW-1-003	Little Madonna	45.00	240.00
79-P-AW-1-004	The Nativity	50.00	140.00
80-P-AW-1-005	Little Pima Drummer	50.00	120.00
81-P-AW-1-006	A Little Prayer	55.00	135.00
Artists of the World	Holiday	De Grazia (signed)	500
76-P-AW-2-001	Festival of Lights(signed)	100.00	320.00
76-P-AW-2-002	Bell of Hope "	100.00	250.00
76-P-AW-2-003	Little Madonna "	100.00	270.00
76-P-AW-2-004	The Nativity "	100.00	195.00
76-P-AW-2-005	Little Pima Drummer "	100.00	190.00
76-P-AW-2-006	A Little Prayer "	100.00	185.00

Company	Series	Artist	Edition limit
Number	Name	Issue Price	Quote
Artists of the World	Children of the World	De Grazia	5,000
76-P-AW-3-001	Los Ninos	35.00	1800.00
77-P-AW-3-002	White Dove	40.00	235.00
Artists of the World	Children of the World	De Grazia	9,500
78-P-AW-4-001	Flower Girl	45.00	205.00
79-P-AW-4-002	Flower Boy	45.00	190.00
80-P-AW-4-003	Little Cocopah	50.00	150.00
81-P-AW-4-004	Beautiful Burden	50.00	145.00
81-P-AW-4-005	Merry Little Indian	55.00	150.00
Artists of the World	Children of the World	De Grazia (signed)	500
78-P-AW-5-001	Flower Girl (signed)	100.00	255.00
79-P-AW-5-002	Flower Boy "	100.00	245.00
80-P-AW-5-003	Little Cocopah Girl "	100.00	200.00
81-P-AW-5-004	Beautiful Burden "	100.00	195.00
81-P-AW-5-005	Merry Little Indian "	100.00	200.00
Bareuther	Christmas	H. Mueller	10,000
67-P-BA-1-001	Stiftskirche	12.00	115.00
68-P-BA-1-002	Kappl	12.00	38.00
69-P-BA-1-003	Christkindlesmarkt	12.00	25.00
70-P-BA-1-004	Chapel in Oberndorf	12.50	20.00
72-P-BA-1-006	Christmas in Munich	14.50	52.00
73-P-BA-1-007	Christmas Sleigh Ride	15.00	30.00
74-P-BA-1-008	Black Forest Church	19.00	26.00
75-P-BA-1-009	Snowman	21.50	25.00
76-P-BA-1-010	Chapel in the Hills	23.50	30.00
77-P-BA-1-011	Story Time	24.50	30.00
78-P-BA-1-012	Mittenwald	27.50	30.00
79-P-BA-1-013	Winter Day	35.00	32.00
80-P-BA-1-014	Mitten Berg	37.50	37.50
81-P-BA-1-015	Walk in the Forest	39.50	39.50
82-P-BA-1-016	Bad Wimpfen	39.50	39.50
Bareuther	Christmas	From Drawing by L. Ricter	10,000
71-P-BA-1-005	Toys for Sale	12.75	25.00
Bareuther	Danish Church		Annual
68-P-BA-2-001	Roskilde Cathedral Fe	12.00	25.00
69-P-BA-2-002	Ribe Cathedral	12.00	25.00
70-P-BA-2-003	Marmor Kirken	13.00	12.00
71-P-BA-2-004	Ejby Church	13.00	16.00
72-P-BA-2-005	Kalundborg Kirken	13.00	22.00
73-P-BA-2-006	Grundtvig Kirken	15.00	20.00
74-P-BA-2-007	Broager Kirken	15.00	20.00
75-P-BA-2-008	St. Knuds Kirken	20.00	20.00
76-P-BA-2-009	Osterlars Kirken	20.00	22.00
77-P-BA-2-010	Budolfi Kirken	15.95	23.00
78-P-BA-2-011	Haderslav Cathedral	19.95	17.00
79-P-BA-2-012	Holmens Church	15.30	20.00
Beleek	Christmas	Undiscl.	7,500
70-P-BE-1-001	Castle Caldwell	25.00	125.00
71-P-BE-1-002	Celtic Cross	25.00	48.00
72-P-BE-1-003	Flight of the Earls	30.00	52.00
73-P-BE-1-004	Tribute to Yeats	38.50	65.00
74-P-BE-1-005	Devenish Island	45.00	200.00
75-P-BE-1-006	The Celtic Cross	48.00	58.00
76-P-BE-1-007	Dove of Peace	55.00	78.00
77-P-BE-1-008	Wren	55.00	59.00
Beleek	Irish Wildlife Christmas	Undiscl.	Undiscl.
78-P-BE-2-001	A Leaping Salmon	55.00	70.00
79-P-BE-2-002	Hare at Rest	58.50	70.00
80-P-BE-2-003	The Hedgehog	66.50	67.00
81-P-BE-2-004	Red Squirrel	78.00	78.00
82-P-BE-2-005	Irish Seal	78.00	78.00
Berlin Design	Christmas	Undiscl.	4,000
70-P-BD-1-001	Christmas in Bernkastel	14.50	145.00
Berlin Design	Christmas	Undiscl.	20,000
71-P-BD-1-002	Christmas in Rothenburg	14.50	28.00
72-P-BD-1-003	Christmas in Michelstadt	15.00	45.00
73-P-BD-1-004	Christmas in Wendelstein	20.00	45.00
74-P-BD-1-005	Christmas in Bremen	25.00	30.00
75-B-BD-1-006	Christmas in Dortland	30.00	30.00
76-P-BD-1-007	Christmas in Augsburg	32.00	30.00
77-P-BD-1-008	Christmas in Hamburg	32.00	34.00
78-P-BD-1-009	Christmas in Berlin	36.00	38.00
79-P-BD-1-010	Christmas in Greetsiel	47.50	48.00
80-P-BD-1-011	Christmas in Mittenberg	50.00	50.00
81-P-BD-1-012	Christmas Eve in Hahnenklee	55.00	55.00
82-P-BD-1-013	Christmas Eve in Wasserberg	55.00	55.00
Berlin Design	Historical	Undiscl.	Annual
75-P-BD-2-001	Washington Crossing the Delaware	30.00	40.00
76-P-BD-2-002	Tom Thumb	32.00	35.00
77-P-BD-2-003	Zeppelin	32.00	35.00
Berlin Design	Historical	Undiscl.	10,000
78-P-BD-3-001	Benz Motor Car in Munich	36.00	36.00
79-P-BD-3-002	Johannes Gutenberg	47.50	48.00
Bing & Grondahl	Christmas	Hallin	Annual
95-P-BG-1-001	Behind the Frozen Window	.50	4200.00
96-P-BG-1-002	New Moon	.50	1500.00
Bing & Grondahl	Christmas	Hallin	Annual
97-P-BG-1-003	Sparrows	.75	1500.00
Bing & Grondahl	Christmas	Garde	Annual
98-P-BG-1-004	Roses & Star	.75	850.00
99-P-BG-1-005	Crows	.75	1500.00
00-P-BG-1-006	Church Bells	.75	860.00
Bing & Grondahl	Christmas	Sabra	Annual
01-P-BG-1-007	Three Wise men	1.00	450.00
Bing & Grondahl	Christmas	D. Jensen	Annual
02-P-BG-1-008	Gothic Church Interior	1.00	450.00
05-P-BG-1-011	Christmas Night	1.00	165.00

Company	Series	Artist	Edition limit
Number	Name	Issue Price	Quote
06-P-BG-1-012	Sleighing to Church	1.00	123.00
15-P-BG-1-021	Dog Outside Window	1.50	180.00
Bing & Grondahl	Christmas	M. Hyldahl	Annual
03-P-BG-1-009	Expectant Children	1.00	300.00
46-P-BG-1-052	Commemoration Cross	5.00	84.00
47-P-BG-1-053	Dybbol Mill	5.00	105.00
48-P-BG-1-054	Watchman	5.50	90.00
49-P-BG-1-055	Landsoldaten	5.50	99.00
50-P-BG-1-056	Kronborg Castle	5.50	168.00
51-P-BG-1-057	Jens Bang	6.00	120.00
Bing & Grondahl	Christmas	C. Olsen	Annual
04-P-BG-1-010	Frederiksberg Hill	1.00	135.00
Bing & Grondahl	Christmas	E. Plockross	Annual
07-P-BG-1-013	Little Match Girl	1.00	150.00
Bing & Grondahl	Christmas	P. Jorgensen	Annual
08-P-BG-1-014	St. Petri Church	1.00	105.00
Bing & Grondahl	Christmas	Aarestrup	Annual
09-P-BG-1-015	Yule Tree	1.50	120.00
Bing & Grondahl	Christmas	C. Ersgaard	Annual
10-P-BG-1-016	The Old Organist	1.50	180.00
Bing & Grondahl	Christmas	H. Moltke	Annual
11-P-BG-1-017	Angels & Shepherds	1.50	120.00
Bing & Grondahl	Christmas	E. Hansen	Annual
12-P-BG-1-018	Going to Church	1.50	99.00
Bing & Grondahl	Christmas	T. Larsen	Annual
13-P-BG-1-019	Bringing Home the Tree	1.50	109.00
14-P-BG-1-020	Amalienborg Castle	1.50	99.00
Bing & Grondahl	Christmas	J.B. Jorgensen	Annual
16-P-BG-1-022	Sparrows at Christmas	1.50	99.00
Bing & Grondahl	Christmas	A. Friis	Annual
17-P-BG-1-023	Christmas Boat	1.50	99.00
18-P-BG-1-024	Fishing Boat	1.50	99.00
19-P-BG-1-025	Outside the Window	2.00	109.00
20-P-BG-1-026	Hare in the Snow	2.00	99.00
21-P-BG-1-027	Pigeons	2.00	75.00
22-P-BG-1-028	Star of Bethlehem	2.00	120.00
23-P-BG-1-029	The Ermitage	2.00	84.00
24-P-BG-1-030	Lighthouse	2.50	85.00
25-P-BG-1-031	Child's Christmas	2.50	90.00
26-P-BG-1-032	Churchgoers	2.50	84.00
27-P-BG-1-033	Skating Couple	2.50	120.00
28-P-BG-1-034	Eskimos	2.50	84.00
29-P-BG-1-035	Fox Outside Farm	2.50	90.00
31-P-BG-1-037	Christmas Train	2.50	105.00
Bing & Grondahl	Christmas	H. Flugenring	Annual
30-P-BG-1-036	Town Hall Square	2.50	120.00
32-P-BG-1-038	Life Boat	2.50	105.00
33-P-BG-1-039	Korsor-Nyborg Ferry	3.00	84.00
Bing & Grondahl	Christmas	I. Tjerne	Annual
34-P-BG-1-040	Church Bell in Tower	3.00	150.00
38-P-BG-1-044	Lighting the Candles	3.00	150.00
39-P-BG-1-045	Ole Lock-Eye, The Sandman	3.00	197.00
Bing & Grondahl	Christmas	O. Larsen	Annual
35-P-BG-1-041	Lillebelt Bridge	3.00	90.00
36-P-BG-1-042	Royal Guard	3.00	89.00
37-P-BG-1-043	Arrival of Christmas Guests	3.00	105.00
40-P-BG-1-046	Christmas Letters	4.00	197.00
41-P-BG-1-047	Horses Enjoying Meal	4.00	420.00
42-P-Bg-1-048	Danish Farm	4.00	150.00
43-P-BG-1-049	Ribe Cathedral	5.00	210.00
44-P-BG-1-050	Sorgenfri Castle	5.00	138.00
45-P-BG-1-051	The Old Water Mill	5.00	59.00
Bing & Grondahl	Christmas	B. Pramvig	Annual
52-P-BG-1-058	Thorvaldsen Museum	6.00	105.00
54-P-BG-1-060	Snowman	7.50	126.00
Bing & Grondahl	Christmas	K. Bonfils	Annual
53-P-BG-1-059	Royal Boat	7.00	90.00
55-P-BG-1-061	Kalundborg Church	8.00	120.00
56-P-BG-1-062	Christmas in Copenhagen	8.50	168.00
57-P-BG-1-063	Christmas Candles	9.00	168.00
58-P-BG-1-064	Santa Claus	9.50	126.00
59-P-BG-1-065	Christmas Eve	10.00	180.00
60-P-BG-1-066	Village Church	10.00	270.00
61-P-BG-1-067	Winter Harmony	10.50	150.00
62-P-BG-1-068	Winter Night	11.00	90.00
Bing & Grondahl	Christmas	H. Thelander	Annual
63-P-BG-1-069	The Christmas Elf	11.00	180.00
64-P-BG-1-070	The Fir Tree and Hare	11.50	69.00
65-P-BG-1-071	Bringing Home the Tree	12.00	69.00
66-P-BG-1-072	Home For Christmas	12.00	66.00
67-P-BG-1-073	Sharing the Joy	13.00	54.00
68-P-BG-1-074	Christmas in Church	14.00	57.00
69-P-BG-1-075	Arrival of Guests	14.00	30.00
70-P-BG-1-076	Pheasants in Snow	14.50	33.00
71-P-BG-1-077	Christmas at Home	15.00	27.00
72-P-BG-1-078	Country Christmas	19.50	21.00
73-P-BG-1-079	Christmas in Greenland	16.50	36.00
74-P-BG-1-080	Christmas in the Village	22.00	22.50
75-P-BG-1-081	Old Water Mill	27.50	30.00
76-P-BG-1-082	Christmas Welcome	27.50	36.00
77-P-BG-1-083	Copenhagen Christmas	29.50	33.00
78-P-BG-1-084	Christmas Tale	32.00	39.00
79-P-BG-1-085	White Christmas	36.50	45.00
80-P-BG-1-086	Christmas in Woods	42.50	42.50
81-P-BG-1-087	Christmas Peace	49.50	49.50
82-P-BG-1-088	Christmas Tree	54.50	54.50
Bing & Grondahl	Jubilee-5 year cycle		Annual
15-P-BG-2-001	First		210.00
20-P-BG-2-002	Church Bells		120.00
25-P-BG-2-003	Dog Outside Window		210.00
30-P-BG-2-004	The Old Organist		250.00
35-P-BG-2-005	Little Match Girl		1000.00

Company	Series	Artist	Edition limit
Number	Name	Issue Price	Quote
40-P-BG-2-006	Three Wise Men		2000.00
45-P-BG-2-007	Amalienborg Castle		325.00
50-P-BG-2-008	Eskimos		275.00
55-P-BG-2-009	Dybbol Mill		275.00
60-P-BG-2-010	Kronborg Castle	25.00	210.00
65-P-BG-2-011	Churchgoers	25.00	130.00
70-P-BG-2-012	Amalienborg Castle	30.00	35.00
75-P-BG-2-013	Horses Enjoying Meal	40.00	50.00
80-P-BG-2-014	Yule Tree	60.00	60.00
Bing & Grondahl	Mother's Day	H. Thelander	Annual
69-P-BG-3-001	Dog and Puppies	9.75	540.00
70-P-BG-3-002	Bird and Chicks	10.00	45.00
71-P-BG-3-003	Cat and Kitten	11.00	22.00
72-P-BG-3-004	Mare and Foal	12.00	19.00
73-P-BG-3-005	Duck and Ducklings	13.00	22.00
74-P-BG-3-006	Bear and Cubs	16.50	24.00
75-P-BG-3-007	Doe and Fawns	19.50	20.00
76-P-BG-3-008	Swan Family	22.50	25.00
77-P-BG-3-009	Squirrel and Young	23.50	26.00
78-P-BG-3-010	Heron	24.50	25.00
79-P-BG-3-011	Fox and Cubs	27.50	29.00
80-P-BG-3-012	Woodpecker and Young	29.50	30.00
81-P-BG-3-013	Hare and Young	36.50	40.00
82-P-BG-3-014	Lioness and Cubs	39.50	39.50
83-P-BG-3-015	Racoon and Young	39.50	39.50
Boehm	Birds of the World(set)	Boehm	4,319
73-P-BM-1-001	Swallow	50.00	50.00
73-P-BM-1-002	Chaffinch	50.00	50.00
73-P-BM-1-003	Coal Tit	50.00	50.00
73-P-BM-1-004	Tree Swallow	50.00	50.00
73-P-BM-1-005	King Fisher	50.00	50.00
73-P-BM-1-006	Gold Crest	50.00	50.00
73-P-BM-1-007	Blue Tit	50.00	50.00
73-P-BM-1-008	Linnet	50.00	50.00
Boehm	Honor America	Boehm	11,033
74-P-BM-2-001	American Bald Eagle	85.00	85.00
Boehm	Fancy Fowl	Boehm	85
74-P-BM-3-001	Pair	2000.00	2000.00
Boehm	Butterfly	Boehm	100
75-P-BM-4-001	Blue Mountain Swallowtails	450.00	450.00
75-P-BM-4-002	Jezebels	450.00	450.00
76-P-BM-4-003	Comma with Loops	450.00	450.00
76-P-BM-4-004	African Butterflies	450.00	450.00
76-P-BM-4-005	Solandras Maxima	450.00	450.00
Boehm	Hard Fruit	Boehm	100
75-P-BM-5-001	Plums	450.00	450.00
75-P-BM-5-002	Pears	450.00	450.00
75-P-BM-5-003	Peaches	450.00	450.00
75-P-BM-5-004	Apples	450.00	450.00
Boehm	Soft Fruit	Boehm	100
75-P-BM-6-001	Loganberries	450.00	450.00
75-P-BM-6-002	Cherries	450.00	450.00
76-P-BM-6-003	Strawberries	450.00	450.00
76-P-BM-6-004	Grapes	450.00	450.00
Boehm	Oriental Birds	Boehm	100
75-P-BM-7-001	Bluebacked Fairy	400.00	400.00
75-P-BM-7-002	Azure-winged Magpies	400.00	400.00
76-P-BM-7-003	Golden-fronted Leafbird	400.00	400.00
76-P-BM-7-004	Golden-throated Barbet	400.00	
Boehm	Seashell	Boehm	100
75-P-BM-8-001	Violet Spider Conch	450.00	450.00
75-P-BM-8-002	Rooster Tail Conch	450.00	450.00
76-P-BM-8-003	Orange Spider Conch	450.00	450.00
76-P-BM-8-004	Cheraga Spider Conch	450.00	450.00
Boehm	Egyptian Commemorative	Boehm	5,000
78-P-BM-9-001	Tutankhamun	125.00	170.00
Boehm	Egyptian Commemorative	Boehm	225
78-P-BM-10-001	Tutankhamun(handpainted)	975.00	975.00
Boehm	Butterflies of the World	Boehm	5,000
78-P-BM-11-001	Monarch & Daisy	62.00	62.00
78-P-BM-11-002	Red Admiral & Thistle	62.00	62.00
Boehm	Favorite Floral	Boehm	25,000
78-P-BM-12-001	Clematis	58.00	58.00
78-P-BM-12-002	Rhododendron	58.00	58.00
79-P-BM-12-003	Boehm Orchid	58.00	58.00
79-P-BM-12-004	Yellow Rose	58.00	58.00
80-P-BM-12-005	Spider Orchid	58.00	58.00
80-P-BM-12-006	Dahlia	58.00	58.00
Boehm	Judaic Commemorative	Boehm	75
79-P-BM-13-001	Rose (handpainted/handmade)	550.00	550.00
Boehm	Judaic Commemorative	Boehm	1,500
79-P-BM-14-001	Blue	45.00	45.00
Boehm/Hamilton Collection	Award Winning Roses	Boehm	15,000
79-P-BH-1-001	Peace Rose	45.00	85.00
79-P-BH-1-002	White Masterpiece	45.00	55.00
79-P-BH-1-003	Tropicana Rose	45.00	55.00
79-P-BH-1-004	Elegance Rose	45.00	55.00
79-P-BH-1-005	Queen Elizabeth Rose	45.00	55.00
79-P-BH-1-006	Royal Highness Rose	45.00	55.00
79-P-BH-1-007	Angle Face Rose	45.00	55.00
79-P-BH-1-008	Mr. Lincoln Rose	45.00	55.00
Boehm/Hamilton Collection	Hummingbird Collection	Boehm	15,000
80-P-BH-2-001	Calliope	62.50	62.50
80-P-BH-2-002	Broadbilled	62.50	62.50
80-P-BH-2-003	Rufous Flame Bearer	62.50	62.50
80-P-BH-2-004	Broadtail	62.50	62.50
80-P-BH-2-005	Streamertail	62.50	62.50
80-P-BH-2-006	Blue Throated	62.50	62.50
80-P-BH-2-007	Crimson Topaz	62.50	62.50
80-P-BH-2-008	Brazilian Ruby	62.00	62.50
Boehm/Hamilton Collection	Waterbirds	Boehm	15,000
81-P-BH-3-001	Canadian Geese	62.50	62.50
81-P-BH-3-002	Wood Ducks	62.50	62.50
81-P-BH-3-003	Hooded Merganser	62.50	62.50
81-P-BH-3-004	Ross's Geese	62.50	62.50
81-P-BH-3-005	Common Mallard	62.50	62.50
81-P-BH-3-006	Canvas Back	62.50	62.50
81-P-BH-3-007	Green Winged Teal	62.50	62.50
81-P-BH-3-008	American Pintail	62.50	62.50
Boehm/Hamilton Collection	Roses of Excellence	Boehm	Year of Issue
81-P-BH-4-001	Love Rose	62.50	62.50
82-P-BH-4-002	White Lightnin	62.50	62.50
83-P-BH-4-003	Brandy	62.50	62.50
Boehm/Hamilton Collection	Blossoms & Berries	Boehm	15,000
82-P-BH-5-001	Winter Holiday Bouquet	62.50	62.50
82-P-BH-5-002	Thanksgiving	62.50	62.50
82-P-BH-5-003	School Days	62.50	62.50
82-P-BH-5-004	Indian Summer	62.50	62.50
82-P-BH-5-005	Mid-Summer	62.50	62.50
82-P-BH-5-006	Autumn	62.50	62.50
82-P-BH-5-007	Warm Days	62.50	62.50
82-P-BH-5-008	Summer Majesty	62.50	62.50
82-P-BH-5-009	Harvest Time	62.50	62.50
82-P-BH-5-010	Spring Images	62.50	62.50
82-P-BH-5-011	Mid-Winter	62.50	62.50
82-P-BH-5-012	Late-Summer	62.50	62.50
Boehm/Hamilton Collection	Life's Best Wishes	Boehm	15,000
82-P-BH-6-001	Longevity	75.00	75.00
82-P-BH-6-002	Happiness	75.00	75.00
82-P-BH-6-003	Fertility	75.00	75.00
82-P-BH-6-004	Prosperity	75.00	75.00
Boehm/Hamilton Collection	Tribute to the Ballet	Boehm	15,000
82-P-BH-7-001	Nutcracker	62.50	62.50
82-P-BH-7-002	Firebird	62.50	62.50
82-P-BH-7-003	Don Quixote	62.50	62.50
82-P-BH-7-004	La Bayadere	62.50	62.50
82-P-BH-7-005	Coppelia	62.50	62.50
82-P-BH-7-006	Sleeping Beauty	62.50	62.50
Boehm/Hamilton Collection	Award Winnig Miniature Roses	Boehm	28 Day Firing
82-P-BH-8-001	Toy Clown	39.50	39.50
82-P-BH-8-002	Rise N' Shine	39.50	39.50
82-P-BH-8-003	Cuddles	39.50	39.50
82-P-BH-8-004	Puppy Love	39.50	39.50
82-P-BH-8-005	Magic Carousel	39.50	39.50
82-P-BH-8-006	Pacesetter	39.50	39.50
82-P-BH-8-007	Gloriglo	39.50	39.50
82-P-BH-8-008	Beauty Secret	39.50	39.50
Carmel Collection	Joys of Christmas	Walczak	19,500
83-P-CC-3-001	Christmas Delight	39.50	39.50
Carmel Collection	Famous Parades	M. Kent	Annual
83-P-CC-1-001	Thanksgiving Day Parade	39.50	39.50
Carmel Collection	First Performances	E. Maxwell	19,500
83-P-CC-2-001	Darling Diana	39.50	39.50
Crown Parian	Freddie the Freeloader	R. Skelton	10,000
79-P-CP-1-001	Freddie in the Bathtub	55.00	240.00
80-P-CP-1-002	Freddies Shack	55.00	116.00
81-P-CP-1-003	Freddie on the Green	60.00	98.00
82-P-CP-1-004	Love That Freddie	60.00	63.00
D'arceau-Limoges	Lafayette	A. Restieau	-
73-P-DL-1-001	The Secret Contract	14.82	42.00
73-P-DL-1-002	North Island Landing	19.82	50.00
74-P-DL-1-003	City Tavern Meeting	19.82	41.00
74-P-DL-1-004	Battle of Brandywine	19.82	50.00
75-P-DL-1-005	Messages to Franklin	19.82	60.00
75-P-DL-1-006	Siege at Yorktown	19.82	45.00
D'arceau-Limoges	Christmas	A. Restieau	-
75-P-DL-2-001	La Fuite En Egypte	24.32	85.00
76-P-DL-2-002	Dans La Creche	24.32	32.00
77-P-DL-2-003	Refus D'hebergement	24.32	37.00
78-P-DL-2-004	La Purification	26.81	27.00
79-P-DL-2-005	L'adoration Des Rois	26.81	28.00
80-P-DL-2-006	Joyeuse Nouvelle	28.74	29.00
81-P-DL-2-007	Guides Par L'etoile	28.74	40.00
82-P-DL-2-008	The Annunciation	30.74	32.00
Designers Collection	Holly Hobbie Custom Edition	Hobbie	42,000
73-P-DC-1-001	Four Season Plates	17.96	17.96
Designers Collection	Holly Hobbie Comerative Collection-Silver Plate	Hobbie	1,000
73-P-DC-2-001	Love is a Precious Thing	200.00	200.00
Designers Collection	A Mother's Remembrance Collection-Floral Plates		13,200
77-P-DC-3-001	(One Pink Rose)	10.00	10.00
Designers Collection	Christmas Keepsakes Collection	Laessig	12,000
77-P-DC-4-001	Never a Christmas Morning	10.00	10.00
78-P-DC-4-002	All Roads Lead Home at Christmas	15.00	15.00
Designers Collection	A Mothers Remembrance Collection-Floral Plates		15,000
78-P-DC-5-001	(Bouquet of Pink Roses)	10.00	10.00
Designers Collection	Love Collection Holly Hobbie Plates	Hobbie	12,000
79-P-DC-6-001	A Gift of Love	15.00	15.00
80-P-DC-6-002	Happy Hearts 1980	20.00	20.00
Designers Collection	A Mother's Remembrance Collection	Trechslin	15,000
79-P-DC-7-001	(Pink Roses)	15.00	15.00
Designers Collection	Christmas Keepsakes Collection	Powell	12,000

Company	Series	Artist	Edition limit
Number	Name	Issue Price	Quote
79-P-DC-8-001	Love is a Gift for All Seasons	20.00	20.00
80-P-DC-8-002	All Things Bright and Beautiful	20.00	20.00
81-P-DC-8-003	Deck the Holidays with Fun and Laughter	20.00	20.00
Designers Collection	Christmas Keepsakes Collection-Ziggy Plates		6,000
79-P-DC-9-001	Peace on Earth 1979	15.00	15.00
Designers Collection	Bas-Relief Annuals Holly Hobbie Plates	Hobbie	15,000
79-P-DC-10-001	First	25.00	25.00
80-P-DC-10-002	Second	25.00	25.00
81-P-DC-10-003	Third	27.50	27.50
82-P-DC-10-004	Fourth	30.00	30.00
83-P-DC-10-005	Fifth	33.00	33.00
Designers Collection	A Mother's Remembrance Collection	Trechslin	12,000
80-P-DC-11-001	Mother's Loving Heart	20.00	20.00
Designers Collection	Christmas Keepsakes Collection- Ziggy Plates		12,000
80-P-DC-12-001	Christmas is Caring	15.00	15.00
81-P-DC-12-002	Christmas is Love	17.50	17.50
82-P-DC-12-003	(Christmas Tree in Woods)	18.00	18.00
83-P-DC-12-004	Peace on Earth 1983	18.00	18.00
Designers Collection	Spring Love Collection	Powell	6,000
80-P-DC-13-001	Spring Love	15.00	15.00
81-P-DC-13-002	Spring Beauty	15.00	15.00
82-P-DC-13-003	Springtime Miracles	15.00	15.00
Designers Collection	Collector's Edition Holly Hobbie Plates	Hobbie	2,500
81-P-DC-14-001	On the Carousel	45.00	45.00
82-P-DC-14-002	Country Morning	45.00	45.00
83-P-DC-14-003	The Recital	45.00	45.00
Designers Collection	Collector's Edition Fine Arts Plates		2,500
81-P-DC-15-001	Unicorn Magic	45.00	45.00
82-P-DC-15-002	Pegasus	45.00	45.00
Designers Collection	Bas-Relief Annuals	Powell	7,500
81-P-DC-16-001	Simple Pleasures	27.50	27.50
Designers Collection	Love Collection Holly Hobbie Plates	Hobbie	9,000
81-P-DC-17-001	Love Shared	20.00	20.00
Designers Collection	A Mother's Remembrance Collection-Holly Hobbie Plates	Hobbie	12,000
81-P-DC-18-001	A Mother's Gift	20.00	20.00
Designers Collection	Love Collection Holly Hobbie Plates	Hobbie	6,000
82-P-DC-19-001	Special Love	20.00	20.00
83-P-DC-19-002	Happy Hearts 1983	20.00	20.00
Designers Collection	Love Collection Ziggy Plates		6,000
82-P-DC-20-001	Begin With Love	20.00	20.00
83-P-DC-20-002	Wishing You Love	18.00	18.00
Designers Collection	Christmas Keepsakes Collection Holly Hobbie Plates	Hobbie	12,000
82-P-DC-21-001	Holiday Fun	20.00	20.00
83-P-DC-21-002	Christmas Greetings	20.00	20.00
Designers Collection	A Mother's Remembrance Collection-Holly Hobbie Plates	Hobbie	10,000
82-P-DC-22-001	Mother's Miracles	20.00	20.00
83-P-DC-22-002	Mother's Joys	20.00	20.00
Designers Collection	A Mother's Remembrance Collection-Cathy Plate	Cathy	10,000
83-P-DC-23-001	No Other Like Mother	18.00	18.00
Designers Collection	Christmas Keepsakes Collection Cathy Plate	Cathy	10,000
83-P-DC-24-001	Special Delivery	18.00	18.00
Di Volteradici	Grand Opera	G. Ruggeri	Undiscl
76-P-VO-1-001	Rigoletto	35.00	176.00
77-P-VO-1-002	Madama Butterfly	35.00	56.00
78-P-VO-1-003	Carmen	40.00	45.00
79-P-VO-1-004	Aida	40.00	46.00
Di Volteradici	Grand Opera	F. Ingargiola	Undiscl.
80-P-VO-1-005	Barber of Seville	40.00	55.00
81-P-VO-1-006	Tosca	40.00	40.00
82-P-VO-1-007	Pagliacci	40.00	40.00
Fairmont	Famous Clowns	R. Skelton	10,000
76-P-FA-1-001	Freddie the Freeloader	55.00	450.00
77-P-FA-1-002	W. C. Fields	55.00	112.00
78-P-FA-1-003	Happy	55.00	105.00
79-P-FA-1-004	The Pledge	55.00	104.00
Fairmont	Spencer Special	I. Spencer	10,000
78-P-FA-3-001	Hug Me	55.00	95.00
78-P-FA-3-002	Sleep Little Baby	65.00	65.00
Fenton Art Glass	American Craftsman Carnival		600
70-P-FG-1-001	Glassmaker	10.00	55.00
Fenton Art Glass	American Craftsman Carnival		200
70-P-FG-2-001	Glassmaker	10.00	70.00
Fenton Art Glass	American Craftsman Carnival		Annual
70-P-FG-3-001	Glassmaker	10.00	130.00
71-P-FG-3-002	Printer	10.00	40.00
72-P-FG-3-003	Blacksmith	10.00	40.00
73-P-FG-3-004	Shoemaker	12.50	20.00

Company	Series	Artist	Edition limit
Number	Name	Issue Price	Quote
74-P-FG-3-005	Cooper	12.50	20.00
75-P-FG-3-006	Silversmith Revere	12.50	20.00
76-P-FG-3-007	Gunsmith	15.00	15.00
77-P-FG-3-008	Potter	15.00	15.00
78-P-FG-3-009	Wheelwright	15.00	15.00
79-P-FG-3-010	Cabinetmaker	15.00	15.00
80-P-FG-3-011	Tanner	16.50	17.00
81-P-FG-3-012	Housewright	17.50	18.00
Fleetwood Collection	Christmas	F. Wegner	5,000
80-P-FC-1-001	The Magi	45.00	75.00
82-P-FC-1-002	The Shepherds	50.00	50.00
Fleetwood Collection	Mother's Day	D. Balke	5,000
80-P-FC-2-001	Cottontails	45.00	75.00
81-P-FC-2-002	Raccoons	45.00	58.00
82-P-FC-2-003	Whitetail Deer	50.00	50.00
Fleetwood Collection	Royal Wedding	J. Mathews	9,500
81-P-FC-3-001	Prince Charles/Lady Diana	49.50	75.00
Fleetwood Collection	Christmas		7,500
81-P-FC-4-001	The Holy Child	49.50	58.00
Fukagawa	Warabe No Haiku Series	Suetomi	Undiscl.
77-P-FU-1-001	Beneath The Plum Branch	38.00	60.00
78-P-FU-1-002	Child of Straw	42.00	42.00
79-P-FU-1-003	Dragon Dance	42.00	52.00
80-P-FU-1-004	Mask Dancing	42.00	95.00
Goebel	M.I.Hummel Collectibles-Annual Plates	M.I. Hummel	Year of Issue
71-P-GC-1-001	Heavenly Angel 264	25.00	790.00
72-P-GC-1-002	Hear Ye, Hear Ye 265	30.00	00.00
73-P-GC-1-003	Globe Trotter 266	32.50	200.00
74-P-GC-1-004	Goose Girl 267	40.00	112.00
75-P-GC-1-005	Ride into Christmas 268	50.00	75.00
76-P-GC-1-006	Apple Tree Girl 269	50.00	90.00
77-P-GC-1-007	Apple Tree Boy 270	52.50	100.00
78-P-GC-1-008	Happy Pastime 271	65.00	105.00
79-P-GC-1-009	Singing Lesson 272	90.00	90.00
80-P-GC-1-010	School Girl 273	100.00	100.00
81-P-GC-1-011	Umbrella Boy 274	100.00	100.00
82-P-GC-1-012	Umbrella Girl 275	100.00	100.00
83-P-GC-1-013	The Postman	108.00	108.00
Goebel	M.I.Hummel Collectibles- Anniversary Plates	M.I. Hummel	Year of Issue
75-P-GC-2-001	Stormy Weather 280	100.00	225.00
80-P-GC-2-002	Spring Dance 281	225.00	225.00
Gorham	Christmas	N. Rockwell	Annual
74-P-GO-1-001	Tiny Tim	12.50	75.00
75-P-GO-1-002	Good Deeds	17.50	65.00
76-P-GO-1-003	Chrsitmastime	19.50	60.00
77-P-GO-1-004	Yuletide Reckoning	19.50	35.00
78-P-GO-1-005	Planning Christmas Visit	24.50	24.50
79-P-GO-1-006	Santa's Helpers	24.50	24.50
80-P-GO-1-007	Letter to Santa	27.50	27.50
81-P-GO-1-008	Santa Plans His Visit	29.50	29.50
82-P-GO-1-009	Jolly Coachman	29.50	29.50
83-P-GO-1-010	Christmas Dancers	29.50	29.50
Gorham	A Boy And His Dog Four Season Plates	N. Rockwell	Annual
71-P-GO-2-001	Boy Meets His Dog	50.00(set)	475.00
71-P-GO-2-002	Adventurers Between Adventures		
71-P-GO-2-003	The Mysterious Malady		
71-P-GO-2-004	Pride of Parenthood		
Gorham	Young Love Four Seasons Plates	N. Rockwell	Annual
72-P-GO-3-001	Downhill Daring	60.00(set)	200.00
72-P-GO-3-002	Beguiling Buttercup		
72-P-GO-3-003	Flying High		
72-P-GO-3-004	A Scholarly Pace		
Gorham	Four Ages of Love	N. Rockwell	Annual
73-P-GO-4-001	Gaily Sharing Vintage Time	60.00(set)	340.00
73-P-GO-4-002	Flowers in Tender Bloom		
73-P-GO-4-003	Sweet Song So Young		
73-P-GO-4-004	Fondly We Do Remember		
Gorham	Grandpa and Me Four Seasons Plates	N. Rockwell	Annual
74-P-GO-5-001	Gay Blades	60.00(set)	170.00
74-P-GO-5-002	Day Dreamers		
74-P-GO-5-003	Goin' Fishing		
74-P-GO-5-004	Pensive Pals		
Gorham	Me & My Pals Four Seasons Plates	N. Rockwell	Annual
75-P-GO-6-001	A Lickin' Good Bath	70.00(set)	190.00
75-P-GO-6-002	Young Man's Fancy		
75-P-GO-6-003	Fisherman's Paradise		
75-P-GO-6-004	Disastrous Daring		
Gorham	Grand Pals Four Seasons Plates	N. Rockwell	Annual
76-P-GO-7-001	Snow Sculpturing	70.00(set)	210.00
76-P-GO-7-002	Soaring Spirits		
76-P-GO-7-003	Fish Finders		
76-P-GO-7-004	Ghostly Gourds		
Gorham	Going on Sixteen Four Seasons Plates	N. Rockwell	Annual
77-P-GO-8-001	Chilling Chore	75.00(set)	200.00
77-P-GO-8-002	Sweet Serenade		
77-P-GO-8-003	Shear Agony		
77-p-Go-8-004	Pilgrimage		
Gorham	Tender Years Four Seasons Plates	N. Rockwell	Annual
78-P-GO-9-001	New Year Look	100.00(set)	115.00
78-P-GO-9-002	Spring Tonic		

Company / Number	Series / Name	Artist / Issue Price	Edition limit / Quote
78-P-GO-9-003	Cool Aid		
78-P-GO-9-004	Chilly Reception		
Gorham	A Helping Hand Four Seasons Plates	N.Rockwell	Annual
79-P-GO-10-001	Year End Count	100.00(set)	125.00
79-P-GO-10-002	Closed for Business		
79-P-GO-10-003	Swatter's Rights		
79-P-GO-10-004	Coal Season's Coming		
Gorham	Dad's Boys Four Seasons Plates	N. Rockwell	Annual
80-P-GO-11-001	Ski Skills	135.00(set)	160.00
80-P-GO-11-002	In His Spirits		
80-P-GO-11-003	Trout Dinner		
80-P-GO-11-004	Careful Aim		
Gorham	Old Timers Four Seasons Plates	N. Rockwell	Annual
81-P-GO-12-001	Canine Solo	100.00	100.00
81-P-GO-12-002	Sweet Surprise		
81-P-GO-12-003	Lazy Days		
81-P-GO-12-004	Fancy Footwork		
Gorham	Life With Father Four Seasons Plates	N. Rockwell	Annual
82-P-GO-13-001	Big Decision	100.00(set)	100.00
82-P-GO-13-002	Blasting Out		
82-P-GO-13-003	Cheering The Champs		
82-P-GO-13-004	A Tough One		
Gorham	Old Buddies Four Seasons Plates	N. Rockwell	Annual
83-P-GO-14-001	Shared Success	115.00(set)	115.00
83-P-GO-14-002	Endless Debate		
83-P-Go-14-003	Hasty Retreat		
83-P-GO-14-004	Final Speech		
Gorham	Bas Relief	N. Rockwell	
81-P-GO-15-001	Sweet Song So Young	100.00	100.00
81-P-GO-15-002	Beguiling Buttercup	62.50	62.50
82-P-GO-15-003	Flowers in Tender Bloom	100.00	100.00
82-P-GO-15-004	Flying High	62.50	62.50
Gorham		N. Rockwell	Annual
74-P-GO-16-001	Weighing In	12.50	50.00
Gorham		N. Rockwell	Annual
74-P-GO-17-001	The Golden Rule	12.50	30.00
Gorham		N. Rockwell	Annual
75-P-GO-18-001	Ben Franklin	19.50	40.00
Gorham	Boy Scout Plates	N. Rockwell	18,500
75-P-GO-19-001	Our Heritage	19.50	60.00
76-P-GO-19-002	A Scout is Loyal	19.50	55.00
77-P-GO-19-003	The Scoutmaster	19.50	60.00
77-P-GO-19-004	A Good Sign	19.50	35.00
78-P-GO-19-005	Pointing the Way	19.50	19.50
78-P-GO-19-006	Campfire Story	19.50	19.50
80-P-GO-19-007	Beyond the Easel	45.00	45.00
Gorham		N. Rockwell	Numbered
76-P-GO-20-001	The Marriage License	37.50	37.50
Gorham	Presidential	N. Rockwell	9,800
76-P-GO-21-001	John F. Kennedy	30.00	55.00
76-P-GO-21-002	Dwight D. Eisenhower	30.00	35.00
Gorham		N. Rockwell	Annual
78-P-GO-22-001	Triple Self Portrait Memorial Plate	37.50	50.00
Gorham	Four Seasons Landscapes	N. Rockwell	Annual
80-P-GO-23-001	Summer Respite	45.00	45.00
81-P-GO-23-002	Autumn Reflection	45.00	45.00
82-P-GO-23-003	Winter Delight	50.00	50.00
Gorham		N. Rockwell	Numbered
80-P-GO-24-001	The Annual Visit	32.50	32.50
Gorham		N.Rockwell	Annual
81-P-GO-25-001	Day in Life of Boy	50.00	50.00
81-P-GO-25-002	Day in Life of Girl	50.00	50.00
Gorham	GAllery of Masters	Rembrandt	10,000
71-P-GO-26-001	Man wit a Gilt Helmet	50.00	50.00
72-P-GO-26-002	Self Portrait wit Saskia	50.00	50.00
Gorham	Gallery of Masters	Gainsborough	7,500
73-P-GO-26-003	The Honorable Mrs. Graham	50.00	50.00
Gorham	Barrymore	Barrymore	15,000
71-P-GO-27-001	Quiet Waters	25.00	25.00
72-P-GO-27-002	San Pedro Harbor	25.00	25.00
Gorham	Barrymore	Barrymore	1,000
72-P-GO-28-001	Nantucket(sterling)	100.00	140.00
72-P-GO-28-002	Little Boatyard(sterling)	100.00	145.00
Gorham	Pewter Bicentennial	N. Rockwell	5,000
71-P-GO-29-001	Burning of the Gaspee	35.00	35.00
72-P-GO-29-002	Boston Tea Party	35.00	35.00
Gorham	Vermeil Bicentennial	N. Rockwell	250
72-P-GO-30-001	1776 Plate	750.00	800.00
Gorham	Silver Bicentennial	N. Rockwell	750
72-P-GO-31-001	1776 Plate	500.00	500.00
72-P-GO-31-002	Burning of the Gaspee	500.00	500.00
73-P-GO-31-003	Boston Tea Party	550.00	575.00
Gorham	China Bicentennial	N. Rockwell	18,500
72-P-GO-32-001	1776 Plate	17.50	35.00
Gorham	China Bicentennial	N. Rockwell	8,000
76-P-GO-32-002	1776 Bicentennial	17.50	35.00
Gorham	Frederick Remington	F.Remington	Annual
73-P-GO-33-001	A New Year on the Cimarron	25.00	35.00
73-P-GO-33-002	Aiding a Comrade	25.00	30.00
73-P-GO-33-003	The Flight	25.00	30.00
73-P-GO-33-004	The Flight For the Water Hole	25.00	30.00
75-P-GO-33-005	Old Ramond	20.00	35.00
75-P-GO-33-006	A Breed	20.00	35.00

Company / Number	Series / Name	Artist / Issue Price	Edition limit / Quote
Gorham	Frederick Remington	F.Remington	5,000
76-P-GO-33-007	Cavalry Officer	37.50	40.00
76-P-GO-33-008	A Trapper	37.50	40.00
Gorham	Moppet Plates		Annual
73-P-GO-34-001	M. Plate(Christmas)	10.00	35.00
74-P-GO-34-002	M. Plate "	12.00	22.00
75-P-GO-34-003	M. Plate "	13.00	15.00
76-P-GO-34-004	M. Plate "	13.00	15.00
77-P-GO-34-005	M. Plate "	13.00	14.00
78-P-GO-34-006	M. Plate "	10.00	10.00
79-P-GO-34-007	M. Plate "	12.00	12.00
80-P-GO-34-008	M. Plate "	12.00	12.00
81-P-GO-34-009	M. Plate "	12.00	12.00
82-P-GO-34-010	M. Plate "	12.00	12.00
83-P-GO-34-011	M. Plate "	12.00	12.00
73-P-GO-34-012	M. Plate Mother's Day	10.00	30.00
74-P-GO-34-013	M. Plate " "	12.00	20.00
75-P-GO-34-014	M. Plate " "	13.00	15.00
76-P-GO-34-015	M. Plate " "	13.00	15.00
77-P-GO-34-016	M. PLate " "	13.00	15.00
78-P-GO-34-017	M. Plate " "	10.00	10.00
Gorham	Moppet Plates		20,000
76-P-GO-001	M. Plate-Anniversary	13.00	13.00
Gorham	Julien Ritter, Fall In Love	J. Ritter	5,000 Sets
77-P-GO-36-001	Enchantment	100.00(set)	100.00
77-P-GO-36-002	Frolic		
77-P-GO-36-003	Gusty Gal		
77-P-GO-36-004	Loney Chill		
Gorham	Julien Ritter	J. Ritter	9,800
77-P-GO-37-001	Christmas Visit	24.50	29.00
Gorham	Julien Ritter To Love A Clown	J. Ritter	5,000 sets
78-P-GO-38-001	Awaited Reunion	120.00(set)	120.00
78-P-GO-38-002	Twosome Time		
78-P-GO-38-003	Showtime Beckons		
78-P-GO-38-004	Together in Memories		
Gorham	Julien Ritter	J. Ritter	7,500
78-P-GO-39-001	Valentine, Fluttering Heart	45.00	45.00
Gorham	Charles Russell	C. Russell	9,800
80-P-GO-40-001	In Without Knocking	38.00	38.00
81-P-GO-40-002	Bronc To Breakfast	38.00	38.00
82-P-GO-40-003	When Ignorance is Bliss	45.00	45.00
83-P-GO-40-004	Cowboy Life	45.00	45.00
Gorham	Christmas/Children's Television Workshop		Annual
81-P-GO-41-001	Sesame Street Christmas	17.50	17.50
82-P-GO-41-002	Sesame Street Christmas	17.50	17.50
83-P-GO-41-003	Sesame Street Christmas	19.50	19.50
Gorham	Bettie Felder	B. Felder	7,500
82-P-GO-42-001	When I Was a Child	42.50	42.50
82-P-GO-42-002	Gather The Children	42.50	42.50
Gorham	John Clymer	J. Clymer	7,500
82-P-GO-43-001	A Fine Welcome	50.00	50.00
83-P-GO-43-002	Winter Trails	50.00	50.00
Gorham/Ghent Collection	American Bicentennial Series	N.Rockwell	10,000
78-P-GN-1-001	April Fool	35.00	60.00
79-P-GN-1-002	April Fool	35.00	35.00
80-P-GN-1-003	April Fool	37.50	38.00
Gorham/Hamilton Collection	The Lewis & Clark Expedition-Trailblazers of the American Northwest Collection	J. Clymer	10 Day Firing
81-P-GA-1-001	Lewis & Clark in the Bitterroots	55.00	55.00
81-P-GA-1-002	Sacajawea At the Big Water	55.00	55.00
81-P-GA-1-003	The Lewis Crossing	55.00	55.00
81-P-GA-1-004	Captain Clark and the Buffalo Gangue	55.00	55.00
82-P-GA-1-005	The Salt Maker	55.00	55.00
82-P-GA-1-006	Up The Jefferson	55.00	55.00
82-P-GA-1-007	Arrival of Sergeant Pryor	55.00	55.00
82-P-GA-1-008	Visitors at Fort Clatsop	55.00	55.00
Ghent Collection	American Bicentennial Wildlife		2,500
76-P-GN-2-001	American Bald Eagle Artist-H. Moeller	95.00	300.00
76-P-GN-2-002	American White-Tailed Deer Artist-E. Bierly	95.00	300.00
76-P-GN-2-003	American Bison Artist- C. Frace	95.00	300.00
76-P-GN-2-004	American Wild Turkey Artist-A. Gilbert	95.00	300.00
Grossman Designs	Tom Sawyer	N. Rockwell	Annual
76-P-GS-1-001	White Washing Fence	25.00	75.00
77-P-GS-1-002	First Smoke	25.00	65.00
77-P-GS-1-003	Take Your Medicine	25.00	50.00
78-P-GS-1 004	Lost in Cave	25.00	50.00
Hackett American Collectors Co.	Endangered Species	S. Mand	7,500
80-P-HA-1-001	California Sea Otters	35.00	75.00
81-P-HA-1-002	Asian Pandas	37.50	38.00
82-P-HA-1-003	Australian Koalas	37.50	38.00
82-P-HA-1-004	River Otters	39.50	40.00
Hackett American Collectors Co.	Playful Memories	S. Etem	10,000
81-P-HA-2-001	Renee	39.50	195.00
82-P-HA-2-002	Jeremy	42.50	120.00
82-P-HA-2-003	Jamie	42.50	43.00
Hamilton Collection	Picasso Series Metal Plates	P. Picasso	5,000
72-P-HC-1-001	Tragedy	125.00	125.00

Company	Series	Artist	Edition limit
Number	**Name**	**Issue Price**	**Quote**
72-P-HC-1-002	Gourmet	125.00	125.00
73-P-HC-1-003	Lovers	125.00	125.00
Hamilton Collection	The Nutcracker Ballet Plate Collection	S. Fisher	28 Day Firing
78-P-HC-2-001	Clara	19.50	125.00
79-P-HC-2-002	Godfather	19.50	65.00
79-P-HC-2-003	Sugar Plum Fairy	19.50	55.00
79-P-HC-2-004	Snow Queen and King	19.50	47.00
80-P-HC-2-005	Waltz of the Flowers	19.50	47.00
80-P-HC-2-006	Clara and the Prince	19.50	47.00
Hamilton Collection	Precious Moments Plate Collection	T. Utz	28 Day Firing
79-P-HC-3-001	Friend in the Sky	21.50	65.00
80-P-HC-3-002	Sand in Her Shoe	21.50	45.00
80-P-HC-3-003	Snow Bunny	21.50	45.00
80-P-HC-3-004	Seashells	21.50	27.00
81-P-HC-3-005	Dawn	21.50	27.00
82-P-HC-3-006	My Kitty	21.50	27.00
Hamilton Collection	Rockwell Copper Christmas Plate Series	N. Rockwell	Year of Issue
78-P-HC-4-001	A Christmas Gift	48.00	48.00
79-P-HC-4-002	The Big Moment	48.00	48.00
80-P-HC-4-003	Santa's Helpers	48.00	48.00
81-P-HC-4-004	Santa	48.00	48.00
Hamilton Collection	Rockwell's "Man's Best Friend" Copper Plate Collection	N. Rockwell	9,500
79-P-HC-5-001	The Hobo	40.00	40.00
79-P-HC-5-002	The Doctor	40.00	40.00
79-P-HC-5-003	Making Friends	40.00	40.00
79-P-HC-5-004	Gone Fishing	40.00	40.00
80-P-HC-5-005	Puppy Love	40.00	40.00
80-P-HC-5-006	The Thief	40.00	40.00
Hamilton Collection	The Greatest Show on Earth Plate Collection	F. Moody	10 Day Firing
81-P-HC-6-001	Clowns	30.00	55.00
81-P-HC-6-002	Elephants	30.00	35.00
81-P-HC-6-003	Aerialists	30.00	30.00
81-P-HC-6-004	Great Parade	30.00	30.00
81-P-HC-6-005	Midway	30.00	30.00
81-P-HC-6-006	Equestrians	30.00	30.00
82-P-HC-6-007	Lion Tamer	30.00	30.00
82-P-HC-6-008	Grande Finale	30.00	30.00
Hamilton Collection	Rockwell Home of the Brave Plate Collection	N. Rockwell	18,000
81-P-HC-7-001	Reminiscing	35.00	45.00
81-P-HC-7-002	Hero's Welcome	35.00	35.00
81-P-HC-7-003	Back to His Old Job	35.00	35.00
81-P-HC-7-004	War Hero	35.00	35.00
82-P-HC-7-005	Willie Gillis in Church	35.00	35.00
82-P-HC-7-006	War Bond	35.00	35.00
82-P-HC-7-007	Uncle Sam Takes Wings	35.00	35.00
82-P-HC-7-008	Taking Mother Over the Top	35.00	35.00
Hamilton Collection	Japanese Floral Calender Plate (Chokin I) Collection	Shuho/Senkin Kage	10 Day Firing
81-P-HC-8-001	New Year's Day	32.50	45.00
82-P-HC-8-002	Early Spring	32.50	32.50
82-P-HC-8-003	Spring	32.50	32.50
82-P-HC-8-004	Girl's Doll Day Festival	32.50	32.50
82-P-HC-8-005	Buddha's Birthday	32.50	32.50
82-P-HC-8-006	Early Summer	32.50	32.50
82-P-HC-8-007	Boy's Doll Day Festival	32.50	32.50
82-P-HC-8-008	Summer	32.50	32.50
82-P-HC-8-009	Autumn	32.50	32.50
83-P-HC-8-010	Fesival of the Full Moon	32.50	32.50
83-P-HC-8-011	Late Autumn	32.50	32.50
83-P-HC-8-012	Winter	32.50	32.50
Hamilton Collection	Treasures of the Chinese Mandarins Collection	From Pieces in Imperial Palace Taiwan	2,500
81-P-HC-9-001	The Bird of Paradise	75.00	105.00
82-P-HC-9-002	The Guardians of Heaven	75.00	75.00
82-P-HC-9-003	The Tree of Immortality	75.00	75.00
82-P-HC-9-004	The Dragon of Eternity	75.00	75.00
Hamilton Collection	Portraits of Childhood Plate Collection	T. Utz	28 Day Firing
81-P-HC-10-001	Butterfly Magic	24.95	39.50
82-P-HC-10-002	Sweet Dreams	24.95	24.95
83-P-HC-10-003	Turtle Talk	24.95	24.95
Hamilton Collection	Carefree Days Plate Collection	Thornton Utz	10 Day Firing
82-P-HC-11-001	Autumn Wanderer	24.50	45.00
82-P-HC-11-002	Best Friends	24.50	35.00
82-P-HC-11-003	Feeding Time	24.50	24.50
82-P-HC-11-004	Bathtime Visitor	24.50	24.50
82-P-HC-11-005	First Catch	24.50	24.50
82-P-HC-11-006	Monkey Business	24.50	24.50
82-P-HC-11-007	Touchdown	24.50	24.50
82-P-HC-11-008	Nature Hunt	24.50	24.50
Haviland	Twelve Days of Christmas	R. Hetreau	30,000
70-P-HA-1-001	Partridge	25.00	215.00
71-P-HA-1-002	Two Turtle Doves	25.00	60.00
72-P-HA-1-003	Three French Hens	27.50	35.00
73-P-HA-1-004	Four Colly Birds	28.50	37.50
74-P-HA-1-005	Five Golden Rings	30.00	37.50
75-P-HA-1-006	Six Geese A'Laying	32.50	31.00
76-P-HA-1-007	Seven Swans	38.00	38.00
77-P-HA-1-008	Eight Maids	40.00	48.00
78-P-HA-1-009	Nine Ladies Dancing	45.00	40.00
79-P-HA-1-010	Ten Lords A'Leaping	50.00	52.50
80-P-HA-1-011	Eleven Pipers Piping	55.00	55.00
81-P-HA-1-012	Twelve Drummers Drumming	60.00	60.00
Haviland & Parlon	Tapestry		10,000
71-P-HD-1-001	Unicorn in Captivity	35.00	200.00
72-P-HD-1-002	Start of the Hunt	35.00	80.00
73-P-HD-1-003	Chase of the Unicorn	35.00	155.00
74-P-HD-1-004	End of the Hunt	37.50	132.00
75-P-HD-1-005	Unicorn Surrounded	40.00	80.00
76-P-HD-1-006	Brought to the Castle	42.50	55.00
Haviland & Parlon	Lady And The Unicorn		20,000
77-P-HD-2-001	To My Only Desire	45.00	72.50
78-P-HD-2-002	Sight	45.00	49.00
79-P-HD-2-003	Sound	47.50	51.00
Haviland & Parlon	Lady And The Unicorn		15,000
80-P-HD-2-004	Touch	52.50	91.00
Haviland & Parlon	Lady And The Unicorn		10,000
81-P-HD-2-005	Scent	59.00	61.00
82-P-HD-2-006	Taste	59.00	59.00
Haviland & Parlon	Christmas Madonnas	Individual	5,000
72-P-HD-3-001	By Raphael	35.00	150.00
73-P-HD-3-002	By Feruzzi	40.00	90.00
74-P-HD-3-003	By Raphael	42.50	75.00
Haviland & Parlon	Christmas Madonnas	Individual	7,500
75-P-HD-3-004	By Murillo	42.50	50.00
76-P-HD-3-005	By Botticelli	45.00	50.00
77-P-HD-3-006	By Bellini	48.00	50.00
78-P-HD-3-007	By Lippi	48.00	55.00
79-P-HD-3-008	By Botticelli	49.50	125.00
Hutschenreuther	Gunther Granget	G. Granget	5,000
72-P-HT-1-001	American Sparrows	50.00	175.00
72-P-HT-1-002	European Sparrows	30.00	70.00
76-P-HT-1-008	Freedom in Flight	100.00	50.00
Hutschenreuther	Gunther Granget	G. Granget	2,500
73-P-HT-1-003	American Kildeer	75.00	100.00
73-P-HT-1-004	American Squirrel	75.00	85.00
73-P-HT-1-005	European Squirrel	35.00	55.00
74-P-HT-1-006	American Partridge	75.00	90.00
75-P-HT-1-007	American Rabbits	90.00	90.00
76-P-HT-1-009	Wrens	100.00	110.00
77-P-HT-1-011	Bears	100.00	100.00
Hutschenreuther	Gunther Granget	G. Granget	200
76-P-HT-1-010	Freedom in Flight(Gold)	200.00	200.00
Hutschenreuther	Gunther Granget	G. Granget	1,000
78-P-HT-1-012	Foxes Spring Journey	125.00	125.00
Incolay	Romantic Poets	G. Appleby	Undiscl.
77-P-IN-1-001	She Walks in Beauty	60.00	270.00
78-P-IN-1-002	A Thing of Beauty	60.00	85.00
79-P-IN-1-003	To A Skylark	65.00	65.00
80-P-IN-1-004	Phantom of Delight	65.00	76.00
Incolay	Romantic Poets	R. Akers	Undiscl.
81-P-IN-1-005	The Kiss	65.00	65.00
Incolay	Romantic Poets		Undiscl.
82-P-IN-1-006	My Heart Leaps UP	70.00	70.00
International	Bicentennial	M. DeOliveira	7,500
72-P-IT-1-001	Signing Declaration	40.00	316.00
73-P-IT-1-002	Paul Revere	40.00	155.00
74-P-IT-1-003	Concord Bridge	40.00	140.00
75-P-IT-1-004	Crossing Delaware	50.00	84.00
76-P-IT-1-005	Valley Forge	50.00	68.00
77-P-IT-1-006	Surrender at Yorktown	50.00	62.00
Knowles	Wizard of Oz	J. Auckland	Undiscl.
77-P-KN-1-001	Over the Rainbow	19.00	225.00
78-P-KN-1-002	If I Only Had A Brain	19.00	45.00
78-P-KN-1-003	If I Only Had A Heart	19.00	50.00
78-P-KN-1-004	If I Were King of the Forest	19.00	34.00
79-P-KN-1-005	Wicked Witch of the West	19.00	32.00
79-P-KN-1-006	Follow The Yellow Brick Road	19.00	50.00
79-P-KN-1-007	Wonderful Wizard of Oz	19.00	25.00
80-P-KN-1-008	The Grand Finale	24.00	24.00
Knowles	Gone With The Wind	R. Kursar	Undiscl.
78-P-KN-2-001	Scarlett	21.50	240.00
79-P-KN-2-002	Ashley	21.50	175.00
80-P-KN-2-003	Melanie	21.50	60.00
81-P-KN-2-004	Rhett	23.50	24.00
82-P-KN-2-005	Mammy Lacing Scarlett	23.50	23.50
83-P-KN-2-006	Melanie Gives Birth	23.50	23.50
Knowles	Csatari Grandparent	J. Csatari	Undiscl.
80-P-KN-3-001	Bedtime Story	18.00	65.00
81-P-KN-3-002	The Skating Lesson	20.00	22.00
82-P-KN-3-003	The Cookie Tasting	20.00	20.00
Konigszelt Bavaria	Hedi Keller Christmas	H. Keller	
79-P-KB-1-001	The Adoration	29.50	130.00
80-P-KB-1-002	Flight Into Egypt	29.50	65.00
81-P-KB-1-003	Return Into Galilee	29.50	30.00
82-P-KB-1-004	Following The Star	29.50	30.00
KPM-Royal Berlin	Christmas		5,000
69-P-KP-1-001	Christmas Star	28.00	380.00
70-P-KP-1-002	Three Kings	28.00	300.00
71-P-KP-1-003	Christmas Tree	28.00	290.00
72-P-KP-1-004	Christmas Angel	31.00	300.00
73-P-KP-1-005	Christ Child on Sled	33.00	280.00
74-P-KP-1-006	Angel & Horn	35.00	180.00
75-P-KP-1-007	Shepherds	40.00	165.00
76-P-KP-1-008	Star of Bethlem	43.00	140.00
77-P-KP-1-009	Mary At Crib	46.00	100.00
78-P-KP-1-010	Three Wise Men	49.00	54.00
79-P-KP-1-011	The Manger	55.00	55.00
80-P-KP-1-012	Shepherds In Fields	55.00	55.00
Lalique	Annual	M. Lalique	2,000
65-P-LA-1-001	Deux Oiseaux	25.00	1600.00
Lalique	Annual	M. Lalique	5,000
66-P-LA-1-002	Dream Rose	25.00	350.00
67-P-LA-1-003	Fish Ballet	25.00	275.00

Company	Series	Artist	Edition limit
Number	**Name**	**Issue Price**	**Quote**
68-P-LA-1-004	Gazelle Fantasie	25.00	130.00
69-P-LA-1-005	Papillon(Buttlerfly)	30.00	120.00
70-P-LA-1-006	Peacock	30.00	110.00
71-P-LA-1-007	Hibou (Owl)	35.00	90.00
72-P-LA-1-008	Coquillage(Shell)	40.00	70.00
73-P-LA-1-009	Jayling	42.50	66.00
74-P-LA-1-010	Silver Pennies	47.50	70.00
75-P-LA-1-011	Fish Duet	50.00	70.00
76-P-LA-1-012	Eagle	60.00	125.00
Lenox	Boehm Birds	E. Boehm	
70-P-LE-1-001	Wood Thrush	35.00	272.00
71-P-LE-1-002	Gold Finch	35.00	100.00
72-P-LE-1-003	Mountain Bluebird	37.50	73.00
73-P-LE-1-004	Meadowlark	50.00	70.00
74-P-LE-1-005	Rufous Hummingbird	45.00	70.00
75-P-LE-1-006	American Redstart	50.00	57.00
76-P-LE-1-007	Cardinals	53.00	58.00
77-P-LE-1-008	Robins	55.00	64.00
78-P-LE-1-009	Mockingbirds	58.00	65.00
79-P-LE-1-010	Golden Crowned Kinglets	65.00	62.00
80-P-LE-1-011	Black-Throated Blue Warblers	80.00	74.00
81-P-LE-1-012	Easterm Phoebes	90.00	95.00
Lihs Lindner	Christmas	J. Neubauer	6,000
72-P-LI-1-001	Little Drummer Boy	25.00	70.00
73-P-LI-1-002	Carolers	25.00	20.00
74-P-LI-1-003	Peace	25.00	32.00
75-P-LI-1-004	Christmas Cheer	30.00	28.00
76-P-LI-1-005	Joy of Christmas	30.00	25.00
77-P-LI-1-006	Holly Jolly Christmas	30.00	25.00
Lihs Lindner	Christmas	J. Neubauer	5,000
78-P-LI-1-007	Holy Night	40.00	37.00
Mingolla/Home Plates	Christmas	Mingolla	1,000
73-P-MI-1-001	Copper, Enamel	95.00	165.00
74-P-MI-1-002	Copper, Enamel	110.00	145.00
75-P-MI-1-003	Copper, Enamel	125.00	145.00
76-P-MI-1-004	Copper, Enamel	125.00	145.00
Mingolla/Home Plates	Christmas	Mingolla	2,000
77-P-MI-1-005	Winter Wonderland (Copper, Enamel)	200.00	200.00
Mingolla/Hone Plates	Christmas	Mingolla	5,000
74-P-MI-2-001	Porcelain	35.00	105.00
75-P-MI-2-002	Porcelain	35.00	45.00
76-P-MI-2-003	Porcelain	35.00	30.00
Norman Rockwell Museum, Inc.	American Family I	N. Rockwell	9,900
79-P-NR-1-001	Baby's First Step	28.50	89.00
79-P-NR-1-002	Happy Berthday, Dear Mother	28.50	55.00
79-P-NR-1-003	Sweet Sixteen	28.50	37.50
79-P-NR-1-004	First Haircut	28.50	35.00
79-P-NR-1-005	First Prom	28.50	35.00
79-P-NR-1-006	Wrapping Christmas Presents	28.50	35.00
79-P-NR-1-007	The Student	28.50	35.00
79-P-NR-1-008	Birthday Party	28.50	35.00
79-P-NR-1-009	Little Mother	28.50	35.00
79-P-NR-1-010	Washing Dog	28.50	35.00
79-P-NR-1-011	Mother's Little Helpers	28.50	35.00
79-P-NR-1-012	Bride and Groom	28.50	35.00
Norman Rockwell Museum, Inc.	Christmas	N. Rockwell	Year of Issue
79-P-NR-2-001	Day After Christmas	75.00	75.00
80-P-NR-2-002	Checking His list	75.00	75.00
81-P-NR-2-003	Ringing In Good Cheer	75.00	75.00
82-P-NR-2-004	Waiting for Santa	75.00	80.00
83-P-NR-2-005	High Hopes	75.00	75.00
Norman Rockwell Museum, Inc.	American Family II	N. Rockwell	22,500
80-P-NR-3-001	New Arrival	35.00	37.50
80-P-NR-3-002	Sweet Dreams	35.00	37.50
80-P-NR-3-003	Little Shaver	35.00	37.50
80-P-NR-3-004	We Missed You Daddy	35.00	37.50
80-P-NR-3-005	Home Run Slugger	35.00	37.50
80-P-NR-3-006	Giving Thanks	35.00	37.50
80-P-NR-3-007	Space Pioneers	35.00	37.50
80-P-NR-3-008	Little Salesman	35.00	37.50
80-P-NR-3-009	Almost Grown Up	35.00	37.50
80-P-NR-3-010	Courageous Hero	35.00	37.50
81-P-NR-3-011	At The Circus	35.00	37.50
81-P-NR-3-012	Good Food, Good Friends	35.00	37.50
Norman Rockwell Museum, Inc.	Classic Plates	N. Rockwell	60 Day Firing
81-P-NR-4-001	Puppy Love	24.50	24.50
81-P-NR-4-002	While The Audience Waits	24.50	24.50
81-P-NR-4-003	Off To School	24.50	24.50
82-P-NR-4-004	Country Doctor	24.50	24.50
82-P-NR-4-005	Spring Fever	24.50	24.50
82-P-NR-4-006	A Dollhouse For Sis	24.50	24.50
Norman Rockwell Museum, Inc.	Mother's Day	N. Rockwell	5,000
82-P-NR-5-001	A Tender Moment	75.00	75.00
Norman Rockwell Museum, Inc.	Celebration	N. Rockwell	9,900
82-P-NR-6-001	Celebration	55.00	55.00
Norman Rockwell Museum, Inc.	World of Children	N. Rockwell	15,000
82-P-NR-7-001	Downhill Racer	45.00	45.00
82-P-NR-7-002	Vacation's Over	45.00	45.00
82-P-NR-7-003	Little Patient	45.00	45.00
82-P-NR-7-004	Bicycle Boys	45.00	45.00
Norman Rockwell Museum, Inc.	Shirley Temple Collectibles Series		22,500
82-P-NR-8-001	Baby Take A Bow	75.00	75.00
83-P-NR-8-002	Curly Top	75.00	75.00

Company	Series	Artist	Edition limit
Number	**Name**	**Issue Price**	**Quote**
83-P-NR-8-003	Stand Up and Cheer	75.00	75.00
Norman Rockwell Museum, Inc.	Shirley Temple Collectibles Series		2,500
82-P-NR-9-001	Baby Take A Bow (autographed)	100.00	125.00
83-P-NR-9-002	Curly Top (autographed)	100.00	100.00
83-P-NR-9-003	Stand Up And Cheer (autographed)	100.00	100.00
Opa's Haus	Annual German Christmas (Weihnachten)		2,500
78-P-OH-1-001	Annual Christmas Plate	65.00	65.00
79-P-OH-1-002	Annual Christmas Plate	65.00	65.00
80-P-OH-1-003	Annual Christmas Plate	65.00	65.00
81-P-OH-1-004	Annual Christmas Plate	65.00	65.00
82-P-OH-1-005	Annual Christmas Plate	65.00	65.00
83-P-OH-1-006	Annual Christmas Plate	65.00	65.00
Pickard	Lockhart Wildlife	J. Lockhart	2,000
70-P-PI-1-001	Woodcock/Ruffled Grouse (pair)	150.00	340.00
71-P-PI-1-002	Teal/Mallard (pair)	150.00	225.00
72-P-PI-1-003	Mockingbird/Cardinal (pair)	162.50	220.00
73-P-PI-1-004	Turkey/Pheasant (pair)	162.50	220.00
74-P-PI-1-005	American Bald Eagle	150.00	630.00
78-P-PI-1-006	American Panther	175.00	195.00
80-P-PI-1-007	Trumpeter Swan	200.00	200.00
Pickard	Lockhart Wildlife	J. Lockhart	2,500
75-P-PI-2-001	White Tailed Deer	100.00	130.00
76-P-PI-2-002	American Buffalo	165.00	195.00
77-P-PI-2-003	Great Horned Owl	100.00	133.00
79-P-PI-2-004	Red Foxes	120.00	124.00
Pickard	Annual Christmas	Raphael	7,500
76-P-PI-3-001	Alba Madonna	60.00	236.00
Pickard	Christmas	L. Lotto	7,500
77-P-PI-3-002	The Nativity	65.00	130.00
Pickard	Christmas	G. David	10,000
78-P-PI-3-003	Rest On Flight Into Egypt	65.00	100.00
Pickard	Christmas	Botticelli	10,000
79-P-PI-3-004	Adoration of the Magi	70.00	68.00
Pickard	Christmas	Sodoma	10,000
80-P-PI-3-005	Madonna and Child	80.00	73.00
Pickard	Christmas	Memling	10,000
81-P-PI-3-006	Madonna and Child	90.00	90.00
Pickard	Children of Renoir	A. Renoir	5,000
78-P-PI-4-001	Girl With Watering Can	50.00	214.00
78-P-PI-4-002	Child in White	50.00	110.00
79-P-PI-4-003	Girl With Hoop	55.00	110.00
79-P-PI-4-004	At The Piano	55.00	118.00
80-P-PI-4-005	Two Little Circus Girls	60.00	90.00
80-P-PI-4-006	Artist's Son Jean	60.00	80.00
Pickard	Mother's Love	Spencer	7,500
80-P-PI-5-001	Miracle	95.00	200.00
81-P-PI-5-002	Story Time	110.00	125.00
82-P-PI-5-003	First Edition	115.00	115.00
Pickard	Children of Mexico	J. Sanchez	5,000
81-P-PI-6-001	Maria	85.00	190.00
81-P-PI-6-002	Miguel	85.00	135.00
82-P-PI-6-003	Regina	90.00	99.00
83-P-PI-6-004	Raphael	90.00	90.00
Porsgrund	Christmas (annual)	G. Bratlie	Undiscl.
68-P-PR-1-001	Church Scene	12.00	194.00
69-P-PR-1-002	Three Kings	12.00	23.00
70-P-PR-1-003	Road To Bethlehem	12.00	14.00
71-P-PR-1-004	A Child Is Born	12.00	19.00
72-P-PR-1-005	Hark The Herald Angels	12.00	24.00
73-P-PR-1-006	Promise of The Savior	12.00	28.00
74-P-PR-1-007	The Shepherds	15.00	43.00
75-P-PR-1-008	Road To Temple	19.50	24.00
76-P-PR-1-009	Jesus And The Elders	22.00	18.00
77-P-PR-1-010	Draught Of The Fish	24.00	18.00
Reco International	The World of Children	J. McClelland	10,000
77-P-RI-1-001	Rainy Day Fun	50.00	225.00
Reco International	The World of Children	J. McClelland	15,000
78-P-RI-1-002	When I Grow Up	50.00	103.00
79-P-RI-1-003	You're Invited	50.00	80.00
80-P-RI-1-004	Kittens For Sale	50.00	65.00
Reco International	Mother Goose	J. Mcclelland	
79-P-RI-2-001	Mary, Mary	22.50	259.00
80-P-RI-2-002	Little Boy Blue	22.50	125.00
81-P-RI-2-003	Little Miss Muffet	24.50	25.00
82-P-RI-2-004	Little Jack Horner	24.50	24.50
83-P-RI-2-005	Little Bo Peep	24.50	24.50
Reco International	Games Children Play	S. Kuck	10,000
79-P-RI-3-001	Me First	45.00	45.00
80-P-RI-3-002	Forever Bubbles	45.00	45.00
81-P-RI-3-003	Skating Pals	45.00	45.00
82-P-RI-3-004	Join me	45.00	45.00
Reco International	Grand Parents	S. Kuck	
81-P-RI-4-001	Grandma's Cookie Jar	37.50	37.50
81-P-RI-4-002	Grandpa And The Doll House	37.50	37.50
Reco International	Little Professionals	S. Kuck	10,000
82-P-RI-5-001	All Is Well	39.50	44.00
83-P-RI-5-002	T.L.C. (Tender Loving Care)	39.50	39.50

Category: Plates

Company Number	Series Name	Artist Issue Price	Edition limit Quote
Reco International	Arabelle and Friends	C. Greunke	15,000
82-P-RI-6-001	Ice Delight	35.00	35.00
83-P-RI-6-002	First Love	35.00	35.00
Reco International	Children's Circus	J. McClelland	
82-P-RI-7-001	Tommy The Clown	29.50	29.50
82-P-RI-7-002	Katie, The Tightrope Walker	29.50	29.50
83-P-RI-7-003	Johnny, The Strongman	29.50	29.50
Reco International Arta Enamel	Christmas		220
73-P-RI-8-001	Nativity	50.00	70.00
Reco International Arta Enamel	Mother's Day		300
73-P-RI-9-001	Family With Puppy	50.00	70.00
Reco International	Bohemia Mother's Day		500
74-P-RI-10-001	1974	130.00	155.00
75-P-RI-10-002	1975	140.00	160.00
76-P-RI-10-003	1976	150.00	160.00
Reco International	Americanna		
72-P-RI-11-001	First Edition Devlin Stuart		325.00
Reco International/ Dresden	Christmas	3,500	
71-P-RI-12-001	Shepherd Scene	15.00	50.00
Reco International/ Dresden	Christmas		6,000
72-P-RI-12-002	Niklas Church	15.00	25.00
73-P-RI-12-003	Schwanstein Church	18.00	35.00
Reco International/ Dresden	Christmas		5,000
74-P-RI-12-004	Village Scene	20.00	30.00
75-P-RI-12-005	Rothenburg Scene	24.00	30.00
76-P-RI-12-006	Village Church	26.00	35.00
77-P-RI-12-007	Old Mill (Issue Closed)	28.00	30.00
Reco International/ Dresden	Mother's Day		8,000
72-P-RI-13-001	Doe and Fawn	15.00	20.00
Reco International/ Dresden	Mother's Day		6,000
73-P-RI-13-002	Mare and Colt	16.00	25.00
Reco International/ Dresden	Mother's Day		5,000
74-P-RI-13-003	Tiger and Cub	20.00	23.00
75-P-RI-13-004	Dachshunds	24.00	28.00
76-P-RI-13-005	Owl and Offspring	26.00	30.00
77-P-RI-13-006	Chamois(Series Closed)	28.00	30.00
Reco International/ Furstenberg	Christmas		7,500
71-P-RI-14-001	Rabbits, FE	15.00	30.00
Reco International/ Furstenberg	Christmas		6,000
72-P-RI-14-002	Snowy Village	15.00	20.00
Reco International/ Furstenberg	Christmas		4,000
73-P-RI-14-003	Christmas Eve	18.00	35.00
74-P-RI-14-004	Sparrows	20.00	30.00
75-P-RI-14-005	Deer Family	22.00	30.00
76-P-RI-14-006	Winter Birds	25.00	25.00
Reco International/ Furstenberg	Deluxe Christmas		1,500
71-P-RI-15-001	Wise Men, FE	45.00	45.00
Reco International/ Furstenberg	Deluxe Christmas		2,000
72-P-RI-15-002	Holy Family	45.00	45.00
73-P-RI-15-003	Christmas Eve	60.00	65.00
Reco International/ Furstenberg	Easter		3,500
71-P-RI-16-001	Sheep, FE	15.00	75.00
Reco International/ Furstenberg	Easter		6,000
72-P-RI-16-002	Chicks	15.00	22.00
Reco International/ Furstenberg	Easter		4,000
73-P-RI-16-003	Bunnies	16.00	40.00
74-P-RI-16-004	Pussywillow	20.00	22.00
75-P-RI-16-005	Easter Window	22.00	26.00
76-P-RI-16-006	Flower Collecting	25.00	25.00
Reco International/ Furstenberg	Mother's Day		6,000
72-P-RI-17-001	Hummingbirds, FE	15.00	35.00
Reco International/ Furstenberg	Mother's Day		5,000
73-P-RI-17-002	Hedgehogs	16.00	23.00
Reco International/ Furstenberg	Mother's Day		4,000
74-P-RI-17-003	Doe and Fawn	20.00	20.00
75-P-RI-17-004	Swans	22.00	23.00
76-P-RI-17-005	Koala Bears	25.00	30.00
Reco International/ Furstenburg	Olympic		5,000
72-P-RI-18-001	Munich	20.00	20.00
76-P-RI-18-002	Montreal	37.50	37.50
Reco Internationas/ Grafburg	Christmas		5,000
75-P-RI-19-001	Black-Capped Chickadee	20.00	60.00
76-P-RI-19-002	Squirrels	22.00	22.00
Reco International/ King's	Christmas		1,500
73-P-RI-20-001	Adoration	100.00	180.00
74-P-RI-20-002	Madonna	150.00	160.00
75-P-RI-20-003	Heavenly Choir	160.00	200.00
76-P-RI-20-004	Siblings	200.00	240.00
Reco International/ King's	Flowers		1,000
73-P-RI-21-001	Carnation	85.00	130.00
74-P-RI-21-002	Red Rose	100.00	145.00
75-P-RI-21-003	Yellow Dahlia	110.00	162.00
76-P-RI-21-004	Bluebells	130.00	165.00
77-P-RI-21-005	Anemones	130.00	175.00
Reco International/ King's	Mother's Day		1,500
73-P-RI-22-001	Dancing Girl	100.00	150.00
74-P-RI-22-002	Dancing Boy	115.00	120.00
75-P-RI-22-003	Motherly Love	140.00	180.00
76-P-RI-22-004	Maiden	180.00	200.00
Reco International	Four Seasons		500
73-P-RI-23-001	Spring	50.00	75.00
73-P-RI-23-002	Summer	50.00	75.00
73-P-RI-23-003	Fall	50.00	75.00
73-P-RI-23-004	Winter	50.00	75.00
Reco International/ Marmot	Father's Day		3,500
70-P-RI-24-001	Stag	12.00	100.00
71-P-RI-24-002	Horse	12.50	40.00
Reco International/ Marmot	Christmas		5,000
70-P-RI-25-001	Polar Bear, FE	13.00	35.00
72-P-RI-25-003	Boy and Grandfather	20.00	30.00
Reco International/ Marmot	Presidents		1,500
71-P-RI-25-002	Washington	25.00	30.00
72-P-RI-25-004	Jefferson	25.00	30.00
73-P-RI-25-005	John Adams	25.00	25.00
Reco International/ Marmot	Christmas		6000
71-P-RI-25-006	American Buffalo	14.50	35.00
Reco International/ Marmot	Christmas		3,000
73-P-RI-25-007	Snowman	22.00	35.00
Reco International/ Marmot	Christmas		2,000
74-P-RI-25-008	Dancing	24.00	30.00
75-P-RI-25-009	Quail	30.00	30.00
76-P-RI-25-010	Windmill	40.00	40.00
Reco International/ Marmot	Mother's Day		6,000
72-P-RI-26-001	Seal, FE	16.00	30.00
Reco International/ Marmot	Mother's Day		3,000
73-P-RI-26-002	Bear With Cub	20.00	140.00
Reco International/ Marmot	Mother's Day		2,000
74-P-RI-26-003	Penguins	24.00	25.00
75-P-RI-26-004	Racoons	30.00	30.00
76-P-RI-26-005	Ducks	40.00	40.00
Reco International/ Moser	Christmas		400
70-P-RI-27-001	Hradcany Castle	75.00	170.00
Reco International/ Moser	Christmas		1,365
71-P-RI-27-002	Karlstein Castle	75.00	80.00
Reco International/ Moser	Christmas		1,000
72-P-RI-27-003	Old Town Hall	85.00	85.00
Reco International/ Moser	Christmas		500
73-P-RI-27-004	Karlovy Vary Castle	90.00	100.00
Reco International/ Moser	Mother's Day		350
71-P-RI-28-001	Peacocks	75.00	100.00

Category: Plates

Company / Number	Series / Name	Artist / Issue Price	Edition limit / Quote
Reco International/ Moser	Mother's Day		750
72-P-RI-28-002	Butterflies	85.00	90.00
Reco International/ Moser	Mother's Day		500
73-P-RI-28-003	Squirrels	90.00	95.00
Reco International/ Royale	Royale		2,000
69-P-RI-29-001	Apollo Moon Landing	30.00	80.00
Reco International/ Royale	Christmas		6,000
69-P-RI-30-001	Christmas Fair	12.00	60.00
73-P-RI-30-005	Christmas Down	20.00	30.00
Reco International/ Royale	Christmas		10,000
70-P-RI-30-002	Vigil Mass	13.00	30.00
Reco International/ Royale	Christmas		8,000
71-P-RI-30-003	Christmas Night	16.00	35.00
72-P-RI-30-004	Elks	16.00	40.00
Reco International/ Royale	Christmas		5,000
74-P-RI-30-006	Village Christmas	22.00	60.00
75-P-RI-30-007	Feeding Time	26.00	30.00
76-P-RI-30-008	Seaport Christmas	27.50	30.00
77-P-RI-30-009	Sledding	30.00	30.00
Reco International/ Royale	Mother's Day		6,000
70-P-RI-31-001	Swan and Young	12.00	80.00
73-P-RI-31-004	Owl Family	18.00	80.00
Reco International/ Royale	Mother's Day		9,000
71-P-RI-31-002	Doe and Fawn	13.00	55.00
72-P-RI-31-003	Rabbits	16.00	40.00
Reco International/ Royale	Mother's Day		5,000
74-P-RI-31-005	Duck and Young	22.00	30.00
75-P-RI-31-006	Lynx and Cubs	26.00	30.00
76-P-RI-31-007	Woodcock and Young	27.50	30.00
77-P-RI-31-008	Koala Bear	30.00	30.00
Reco International/ Royale	Father's Day		5,000
70-P-RI-32-001	Frigate Constitution	13.00	60.00
71-P-RI-32-002	Man Fishing	13.00	35.00
72-P-RI-32-003	Mountaineer	16.00	50.00
Reco International/ Royale	Father's Day		4,000
73-P-RI-32-004	Camping	18.00	25.00
Reco International/ Royale	Father's Day		2,500
74-P-RI-32-005	Eagle	22.00	35.00
75-P-RI-32-006	Regatta	26.00	30.00
76-P-RI-32-007	Hunting	27.50	30.00
77-P-RI-32-008	Fishing	30.00	30.00
Reco International/ Royale	Game Plates		500
72-P-RI-33-001	Setters	180.00	200.00
73-P-RI-33-002	Fox	200.00	250.00
Reco International/ Royale Germania	Annual		600
70-P-RI-34-001	Orchid	200.00	650.00
73-P-RI-34-004	Tulips	275.00	310.00
Reco International/ Royale	Game Plates		250
74-P-RI-33-003	Osprey	250.00	250.00
75-P-RI-33-004	California Quail	265.00	265.00
Reco International/ Royale Germania	Annual		1,000
71-P-RI-34-002	Cyclamen	200.00	325.00
72-P-RI-34-003	Silver Thistle	250.00	290.00
Reco International/ Royale Germania	Annual		500
74-P-RI-34-005	Sunflowers	300.00	320.00
Reco International/ Royale Germania	Annual		350
75-P-RI-34-006	Snowdrops	450.00	500.00
76-P-RI-34-007	Flaming Heart	450.00	450.00
Reco International/ Royale Germania	Mother's Day		250
71-P-RI-35-001	Roses	135.00	650.00
Reco International/ Royale Germania	Mother's Day		750
72-P-RI-35-002	Elephant and Youngster	180.00	250.00
Reco International/ Royale Germania	Mother's Day		600
73-P-RI-35-003	Koala Bear and Cub	200.00	225.00
Reco International/ Royale Germania	Mother's Day		500
74-P-RI-35-004	Squirrels	240.00	250.00
Reco International/ Royale Germania	Mother's Day		350
75-P-RI-35-005	Swan and Young	350.00	360.00
Reco International/ Tirschenreuth	Christmas		3,500
69-P-RI-36-001	Homestead	12.00	25.00
70-P-RI-36-002	Church	12.00	15.00
71-P-RI-36-003	Star of Bethelem	12.00	15.00
72-P-RI-36-004	Elk	13.00	15.00
Reco International/ Tirschenreuth	Christmas		
73-P-RI-36-005	Christmas	14.00	15.00
Reco International/ Tirschenreuth	Western		1,000
74-P-RI-37-001	Mountain Man	165.00	165.00
Reece, Maynard	Waterfowl		900
73-P-RE-1-001	Mallards & Wood Ducks (pair)	250.00	375.00
74-P-RE-1-002	Canvasback & Canadian Geese(pair)	250.00	375.00
75-P-RE-1-003	Pintails & Teal (pair)	250.00	425.00
Reed & Barton	Audubon		5,000
70-P-RB-1-001	Pine Siskin	60.00	175.00
71-P-RB-1-002	Red-shouldered Hawk	60.00	75.00
72-P-RB-1-003	Stilt Sandpiper	60.00	70.00
73-P-RB-1-004	Red Cardinal	60.00	65.00
74-P-RB-1-005	Boreal Chickadee	65.00	65.00
75-P-RB-1-006	Yellow-Breasted Chat	65.00	65.00
76-P-RB-1-007	Bay-Breasted Warbler	65.00	65.00
77-P-RB-1-008	Purple Finch	65.00	65.00
Reed & Barton	Christmas Carols		2,500
70-P-RB-2-001	Partridge In A Pear Tree	65.00	210.00
Reed & Barton	Christmas Carols		7,500
71-P-RB-2-002	We Three Kings of Orient Are	60.00	75.00
72-P-RB-2-003	Hark The Herald Angels Sing	60.00	65.00
Rockwell Society	Christmas	N. Rockwell	Firing Period
74-P-RK-1-001	Scotty Gets His Tree	24.50	160.00
75-P-RK-1-002	Angel With Black Eye	24.50	99.00
76-P-RK-1-003	Golden Christmas	24.50	58.00
77-P-RK-1-004	Toy Shop Window	24.50	50.00
78-P-RK-1-005	Christmas Dream	24.50	60.00
79-P-RK-1-006	Sonbody's Up There	24.50	30.00
80-P-RK-1-007	Scotty Plays Santa	24.50	42.00
81-P-RK-1-008	Wrapped Up in Christmas	24.50	28.00
82-P-RK-1-009	Christas Courtship	24.50	25.50
Rockwell Society	Mother's Day	N. Rockwell	Firing Period
76-P-RK-2-001	A Mother's Love	24.50	115.00
77-P-RK-2-002	Faith	24.50	72.00
78-P-RK-2-003	Bedtime	24.50	104.00
79-P-RK-2-004	Reflections	24.50	38.00
80-P-RK-2-005	A Mother's Pride	24.50	27.00
81-P-RK-2-006	After The Party	24.50	29.00
82-P-RK-2-007	The Cooking Lesson	25.50	25.50
83-P-RK-2-008	Add Two Cups & Love	25.50	25.50
Rockwell Society	Heritage	N. Rockwell	Firing Period
77-P-RK-3-001	Toy Maker	14.50	240.00
78-P-RK-3-002	Cobbler	19.50	155.00
79-P-RK-3-003	Lighthouse Keeper's Daughter	19.50	98.00
80-P-RK-3-004	Shop Builder	19.50	65.00
81-P-RK-3-005	Music Maker	19.50	28.00
82-P-RK-3-006	Tycoon	19.50	19.50
83-P-RK-3-007	Painter	19.50	19.50
Roman Inc.	The Masterpiece Collection	Fra Filippo Lippe	5,000
79-P-RO-1-001	Adoration	65.00	65.00
Roman Inc.	The Masterpiece Collection	P. Mignard	5,000
80-P-RO-1-002	Madonna With Grapes	87.50	87.50
Roman Inc.	The Masterpiece Collection	G. delle Notti	5,000
81-P-RO-1-003	The Holy Family	95.00	95.00
Roman Inc.	The Masterpiece Collection(4th Ed)	R. Ferruzzi	5,000
82-P-RO-1-004	Madonna Of The Streets	85.00	85.00
Roman Inc.	A Child's World	F. Hook	15,000
80-P-RO-2-001	Little Children, Come To Me	45.00	45.00
Roman Inc.	A Child's Play	F. Hook	By Time
82-P-RO-3-001	Breezy Day	29.95	29.95
82-P-RO-3-002	Kite Flying	29.95	29.95

Company	Series	Artist	Edition limit
Number	**Name**	**Issue Price**	**Quote**
Roman Inc.	Frances Hook Collection (1st Set)	F. Hook	15,000
82-P-RO-4-001	I Wish, I Wish	24.95	24.95
82-P-RO-4-002	Baby Blossoms	24.95	24.95
82-P-RO-4-003	Daisy Dreamer	24.95	24.95
82-P-RO-4-004	Trees So Tall	24.95	24.95
Roman Inc.	Frances Hook Collection (2nd Set)	F. Hook	15,000
83-P-RO-5-001	Caught It Myself	24.95	24.95
83-P-RO-5-002	Winter Wrappings	24.95	24.95
83-P-RO-5-003	So Cuddly	24.95	24.95
83-P-RO-5-004	Can I Keep Him ?	24.95	24.95
Roman Inc.	Petty Girls of the Ice Capades	G. Petty	By Time
83-P-RO-6-001	Ice Princess	24.50	24.50
Roman Inc.	The Ice Capades Clown		By Time
83-P-RO-7-001	Presenting Freddie Trenkler	24.50	24.50
Rorstrand	Christmas	G. Nylund	Annual
68-P-RR-1-001	Bringing Home The Tree	12.00	570.00
69-P-RR-1-002	Fisherman Sailing Home	13.50	95.00
70-P-RR-1-003	Nils With His Geese	13.50	32.00
71-P-RR-1-004	Nils In Lapland	15.00	28.00
72-P-RR-1-005	Dalecarlian Fiddler	15.00	30.00
73-P-RR-1-006	Farm In Smaland	16.00	104.00
74-P-RR-1-007	Vadslena	19.00	58.00
75-P-RR-1-008	Nils In Vastmanland	20.00	36.00
76-P-RR-1-009	Nils in Uapland	20.00	28.00
77-P-RR-1-010	Nils In Varmland	29.50	26.00
78-P-RR-1-011	Nils In Fjallbacka	22.50	33.00
79-P-RR-1-012	Nils In Vaestergoetland	38.50	35.00
80-P-RR-1-013	Nils In Halland	55.00	51.00
81-P-RR-1-014	Nils In Gotland	55.00	55.00
82-P-RR-1-015	Nils At Skansen	47.50	47.50
Rosenthal	Christmas		Annual
10-P-RL-1-001	Winter Peace		550.00
11-P-RL-1-002	Three Wise Men		325.00
12-P-RL-1-003	Stardust		255.00
13-P-RL-1-004	Christmas Lights		235.00
14-P-RL-1-005	Christmas Song		350.00
15-P-RL-1-006	Walking To Church		180.00
16-P-RL-1-007	Christmas During War		240.00
17-P-RL-1-008	Angel of Peace		200.00
18-P-RL-1-009	Peace on Earth		200.00
19-P-RL-1-010	St. Christopher With Christ Child		225.00
20-P-RL-1-011	Manger In Bethlehem		325.00
21-P-RL-1-012	Christmas in Mountains		200.00
22-P-RL-1-013	Advent Branch		200.00
23-P-RL-1-014	Children in Winter Woods		200.00
24-P-RL-1-015	Deer in the Woods		200.00
25-P-RL-1-016	Three Wise Men		200.00
26-P-RL-1-017	Christmas in Mountains		195.00
27-P-RL-1-018	Station On The Way		200.00
28-P-RL-1-019	Chalet Christmas		185.00
24-P-RL-1-020	Christmas In Alps		225.00
30-P-RL-1-021	Group of Deer Under Pines		225.00
31-P-RL-1-022	Path Of The Magi		225.00
32-P-RL-1-023	Christ Child		185.00
33-P-RL-1-024	Thru The Night To Light		190.00
34-P-RL-1-025	Christmas Peace		190.00
35-P-RL-1-026	Christmas By The Sea		190.00
36-P-RL-1-027	Nurnberg Angel		195.00
37-P-RL-1-028	BerchtesGarden		195.00
38-P-RL-1-029	Christmas In The Alps		195.00
39-P-RL-1-030	Schneekoppe Moutain		195.00
40-P-RL-1-031	Marien Church In Danzig		250.00
41-P-RL-1-032	Strassburg Cathedral		250.00
42-P-RL-1-033	Marianburg Castle		300.00
43-P-RL-1-034	Winter Idyll		300.00
44-P-RL-1-035	Wood Scape		300.00
45-P-RL-1-036	Christmas Peace		400.00
46-P-RL-1-037	Christmas In An Alpine Valley		240.00
47-P-RL-1-038	Dillingen Madonna		985.00
48-P-RL-1-039	Message To The Shepherds		875.00
49-P-RL-1-040	The Holy Family		185.00
50-P-RL-1-041	Christmas In The Forest		185.00
51-P-RL-1-042	Star of Bethlem		450.00
52-P-RL-1-043	Christmas In The Alps		195.00
53-P-RL-1-044	The Holy Light		195.00
54-P-RL-1-045	Christmas Eve		195.00
55-P-RL-1-046	Christmas In A Village		195.00
56-P-RL-1-047	Christmas In The Alps		195.00
57-P-RL-1-048	Christmas By the Sea		195.00
58-P-RL-1-049	Christmas Eve		195.00
59-P-RL-1-050	Midnight Mass		195.00
60-P-RL-1-051	Christmas In A Small Village		195.00
61-P-RL-1-052	Solitary Christmas		225.00
62-P-RL-1-053	Christmas Eve		195.00
63-P-RL-1-054	Silent Night		195.00
64-P-RL-1-055	Christmas Market In Nurnberg		225.00
65-P-RL-1-056	Christmas Munich		185.00
66-P-RL-1-057	Christmas In Ulm		275.00
67-P-RL-1-058	Christmas In Reginburg		185.00
68-P-RL-1-059	Christmas In Bremen		195.00
69-P-RL-1-060	Christmas In Rothenburg		220.00
70-P-RL-1-061	Christmas In Cologne		175.00
71-P-RL-1-062	Christmas In Garmisch	42.00	100.00
72-P-RL-1-063	Christmas In Franconia	50.00	95.00
73-P-RL-1-064	Lubeck-Holstein	77.00	105.00
74-P-RL-1-065	Christmas In Wurzburg	85.00	100.00
75-P-RL-1-066	Freiburg	75.00	80.00
76-P-RL-1-067	Cochem	95.00	85.00
77-P-RL-1-068	Hannover	125.00	115.00
78-P-RL-1-069	Aachen	150.00	120.00
79-P-RL-1-070	Cathedral In Luxenbourg	165.00	155.00
80-P-RL-1-071	Christmas In Brussels	190.00	190.00
81-P-Rl-1-072	Christmas In Trier	190.00	190.00

Company	Series	Artist	Edition limit
Number	**Name**	**Issue Price**	**Quote**
Rosenthal	Wiinbland Christmas	B. Wiinblad	Undiscl.
71-P-RL-2-001	Maria & Child	100.00	1375.00
72-P-RL-2-002	Caspar	100.00	600.00
73-P-RL-2-003	Melchior	125.00	500.00
74-P-RL-2-004	Balthazar	125.00	550.00
75-P-RL-2-005	The Annunciation	195.00	235.00
76-P-RL-2-006	Angel With Trumpet	195.00	235.00
77-P-RL-2-007	Adoration of Shepherds	225.00	260.00
78-P-RL-2-008	Angel With Harp	275.00	278.00
79-P-RL-2-009	Exodus From Egypt	310.00	310.00
80-P-RL-2-010	Angel With Glockenspiel	360.00	360.00
81-P-RL-2-011	Christ Child Visits Temple	375.00	375.00
82-P-RL-2-012	Christening of Christ	375.00	400.00
Rosenthal	Nobility of Children	E. Hibel	12,750
76-P-RL-3-001	La Contessa Isabella	120.00	265.00
77-P-RL-3-002	La Marquis Maurice-Peter	120.00	150.00
78-P-RL-3-003	Baronesse	130.00	180.00
79-P-RL-3-004	Chief Red Feather	140.00	140.00
Rosenthal	Oriental Gold	E. Hibel	2,000
76-P-RL-4-001	Yasuko	275.00	1500.00
77-P-RL-4-002	Mr. Obata	275.00	650.00
78-P-RL-4-003	Sakura	295.00	650.00
79-P-RL-4-004	Michio	325.00	500.00
Royal Bayreuth	Christmas		4,000
72-P-RL-5-001	Carriage In The Village	15.00	80.00
73-P-RL-5-002	Snow Scene	16.50	20.00
74-P-RL-5-003	The Old Mill	24.00	20.00
75-P-RL-5-004	Forest Chalet "Serenity"	27.50	20.00
Royal Bayreuth	Christmas		5,000
76-P-RL-5-005	Christmas In The Country	40.00	30.00
77-P-RL-5-006	Peace On Earth	40.00	30.00
78-P-RL-5-007	Peaceful Interlude	45.00	50.00
79-P-RL-5-008	Homeward Bound	50.00	50.00
Royal Copenhagen	Christmas	C. Thomsen	Annual
08-P-RC-1-001	Madonna And Child	1.00	1800.00
10-P-RC-1-003	The Magi	1.00	135.00
12-P-RC-1-005	Christmas Tree	1.00	160.00
Royal Copenhagen	Christmas	S. Ussing	Annual
09-P-RC-1-002	Danish Landscape	1.00	150.00
Royal Copenhagen	Christmas	O. Jensen	Annual
11-P-RC-1-004	Danish Landscape	1.00	160.00
17-P-RC-1-010	Our Savior Church	2.00	95.00
18-P-RC-1-011	Sheep And Shepherds	2.00	95.00
19-P-RC-1-012	In The Park	2.00	95.00
21-P-RC-1-014	Aabenraa Market Place	2.00	85.00
23-P-RC-1-016	Danish Landscape	2.00	90.00
25-P-RC-1-018	Christianshavn	2.00	100.00
29-P-RC-1-022	Grundtvig Church	2.00	85.00
32-P-RC-1-025	Frederiksberg Gardens	2.50	110.00
34-P-RC-1-027	The Hermitage Castle	2.50	130.00
Royal Copenhagen	Christmas	A. Boesen	Annual
13-P-RC-1-006	Frederick Church Spire	1.50	150.00
14-P-RC-1-007	Holy Spirit Church	1.50	125.00
Royal Copenhagen	Christmas	A. Krog	Annual
15-P-RC-1-008	Danish Landscape	1.50	140.00
Royal Copenhagen	Christmas	R. Bocher	Annual
16-P-RC-1-009	Shepherd At Christmas	1.50	95.00
26-P-RC-1-019	Christianshavn Canal	2.00	90.00
36-P-RC-1-029	Roskilde Cathedral	2.50	140.00
45-P-RC-1-038	A Peaceful Motif	4.00	370.00
51-P-RC-1-043	Christmas Angel	5.00	410.00
Royal Copenhagen	Christmas	G. Rode	Annual
20-P-RC-1-013	Mary and Child Jesus	2.00	105.00
28-P-RC-1-021	Vicar's Family	2.00	90.00
31-P-RC-1-024	Mother And Child	2.50	110.00
Royal Copenhagen	Christmas	E. Selschau	Annual
22-P-RC-1-015	Three Singing Angels	2.00	85.00
Royal Copenhagen	Christmas	B. Olsen	Annual
24-P-RC-1-017	Sailing Ship	2.00	105.00
27-P-RC-1-020	Ship's Boy at Tiller	2.00	200.00
30-P-RC-1-023	Fishing Boats	2.50	100.00
33-P-RC-1-026	Benjamin Olsen	2.50	125.00
35-P-RC-1-020	Kronborg Castle	2.50	150.00
Royal Copenhagen	Christmas	N. Thorsson	Annual
37-P-RC-1-030	Main Street Copenhagen	2.50	140.00
42-P-RC-1-035	Bell Tower	4.00	430.00
43-P-RC-1-036	Flight Into Egypt	4.00	500.00
46-P-RC-1-039	Zealand Village Church	4.00	170.00
Royal Copenhagen	Christmas	H. Nielsen	Annual
38-P-RC-1-031	Round Church Osterlars	3.00	290.00
Royal Copenhagen	Christmas	S. Nielsen	Annual
39-P-RC-1-032	Greenland Pack-Ice	3.00	275.00
Royal Copenhagen	Christmas	K. Lange	Annual
40-P-RC-1-033	The Good Shepherd	3.00	375.00
47-P-RC-1-040	The Good Shepherd	4.50	225.00
52-P-RC-1-044	Christmas In The Forest	5.00	140.00
54-P-RC-1-046	Amalienborg Palace	6.00	150.00
55-P-RC-1-047	Fano Girl	7.00	235.00
56-P-RC-1-048	Rosenborg Castle	7.00	250.00
61-P-RC-1-053	Training Ship	10.00	235.00
63-P-RC-1-055	Hojsager Mill	11.00	110.00
64-P-RC-1-056	Fetching The Tree	11.00	90.00
65-P-RC-1-057	Little Skaters	12.00	80.00
66-P-RC-1-058	Blackbird	12.00	65.00
67-P-RC-1-059	The Royal Oak	13.00	50.00
68-P-RC-1-060	The Last Umiak	13.00	34.00
69-P-RC-1-061	The Old Farmyard	14.00	35.00
70-P-RC-1-062	Christmas Rose & Cat	14.00	30.00
71-P-RC-1-063	Hare In Winter	15.00	25.00
72-P-RC-1-064	In The Desert	16.00	25.00
73-P-RC-1-065	Train Homeward Bound	22.00	28.00

Category: Plates

Company / Number	Series / Name	Artist / Issue Price	Edition limit / Quote
74-P-RC-1-066	Winter Twilight	22.00	22.00
75-P-RC-1-067	Queen's Palace	27.50	25.00
Royal Copenhagen	Christmas	T. Kjolner	Annual
41-P-RC-1-034	Danish Village Church	3.00	390.00
48-P-RC-1-041	Nodebo Church	4.50	235.00
53-P-RC-1-045	Frederiksberg Castle	6.00	130.00
Royal Copenhagen	Christmas	V. Olson	Annual
44-P-RC-1-037	Danish Winter Scene	4.00	200.00
50-P-RC-1-043	Boeslunde Church	5.00	270.00
Royal Copenhagen	Christmas	H. Hansen	Annual
49-P-RC-1-042	Our Lady's Cathedral	5.00	225.00
57-P-RC-1-049	The Good Shepherd	8.00	125.00
58-P-RC-1-050	Sunshine Over Greenland	9.00	160.00
59-P-RC-1-051	Christmas Night	9.00	190.00
60-P-RC-1-052	The Stag	10.00	240.00
Royal Copenhagen	Christmas		Annual
62-P-RC-1-054	The Little Mermaid	11.00	205.00
Royal Copenhagen	Christmas	S. Vestergaard	Annual
76-P-RC-1-068	Danish Watermill	27.50	39.00
Royal Copenhagen	Christmas	K. Lange	Annual
77-P-RC-1-069	Immervad Bridge	32.00	32.00
78-P-RC-1-070	Greenland Scenery	35.00	35.00
79-P-RC-1-071	Choosing Christmas Tree	42.50	42.50
80-P-RC-1-072	Bringing Home The Tree	49.50	49.50
81-P-RC-1-073	Admiring Christmas Tree	52.50	52.50
82-P-RC-1-074	Waiting For Christmas	54.50	54.50
Royal Copenhagen	Mother's Day	K. Svennson	Annual
71-P-RC-2-001	American Mother	12.50	20.00
72-P-RC-2-002	Oriental Mother	14.00	12.00
Royal Copenhagen	Mother's Day	A. Ungermann	Annual
73-P-RC-2-003	Danish Mother	16.00	16.00
74-P-RC-2-004	Greenland Mother	16.50	16.50
75-P-RC-2-005	Bird In Nest	20.00	20.00
76-P-RC-2-006	Mermaids	20.00	20.00
77-P-RC-2-007	The Twins	24.00	24.00
Royal Copenhagen	Mother's Day	S. Olsen	Annual
78-P-RC-2-008	Mother & Child	26.00	26.00
79-P-RC-2-009	A Loving Mother	29.50	29.50
80-P-RC-2-010	An Outing With Mother	37.50	37.50
81-P-RC-2-011	Reunion	39.00	39.00
82-P-RC-2-012	Children's Hour	39.00	39.00
Royal Cornwall	Creation	Koutsis	10,000
77-P-RI-1-001	In The Beginning	37.50	90.00
77-P-RL-1-002	In His Image	45.00	130.00
78-P-RL-1-003	Adam's Rib	45.00	125.00
78-P-RL-1-004	Banished From Eden	45.00	125.00
78-P-RL-1-005	Noah And The Ark	45.00	120.00
80-P-RL-1-006	Tower Of Babel	45.00	75.00
80-P-RL-1-007	Sodom And Gomorrah	45.00	75.00
80-P-RL-1-008	Jacob's Wedding	45.00	75.00
80-P-RL-1-009	Rebekah At The Well	45.00	75.00
80-P-RL-1-010	Jacob's Ladder	45.00	75.00
80-P-RL-1-011	Joseph's coat of Many Colors	45.00	75.00
80-P-RL-1-012	Joseph Interprets Pharaoh's Dream	45.00	75.00
Royal Cornwall	Creation Calhoun Charter Release	Koutsis	19,500
77-P-RL-2-001	In The Beginning	29.50	152.00
77-P-RL-2-002	In His Image	29.50	120.00
77-P-RL-2-003	Adam's Rib	29.50	100.00
77-P-RL-2-004	Banished From Eden	29.50	90.00
77-P-RL-2-005	Noah And The Ark	29.50	90.00
78-P-RL-2-006	Tower Of Babel	29.50	80.00
78-P-RL-2-007	Sodom & Gomorrah	29.50	80.00
78-P-RL-2-008	Jacob's Wedding	29.50	80.00
78-P-RL-2-009	Rebekah At The Well	29.50	80.00
78-P-RL-2-010	Jacob's Ladder	29.50	80.00
78-P-RL-2-011	Joseph's Coat Of Many Colors	29.50	80.00
78-P-RL-2-012	Joseph Interprets Pharaoh's Dream	29.50	80.00
Royal Devon	Royal Devon Rockwell Christmas	N. Rockwell	Year Of Issue
75-P-RD-1-001	Downhill Daring	24.50	69.00
76-P-RD-1-002	The Christmas Gift	24.50	82.50
77-P-RD-1-003	The Big Moment	27.50	80.00
78-P-RD-1-004	Puppets For Christmas	27.50	40.00
79-P-RD-1-005	One Present Too Many	31.50	33.00
80-P-RD-1-006	Gramps Meets Gramps	33.00	33.00
Royal Devon	Mother's Day Rockwell Plates	N. Rockwell	Year Of Issue
75-P-RD-2-001	Doctor And Doll	23.50	95.00
75-P-RD-2-022	Puppy Love	24.50	75.00
75-P-RD-2-003	The Family	24.50	82.50
75-P-RD-2-004	Mother's Day Off	27.00	70.00
75-P-RD-3-005	Mother's Evening Out	30.00	33.00
75-P-RD-3-006	Mother's Treat	32.50	32.50
Royal Worcester	Bicentennial	P. Baston	10,000
72-P-RW-1-001	Boston Tea Party	45.00	250.00
73-P-RW-1-002	Paul Revere	45.00	230.00
74-P-RW-1-003	Concord Bridge	50.00	80.00
75-P-RW-1-004	Signing Declaration	65.00	60.00
76-P-RW-1-005	Crossing Delaware	65.00	75.00
Royal Worcester	Doughty Bird	D. Doughty	2,750
72-P-RW-2-001	Redstarts & Beech	125.00	195.00
Royal Worcester	Doughty Bird	D. Doughty	3,000
73-P-RW-2-002	Myrtle Warbler & Cherry	175.00	195.00
74-P-RW-2-003	Blue-Grey Gnatcatchers	195.00	195.00
75-P-RW-2-004	Blackburnian Warbler	195.00	195.00
76-P-RW-2-005	Blue-Winged Sivas & Bamboo	195.00	195.00
77-P-RW-2-006	Paradise Wydah	195.00	195.00
78-P-RW-2-007	Bluetits & Witch Hazel	195.00	195.00
79-P-RW-2-008	Mountain Bluebird & Pine	195.00	195.00

Company / Number	Series / Name	Artist / Issue Price	Edition limit / Quote
80-P-RW-2-009	Cerulean Warblers & Beech	315.00	310.00
81-P-RW-2-010	Willow Warbler	330.00	330.00
82-P-RW-2-011	Ruby-crowned Kinglets	330.00	330.00
Schmid	Christmas	B. Hummel	Annual
71-P-SH-1-001	Angel	15.00	66.00
72-P-SH-1-002	Angel With Flute	15.00	31.00
73-P-SH-1-003	The Nativity	15.00	205.00
74-P-SH-1-004	The Guardian Angel	18.50	30.00
75-P-SH-1-005	Christmas Child	25.00	30.00
76-P-SH-1-006	Sacred Journey	27.50	57.50
77-P-SH-1-007	Herald Angel	27.50	40.00
78-P-SH-1-008	Heavenly Trio	32.50	30.00
79-P-SH-1-009	Starlight Angel	38.00	35.00
80-P-SH-1-010	Parade Into Toyland	45.00	60.00
81-P-SH-1-011	A Time To Remember	45.00	45.00
82-P-SH-1-012	Angelic Procession	45.00	45.00
Schmid	Peanuts Christmas	C. Schulz	Annual
72-P-SC-2-001	Snoopy Guides the Sleigh	10.00	68.00
73-P-SC-2-002	Christmas Eve At Doghouse	10.00	100.00
74-P-SC-2-003	Christmas At Fireplace	10.00	56.00
75-P-SC-2-004	Woodstock's Santa Claus	12.50	21.00
76-P-SC-2-005	Woodstock's Christmas	13.00	25.00
77-P-SC-2-006	Deck The Doghouse	13.00	21.00
78-P-SC-2-007	Filling the Stocking	15.00	18.00
Schmid	Mother's Day	B. Hummel	Annual
72-P-SC-3-001	Playing Hooky	15.00	40.00
73-P-SC-3-002	Little Fisherman	15.00	78.00
74-P-SC-3-003	Bumblebee	18.50	35.00
75-P-SC-3-004	Message of Love	25.00	35.00
76-P-SC-3-005	Devotion For Mother	27.50	35.00
77-P-SC-3-006	Moonlight Return	27.50	35.50
78-P-SC-3-007	Afternoon Stroll	32.50	35.00
79-P-SC-3-008	Cherub's Gift	38.00	40.00
80-P-SC-3-009	Mother's Little Helpers	45.00	45.00
81-P-SC-3-010	Playtime	45.00	45.00
82-P-SC-3-011	The Flower Basket	45.00	45.00
83-P-SC-3-012	Spring Bouquet	45.00	45.00
Schmid	Disney Christmas	Disney	Annual
73-P-SC-4-001	Sleigh Ride	10.00	310.00
74-P-SC-4-002	Decorating The Tree	10.00	53.00
75-P-SC-4-003	Caroling	12.50	20.00
76-P-SC-4-004	Building A Snowman	13.00	18.00
77-P-SC-4-005	Down The Chimney	13.00	16.00
78-P-SC-4-006	Night Before Christmas	15.00	21.00
Schimd	Disney Mother's Day	Disney	Annual
71-P-SJ-1-002	Little Match Girl	15.00	35.00
76-P-SJ-1-007	The Snow Queen	27.50	30.00
Svend Jensen	Christmas	E. Eriksen	Annual
72-P-SJ-1-003	Maid Of Copenhagen	16.50	30.00
Svend Jensen	Christmas	S. Otto	Annual
73-P-SJ-1-004	The Fir Tree	22.00	30.00
74-P-SJ-1-005	The Chimney Sweep	25.00	30.00
75-P-SJ-1-006	The Ugly Duckling	27.50	25.00
77-P-SJ-1-008	Snowman	29.50	25.00
78-P-SJ-1-009	Last Dream Of Old Oak	32.00	25.00
79-P-SJ-1-010	The Old Street Lamp	36.50	36.50
80-P-SJ-1-011	Willie Winky	42.50	42.50
81-P-SJ-1-012	Uttermost Parts Of The Sea	49.50	49.50
82-P-SJ-1-013	Twelve By The Mailcoach	54.50	54.50
U.S. Historical Society	Patriot Plates		2,500
73-P-US-1-001	George Washington	75.00	150.00
73-P-US-1-002	Benjamin Franklin	75.00	150.00
73-P-US-1-003	Thomas Jefferson	75.00	150.00
73-P-US-1-004	Patrick Henry	75.00	150.00
73-P-US-1-005	Abigail Adams	75.00	150.00
73-P-US-1-006	Alexander Hamilton	75.00	150.00
73-P-US-1-007	Thomas Paine	75.00	150.00
73-P-US-1-008	John Marshall	75.00	150.00
73-P-US-1-009	John Paul Jones	75.00	150.00
73-P-US-1-010	Samuel Adams	75.00	150.00
73-P-US-1-011	John Hancock	75.00	150.00
73-P-US-1-012	Nathanael Greene	75.00	150.00
U.S.Historical Society	Young America	W. Homer	2,500
73-P-US-2-001	Young America of Winslow Homer- (6 plates)	425.00	1100.00
U.S. Historical Society	Annual Stained Glass and Pewter Christmas Plate		10,000
78-P-US-3-001	The Nativity- Caterbury Cathedral	97.00	150.00
79-P-US-3-002	Flight Into Egypt- St. Johns, New York	97.00	150.00
80-P-US-3-003	Madonna And Child- Washington Cathedral	125.00	150.00
81-P-US-3-004	The Magi- St. Pauls San Francisco	125.00	150.00
82-P-US-3-005	Flight Into Egypt- Los Angeles Cathedral	135.00	175.00
83-P-US-3-006	The Shepherds At Bethlehem- St. Johns, New Orleans	135.00	135.00
U.S. Historical Society	Christmas	W. Tower	10,000
80-P-UH-4-001	Washington Cathedral	125.00	150.00
81-P-UH-4-002	The Magi	125.00	125.00
U.S. Historical Society	Stained Glass and Pewter Plates		10,000
82-P-US-5-001	Spring Flowers	135.00	135.00
83-P-US-5-002	U.S.S. Constitution (Old Ironsides)	135.00	135.00
U.S. Historical Society	The Christmas Carol Plate	J. Landis	10,000
82-P-US-6-001	Deck The Halls With Boughs of Holly	55.00	65.00

Category: Plates

Company / Number	Series / Name	Artist / Issue Price	Edition limit / Quote
Company	**Series**	**Artist**	**Edition limit**
Number	**Name**	**Issue Price**	**Quote**
U.S. Historical Society	The Christmas Carol Plate	Jack Woodson	10,000
83-P-US-6-002	Oh, Christmas Tree	55.00	55.00
Vague Shadows, Ltd	Chieftain	G. Perillo	7,500
79-P-VS-1-001	Chief Sitting Bull	65.00	280.00
79-P-VS-1-002	Chief Joseph	65.00	90.00
80-P-VS-1-003	Chief Red Cloud	65.00	65.00
80-P-VS-1-004	Geronimo	65.00	65.00
81-P-VS-1-005	Chief Crazy Horse	65.00	65.00
Vague Shadows, Ltd	The Plainsmen	G. Perillo	2,500
78-P-VS-2-001	Buffalo Hunt	300.00	310.00
79-P-VS-2-002	The Proud One	300.00	300.00
Vague Shadows, Ltd	The Professionals	G. Perillo	15,000
79-P-VS-3-001	The Big Leaguer	29.95	90.00
80-P-VS-3-002	Ballerina's Dilemma	32.50	32.50
81-P-VS-3-003	Quarterback	32.50	32.50
81-P-VS-3-004	Rodeo Joe	35.00	35.00
82-P-VS-3-005	Major Leaguer	35.00	35.00
Val St. Lambert	Annual Old Masters		5,000
69-P-SL-1-001	Rubens & Rembrandt(pr)	50.00	120.00
69-P-SL-1-002	Van Gogh & Van Dyck(pr)	50.00	85.00
70-P-SL-1-003	Da Vinci & Michelangelo(pr)	50.00	90.00
71-P-SL-1-004	El Greco & Goya (pr)	50.00	85.00
72-P-SL-1-005	Reynolds, Gainsborough(pr)	50.00	70.00
Val St. Lambert	American Heritage		500
69-P-SL-2-001	Pilgrim Father's	200.00	450.00
70-P-SL-2-002	Paul Revere's Ride	200.00	225.00
71-P-SL-2-003	Washington On Delaware	200.00	225.00
Veneto Flair	-	V. Tiziano	500
71-P-VE-1-001	Madonna (Bellini)	45.00	440.00
Veneto Flair	Christmas		1,500
71-P-VE-2-001	Three Kings	55.00	160.00
Veneto Flair	Christmas		2,000
72-P-VE-3-001	Shepherds	55.00	90.00
73-P-VE-3-002	Christ Child	55.00	55.00
Veneto Flair	Christmas		-
74-P-VE-3-004	Angel	55.00	55.00
Veneto Flair	Wildlife		500
71-P-VE-4-001	Deer	37.50	450.00
Veneto Flair	Wildlife		1,000
72-P-VE-4-002	Elephant	37.50	275.00
Veneto Flair	Wildlite		2,000
73-P-VE-4-003	Puma	37.50	65.00
74-P-VE-4-004	Tiger	40.00	50.00
Veneto Flair	Dogs	V. Tiziano	2,000
72-P-VE-5-001	German Shepherd	37.50	79.00
73-P-VE-5-002	Poodle	37.50	45.00
73-P-VE-5-003	Doberman	37.50	32.00
73-P-VE-5-004	Collie	40.00	42.00
73-P-VE-5-005	Dachshund	45.00	43.00
Veneto Flair	Birds		2,000
72-P-VE-6-001	Owl	37.50	100.00
72-P-VE-6-002	Falcon	37.50	55.00
73-P-VE-6-003	Mallard	45.00	60.00
Veneto Flair	Easter		2,000
73-P-VE-7-001	Rabbits	50.00	90.00
74-P-VE-7-002	Chicks	50.00	55.00
75-P-VE-7-003	Lamb	50.00	55.00
76-P-VE-7-004	Composite	55.00	55.00
Viletta	Disneyland		3,000
76-P-VI-1-001	Signing The Declaration	15.00	100.00
76-P-VI-1-002	Crossing The Delaware	15.00	100.00
76-P-VI-1-003	Betsy Ross	15.00	100.00
76-P-VI-1-004	Spirit of '76	15.00	100.00
Viletta	Disneyland		5,000
79-P-VI-1-001	Mickey's 50th Anniversary	37.00	37.00
Viletta	Zolan's Children	D. Zolan	Undiscl.
78-P-VI-2-001	Erik & Dandelion	19.00	201.00
79-P-VI-2-002	Sabrina In The Grass	22.00	195.00
80-P-VI-2-003	By Myself	24.00	45.00
81-P-VI-2-004	For You	24.00	27.00
Villeroy & Boch	Russian Fairytales Snow Maiden	B. Zvorykin	27,500
81-P-VB-1-001	The Snow Maiden	70.00	90.00
81-P-VB-1-002	Snegurochka At The Court Of Tsar Berendei	70.00	74.00
81-P-VB-1-003	Snegurochka And Lei, The Shepherd Boy	70.00	72.00
Villeroy & Boch	Russian Fairtales The Red Knight	B. Zvorykin	27,500
81-P-VB-2-001	Vassilissa The Fair	70.00	70.00
81-P-VB-2-002	Vassilissa And Her Stepsisters	70.00	70.00
81-P-VB-2-003	Vassilissa Is Presented To The Tsar	70.00	70.00
Villeroy & Boch	Russian Fairytales The Firebird	B. Zvorykin	27,500
81-P-VB-3-001	In Search Of The Firebird	70.00	70.00
81-P-VB-3-002	Ivan And Tsarevna On The Grey Wolf	70.00	70.00
81-P-VB-3-003	The Wedding Of Tsarevna Elena The Fair	70.00	70.00
Villeroy & Boch	Russian Fairytales Maria Morevna	B. Zvorykin	27,500
82-P-VB-4-001	Maria Morevna And Tsarevich Ivan	70.00	70.00

Category: Figurine

Company / Number	Series / Name	Artist / Issue Price	Edition limit / Quote
Company	**Series**	**Artist**	**Edition limit**
Number	**Name**	**Issue Price**	**Quote**
82-P-VB-4-002	Koshchey Carries Off Maria Morevna	70.00	70.00
82-P-VB-4-003	Tsarevich Ivan And The Beautiful Castle	70.00	70.00
Villeroy & Boch	Flower Fairy	C. Barker	21 Day Firing
79-P-VB-5-001	Lavender	35.00	35.00
80-P-VB-5-002	Sweet Pea	35.00	35.00
80-P-VB-5-003	Candytuft	35.00	35.00
81-P-VB-5-004	Heliotrope	35.00	35.00
81-P-VB-5-005	Blackthorn	35.00	35.00
81-P-VB-5-006	Appleblossom	35.00	35.00
Villeroy & Boch	Fairyland Lovers	E. Dulac	10 Day Firing
82-P-VB-6-001	The Prince & Sleeping Beauty	39.00	39.00
82-P-VB-6-002	Ivan And The Chestnut Horse	39.00	39.00
82-P-VB-6-003	The Princess And The Enchanted Stag	39.00	39.00
82-P-VB-6-004	The Goose Girl	39.00	39.00
83-P-VB-6-005	Cinderella	39.00	39.00
83-P-VB-6-006	Prince Ahmed and Peri Banu	39.00	39.00
83-P-VB-6-007	Ta-Khai And The Bird Feng	39.00	39.00
83-P-VB-6-008	The Fisherman And The Dragon King's Daughter	39.00	39.00
Villeroy & Boch	Fairies Of The Fields And Flowers	C. Barker	10 Day Firing
82-P-VB-7-001	Ragged Robin	49.00	49.00
82-P-VB-7-002	Willow Fairy	49.00	49.00
82-P-VB-7-003	Elderberry	49.00	49.00
82-P-VB-7-004	Vetch	49.00	49.00
83-P-VB-7-005	Narcissus	49.00	49.00
83-P-VB-7-006	Nasturtium	49.00	49.00
83-P-VD 7 007	Phlox	49.00	49.00
83-P-VB-7-008	Gorse	49.00	49.00
Villeroy & Boch	World Wildlife Series	W. Weber	-
82-P-VB-8-001	Panda	38.00	38.00
83-P-VB-8-002	Tiger	38.00	38.00
84-P-VB-8-003	Otter	38.00	38.00
85-P-VB-8-004	Orangutang	38.00	38.00
Villeroy & Boch	Unicef series	K. Blume	Year Of Issue
77-P-VB-9-001	Europe	30.00	30.00
78-P-VB-9-002	Asia	30.00	30.00
79-P-VB-9-003	Africa	30.00	30.00
80-P-VB-9-004	Malaysia	30.00	30.00
81-P-VB-9-005	India	35.00	35.00
82-P-VB-9-006	Mexico	35.00	35.00
79-P-VB-9-007	International Year Of The Child	35.00	35.00
Villeroy & Boch	Famous Sea Battles	J. Van Zundert	Year Of Issue
82-P-VB-10-001	Battle of Trafalgar	42.00	42.00
82-P-VB-10-002	Battle of Flamborough	42.00	42.00
82-P-VB-10-003	Battle of Lepanto 1571	42.00	42.00
Wedgwood	Christmas	T. Harper	Annual
69-P-WE-1-001	Windsor Castle	25.00	285.00
70-P-WE-1-002	Trafalgar Square	30.00	35.00
71-P-WE-1-003	Picadilly Circus	30.00	42.50
72-P-WE-1-004	St. Paul's Cathedral	35.00	42.50
73-P-WE-1-005	Tower Of London	40.00	47.00
74-P-WE-1-006	Houses Of Parliment	40.00	40.00
75-P-WE-1-007	Tower Bridge	45.00	40.00
76-P-WE-1-008	Hampton Court	50.00	47.50
77-P-WE-1-009	Westminster Abbey	55.00	44.00
78-P-WE-1-010	Horse Guards	60.00	50.00
Wedgwood	Christmas	Undisc.	Annual
79-P-RW-1-011	Buckingham Palace	65.00	65.00
80-P-RW-1-012	St. James Palace	70.00	70.00
81-P-RW-1-013	Marble Arch	75.00	75.00
82-P-RW-1-014	Lambeth Palace	80.00	80.00

Category: Figurines

Company / Number	Series / Name	Artist / Issue Price	Edition limit / Quote
*Boehm Studios		Boehm	Year of Issue
83-F-BH-001	Great Egret	1,200.00	1,200.00
Boehm/Am.Express		Boehm	To Amex Cardholders
83-F-BH-2 001	American Express Rose	195.00	195.00
Boehm/Hamilton Collection	Classic Moments In Ballet	Boehm	7,500
81-F-BH-3-001	Giselle	120.00	120.00
81-F-BH-3-002	Swan Lake	120.00	120.00
81-F-BH-3-003	Don Quixote	120.00	120.00
81-F-BH-3-004	Nutcracker	120.00	120.00
Boehm/Hamilton Collection	Annual Ballet Classics	Boehm	Annual
82-F-BH-4-001	Firebird	140.00	140.00
82-F-BH-4-002	Coppelia	140.00	140.00
Boehm/Hamilton Collection	Romantic Moments in Ballet	Boehm	5,000
82-F-BH-5-001	Romeo	240.00	240.00
82-F-BH-5-002	Odette	240.00	240.00
82-F-BH-5-003	Nutcracker Prince	240.00	240.00
82-F-BH-5-004	Giselle	240.00	240.00
Boehm/Hamilton Collection	The First Noel	Boehm	Date of Issue
82-F-BH-6-001	The Holy Family	135.00	135.00
82-F-BH-6-002	Angel & Shepherds	135.00	135.00
82-F-BH-6-003	Townsfolk & Animals	135.00	135.00
Boehm/Hamilton Collection	Roses of Distinction	Boehm	9,800
83-F-BH-7-001	Peace Rose	135.00	135.00
83-F-BH-7-002	White Masterpiece Rose	135.00	135.00
*Boehm/Hamilton Collection	Wildflowers By the Sea	Boehm	9,800

*Please note: More Boehm figurines are listed on the last page of the index.

Category: Figurine

Company / Number	Series / Name	Artist / Issue Price	Edition limit / Quote
83-F-BH-8-001	Periwinkle	95.00	95.00
Brantwood Treins	Various	N. Rockwell	15,000
80-F-BT-1-001	Doctor & The Doll	89.50	70.00
80-F-BT-1-002	Toymaker	79.50	90.00
Brown & Bigelow	Various	N. Rockwell	
79-F-BB-1-001	The Runaway	90.00	90.00
Brown & Bigelow	Various	N. Rockwell	1,500
82-F-HP-2-001	The Horse Trader	180.00	
80-F-HP-2-002	The Country Pedlar	160.00	220.00
81-F-HP-2-003	The Traveling Salesman	175.00	175.00
Burgues	Burgues Porcelains	I. Burgues	350
xx-F-BU-1-001	American Goldfinches with Morning Glories	1,250.00	1,700.00
xx-F-BU-1-002	Anemone	550.00	600.00
xx-F-BU-1-003	Carolina Wren with White Dogwood	750.00	825.00
xx-F-BU-1-004	King Penguins	850.00	925.00
76-F-BU-1-005	Pileated Woodpecker	225.00	225.00
xx-F-BU-1-006	Pink Lady Slipper Orchid	800.00	875.00
xx-F-BU-1-007	Redheaded Woodpecker	1,100.00	1,200.00
xx-F-BU-1-008	Rufous Hummingbird, Allamanda		300.00
xx-F-BU-1-009	Saw-Whet Owl		275.00
xx-F-BU-1-010	Young Saw-Whet Owl	500.00	550.00
Burgues	Burgues Porcelains	I. Burges	10
76-F-BU-1-011	American Wild Goat		1,000.00
Burgues	Burgues Porcelains	I. Burgues	200
76-F-BU-1-012	Anniversary Orchid		75.00
xx-F-BU-1-013	Baltimore Oriole, Juvenile	750.00	825.00
xx-F-BU-1-014	Crab-Eater Seals	1,250.00	1,375.00
xx-F-BU-1-015	Cymbidium Orchid		75.00
78-F-BU-1-016	Ectasy, Paphiopedilum Orchid		90.00
xx-F-BU-1-017	Hibiscus		85.00
xx-F-BU-1-018	Imperial Gold Lily		225.00
78-F-BU-1-019	Perfection, Paphiopedilum Orchid		90.00
xx-F-BU-1-020	Pink Glory Lily		225.00
xx-F-BU-1-021	Rhododendron	375.00	400.00
78-F-BU-1-022	Springtime, Paphiopedilum Orchid		90.00
78-F-BU-1-023	Sunny Glow, Paphiopedilum Orchid		90.00
xx-F-BU-1-024	Water Lily	175.00	275.00
Burgues	Burgues Porcelains	I. Burgues	Year
76-F-BU-1-025	Barn Swallows, Pewter, American Express	100.00	150.00
76-F-BU-1-026	Great White Heron, Pewter, American Express	100.00	160.00
76-F-BU-1-027	Pygmy Owl, Pewter, American Express	100.00	100.00
76-F-BU-1-028	Wood Ducks, Pewter, American Express	100.00	100.00
Burgues	Burgues Porcelains	I. Burgues	500
77-F-BU-1-029	Barrel Cactus	200.00	225.00
xx-F-BU-1-030	Cardinal, Juvenile	250.00	275.00
xx-F-BU-1-031	Cave Swallow, Male and Female	750.00	2,800.00
xx-F-BU-1-032	Clematis Sieboldi	175.00	190.00
xx-F-BU-1-033	Robin with Marsh Marigolds	550.00	490.00 - 600.00
xx-F-BU-1-034	Snow Bunting with Trumpet Honeysuckle	350.00	200.00 - 385.00
xx-F-BU-1-035	Snowy Owl	450.00	260.00 - 495.00
xx-F-BU-1-036	Wood Thrush, Juvenile	225.00	265.00
xx-F-BU-1-037	Yellow-Billed Cuckoo	400.00	450.00
Burgues	Burgues Porcelains	I. Burgues	950
xx-F-BU-1-038	Bay-Breasted Warbler	175.00	190.00
76-F-BU-1-039	Black-Capped Chickadee	145.00	160.00
xx-F-BU-1-040	Black-Tailed Prairie Dog	195.00	1,375.00
xx-F-BU-1-041	Chestnut-Backed Chickadee		160.00
xx-F-BU-1-042	Chestnut-Sided Warbler		190.00
xx-F-BU-1-043	Lucy's Warbler		190.00
76-F-BU-1-044	Magnolia Warbler	145.00	160.00
76-F-BU-1-045	Parula Warbler	190.00	175.00 - 190.00
76-F-BU-1-046	Polar Bear	215.00	215.00
76-F-BU-1-047	Polar Bear, Cubs	185.00	185.00
xx-F-BU-1-048	Red-Breasted Nuthatch	225.00	250.00
76-F-BU-1-049	Red Squirrel	195.00	195.00
xx-F-BU-1-050	Robin, Juvenile	150.00	175.00
xx-F-BU-1-051	Snow Bunting, Juvenile	165.00	185.00
xx-F-BU-1-052	Wood Duckling		175.00
xx-F-BU-1-053	Yellow-Billed Cuckoo, Juvenile	175.00	190.00
78-F-BU-1-054	Young Cottontail	185.00	185.00
76-F-BU-1-055	Young Walrus	225.00	225.00
Burgues	Burgues Porcelains	I. Burgues	750
xx-F-BU-1-056	Belted Kingfisher Fledgling	350.00	500.00
xx-F-BU-1-057	Chipmunk with Acorn	150.00	350.00
Burgues	Burgues Porcelains	I. Burgues	250
xx-F-BU-1-058	Bighorn Sheep	2,750.00	3,100.00
xx-F-BU-1-059	Canyon Wren	850.00	925.00
xx-F-BU-1-060	Daffodil Manco	450.00	500.00
xx-F-BU-1-061	Junco on Snow	600.00	650.00
xx-F-BU-1-062	Lily Harlequin	575.00	635.00
xx-F-BU-1-063	Pricklly Pear Cactus	900.00	995.00
73-F-BU-1-064	White-Throated Sparrow	800.00	800.00 - 875.00
Burgues	Burgues Porcelains	I. Burgues	25
xx-F-BU-1-065	Bighorn Sheep, Glazed	3,000.00	3,400.00
Burgues	Burgues Porcelains	I. Burgues	300
xx-F-BU-1-066	Burro, Young	1,250.00	1,250.00
78-F-BU-1-067	Heavenly Blue Morning Glory	200.00	200.00
xx-F-BU-1-068	Ruby-Throated Hummingbird	600.00	650.00
xx-F-BU-1-069	Young Burro	1,250.00	1,375.00
Burgues	Burgues Porcelains	I. Burgues	50
xx-F-BU-1-070	Cassin's Kingbird	750.00	825.00
76-F-BU-1-071	Spirit of Freedom, Equus Caballus, Color	1,500.00	1,500.00
76-F-BU-1-072	Spirit of Freedom, Equus Caballus, White	1,000.00	1,000.00
Burgues	Burgues Porcelains	I. Burgues	100
xx-F-BU-1-073	Chanticleer	1,300.00	1,850.00
xx-F-BU-1-074	Golden-Winged Warbler In Nest	1,100.00	1,650.00
Burgues	Burgues	I. Burgues	75
xx-F-BU-1-075	Chickadee on Dogwood	950.00	1,100.00
73-F-BU-1-076	Lilac Charm Rose	700.00	775.00
xx-F-BU-1-077	Water Lily Fire Crest	1,250.00	1,375.00
xx-F-BU-1-078	White-Breasted Nuthatches	3,500.00	3,850.00
xx-F-BU-1-079	Yellow Warbler	700.00	950.00
Burgues	Burgues Porcelains	I. Burgues	540
xx-F-BU-1-080	Chipmunk with Fly Amanita	400.00	500.00
xx-F-BU-1-081	Golden-Crowned Kinglet	500.00	550.00
Burgues	Burgues Porcelains	I. Burgues	30
xx-F-BU-1-082	Madonna	125.00	2,700.00
Burgues	Burgues Porcelains	I. Burgues	150
73-F-BU-1-083	Magnolia, Oriental Strain	1,600.00	1,750.00
xx-F-BU-1-084	Veiltail Goldfish, Clear Glaze	875.00	1,100.00
xx-F-BU-1-085	Veiltail Goldfish, Decorated	875.00	950.00
xx-F-BU-1-086	Wild Rose	2,500.00	2,750.00
Creative World	Woodcarvings	N. Rockwell	2,500
79-F-CW-1-001	Little Leaguer	175.00	180.00
79-F-CW-1-002	First Formal	190.00	195.00
Cybis	Animal Kingdom	Cybis	100
xx-F-CY-1-001	Bull	150.00	4,500.00
xx-F-CY-1-002	Elephant	600.00	5,000.00
xx-F-CY-1-003	Horse	150.00	2,000.00
xx-F-CY-1-004	Nashua	2,000.00	3,000.00
Cybis	Animal Kingdom	Cybis	250
xx-F-CY-1-005	American White Buffalo	1,250.00	4,000.00
Cybis	Animal Kingdom	Cybis	350
xx-F-CY-1-006	Stallion	475.00	850.00
xx-F-CY-1-007	Thoroughbred	425.00	1,500.00
Cybis	Biblical	Cybis	Few
xx-F-CY-2-001	Madonna, House of Gold	125.00	4,000.00
Cybis	Biblical	Cybis	10
xx-F-CY-2-002	Holy Child of Prague	1,500.00	75,000.00
Cybis	Biblical	Cybis	50
xx-F-CY-2-003	Exodus	350.00	2,600.00
xx-F-CY-2-004	Flight Into Egypt	175.00	2,500.00
xx-F-CY-2-005	The Prophet	250.00	3,500.00
Cybis	Biblical	Cybis	500
76-F-CY-2-006	Noah	975.00	2,400.00
Cybis	Biblical	Cybis	750
xx-F-CY-2-007	Moses, The Great Lawgiver	250.00	3,500.00
Cybis	Birds & Flowers	Cybis	50
xx-F-Cy-3-001	Great Horned Owl (color)	3,250.00	7,500.00
Cybis	Birds & Flowers	Cybis	75
xx-F-Cy-3-002	American White Turkey	1,450.00	1,600.00
xx-F-CY-3-003	American Wild Turkey	1,950.00	2,200.00
Cybis	Birds & Flowers	Cybis	100
xx-F-Cy-3-004	Golden Clarion Lily	250.00	4,500.00
Cybis	Birds & Flowers	Cybis	150
xx-F-CY-3-005	Great Horned Owl (white)	1,950.00	4,500.00
xx-F-CY-3-006	Pheasant	750.00	5,000.00
Cybis	Birds & Flowers	Cybis	200
xx-F-CY-3-007	Blue-Gray Gnatcatchers	400.00	2,500.00
xx-F-CY-3-008	Golden Winged Warbler	1,075.00	1,150.00
Cybis	Birds & Flowers	Cybis	250
xx-F-CY-3-009	Iris	500.00	4,500.00
Cybis	Birds & Flowers	Cybis	275
xx-F-CY-3-010	Blue Headed Vireo with Lilac	1,200.00	2,200.00
Cybis	Birds & Flowers	Cybis	350
xx-F-CY-3-011	Autumn Dogwood	1,100.00	1,200.00
xx-F-CY-3-012	Clematis with House Wren	1,300.00	1,400.00
xx-F-CY-3-013	Dahlia	450.00	1,800.00
xx-F-CY-3-014	Dutch Crocus	550.00	750.00
xx-F-CY-3-015	Great White Heron	850.00	3,750.00
xx-F-CY-3-016	Skylarks	300.00	1,800.00
Cybis	Birds & Flowers	Cybis	400
xx-F-CY-3-017	American Crested Iris	975.00	1,150.00
xx-F-CY-3-018	Apple Blossoms	350.00	550.00
xx-F-CY-3-019	Sandpipers	700.00	1,500.00
Cybis	Birds & Flowers	Cybis	500
xx-F-CY-3-020	Calla Lily	750.00	1,750.00
xx-F-CY-3-021	Christmas Rose	250.00	750.00
xx-F-CY-3-022	Little Blue Heron	425.00	1,500.00
xx-F-CY-3-023	Narcissus	350.00	550.00
xx-F-CY-3-024	Turtle Doves	350.00	5,000.00
xx-F-CY-3-025	Wood Duck	325.00	800.00
Cybis	Birds & Flowers	Cybis	750
xx-F-CY-3-026	Pansies, Chinolina Lady	295.00	400.00
Cybis	Birds & Flowers	Cybis	1,000
xx-F-CY-3-027	Pansies, China Maid	275.00	350.00
Cybis	Carousel - Circus	Cybis	150
xx-F-CY-4-001	Circus Rider	2,275.00	3,000.00
Cybis	Carousel - Circus	Cybis	325
xx-F-CY-4-002	Carousel Goat	875.00	1,200.00
xx-F-CY-4-003	Carousel Horse	925.00	3,000.00

Company / Number	Series / Name	Artist / Issue Price	Edition limit / Quote
Cybis	Carousel - Circus	Cybis	350
75-F-CY-4-004	Bicentennial Horse Ticonderoga	925.00	3,000.00
Cybis	Carousel - Circus	Cybis	1,000
xx-F-CY-4-005	Performing Pony, Poppy	325.00	1,200.00
Cybis	Children to Cherish	Cybis	239
xx-F-CY-5-001	Baby Bust	375.00	1,000.00
Cybis	Children to Cherish	Cybis	500
xx-F-CY-5-002	Mary, Mary	475.00	750.00
Cybis	Children to Cherish	Cybis	1,000
xx-F-CY-5-003	Rapunzel/Apricot	475.00	1,000.00
Cybis	Commemorative	Cybis	10
xx-F-CY-6-001	Chess Set	30,000.00	60,000.00
Cybis	Commemorative	Cybis	100
71-F-CY-6-002	Cree Indian, Cree Indian	2,500.00	5,500.00
Cybis	Commemorative	Cybis	200
xx-F-CY-6-003	Columbia	1,000.00	2,500.00
Cybis	Commemorative	Cybis	250
xx-F-CY-6-004	Conductor's Hands	250.00	1,500.00
Cybis	Fantasia	Cybis	200
77-F-CY-6-005	Oceania	1,250.00	1,500.00
Cybis	Fantasia	Cybis	500
73-F-CY-7-001	Cybele	675.00	800.00
xx-F-CY-7-002	Pegasus	1,450.00	3,750.00
78-F-CY-7-003	Satin	1,100.00	2,250.00
xx-F-CY-7-004	Unicorn	1,250.00	3,750.00
Cybis	Land of Chimeric	Cybis	750
xx-F-CY-8-001	Queen Titania	725.00	2,100.00
Cybis	North American Indian	Cybis	200
77-F-CY-9-001	Crow Dancer, Great Thunder	3,875.00	6,000.00
xx-F-CY-9-002	Eskimo Mother	1,875.00	2,500.00
Cybis	Portraits in Porcelain	Cybis	200
xx-F-CY-10-001	Ballet - Prince Florimund	975.00	1,000.00
xx-F-CY-10-002	Ballet - Princess Aurora	1,125.00	1,500.00
Cybis	Portraits in Porcelain	Cybis	283
xx-F-CY-10-001	Folk Singer	300.00	850.00
Cybis	Portraits in Porcelain	Cybis	350
xx-F-CY-10-002	Chinese Goddess 'Kwan Yin'	1,250.00	2,000.00
Cybis	Portraits in Porcelain	Cybis	500
81-F-CY-10-003	Berengaria	1,450.00	2,250.00
xx-F-CY-10-004	Hamlet	350.00	1,750.00
xx-F-CY-10-005	Scarlett	450.00	3,000.00
xx-F-CY-10-006	Beatrice	225.00	1,500.00
Cybis	Portraits in Porcelain	Cybis	750
xx-F-CY-10-007	Eleanor of Aquitaine	875.00	2,800.00
xx-F-CY-10-008	Portia	825.00	3,250.00
xx-F-CY-10-009	Queen Esther	925.00	1,600.00
Cybis	Portraits in Porcelain	Cybis	800
xx-F-CY-10-010	Guinevere	250.00	1,400.00
xx-F-CY-10-011	Juliet	175.00	4,000.00
xx-F-CY-10-012	Ophelia	650.00	3,500.00
Cybis	Theatre of Porcelain	Cybis	250
78-F-CY-11-001	Court Jester	1,450.00	1,750.00
The Danbury Mint	Rockwell Figurines	N. Rockwell	Ltd. Production
80-F-DM-1-001	Trick or Treat	55.00	60.00
80-F-DM-1-002	Gramps at the Reins	55.00	60.00
80-F-DM-1-003	Grandpa Snowman	55.00	60.00
80-F-DM-1-004	Caught in the Act	55.00	60.00
80-F-DM-1-005	Boy on Stilts	55.00	60.00
80-F-DM-1-006	Young Love	55.00	60.00
Dave Grossman Designs	Dave Grossman Figurines	N. Rockwell	1,000
74-F-DG-1-001	Doctor & Doll	300.00	1,200.00
75-F-DG-1-002	Barbershop Quartet	175.00	1,000.00
75-F-DG-1-003	No Swimming	150.00	300.00
75-F-DG-1-004	100th Year of Baseball	125.00	300.00
75-F-DG-1-005	See America First	100.00	300.00
79-F-DG-1-006	Leapfrog	440.00	800.00
80-F-DG-1-007	Dreams of Long Ago	500.00	650.00
Dave Grossman Designs	Dave Grossman Figurines	N. Rockwell	7,500
75-F-DG-1-008	Whitewashing the Fence	60.00	285.00
76-F-DG-1-009	First Smoke	60.00	180.00
77-F-DG-1-010	Take Your Medicine	63.00	135.00
78-F-DG-1-011	Lost in the Cave	70.00	135.00
Dave Grossman Designs	Dave Grossman Figurines	N. Rockwell	5,000
78-F-DG-1-012	Young Doctor	100.00	120.00
Dave Grossman Designs	Dave Grossman Figurines	N. Rockwell	10,000
80-F-DG-1-013	Listening	100.00	120.00
80-F-DG-1-014	The Secret	100.00	120.00
81-F-DG-1-015	No Kings Nor Dukes	100.00	120.00
81-F-DG-1-016	The Snake Escapes	100.00	120.00
Dave Grossman Designs	Dave Grossman Figurines	N. Rockwell	Year of Issue
81-F-DG-1-017	Young Artist	96.00	115.00
Designers Collection	A Holly Hobbie Creation Collection	Hobbie	15,000
73-F-DC-1-001	Girl with Packages	18.50	18.50
73-F-DC-1-002	Blue Girl	18.50	18.50
73-F-DC-1-003	Girl with Bonnet of Flowers	18.50	18.50
73-F-DC-1-004	Girl with Tote	18.50	18.50
73-F-DC-1-005	Girl Holding Cat	18.50	18.50
73-F-DC-1-006	Girl with Basket of Kittens	18.50	18.50
Designers Collection	A Holly Hobby Creation Keepsake Collection	Hobbie	6,000
74-F-DC-2-001	Boy with Dog	18.50	18.50
74-F-DC-2-002	Girl at Pump	18.50	18.50
74-F-DC-2-003	Girl Sewing	18.50	18.50
74-F-DC-2-004	Girl Holding Bouquet	18.50	18.50
74-F-DC-2-005	Girl Holding Skirt Dancing	18.50	18.50

Company / Number	Series / Name	Artist / Issue Price	Edition limit / Quote
74-F-DC-2-006	Girl with Mixing Bowl	18.50	18.50
Designers Collection	Christmas Keepsakes Collection - Holly Hobbie Figurines	Hobbie	4,500
76-F-DC-3-001	Christmas Keepsake 1976	17.50	17.50
Designers Collection	Christmas Keepsakes Collection - Holly Hobbie Figurines	Hobbie	9,000
77-F-DC-3-002	Christmas Keepsake 1977	25.00	25.00
78-F-DC-3-003	Christmas Fun	35.00	35.00
Designers Collection	Christmas Keepsake Collection - Holly Hobbie Figurines	Hobbie	6,000
79-F-DC-3-004	Joy to the World	35.00	35.00
80-F-DC-3-005	Christmas is Love	45.00	45.00
Designers Collection	Christmas Keepsakes Collection - Holly Hobbie Figurines	Hobbie	15,000
81-F-DC-3-006	Christmas Surprise	52.50	52.50
82-F-DC-3-007	Holiday Fun	55.00	55.00
83-F-DC-3-008	Christmas Greetings	67.50	67.50
Designers Collection	Holly Hobbie Commemorative Collection Bicentennial	Hobbie	2,000
76-F-DC-4-001	3 Figure Fife & Drum	40.00	40.00
Designers Collection	A Mother's Remembrance Collection - Holly Hobbie Figurines	Hobbie	3,000
76-F-DC-5-001	A Mother is Love	7.50	7.50
Designers Collection	A Mother's Remembrance Collection - Holly Hobbie Figurines	Hobbie	6,000
77-F-DC-5-002	A Mother's Remembrance	16.00	16.00
Designers Collection	A Mother's Remembrance Collection - Holly Hobbie Figurines	Hobbie	7,500
78-F-DC-5-003	Mothers Stitch a Bond of Love	30.00	30.00
79-F-DC-5-004	A Mother's Love	35.00	35.00
80-F-DC-5-005	Mother's Sweet Love	35.00	35.00
81-F-DC-5-006	A Mother's Gift	45.00	45.00
82-F-DC-5-007	Mother's Miracles	45.00	45.00
83-F-DC-5-008	Mother's Joys	45.00	45.00
Designers Collection	Holly Hobbie Fine Pewter Collection	Hobbie	6,000
77-F-DC-6-001	Sweet Dreams	27.50	40.00
77-F-DC-6-002	Happy Times	27.50	40.00
77-F-DC-6-003	Kind Heart	27.50	40.00
77-F-DC-6-004	Treasures	27.50	40.00
77-F-DC-6-005	Love	27.50	40.00
77-F-DC-6-006	Best Friends	27.50	40.00
79-F-DC-6-007	The Gentle Touch	40.00	40.00
79-F-DC-6-008	Just Friends	40.00	40.00
79-F-DC-6-009	Winter Magic	25.00	25.00
Designers Collection	Holly Hobbie Fine Pewter Collection	Hobbie	8,000
79-F-DC-6-010	Little Blessings	40.00	40.00
Designers Collection	Holly Hobbie Precious Moments Collection Series I	Hobbie	17,500
77-F-DC-7-001	The Caring Heart	25.00	30.00
77-F-DC-7-002	Carefree Days	25.00	30.00
77-F-DC-7-003	That Special Touch	25.00	30.00
77-F-DC-7-004	That Perfect Blend	25.00	30.00
77-F-DC-7-005	A Secret Shared	25.00	30.00
77-F-DC-7-006	The Simple Things	25.00	30.00
Designers Collection	Holly Hobbie Precious Moments Collection - Series II	Hobbie	17,50
79-F-DC-8-001	A Moment Shared	30.00	45.00
79-F-DC-8-002	Togetherness	30.00	45.00
79-F-DC-8-003	Caring	30.00	45.00
Designers Collection	Holly Hobbie Precious Moments Collection - Series III	Hobbie	17,500
79-F-DC-9-001	Showers of Sunshine	22.50	25.00
79-F-DC-9-002	Simple Pleasures	20.00	22.50
79-F-DC-9-003	Pleasant Dreams	20.00	22.50
Designers Collection	Holly Hobbie Precious Moments Collection - Series IV	Hobbie	17,500
80-F-DC-10-001	Farmyard Fun	40.00	45.00
80-F-DC-10-002	Sunshine Fun-Time	40.00	45.00
80-F-DC-10-003	Sweet Joys	40.00	45.00
Designers Collection	Holly Hobbie Precious Moments Collection - Series V First Edition	Hobbie	17,500
83-F-DC-11-001	A Pleasant Task	48.00	48.00
Designers Collection	Christmas Keepsake Collection - Holly Hobbie Mini Figurine	Hobbie	12,000
78-F-DC-12-001	A Christmas Prayer 1978	7.50	7.50
Designers Collection	Holly Hobbie Sweet Remembrance Collection - Series I	Hobbie	12,000
78-F-DC-13-001	Happy Days	20.0	40.00
78-F-DC-13-002	Loving Ways	20.00	40.00
78-F-DC-13-003	Good Times	20.00	40.00
Designers Collection	Holly Hobbie Sweet Remembrance Collection - Series II	Hobbie	12,000
79-F-DC-14-001	Going Places	30.00	40.00
79-F-DC-14-002	Friends Forever	30.00	40.00
79-F-DC-14-003	All Better	30.00	40.00
Designers Collection	Holly Hobbie Sweet Remembrance Collection - Series III	Hobbie	12,000
80-F-DC-15-001	Homemade Fun	40.00	40.00
80-F-DC-15-002	Good Friends & Fun	48.00	48.00
80-F-DC-15-003	Stitching Fun	50.00	50.00

Company	Series	Artist	Edition limit
Number	Name	Issue Price	Quote
Designers Collection	Love Collection Holly Hobbie Figurines	Hobbie	6,000
78-F-DC-16-001	A Gift of Love 1978	30.00	30.00
80-F-DC-16-002	Happy Hearts 1980	30.00	30.00
82-F-DC-16-003	Special Love	45.00	45.00
83-F-DC-16-004	Happy Hearts 1983	50.00	50.00
Designers Collection	Love Collection Holly Hobbie Figurines	Hobbie	7,500
81-F-DC-17-001	Love Shared	40.00	40.00
Designers Collection	Wedding/Anniversary Keepsakes Collection Holly Hobbie Figurines	Hobbie	6,000
78-F-DC-18-001	Love is for Sharing	25.00	25.00
Designers Collection	Wedding/Anniversary Keepsakes Collection Holly Hobbie Figurines	Hobbie	12,000
80-F-DC-19-001	The Music of Love	35.00	35.00
Designers Collection	Holly Hobbie Blue Girl Collection	Hobbie	45,000
79-F-DC-20-001	Blue Girl	15.00	25.00
Designers Collection	Holly Hobbie Blue Girl Collection	Hobbie	20,000
83-F-DC-20-002	Blue Girl	25.00	25.00
Designers Collection	Holly Hobbie Classics Collection - Series I	Hobbie	20,000
79-F-DC-21-001	Gentle Hearts	45.00	60.00
79-F-DC-21-002	Reveries	45.00	60.00
79-F-DC-21-003	Windy Weather	45.00	60.00
Designers Collection	Holly Hobbie Classics Collection - Series II	Hobbie	20,000
80-F-DC-22-001	Yesterday's Memories	50.00	60.00
80-F-DC-22-002	The Heart's Treasures	50.00	60.00
80-F-DC-22-003	Meadow Flowers	50.00	60.00
Designers Collection	Holly Hobbie Classics Collection - Series III	Hobbie	20,000
81-F-DC-23-001	A Day to Enjoy	60.00	60.00
81-F-DC-23-002	Companions	60.00	60.00
81-F-DC-23-003	Memories of Gold	60.00	60.00
Designers Collection	Holly Hobbie Classics Collection - Series IV	Hobbie	20,000
83-F-DC-24-001	Friendship's Bouquet	60.00	60.00
Designers Collection	Christmas Keepsakes Collection Holly Hobbie Baby's First Christmas Figurines	Hobbie	24,000
80-F-DC-25-001	Baby's First Christmas	12.00	12.00
81-F-DC-25-002	Christmas Magic	15.00	15.00
82-F-DC-25-003	Baby's Joy	15.00	15.00
83-F-DC-25-004	Little One	15.00	15.00
Designers Collection	Holly Hobbie Grandparent Keepsakes Collection	Hobbie	12,000
81-F-DC-26-001	Grandparent's Keepsake 1981	40.00	40.00
82-F-DC-26-002	Grandparent's Keepsake 1982	45.00	45.00
83-F-DC-26-003	Grandma's Love	48.00	48.00
Designers Collection	Holly Hobbie Autumn Keepsake Collection	Hobbie	10,000
81-F-DC-27-001	Thankful Hearts	50.00	50.00
82-F-DC-27-002	Harvest of Happiness	65.00	65.00
83-F-DC-27-003	Harvest Prayer	50.00	50.00
Designers Collection	Holly Hobbie Baby Keepsakes Collection	Hobbie	15,000
81-F-DC-28-001	Little Blessings	25.00	25.00
83-F-DC-28-002	Bundle of Joy	35.00	35.00
Designers Collection	Collector's Edition Fine Arts Figurines	Hobbie	2,500
81-F-DC-29-001	Unicorn Magic	65.00	130.00
82-F-DC-29-002	Pegasus	75.00	100.00
Designers Collection	Collector's Edition Holly Hobbie Figurines	Hobbie	2,500
81-F-DC-30-001	On The Carousel	125.00	225.00
82-F-DC-30-002	Country Morning	125.00	125.00
83-F-DC-30-003	The Recital	125.00	125.00
Designers Collection	Spring Love Collection Holly Hobbie Figurines	Hobbie	15,000
82-F-DC-31-001	Joyful Spring	45.00	45.00
Designers Collection	Holly Hobbie Commemorative Collection - Fifteenth Anniversary	Hobbie	25,000
83-F-DC-32-001	Blue Girl	60.00	60.00
Designers Collection	Holly Hobbie Commemorative Collection - Fifteenth Anniversary	Hobbie	10,000
83-F-DC-32-002	Waltz of the Flowers	55.00	55.00
83-F-DC-32-003	Beautiful Dreamer	38.00	38.00
Franklin Mint	Joys of Childhood	Rockwell	3,700
76-F-FM-1-001	Hopscotch	120.00	175.00
76-F-FM-1-002	The Fishing Hole	120.00	175.00
76-F-FM-1-003	Dressing Up	120.00	175.00
76-F-FM-1-004	The Stilt Walker	120.00	175.00
76-F-FM-1-005	Trick or Treat	120.00	175.00
76-F-FM-1-006	Time Out	120.00	175.00
76-F-FM-1-007	The Marble Champ	120.00	175.00
76-F-FM-1-008	The Nurse	120.00	175.00
76-F-FM-1-009	Ride 'Em Coyboy	120.00	175.00
76-F-FM-1-010	Coasting Along	120.00	175.00
Goebel Collectors Club	Goebel Collectors Club Exclusives	M. I. Hummel	Closed
xx-F-GC-1-001	Valentine Gift 387	45.00	325.00
xx-F-GC-1-002	Smiling Through Plaque 690	50.00	85.00
xx-F-GC-1-003	Valentine Joy 399	95.00	150.00
xx-F-GC-1-004	Daisies Don't Tell 380	80.00	125.00
xx-F-GC-1-005	It's Cold	80.00	80.00
xx-F-GC-1-006	What Now? 422	90.00	90.00
xx-F-GC-2-001	A Fair Measure 345		115.50

Company	Series	Artist	Edition limit
Number	Name	Issue Price	Quote
xx-F-GC-2-002	Accordian Boy 185		72.00
xx-F-GC-2-003	Adoration 23/1		155.00
xx-F-GC-2-004	Adoration 23/111		220.50
xx-F-GC-2-005	Adventure Bound 347		1,790.00
xx-F-GC-2-006	Angel Duet 261		88.00
xx-F-GC-2-007	Angel Serenade 214D		33.00
xx-F-GC-2-008	Angel Serenade with Lamb 83		84.00
xx-F-GC-2-009	Angel with Accordian 238/B		23.00
xx-F-GC-2-010	Angel with Lute 238/A		23.00
xx-F-GC-2-011	Angel with Trumpet 238/C		23.00
xx-F-GC-2-012	Angelic Song 144		63.00
xx-F-GC-2-013	Apple Tree Boy 142/3/0		55.00
xx-F-GC-2-014	Apple Tree Boy 142/1		105.00
xx-F-GC-2-015	Apple Tree Boy 142/V		525.00
xx-F-GC-2-016	Apple Tree Boy 142/X		13,100.00
xx-F-GC-2-017	Apple Tree Girl 141/3/0		55.00
xx-F-GC-2-018	Apple Tree Girl 141/1		105.00
xx-F-GC-2-019	Apple Tree Girl 141/V		525.00
xx-F-GC-2-020	Apple Tree Girl 141/X		13,100.00
xx-F-GC-2-021	Artist 304		94.50
xx-F-GC-2-022	Auf Wiedersehen 153/0		94.50
xx-F-GC-2-023	Auf Wiedersehen 153/1		125.00
xx-F-GC-2-024	Autumn Harvest 355		88.00
xx-F-GC-2-025	Baker 128		72.00
xx-F-GC-2-026	Band Leader 129		88.00
xx-F-GC-2-027	Barnyard Hero 195/2/0		72.00
xx-F-GC-2-028	Barnyard Herd 195/1		125.00
xx-F-GC-2-029	Bashful 377		77.50
xx-F-GC-2-030	Begging His Share 9		88.00
xx-F-GC-2-031	Be Patient 197/2/0		77.50
xx-F-GC-2-032	Be Patient 197/1		105.00
xx-F-GC-2-033	Big Housecleaning 363		115.50
xx-F-GC-2-034	Bird Duet 169		66.00
xx-F-GC-2-035	Bird Watcher 300		100.00
xx-F-GC-2-036	Birthday Serenade 218/2/0		77.50
xx-F-GC-2-037	Birthday Serenade 218/0		125.00
xx-F-GC-2-038	Blessed Event 333		147.00
xx-F-GC-2-039	Bookworm 8		88.00
xx-F-GC-2-040	Bookworm 3/1		140.00
xx-F-GC-2-041	Bookworm 3/11		630.00
xx-F-GC-2-042	Bookworm 3/111		680.00
xx-F-GC-2-043	Boots 143/0		72.00
xx-F-GC-2-044	Boots 143/1		110.00
xx-F-GC-2-045	Botanist 351		88.00
xx-F-GC-2-046	Boy with Accordian 390		31.50
xx-F-GC-2-047	Boy with Horse 239C		25.00
xx-F-GC-2-048	Boy with Toothache 217		77.50
xx-F-GC-2-049	Brother 95		66.00
xx-F-GC-2-050	Builder 305		94.50
xx-F-GC-2-051	Busy Student 367		72.00
xx-F-GC-2-052	Carnival 328		77.50
xx-F-GC-2-053	Celestial Musician 188		115.50
xx-F-GC-2-054	Chick Girl 57/0		66.00
xx-F-GC-2-055	Chick Girl 57/1		105.00
xx-F-GC-2-056	Chicken-Licken 385		125.00
xx-F-GC-2-057	Chimney Sweep 12/2/0		39.00
xx-F-GC-2-058	Chimney Sweep 12/1		72.00
xx-F-GC-2-059	Christ Child 18		52.50
xx-F-GC-2-060	Christmas Song 343		90.00
xx-F-GC-2-061	Cinderella 337		115.50
xx-F-GC-2-062	Close Harmony 336		125.00
xx-F-GC-2-063	Confidentially 314		94.50
xx-F-GC-2-064	Congratulations 17/0		66.00
xx-F-GC-2-065	Coquettes 179		105.00
xx-F-GC-2-066	Crossroads 331		185.00
xx-F-GC-2-067	Culprits 56/A		105.00
xx-F-GC-2-068	Doctor 127		63.00
xx-F-GC-2-069	Doll Bath 319		94.50
xx-F-GC-2-070	Doll Mother 67		94.50
xx-F-GC-2-071	Duet 130		105.00
xx-F-GC-2-072	Easter Greetings 378		88.00
xx-F-GC-2-073	Easter Time 384		125.00
xx-F-GC-2-074	Eventide 99		125.00
xx-F-GC-2-075	Farewell 65		110.00
xx-F-GC-2-076	Farm Boy 66		88.00
xx-F-GC-2-077	Favorite Pet 361		100.00
xx-F-GC-2-078	Feathered Friend 344		110.00
xx-F-GC-2-079	Feeding Time 199/0		88.00
xx-F-GC-2-080	Feeding Time 199/0		88.00
xx-F-GC-2-081	Feeding Time 199/1		94.50
xx-F-GC-2-082	Festival Harmony, with Mandolin 172/0		115.50
xx-F-GC-2-083	Festival Harmony, with Mandolin 172/11		220.50
xx-F-GC-2-084	Festival Harmony, with Flute 173/0		115.50
xx-F-GC-2-085	Festival Harmony, with Flute 173/11		220.50
xx-F-GC-2-086	Flower Vendor 381		100.00
xx-F-GC-2-087	Follow the Leader 369		450.00
xx-F-GC-2-088	For Father 87		83.00
xx-F-GC-2-089	For Mother 257		63.00
xx-F-GC-2-090	Forest Shrine 183		273.00
xx-F-GC-2-091	Friends 136/1		88.00
xx-F-GC-2-092	Friends 136/V		525.00
xx-F-GC-2-093	Gay Adventure 356		75.00
xx-F-GC-2-094	Girl with Doll 239/B		25.00
xx-F-GC-2-095	Girl with Music 389		31.50
xx-F-GC-2-096	Girl with Nosegay 239A		25.00
xx-F-GC-2-097	Girl with Trumpet 391		31.50
xx-F-GC-2-098	Globe Trotter 79		72.00
xx-F-GC-2-099	Going to Grandma's 52/0		100.00
xx-F-GC-2-100	Going to Grandma's 52/1		240.00
xx-F-GC-2-101	Good Friends 182		83.00
xx-F-GC-2-102	Good Hunting 307		94.50
xx-F-GC-2-103	Good Night 214C		39.00
xx-F-GC-2-104	Good Shepherd 42/0		66.00
xx-F-GC-2-105	Goose Girl 47/3/0		66.00
xx-F-GC-2-106	Goose Girl 47/0		90.00
xx-F-GC-2-107	Goose Girl 47/11		200.00
xx-F-GC-2-108	Guiding Angel 357		42.00
xx-F-GC-2-109	Happiness 86		55.00
xx-F-GC-2-110	Happy Birthday 176/0		94.50

Company	Series	Artist	Edition limit
Number	**Name**	**Issue Price**	**Quote**
xx-F-GC-2-111	Happy Birthday 176/1		136.50
xx-F-GC-2-112	Happy Days 150/2/0		83.00
xx-F-GC-2-113	Happy Days 150/0		125.00
xx-F-GC-2-114	Happy Days 150/1		240.00
xx-F-GC-2-115	Happy Pastime 69		66.00
xx-F-GC-2-116	Happy Traveller 109/0		55.00
xx-F-GC-2-117	Hear Ye! Hear Ye! 15/0		88.00
xx-F-GC-2-118	Hear Ye! Hear Ye! 15/1		100.00
xx-F-GC-2-119	Hear Ye! Hear Ye! 15/11		185.00
xx-F-GC-2-120	Heavenly Angel 21/0		42.00
xx-F-GC-2-121	Heavenly Angel 21/01/2		73.50
xx-F-GC-2-122	Heavenly Angel 21/1		88.00
xx-F-GC-2-123	Heavenly Angel 21/11		184.00
xx-F-GC-2-124	Heavenly Lullaby 262		80.00
xx-F-GC-2-125	Heavenly Protection 88/1		155.00
xx-F-GC-2-126	Heavenly Protection 88/11		231.00
xx-F-GC-2-127	Hello 124/0		77.50
xx-F-GC-2-128	Hello 124/1		110.00
xx-F-GC-2-129	Holy Child 70		63.00
xx-F-GC-2-130	Home from Market 198/2/0		55.00
xx-F-GC-2-131	Home from Market 198/1		88.00
xx-F-GC-2-132	Homeward Bound 334		157.50
xx-F-GC-2-133	"Hummel" Display Plaque 187/C		42.00
xx-F-GC-2-134	Infant of Krumbad 78/1/11		21.00
xx-F-GC-2-135	Infant of Krumbad 78/11/11		26.50
xx-F-GC-2-136	Infant of Krumbad 78/111/11		31.50
xx-F-GC-2-137	In Tune 414		120.00
xx-F-GC-2-138	Joyful 53		44.00
xx-F-GC-2-139	Joyous News 27/11		94.50
xx-F-GC-2-140	Just Resting 112/3/0		63.00
xx-F-GC-2-141	Just Resting 112/1		94.50
xx-F-GC-2-142	Kiss Me 311		94.50
xx-F-GC-2-143	Knitting Lesson 256		220.00
xx-F-GC-2-144	Latest News 184/0		115.50
xx-F-GC-2-145	Let's Sing 110/0		50.00
xx-F-GC-2-146	Let's Sing 110/1		72.00
xx-F-GC-2-147	Letter to Santa Claus 340		137.00
xx-F-GC-2-148	Little Band 392		132.00
xx-F-GC-2-149	Little Bookkeeper 306		115.50
xx-F-GC-2-150	Little Cellist 89/1		88.00
xx-F-GC-2-151	Little Cellist 89/11		195.00
xx-F-GC-2-152	Little Drummer 240		55.00
xx-F-GC-2-153	Little Fiddler 4		72.00
xx-F-GC-2-154	Little Fiddler 2/0		94.50
xx-F-GC-2-155	Little Fiddler 2/1		185.00
xx-F-GC-2-156	Little Fiddler 2/11		630.00
xx-F-GC-2-157	Little Fiddler 2/111		680.00
xx-F-GC-2-158	Little Gabriel 32		55.00
xx-F-GC-2-159	Little Gardener 74		55.00
xx-F-GC-2-160	Little Goat Herder 200/0		83.00
xx-F-GC-2-161	Little Goat Herder 200/1		94.50
xx-F-GC-2-162	Little Guardian 145		63.00
xx-F-GC-2-163	Little Helper 73		55.00
xx-F-GC-2-164	Little Hiker 16/2/0		44.00
xx-F-GC-2-165	Little Hiker 16/1		77.50
xx-F-GC-2-166	Little Nurse 376		100.00
xx-F-GC-2-167	Little Pharmacist 322		100.00
xx-F-GC-2-168	Little Scholar 80		72.00
xx-F-GC-2-169	Little Shopper 96		55.00
xx-F-GC-2-170	Little Sweeper 171		55.00
xx-F-GC-2-171	Little Tailor 308		105.00
xx-F-GC-2-172	Little Thrifty 118		66.00
xx-F-GC-2-173	Little Tooter 214H		50.00
xx-F-GC-2-174	Lost Sheep 68/2/0		55,00
xx-F-GC-2-175	Lost Sheep 68/0		77.50
xx-F-GC-2-176	Lost Stocking 374		63.00
xx-F-GC-2-177	Mail is Here 226		265.00
xx-F-GC-2-178	March Winds 43		55.00
xx-F-GC-2-179	Max & Moritz 123		77.50
xx-F-GC-2-180	Meditation 13/2/0		55.00
xx-F-GC-2-181	Meditation 13/0		77.50
xx-F-GC-2-182	Meditation 13/11		200.00
xx-F-GC-2-183	Meditation 13V		680.00
xx-F-GC-2-184	Merry Wanderer 11/2/0		55.00
xx-F-GC-2-185	Merry Wanderer 11/0		72.00
xx-F-GC-2-186	Merry Wanderer 7/0		100.00
xx-F-GC-2-187	Mery Wanderer 7/1		185.00
xx-F-GC-2-188	Merry Wanderer 7/11		630.00
xx-F-GC-2-189	Merry Wanderer 7/111		680.00
xx-F-GC-2-190	Merry Wanderer 7X		13,000.00
xx-F-GC-2-191	Mischief Maker 342		110.00
xx-F-GC-2-192	Mother's Darling 175		88.00
xx-F-GC-2-193	Mother's Helper 133		88.00
xx-F-GC-2-194	Mountaineer 315		94.50
xx-F-GC-2-195	Not for You 317		94.50
xx-F-GC-2-196	On Holiday 350		90.00
xx-F-GC-2-197	On Secret Path 386		115.50
xx-F-GC-2-198	Out of Danger 56/B		105.00
xx-F-GC-2-199	Photographer 178		105.00
xx-F-GC-2-200	Playmates 58/0		66.00
xx-F-GC-2-201	Playmates 58/1		100.00
xx-F-GC-2-202	Postman 119		83.00
xx-F-GC-2-203	Prayer Before Battle 20		72.00
xx-F-GC-2-204	Puppy Love 1		77.50
xx-F-GC-2-205	Retreat to Safety 201/2/0		72.00
xx-F-GC-2-206	Retreat to Safety 201/1		125.00
xx-F-GC-2-207	Ride into Christmas 396/2/0		100.00
xx-F-GC-2-208	Ride into Christmas 396		185.00
xx-F-GC-2-209	Ring Around the Rosie 348		1,310.00
xx-F-GC-2-210	Run-A-Way 327		115.50
xx-F-GC-2-211	St. George 55		144.00
xx-F-GC-2-212	St. Joseph, color, 214/B/11		83.00
xx-F-GC-2-213	School Boy 82/2/0		55.00
xx-F-GC-2-214	School Boy 82/0		72.00
xx-F-GC-2-215	School Boy 82/11		195.00
xx-F-GC-2-216	School Boys 170/1		525.00
xx-F-GC-2-217	School Girl 81/2/0		55.00
xx-F-GC-2-218	School Girl 81/0		72.00
xx-F-GC-2-219	School Girls 177/1		525.00
xx-F-GC-2-220	Sensitive Hunter 6/0		72.00
xx-F-GC-2-221	Sensitive Hunter 6/1		94.50
xx-F-GC-2-222	Sensitive Hunter 6/11		175.00
xx-F-GC-2-223	Serenade 85/0		55.00
xx-F-GC-2-224	Serenade 85/11		195.00
xx-F-GC-2-225	Shepherd's Boy 64		88.00
xx-F-GC-2-226	She Loves Me, She Love Me Not 174		72.00
xx-F-GC-2-227	Shining Light 358		42.00
xx-F-GC-2-228	Signs of Spring 203/2/0		72.00
xx-F-GC-2-229	Signs of Spring 203/1		94.50
xx-F-GC-2-230	Singing Lesson 63		55.00
xx-F-GC-2-231	Sister 98/2/0		55.00
xx-F-GC-2-232	Sister 98/0		66.00
xx-F-GC-2-233	Skier 59		88.00
xx-F-GC-2-234	Smart Little Sister 346		94.50
xx-F-GC-2-235	Soldier Boy 332		72.00
xx-F-GC-2-236	Soloist 135		55.00
xx-F-GC-2-237	Spring Cheer 72		55.00
xx-F-GC-2-238	Spring Dance 353/0		115.50
xx-F-GC-2-239	Spring Dance 353/1		265.00
xx-F-GC-2-240	Star Gazer 132		88.00
xx-F-GC-2-241	Stitch in Time 255		94.50
xx-F-GC-2-242	Stormy Weather 71		200.00
xx-F-GC-2-243	Street Singer 131		66.00
xx-F-GC-2-244	Strolling Along 5		72.00
xx-F-GC-2-245	Surprise 94/3/0		66.00
xx-F-GC-2-246	Surprise 94/1		94.50
xx-F-GC-2-247	Sweet Greetings 352		90.00
xx-F-GC-2-248	Sweet Music 186		83.00
xx-F-GC-2-249	Telling Her Secret 196/0		125.00
xx-F-GC-2-250	Telling Her Secret 196/1		240.00
xx-F-GC-2-251	Thoughtful 415		110.00
xx-F-GC-2-252	Timid Little Sister 394		200.00
xx-F-GC-2-253	To Market 49/3/0		77.50
xx-F-GC-2-254	To Market 49/0		115.50
xx-F-GC-2-255	To Market 49/1		240.00
xx-F-GC-2-256	Trumpet Boy 97		55.00
xx-F-GC-2-257	Tuneful Angel 359		42.00
xx-F-GC-2-258	Umbrella Boy 152/A/0		265.00
xx-F-GC-2-259	Umbrella Boy 152/A/11		750.00
xx-F-GC-2-260	Umbrella Girl 152/B/0		266.00
xx-F-GC-2-261	Umbrella Girl 152/B/11		750.00
xx-F-GC-2-262	Village Boy 51/3/0		39.00
xx-F-GC-2-263	Village Boy 51/2/0		55.00
xx-F-GC-2-264	Village Boy 51/0		88.00
xx-F-GC-2-265	Village Boy 51/1		110.00
xx-F-GC-2-266	Visiting an Invalid 382		94.50
xx-F-GC-2-267	Volunteers 50/2/0		105.00
xx-F-GC-2-268	Volunteers 50/0		136.50
xx-F-GC-2-269	Volunteers 50/1		240.00
xx-F-GC-2-270	Waiter 154/0		88.0
xx-F-GC-2-271	Waiter 154/1		110.00
xx-F-GC-2-272	Wash Day 321		94.50
xx-F-GC-2-273	Watchful Angel 194		136.50
xx-F-GC-2-274	Wayside Devotion 28/11		165.00
xx-F-GC-2-275	Wayside Devotion 28/111		231.00
xx-F-GC-2-276	Wayside Harmony 111/3/0		63.00
xx-F-GC-2-277	Wayside Harmony 111/1		94.50
xx-F-GC-2-278	Weary Wanderer 204		88.00
xx-F-GC-2-279	We Congratulate 214/E		66.00
xx-F-GC-2-280	We Congratulate 220		72.00
xx-F-GC-2-281	Which Hand? 258		63.00
xx-F-GC-2-282	Whitsuntide 163		125.00
xx-F-GC-2-283	Worship 84/0		68.50
xx-F-GC-2-284	Worship 84/V		630.00
Goebel	M. I. Hummel Collectibles Figurines	M. I. Hummel	Closed
xx-F-GC-3-001	Happy Traveler 109/11		195.00
xx-F-GC-3-002	School Boys 170/111		1,310.00
xx-F-GC-3-003	School Girls 177/111		1,310.00
Goebel	M. I. Hummel Collectibles Nativity Components	M. I. Hummel	Open
xx-F-GC-4-001	Madonna & Child 214 AM & K 2 Pieces color		110.00
xx-F-GC-4-002	Madonna 214/A/M/11		83.00
xx-F-GC-4-003	Infant Jesus 214/A/K		27.50
xx-F-GC-4-004	St. Joseph color 214/B/11		83.00
xx-F-GC-4-005	Goodnight 214/C/11		39.00
xx-F-GC-4-006	Angel Serenade 214/D/11		33.00
xx-F-GC-4-007	We Congratulate 214/E/11		66.00
xx-F-GC-4-008	Shepherd with Sheep 214/F/11 1 Piece		88.00
xx-F-GC-4-009	Shepherd Boy 214/G/11		50.00
xx-F-GC-4-010	Little Tooter 214/H/11		30.50
xx-F-GC-4-011	Donkey 214/J/11		30.50
xx-F-GC-4-012	Ox 214/K/11		83.00
xx-F-GC-4-013	King (standing) 214/L/11		83.00
xx-F-GC-4-014	King (kneeling on one knee) 214/M/11		83.00
xx-F-GC-4-015	King (kneeling on two knees) 214/N/11		77.00
xx-F-GC-4-016	Lamb 214/0/11		9.00
xx-F-GC-4-017	Flying Angel/color 366		55.00
xx-F-GC-4-018	Madonna 260A		290.00
xx-F-GC-4-019	St. Joseph 260B		290.00
xx-F-GC-4-020	Infant Jesus 260C		60.00
xx-F-GC-4-021	Good Night 260D		75.50
xx-F-GC-4-022	Angel Serenade 260E		66.00
xx-F-GC-4-023	We Congratulate 260F		200.00
xx-F-GC-4-024	Shepherd, standing 260G		315.00
xx-F-GC-4-025	Sheep (standing) with Lamb 260H		55.00
xx-F-GC-4-026	Shepherd Boy (kneeling)260J		174.00
xx-F-GC-4-027	Little Tooter 260K		84.00
xx-F-GC-4-028	Donkey 260L		66.00
xx-F-GC-4-029	Ox 260M		84.00
xx-F-GC-4-030	Moorish King 260N		290.00
xx-F-GC-4-031	KIng (standing) 260 O		290.00
xx-F-GC-4-032	King (kneeling) 260P		273.00
xx-F-GC-4-033	Sheep (lying) 260R		27.50
Goebel	M. I. Hummel Collectibles Nativity Sets	M. I. Hummel	Open
xx-F-GC-4-034	Holy Family 3 Pieces 214/A & B/11		197.50
xx-F-GC-4-035	12 Piece Set, Figurines Only, Color, 214/A,B,F,G,J, K,L,M,N,O/11 366		709.50

Company / Number	Series / Name	Artist / Issue Price	Edition limit / Quote
xx-F-GC-4-036	16 Piece Set, Figurines Only, Color, 214/A,B,C,D, E,F,G,H,J,K,L,M,N,O/11 366		888.50
xx-F-GC-4-037	17 Piece Set, Large Color 16 Figurines & Stable 260 A-S		2,930.00
Goebel	M. I. Hummel Collectibles Nativity Stables	M. I. Hummel	Open
xx-GC-4-038	Stable only to fit 12 or 16 piece HUM214 Set 214/SI		55.00
xx-GC-4-039	Stable only to fit 3 piece HUM214 Set 214/S11		31.50
xx-GC-4-040	Stable only to fit 16 piece HUM260 Set 260/S		290.00
Goebel	M. I. Hummel Collectibles Madonna Figurines	M. I. Hummel	Open
xx-F-GC-5-001	Flower Madonna, color, 10/1/11		130.00
xx-F-GC-5-002	Flower Madonna, white 10/1/W		70.00
xx-F-GC-5-003	Flower Madonna, color 10/111/11		315.00
xx-F-GC-5-004	Flower Madonna, white 10/111/W		175.00
xx-F-GC-5-005	Madonna with Halo, color 45/0/6		42.00
xx-F-GC-5-006	Madonna with Halo, color 45/1/6		52.50
xx-F-GC-5-007	Madonna with Halo, white 45/0/W		26.50
xx-F-GC-5-008	Madonna with Halo, white 45/1/W		31.50
xx-F-GC-5-009	Madonna with Halo 45/111/W		70.00
xx-F-GC-5-010	Madonna with Halo 45/111/6		105.00
xx-F-GC-5-011	Madonna Praying, color 46/0/6		42.00
xx-F-GC-5-012	Madonna Praying, color 46/1/6		52.50
xx-F-GC-5-013	Madonna Praying, color 46/111/6		105.00
xx-F-GC-5-014	Madonna Praying, white 46/0/W		26.50
xx-F-GC-5-015	Madonna Praying, white 46/1/W		31.50
xx-F-GC-5-016	Madonna Praying, white 46/111/W		73.50
xx-F-GC-5-017	Madonna Holding Child color 151/11		472.50
xx-F-GC-5-018	Madonna Holding Child white 151/W		175.00
xx-F-GC-5-019	Madonna 214/A/M 11		83.00
xx-F-GC-5-020	Madonna with Child 2 Pieces, color 214/AM & K		110.00
Goebel Hummelwerk	Goebel Figurines	N. Rockwell	500
63-F-GH-1-001	Little Veterinarian (Mysterious Malady)	15.00	400.00
63-F-GH-1-002	Boyhood Dreams (Adventurers between Adventures)	12.00	400.00
63-F-GH-1-003	Mother's Helper (Pride of Parenthood)	15.00	400.00
63-F-GH-1-004	His First Smoke	9.00	400.00
63-F-GH-1-005	My New Pal (A Boy Meets His Dog)	12.00	400.00
63-F-GH-1-006	Home Cure	16.00	400.00
63-F-GH-1-007	Timely Assistance (Love Aid)	16.00	400.00
63-F-GH-1-008	She Loves Me (Day Dreamer)	8.00	400.00
63-F-GH-1-009	Buttercup Test (Beguiling Buttercup)	10.00	400.00
63-F-GH-1-010	First Love (A Scholarly Pace)	30.00	400.00
63-F-GH-1-011	Canine Solo	16.00	400.00
63-F-GH-1-012	Patient Anglers (Fisherman's Paradise)	18.00	400.00
63-F-GH-1-013	Advertising Plaque		600.00
Gorham	A Boy And His Dog (Four Seasons)	N. Rockwell	2,500 sets Annual
72-F-GO-1-001	A Boy Meets His Dog	200.00 set	1520.00 Set
72-F-GO-1-002	Adventures Between Adventures		
72-F-GO-1-003	The Mysterious Malady		
72-F-GO-1-004	Pride Of Parenthood		
Gorham	Young Love (Four Seasons)	N. Rockwell	2,500 sets Annual
73-F-GO-2-001	Downhill Daring	250.00 set	1020.00 Set
73-F-GO-2-002	Beguiling Buttercup		
73-F-GO-2-003	Flying High		
73-F-GO-2-004	A Scholarly Pace		
Gorham	Four Ages of Love (Four Seasons)	N. Rockwell	2,500 sets Annual
74-F-GO-3-001	Gaily Sharing Vintage Times	300.00 set	1170.00 set
74-F-GO-3-002	Sweet Song So Young		
74-F-GO-3-003	Flowers In Tender Bloom		
74-F-GO-3-004	Fondly Do We Remember		
Gorham	Grandpa And Me (Four Seasons)	N. Rockwell	2,500 sets Annual
75-F-GO-4-001	Gay Blades	300.00 set	850.00 set
75-F-GO-4-002	Day Dreamers		
75-F-GO-4-003	Goin Fishing		
75-F-GO-4-004	Pensive Pals		
Gorham	Me And My Pal (Four Seasons)	N. Rockwell	2,500 sets Annual
76-F-GO-5-001	A Licking Good Bath	300.00 set	850.00 set
76-F-GO-5-002	Young Man's Fancy		
76-F-GO-5-003	Fisherman's Paradise		
76-F-GO-5-004	Disastrous Daring		

Company / Number	Series / Name	Artist / Issue Price	Edition limit / Quote
Gorham	Grand Pals (Four Seasons)	N. Rockwell	2,500 sets Annual
77-F-GO-6-001	Snow Sculpturing	350.00 set	600.00 set
77-F-GO-6-002	Soaring Spirits		
77-F-GO-6-003	Fish Finders		
77-F-GO-6-004	Ghostly Gourds		
Gorham	Going On Sixteen (Four Seasons)	N. Rockwell	2,500 sets Annual
78-F-GO-7-001	Chilling Chore	400.00 set	600.00 set
78-F-GO-7-002	Sweet Serenade		
78-F-GO-7-003	Shear Agony		
78-F-GO-7-004	Pilgrimage		
Gorham	Tender Years (Four Seasons)	N. Rockwell	-
79-F-GO-8-001	New Year Look	500.00 set	600.00 set
79-F-GO-8-002	Spring Tonic		
79-F-GO-8-003	Cool Aid		
79-F-GO-8-004	Chilly Reception		
Gorham	A Helping Hand (Four Seasons)	N. Rockwell	2,500 sets Annual
80-F-GO-9-001	Year End Count	650.00 set	650.00 set
80-F-GO-9-002	Closed For Business		
80-F-GO-9-003	Swatter's Right		
80-F-GO-9-004	Coal Season's Coming		
Gorham	"Dad's Boy" (Four Seasons)	N. Rockwell	2,500 sets
81-F-GO-10-001	Ski Skills	750.00 set	750.00
81-F-GO-10-002	In His Spirit		
81-F-GO-10-003	Trout Dinner		
81-F-GO-10-004	Careful Aim		
Gorham	Rockwell	N. Rockwell	
74-F-GO-11-001	Weighing In	40.00	80.00
74-F-GO-11-002	Missing Tooth	30.00	70.00
74-F-GO-11-003	Tiny Tim	30.00	75.00
74-F-GO-11-004	At The Vets	25.00	65.00
74-F-GO-11-005	Fishing	50.00	100.00
75-F-GO-11-006	Batter Up	40.00	90.00
75-F-GO-11-007	Skating	37.50	85.00
75-F-GO-11-008	Captain	45.00	95.00
75-F-GO-11-009	Boy And His Dog	37.50	85.00
75-F-GO-11-010	No Swimming	35.00	80.00
75-F-GO-11-011	Old Mill Pond	45.00	95.00
76-F-GO-11-012	Saying Grace	75.00	120.00
76-F-GO-11-013	God Rest Ye Merry Gentlemen	50.00	800.00
76-F-GO-11-014	Tackled(Ad Stand)	35.00	55.00
76-F-GO-11-015	Independence	40.00	150.00
76-F-GO-11-016	Marriage License	50.00	110.00
76-F-GO-11-017	The Occulist	50.00	175.00
81-F-GO-11-018	Day In The Life Boy II	75.00	85.00
81-F-GO-11-019	Wet Sport	85.00	85.00
82-F-GO-11-020	April Fool's (At The Curiosity Shop)	55.00	110.00
82-F-GO-11-021	Tackled(Rockwell Name Signed)	45.00	70.00
82-F-GO-11-022	A Day In The Life Boy III	85.00	85.00
82-F-GO-11-023	A Day In The Life Girl III	85.00	85.00
Gorham	Rockwell	N. Rockwell	Dated 1981 7,500
81-F-GO-11-024	Christmas Dancers	130.00	130.00
Gorham	Rockwell	N. Rockwell	5,000
82-F-GO-11-025	Marriage License	110.00	400.00
82-F-GO-11-026	Saying Grace	110.00	450.00
82-F-GO-11-027	Triple Self Portrait	300.00	500.00
Gorham	Rockwell	N. Rockwell	Annual 7,500
80-F-GO-11-028	Jolly Coachman	75.00	125.00
82-F-GO-11-029	Merrie Christmas	75.00	75.00
Gorham	Rockwell	N. Rockwell	7,500 Numbered
83-F-GO-11-030	Facts of Life	110.00	110.00
83-F-GO-11-031	Antique Dealer	130.00	130.00
Gorham	Rockwell	N. Rockwell	Annual 7,500 Numbered
83-F-GO-11-032	Christmas Goose	75.00	75.00
Gorham	Minature Christmas Figurines	N. Rockwell	-
79-F-GO-12-001	Tiny Tim	15.00	15.00
80-F-GO-12-002	Santa Plans His Trip	15.00	15.00
81-F-GO-12-003	Yuletide Reconing	20.00	20.00
82-F-GO-12-004	Checking Good Deeds	20.00	20.00
Gorham	Miniatures	N. Rockwell	
81-F-GO-13-001	Young Man's Fancy	55.00	55.00
81-F-GO-13-002	Beguiling Buttercup	45.00	45.00
81-F-GO-13-003	Gay Blades	45.00	45.00
81-F-GO-13-004	Sweet Song So Young	55.00	55.00
81-F-GO-13-005	Snow Sculpture	45.00	45.00
81-F-GO-13-006	Sweet Serenade	45.00	45.00
81-F-GO-13-007	At The Vets	27.50	27.50
81-F-GO-13-008	Boy Meets His Dog	37.50	37.50
81-F-GO-13-009	Downhill Daring	45.00	45.00
81-F-GO-13-010	Flowers In Tender Bloom	60.00	60.00
82-F-GO-13-011	Triple Self Portrait	60.00	60.00
82-F-GO-13-012	Marriage License	60.00	60.00
82-F-GO-13-013	The Runaway	50.00	50.00
82-F-GO-13-014	Vintage Times	50.00	50.00
82-F-GO-13-015	The Annual Visit	50.00	50.00
83-F-GO-13-016	Trout Dinner	60.00	60.00
Gorham	Old Timers (Four Seasons Miniatures)	N. Rockwell	2,500 Annual
82-F-GO-14-001	Canine Solo	250.00 set	250.00 set
82-F-GO-14-002	Sweet Surprise		
82-F-GO-14-003	Lazy Days		
82-F-GO-14-004	Fancy Footwork		
Gorham	Life With Father (Four Seasons-Miniatures)	N. Rockwell	2,500 Annual

Company / Number	Series / Name	Artist / Issue Price	Edition limit / Quote
83-F-GO-15-001	Big Decision	250.00 set	250.00 set
83-F-GO-15-002	Blasting Out		
83-F-GO-15-003	Cheering The Champs		
83-F-GO-15-004	A Tough One		
Gorham	Vasari Figurines	Vasari	250
71-F-GO-16-001	Mercenary Warrior	250.00	250.00
71-F-GO-16-002	Ming Warrior	200.00	200.00
71-F-GO-16-003	Swiss Warrior	250.00	Unknown
73-F-GO-16-004	Austrian Hussar	300.00	300.00
73-F-GO-16-005	D'Artagnan	250.00	400.00
73-F-GO-16-006	English Crusader	250.00	250.00
73-F-GO-16-007	French Crusader	250.00	250.00
73-F-GO-16-008	German Hussar	250.00	250.00
73-F-GO-16-009	German Mercenary	250.00	250.00
73-F-GO-16-010	Italian Crusader	250.00	250.00
73-F-GO-16-011	Pirate	200.00	200.00
73-F-GO-16-012	Porthos	250.00	250.00
73-F-GO-16-013	Roman Centurion	200.00	200.00
73-F-GO-16-014	Spanish Grandee	200.00	200.00
73-F-GO-16-015	The Cossack	250.00	250.00
73-F-GO-16-016	Venetian Nobleman	200.00	200.00
73-F-GO-16-017	Viking	200.00	200.00
Gorham	Vasari Figurines	Vasari	200
73-F-GO-16-018	Cellini	400.00	400.00
73-F-GO-16-019	Christ	250.00	250.00
73-F-GO-16-020	Creche	500.00	500.00
73-F-GO-16-021	Leoanrdo Da Vinci	250.00	250.00
73-F-GO-16-022	Michelangelo	250.00	250.00
73-F-GO-16-023	Three kings, set of 3	750.00	750.00
73-F-GO-16-024	Three Musketeers, set of 3	750.00	750.00
Granget	Granget Porcelains	Granget	750
74-F-GR-2-001	Blue Titmouse, Lively Fellow	1295.00	1295.00
74-F-GR-2-002	Chaffinch, Spring Melody	1675.00	1675.00
74-F-GR-2-003	Goldfinch, Morning Hour	1250.00	1250.00
74-F-GR-2-004	Great Titmouse Adults, Busy Activity	2175.00	2175.00
74-F-GR-2-005	Robin, A Day Begins	1795.00	1795.00
Granget	Granget Porcelains	Granget	200
76-F-GR-2-006	American Bald Eagle, Freedom in Flight	3400.00	3400.00
XX-F-GR-2-007	Woodcocks, A Family Affair	-	1000.00 to 1500.00
Granget	Granget Porcelains	Granget	150
76-F-GR-2-008	American Robin, It's Spring Again	1950.00	1950.00
XX-F-GR-2-009	Canadian Geese, Heading South	4650.00	4650.00
XX-F-GR-2-010	Great Blue Herons,the Challenge	-	7400.00 to 9000.00
XX-F-GR-2-011	Red Deer Stag, The Royal Stag	4850.00	4850.00
XX-F-GR-2-012	Ruffed Grouse	2000.00	2000.00
XX-F-GR-2-013	Spring Bok, The Sentinel	2000.00	2000.00
Granget	Granget Porcelains	Granget	350
76-F-GR-2-014	Bluebirds, Reluctant Fledgling	1750.00	1750.00
XX-F-GR-2-015	Pintail Ducks, Safe at Home	-	4000.00
77-F-GR-2-016	Reluctant Fledgling	1750.00	1750.00
Granget	Granget Porcelains	Granget	
XX-F-GR-2-017	Bobwhite Quail, Off Season	-	2700.00 to 3300.00
XX-F-GR-2-018	Dolphin Group	-	1750.00 to 1900.00
XX-F-GR-2-019	Halla	-	1300.00 to 1400.00
XX-F-GR-2-020	Stag	-	4000.00 to 4850.00
Granget	Granget Porcelains	Granget	500
XX-F-GR-2-021	California Sea Lions, Sea Frolic	1375.00	1375.00
XX-F-GR-2-022	Dolphins, Play Time, Undecorated	3500.00	3000.00 to 3500.00
XX-F-GR-2-023	Open Jumper, The Champion	1350.00	1350.00
Granget	Granget Porcelains	Granget	175
XX-F-GR-2-024	Cedar Waxwings, Anxious Moments	2675.00	2675.00
XX-F-GR-2-025	Mallard Family, First Lesson	-	2350.00 to 2850.00
XX-F-GR-2-026	Meadowlark, Spring Is Here	2450.00	2450.00
XX-F-GR-2-027	Screech Owl With Chickadees, Disdain		2200.00 to 3150.00
Granget	Granget Porcelains	Granget	100
XX-F-GR-2-028	Dolphins, Play Time, Decorated	9000.00	Unknown
76-F-GR-2-029	Secretary Bird, The Contest	6000.00	6000.00
Granget	Granget Porcelains	Granget	1200
76-F-GR-2-030	Dougle Eagle, 24k Gold Vermeil On Pewter	250.00	250.00
Granget	Granget Porcelains	Granget	700
74-F-GR-2-031	Golden-Crested Wrens, Tiny Acrobats	2060.00	2060.00
Granget	Granget Porcelains	Granget	600
74-F-GR-2-032	Kingfisher, Detected Prey	1975.00	1975.00

Company / Number	Series / Name	Artist / Issue Price	Edition limit / Quote
Granget	Granget Porcelains	Granget	250
XX-F-GR-2-033	Mourning Doves, Engaged	-	1200.00 to 1750.00
XX-F-GR-2-034	Peregrine Falcon, Wood, 20 Inches	2000.00	2000.00
Granget	Granget Porcelains	Granget	2500
XX-F-GR-2-035	Pergrine Falcon, Wood 10 Inches	500.00	500.00
Granget	Granget Porcelains	Granget	1500
XX-F-GR-2-036	Peregrine Falcon, Wood 12.5 Inches	700.00	700.00
Granget	Granget Porcelains	Granget	125
XX-F-GR-2-037	Ring-necked Pheasants, Take Cover		3800.00 to 6350.00
Granget	Granget Wood Carvings	Granget	250
XX-F-GR-3-001	Barn Owl, 20 Inches	2000.00	2000.00
73-F-GR-3-002	Black Grouse, Large	2800.00	3500.00
73-F-GR-3-003	Golden Eagle, large	2000.00	2500.00
73-F-GR-3-004	Lynx, Large	1600.00	2000.00
73-F-GR-3-005	Mallard, Large	2000.00	2250.00
XX-F-GR-3-006	Peregrine Falcon, Large	2250.00	2250.00
73-F-GR-3-007	Rooster, Large	2400.00	2800.00
Granget	Granget Wood Carvings	Granget	1000
73-F-GR-3-008	Black Grouse, Small	700.00	700.00
73-F-GR-3-009	Fox, Small	650.00	650.00 to 750.00
73-F-GR-3-010	Golden Eagle, Small	550.00	750.00
73-F-GR-3-011	Lynx, Small	400.00	400.00
73-F-GR-3-012	Mallard, Small	500.00	500.00
73-F-GR-3-013	Partridge, Small	550.00	550.00
XX-F-GR-3-014	Peregrine Falcon, Small	500.00	500.00
73-F-GR-3-015	Rooster, Small	600.00	650.00
73-F-GR-3-016	Wild Boar, Small	275.00	275.00
XX-F-GR-3-017	Wild Sow With Young, Large	2800.00	2800.00
Granget	Granget Wood Carvings	Granget	200
73-F-GR-3-018	Fox, Large	2800.00	2800.00 to 3200.00
73-F-GR-3-019	Partridge, Large	2400.00	2800.00
73-F-GR-3-020	Wild Boar, Large	2400.00	2400.00
XX-F-GR-3-021	Wild Sow With Young, Small	600.00	600.00
Granget	Granget Wood Carvings	Granget	2500
XX-F-GR-3-022	Barn Owl, 10 Inches	600.00	600.00
Granget	Granget Wood Carvings	Granget	1500
XX-F-GR-3-023	Barn Owl, 12.5 Inches	700.00	700.00
XX-F-GR-3-024	Peregrine Falcon, Medium	700.00	700.00
Granget	Granget Wood Carvings	Granget	-
XX-F-GR-3-025	Ring-Necked Pheasant, Large	2250.00	2250.00
XX-F-GR-3-026	Ring-Necked Pheaseant, Small	500.00	500.00
Hamilton Collection	The Audubon Bronzes	H. and N. Deaton	7,500
78-F-HC-1-001	Rabbit	55.00	57.50
78-F-HC-1-002	Gray Fox	55.00	57.50
78-F-HC-1-003	Eastern Grey Squirrel	55.00	57.50
78-F-HC-1-004	Ringtailed Cat	55.00	57.50
78-F-HC-1-005	Eastern Racoon	55.00	57.50
78-F-HC-1-006	Texas Nine Banded Armadillo	55.00	57.50
Hamilton Collection	American Wildlife Bronze Collection	H. and N. Deaton	7,500
79-F-HC-2-001	Cougar	60.00	105.00
79-F-HC-2-002	White-Tailed Deer	60.00	95.00
79-F-HC-2-003	Bobcat	60.00	75.00
80-F-HC-2-004	Beaver	60.00	65.00
80-F-HC-2-005	Polar Bear	60.00	65.00
80-F-HC-2-006	Sea Otter	60.00	65.00
Hamilton Collection	The Art Of The Carousel	P. Cozzolino	7,500
80-F-HC-3-001	Lead Horse	135.00	175.00
80-F-HC-3-002	Majestic Lion	135.00	140.00
80-F-HC-3-003	Laughing Horse	135.00	135.00
81-F-HC-3-004	White Rabbit	135.00	135.00
81-F-HC-3-005	Patriotic Horse	135.00	135.00
81-F-HC-3-006	Dancing Bear	135.00	135.00
Hamilton Collection	America's Majestic Owls Collection	J. Dixon	7,500
81-F-HC-4-001	Snowy Owl	120.00	120.00
81-F-HC-4-002	Barn Owl	120.00	120.00
81-F-HC-4-003	Great Horned Owl	120.00	120.00
81-F-HC-4-004	Great Gray Owl	120.00	120.00
81-F-HC-4-005	Screech Owl	120.00	120.00
81-F-HC-4-006	Burrowing Owl	120.00	120.00
Hamilton Collection	The Heralds Of Spring Songbird Collection	R. Palmer	7,500
81-F-HC-5-001	Eastern Bluebird	120.00	120.00
81-F-HC-5-002	Black-capped Chickadee	120.00	120.00
81-F-HC-5-003	American Goldfinch	120.00	120.00
81-F-HC-5-004	Purple Finch	120.00	120.00
81-F-HC-5-005	Tufted Titmouse	120.00	120.00
81-F-HC-5-006	Tree Swallow	120.00	120.00
Hamilton Collection	Rockwell Home of the Brave Figurine Collection	N. Rockwell	7,500
82-F-HC-6-001	Reminiscing	75.00	75.00
82-F-HC-6-002	Hero's Welcome	75.00	75.00
82-F-HC-6-003	Uncle Sam Takes Wings	75.00	75.00
82-F-HC-6-004	Back To His Old Job	75.00	75.00
82-F-HC-6-005	Willie Gillis In Church	75.00	75.00
82-F-HC-6-006	Taking Mother Over The Top	75.00	75.00
Hutschenreuther Porcelain Co.	Hutschenreuther Figurines		500
77-F-HU-1-001	Catherine The Great	500.00	875.00
77-F-HU-1-002	Helen Of Troy	500.00	925.00

Category: Figurine

Company / Number	Series / Name	Artist / Issue Price	Edition limit / Quote
Company	Series	Artist	Edition limit
Number	Name	Issue Price	Quote
77-F-HU-1-003	Jennie Churchhill	500.00	925.00
77-F-HU-1-004	Queen Isabelle	500.00	925.00
Ispanky	Ispanky Porcelains	L. Ispanky	600
67-F-IS-1-001	Drummer Boy, White	150.00	175.00 to 185.00
75-F-IS-1-002	Healing Hand, Decorated	750.00	750.00 to 1250.00
75-F-IS-1-003	Healing Hand, White	650.00	800.00
78-F-IS-1-004	Spring Fever	650.00	935.00 to 1050.00
Ispanky	Ispanky Porcelains	Ispanky	500
XX-F-IS-1-005	Princess Of The Nile	275.00	275.00
67-F-IS-1-006	Artist Girl	200.00	1200.00 to 1800.00
67-F-IS-1-007	Ballerina	350.00	900.00 to 1000.00
67-F-IS-1-008	Ballet Dancers	350.00	900.00 to 1000.00
67-F-IS-1-009	Morning	300.00	1200.00 to 1500.00
67-F-IS-1-010	Romeo And Juliet, Decorated	375.00	750.00 to 850.00
67-F-IS-1-011	King Arthur	300.00	575.00 to 750.00
69-F-IS-1-012	Autumn Wind	300.00	1200.00 to 1500.00
69-F-IS-1-013	Storm	400.00	600.00 to 850.00
71-F-IS-1-014	Debutante	350.00	225.00 to 625.00
71-F-IS-1-015	Mr. & Mrs. Otter	250.00	400.00 to 600.00
72-F-IS-1-016	Princess And the Frog	675.00	675.00
72-F-IS-1-017	Annabel Lee	750.00	750.00
73-F-IS-1-018	Abraham	600.00	1250.00 to 1400.00
73-F-IS-1-019	Lorelei	550.00	550.00 to 650.00
74-F-IS-1-020	Dianne	500.00	700.00 to 900.00
74-F-IS-1-021	Belle Of The Ball	550.00	550.00 to 950.00
74-F-IS-1-022	Second Base	650.00	750.00 to 950.00
75-F-IS-1-023	Madonna, The Blessed Saint, Decorated	295.00	295.00 to 350.00
75-F-IS-1-024	Madonna, The Blessed Saint, White	195.00	195.00 to 250.00
Ispanky	Ispanky Porcelains	L. Ispanky	150
67-F-IS-1-025	Cavalry Scout, White	675.00	900.00
67-F-IS-1-026	Great Spirit, White	750.00	750.00
67-F-IS-1-027	Hunt, White	1200.00	1200.00 to 1485.00
67-F-IS-1-028	On The Trail, White	750.00	750.00 to 1125.00
67-F-IS-1-029	Pack Horse, White	500.00	350.00
67-F-IS-1-030	Pioneer Woman, White	225.00	275.00 to 350.00
Ispanky	Ispanky Porcelains	L. Ispanky	200
67-F-IS-1-031	Cavalry Scout, Decorated	1000.00	1200.00
67-F-IS-1-032	Drummer Boy, Decorated	250.00	250.00 to 285.00
67-F-IS-1-033	Forty-Niner, Decorated	450.00	650.00
67-F-IS-1-034	Hunt, Decorated	2000.00	2600.00 to 3850.00
67-F-IS-1-035	Pack Horse, Decorated	700.00	1250.00
67-F-IS-1-036	Pilgrim Family, Decorated	500.00	500.00 to 750.00
67-F-IS-1-037	Pioneer Scout, Decorated	1000.00	1000.00
67-F-IS-1-038	Pioneer Scout, White	675.00	405.00
67-F-IS-1-039	Pioneer Woman, Decorated	350.00	350.00 to 430.00
68-F-IS-1-040	Queen Of Spring	750.00	1200.00
69-F-IS-1-041	Great Spirit, Decorated	1500.00	1500.00 to 1850.00
69-F-IS-1-042	Mermaid Group, Decorated	1000.00	1000.00 to 1800.00
69-F-IS-1-043	Mermaid Group, White	950.00	950.00
70-F-IS-1-044	Celeste	475.00	250.00 to 500.00
70-F-IS-1-045	On The Trail, Decorated	1700.00	1700.00
70-F-IS-1-046	Reverie	200.00	500.00 to 850.00
Ispanky	Ispanky Porcelains	L. Ispanky	250
67-F-IS-1-047	Bird Of Paradise	1500.00	1500.00
67-F-IS-1-048	Dutch Iris	1400.00	1400.00 to 1500.00
69-F-IS-1-049	Daffodils	950.00	450.00 to 950.00
70-F-IS-1-050	King & Queen, pair	750.00	1200.00
71-F-IS-1-051	Freedom	300.00	500.00
74-F-IS-1-052	King Lear & Cordelia	1250.00	1250.00 to 1500.00
75-F-IS-1-053	Apotheosis Of The Sculptor	495.00	800.00
76-F-IS-1-054	Orchids	1000.00	1400.00
Ispanky	Ispanky Porcelains	L. Ispanky	300
67-F-IS-1-055	Love	375.00	950.00
67-F-IS-1-056	Meditation	350.00	450.00 to 600.00
68-F-IS-1-057	Horse	300.00	350.00 to 600.00
68-F-IS-1-058	Pegasus, Decorated	375.00	800.00
68-F-IS-1-059	Pegasus, White	300.00	800.00
69-F-IS-1-060	Isaiah	475.00	1100.00
70-F-IS-1-061	Dawn	500.00	500.00 to 900.00
70-F-IS-1-062	Evening	375.00	650.00
70-F-IS-1-063	Thrasher	1000.00	1000.00
71-F-IS-1-064	Christine	350.00	700.00 to 800.00
71-F-IS-1-065	Eternal Love	400.00	400.00 to 650.00
71-F-IS-1-066	Swan Lake	1000.00	2000.00
72-F-IS-1-067	Madame Butterfly	1500.00	1000.00 to 1500.00
73-F-IS-1-068	Rebekah	400.00	400.00 to 550.00
XX-F-IS-1-069	Owl	750.00	750.00 to 825.00
Ispanky	Ispanky Porcelains	L. Ispanky	350
67-F-IS-1-070	Forty-Niner, White	250.00	250.00
67-F-IS-1-071	Pilgrim Family, White	350.00	250.00 to 350.00
69-F-IS-1-072	Maria	750.00	750.00 to 1000.00
70-F-IS-1-073	Icarus	350.00	650.00
71-F-IS-1-074	Betsy Ross	750.00	750.00 to 1325.00
73-F-IS-1-075	Aaron	1200.00	2100.00 to 2400.00
73-F-IS-1-076	Maid Of The Mist	450.00	450.00 to 750.00
74-F-IS-1-077	Banbury Cross	550.00	550.00 to 1025.00
74-F-IS-1-078	Hamlet And Ophelia	1250.00	1250.00 to 1500.00
75-F-IS-1-079	Joshua	750.00	1200.00
Ispanky	Ispanky Porcelains	L. Ispanky	400
XX-F-IS-1-080	Rosh Hashana, White Beard	275.00	1300.00
67-F-IS-1-081	Moses	400.00	1800.00
71-F-IS-1-082	David	450.00	450.00 to 600.00
71-F-IS-1-083	Jessamy 1	450.00	450.00 to 600.00
72-F-IS-1-084	Cinderella	375.00	375.00
72-F-IS-1-085	Spring Ballet	450.00	450.00 to 600.00
73-F-IS-1-086	Texas Rangers	1650.00	990.00 to 1650.00
76-F-IS-1-087	Lydia	450.00	450.00 to 835.00
Ispanky	Ispanky Porcelains	L. Ispanky	100
XX-F-IS-1-088	Exodus, Bronze	1500.00	1500.00
67-F-IS-1-089	Promises	225.00	2000.00 to 2500.00
70-F-IS-1-090	Horsepower	1650.00	1650.00 to 3125.00
70-F-IS-1-091	Peace, Decorated	375.00	350.00 to 700.00
70-F-IS-1-092	Peace, White	300.00	300.00 to 450.00
73-F-IS-1-093	Emerald Dragon	2500.00	3250.00
77-F-IS-1-094	Serene Highness	2500.00	2500.00 to 4250.00
Ispanky	Ispanky Porcelains	L. Ispanky	50
67-F-IS-1-095	Tulips, Red	1800.00	4500.00
67-F-IS-1-096	Tulips, Yellow	1800.00	4500.00
72-F-IS-1-097	Spring Bouquet	3000.00	10000.00
Ispanky	Ispanky Porcelains	L. Ispanky	1
71-F-IS-1-098	Peace Riders	35000.00	35000.00
Ispanky	**Ispanky Porcelains**	**L. Ispanky**	**15**
71-F-IS-1-099	**Beauty And The Beast**	**4500.00**	**4500.00**
71-F-IS-1-100	**Excalibur**	**3500.00**	**3500.00**
71-F-IS-1-101	**Felicia**	**2500.00**	**2500.00**
71-F-IS-1-102	**Quest**	**1500.00**	**1500.00**
71-F-IS-1-103	**Tekieh**	**1800.00**	**1800.00**
Ispanky	Ispanky Porcelains	L. Ispanky	450
72-F-IS-1-104	Spirit Of The Sea	500.00	190.00 to 500.00
73-F-IS-1-105	Love Letters	750.00	750.00
74-F-IS-1-106	Holy Family, Decorated	900.00	900.00 to 1125.00
74-F-IS-1-107	Holy Family, White	750.00	700.00 to 925.00
Ispanky	Ispanky Porcelains	L. Ispanky	750
73-F-IS-1-108	Messiah	450.00	450.00
Ispanky	Ispanky Porcelains	L. Ispanky	500
75-F-IS-1-109	Madonna with Halo, Decorated	350.00	350.00
75-F-IS-1-110	Madonna with Halo, White	250.00	250.00
77-F-IS-1-111	Memories	600.00	825.00 to 900.00
77-F-IS-1-112	Thunder	500.00	695.00 to 800.00
78-F-IS-1-113	Romance	800.00	1000.00
78-F-IS-1-114	Ten Commandments, Decorated	950.00	950.00 to 1525.00
Ispanky	Ispanky Porcelains	L. Ispanky	800
78-F-IS-1-115	Little Mermaid	350.00	350.00 to 520.00
76-F-IS-1-116	Piano Girl	300.00	435.00 to 665.00
77-F-IS-1-117	Sophistication	350.00	390.00 to 575.00
Ispanky	Ispanky Porcelains	L. Ispanky	1000
77-F-IS-1-118	Daisy	325.00	365.00 to 575.00
77-F-IS-1-119	Day Dreams	300.00	420.00 to 520.00
77-F-IS-1-120	Morning Glory	325.00	325.00 to 620.00
77-F-IS-1-121	Poppy	325.00	365.00 to 620.00
77-F-IS-1-122	Snow Drop	325.00	365.00 to 430.00
76-F-IS-1-123	Swanilda	285.00	650.00
77-F-IS-1-124	Water Lily	325.00	325.00/ 365.00
Ispanky	Ispanky Porcelains	L. Ispanky	700
78-F-IS-1-125	My Name Is Iris	500.00	755.00
78-F-IS-1-126	Narcissus	500.00	500.00
78-F-IS-1-127	Ten Commandments, White	600.00	600.00 to 850.00

Company / Number	Series / Name	Artist / Issue Price	Edition limit / Quote
Ispanky	Ispanky Porcelains	L. Ispanky	2
XX-F-IS-1-128	Rosh Hashana, Gray Beard	275.00	10,000.00
Jean Paul Loup/ Betournes	Jean Paul Loup/Betournes Enamel on Copper Paintings	J. Loup	150
XX-F-JL-1-001	SaCrafts, The Butcher	200.00	Unknown
XX-F-JL-1-002	SaCrafts, The Mower	200.00	Unknown
XX-F-JL-1-003	SaCrafts, The Plowman	200.00	Unknown
XX-F-JL-1-004	SaCrafts, The Reaper	200.00	Unknown
XX-F-JL-1-005	SaCrafts, The Sower	200.00	Unknown
XX-F-JL-1-006	SaCrafts, The Vinedresser	200.00	Unknown
Jean Paul Loup/ Betournes	Jean Paul Loup/Betournes Enamel on Copper Paintings	J. Loup	200
XX-F-JL-2-001	Four Seasons, Autumn	250.00	Unknown
XX-F-JL-2-002	Four Seasons, Spring	250.00	Unknown
XX-F-JL-2-003	Four Seaons, Summer	250.00	Unknown
XX-F-JL-2-004	Four Seasons, Winter	250.00	Unknown
Kaiser	Kaiser Porcelains		1500
70-F-KA-1-001	Cardinal, Color	60.00	350.00
70-F-KA-1-002	Owl, Color	150.00	350.00
70-F-KA-1-003	Pigeon Group, Color	150.00	350.00
70-F-KA-1-004	Wild Ducks, Color	150.00	500.00
71-F-KA-1-005	Cardinal With Wood Base, Color	225.00	225.00
72-F-KA-1-006	Kingfisher, Color	140.00	350.00
74-F-KA-1-007	Blue Jay With Wood Base	475.00	650.00
74-F-KA-1-008	Hummingbirds With Wood Base	450.00	625.00
75-F-KA-1-009	Peregrine Falcon, Color, Wood Base	850.00	1000.00
75-F-KA-1-010	Sparrow, Color, Wood Base	300.00	350.00
77-F-KA-1-011	Arabian Stallion, one Leg Up, White	250.00	250.00
77-F-KA-1-012	Canadian Geese	1500.00	1750.00
77-F-KA-1-013	Pheasant	3200.00	3200.00
77-F-KA-1-014	Robin	340.00	375.00
Kaiser	Kaiser Porcelains		2000
XX-F-KA-1-015	Owl, Horned	650.00	650.00
70-F-KA-1-016	Baltimore Oriole, Color	60.00	80.00 to 100.00
70-F-KA-1-017	Blue Jay, Color	60.00	85.00 to 100.00
70-F-KA-1-018	Robin & Worm, Color	60.00	80.00 to 90.00
70-F-KA-1-019	Scarlet Tanager, Color	60.00	80.00 to 90.00
71-F-KA-1-020	Kingfisher, White	45.00	55.00 to 60.00
71-F-KA-1-021	Wild Ducks, White	75.00	175.00
72-F-KA-1-022	Owl, White	70.00	160.00
72-F-KA-1-023	Pigeon Group, White	60.00	140.00
77-F-KA-1-024	German Shepherd, White	185.00	185.00
77-F-KA-1-025	Irish Setter, White	185.00	185.00
77-F-KA-1-026	Screech Owl, White	85.00	85.00
Kaiser	Kaiser Porcelains		1200
XX-F-KA-1-027	Titmouse	265.00	265.00
70-F-KA-1-028	Eagle, White	250.00	200.00
74-F-KA-1-029	Baby Titmice, White	200.00	200.00
75-F-KA-1-030	Mare & Colt, Wood Base	650.00	775.00
75-F-KA-1-031	Owl, White, Wood Base	300.00	400.00
76-F-KA-1-032	Mother Bear & Cub, White Wood Base	125.00	160.00
77-F-KA-1-033	Pelican	925.00	925.00
Kaiser	Kaiser Porcelains		400
70-F-KA-1-034	Eagle, Color	500.00	500.00 to 650.00
Kaiser	Kaiser Porcelains		5000
71-F-KA-1-035	Porpoises, Group of 3, White	85.00	375.00
72-F-KA-1-036	Pony Group, White	50.00	150.00
Kaiser	Kaiser Porcelains		600
72-F-KA-1-037	Arabain Stallion, Color	250.00	300.00 to 500.00
Kaiser	Kaiser Porcelains		1000
XX-F-KA-1-038	American Eagle, 11 Inches		Unknown
72-F-KA-1-039	Pony Group, Color	150.00	350.00
73-F-KA-1-040	Roadrunner, Color	350.00	500.00
74-F-KA-1-041	Robin With Wood Base	260.00	390.00
77-F-KA-1-042	Baltimore Oriole	280.00	280.00
77-F-KA-1-043	German Shepherd, Color	250.00	290.00
77-F-KA-1-044	Irish Setter, Color	290.00	290.00
77-F-KA-1-045	Screech Owl, Color	175.00	175.00
Kaiser	Kaiser Porcelains		800
XX-F-KA-1-046	American Eagle, 16.5 Inches	1850.00	1850.00
XX-F-KA-1-047	Titmouse, Baby, Color		Unknown
73-F-KA-1-048	Goshawk, Color	1200.00	2000.00
73-F-KA-1-049	Seagull, Color	850.00	1150.00
73-F-KA-1-050	Tay-Kaiser Eagle, Color	1300.00	1300.00
74-F-KA-1-051	Baby Titmice, Color	400.00	500.00
75-F-KA-1-052	Lipizzaner Horse, Color, Wood Base	625.00	800.00
75-F-KA-1-053	Owl, Color, Wood Base	850.00	1150.00
75-F-KA-1-054	Wood Ducks, Color, Wood Base	1450.00	1675.00
75-F-KA-1-055	Woodpeckers, Color, Wood Base	900.00	1000.00
76-F-KA-1-056	Mother Bear & Cub, Color, Wood Base	400.00	550.00
76-F-KA-1-057	Porpoises, Group of 5, White, Wood Base	850.00	1100.00
Kaiser	Kaiser Porcelains		950
73-F-KA-1-058	Encroachment, Color	900.00	1100.00
73-F-KA-1-059	Flushed, Color	1000.00	1150.00
73-F-KA-1-060	Waiting For Mother, Color	550.00	650.00
Kaiser	Kaiser Porcelains		700
73-F-KA-1-061	Goshawk, White	550.00	800.00
73-F-KA-1-062	Seagull, White	550.00	850.00
Kaiser	Kaiser Porcelains		2500
73-F-KA-1-063	Bluebird, Color	120.00	225.00
77-F-KA-1-064	Lady, Victorian, Dog	450.00	450.00
77-F-KA-1-065	Lady, Victorian, Tennis	450.00	450.00
77-F-KA-1-066	Lady, Victorian, Umbrella	450.00	450.00
Kaiser	Kaiser Porcelains		2200
75-F-KA-1-067	Lipizzaner Horse, White, Wood Base	275.00	350.00
Kaiser	Kaiser Porcelains		3000
75-F-KA-1068	Porpoises, Group of 4, White, Wood Base	75.00	460.00
76-F-KA-1-069	Four Dolphins		Unknown
77-F-KA-1-070	Eagle	450.00	500.00
Kaiser	Kaiser Porcelains		500
77-F-KA-1-071	Arabian Stallion, One Leg Up, Color	600.00	600.00
Kaiser	Kaiser Porcelains		1060
77-F-KA-1-072	Seated Poodle	160.00	160.00
Kaiser	Kaiser Porcelains		4000
XX-F-KA-1-073	American Eagle, 11 Inches, White	260.00	260.00
Lladro	Lladro Porcelains		150
XX-F-LL-1-001	Allegory For Peace	550.00	550.00
Lladro	Lladro Porcelains		750
XX-F-LL-1-002	Antique Automobile	1100.00	1100.00
XX-F-LL-1-003	Eagle Owl	650.00	650.00
XX-F-LL-1-004	Eagles	900.00	900.00 to 1000.00
XX-F-LL-1-005	Girl With Guitar	650.00	850.00
XX-F-LL-1-006	Hamlet	350.00	350.00
XX-F-LL-1-007	Hansom Carriage	1250.00	1250.00
XX-F-LL-1-008	Othello & Desdemona	350.00	350.00
XX-F-LL-1-009	Peasant Woman	500.00	500.00
XX-F-LL-1-010	Soccer Players	2750.00	2750.00
XX-F-LL-1-011	Turtle Doves	675.00	675.00
Lladro	Lladro Porcelains		600
XX-F-LL-1-012	Eve At The Tree	450.00	600.00
Lladro	Lladro Porcelains		500
XX-F-LL-1-013	The Forest	1500.00	1500.00
XX-F-LL-1-014	Seabirds With Nest	600.00	600.00
XX-F-LL-1-015	Three Graces	950.00	1100.00
XX-F-LL-1-016	Young Oriental Man	500.00	650.00
Lladro	Lladro Porcelains		800
XX-F-LL-1-017	Hunting Scene	850.00	850.00
Lladro	Lladro Porcelains		1200
XX-F-LL-1-018	Judge	325.00	325.00
Lladro	Lladro Porcleains		400
XX-F-LL-1-019	Lyncmuse	750.00	750.00 to 800.00
Lladro	Lladro Porcelains		300
XX-F-LL-1-020	Madonna With Child	450.00	450.00
XX-F-LL-1-021	Madonna With Child, Seated	400.00	400.00
Lladro	Lladro Porcelains		1500
XX-F-LL-1-022	Man From La Mancha	800.00	800.00
Lladro	Lladro Porcelains		350
XX-F-LL-1-023	Oriental Horse	1100.00	1200.00
XX-F-LL-1-024	Turkey Group	650.00	1300.00
Lynell Studios	Rockwell	N. Rockwell	10,000
81-F-LS-1-001	Snow Queen	85.00	85.00
81-F-LS-1-002	Cradle of Love	85.00	85.00
Lynell Studies	Rockwell	N. Rockwell	7,500
81-F-LS-1-003	Scotty	125.00	125.00
Moussalli	Moussalli Porcelains	Moussalli	250
69-F-MO-1-001	Black-Capped Chickadee	550.00	700.00 to 1150.00
Moussalli	Moussalli Porcelains	Moussalli	500
XX-F-MO-1-002	American Redstart With Cherries	60.00	150.00
XX-F-MO-1-003	Canadian Warbler	180.00	200.00 to 250.00
XX-F-MO-1-004	Hummingbird In Forsythia	250.00	150.00 to 325.00
XX-F-MO-1-005	Hummingbird And Honeysuckle	250.00	275.00 to 325.00
XX-F-MO-1-006	Olive Warbler	200.00	225.00 to 250.00
XX-F-MO-1-007	Slate Colored Junco	180.00	200.00 to 250.00
XX-F-MO-1-008	Wren On A Rock	170.00	300.00
69-F-MO-1-009	Eastern Bluebird On Rock	250.00	350.00
69-F-MO-1-010	Yellow-Throated Warbler	120.00	180.00 to 450.00
72-F-MO-1-011	American Red Start With Flowers	600.00	600.00
72-F-MO-1-012	House Wren	250.00	275.00 to 325.00
Moussalli	Moussalli Porcelains	Moussalli	300
XX-F-MO-1-013	Baltimore Oriole	650.00	625.00
74-F-MO-1-014	Bay-Breasted Warbler	325.00	325.00
XX-F-MO-1-015	Cardinal	600.00	700.00 to 800.00
74-F-MO-1-016	Flycatcher	360.00	360.00
71-F-MO-1-017	Redbreasted Grosbeak	435.00	435.00
74-F-MO-1-018	Red-Faced Warbler	435.00	435.00
XX-F-MO-1-019	Red-Winged Blackbird	700.00	625.00 to 1200.00
XX-F-MO-1-020	Say's Phoebe	360.00	360.00
XX-F-MO-1-021	Scarlet Tanager	360.00	175.00
XX-F-MO-1-022	Wheatear	350.00	400.00 to 450.00
XX-F-MO-1-023	Wren On Magnolia Branch	600.00	725.00 to 775.00
Moussalli	Moussalli Porcelains	Moussalli	150
XX-F-MO-1-024	Golden Finch	550.00	275.00
72-F-MO-1-025	Indigo Bunting	650.00	325.00
72-F-MO-1-026	Tufted Titmouse	650.00	325.00

Company / Number	Series / Name	Artist / Issue Price	Edition limit / Quote
Company	Series	Artist	Edition limit
Number	Name	Issue Price	Quote
Moussalli	Mousalli Porcelains	Moussalli	400
74-F-MO-1-027	Golden-Crowned Kinglet	225.00	225.00
Moussalli	Moussalli Porcelains	Moussalli	200
XX-F-MO-1-028	Redheaded Woodpecker	450.00	525.00 to 575.00
74-F-MO-1-029	Snow Bunting	830.00	830.00
Moussalli	Moussalli Porcelains	Moussalli	
XX-F-MO-1-030	Anna's Hummingbird	250.00	125.00 to 250.00
XX-F-MO-1-031	Baltimore Oriole With Snake		1200.00
XX-F-MO-1-032	Bluebird On Crabapple Tree		1000.00
Norman Rockwell Museum, Inc.	American Family I	N. Rockwell	22,500
79-F-NR-1-001	Baby's First Step	90.00	250.00
80-F-NR-1-002	Happy Berthday, Dear Mother	90.00	160.00
80-F-NR-1-003	Sweet Sixteen	90.00	110.00
80-F-NR-1-004	First Haircut	90.00	110.00
80-F-NR-1-005	First Prom	90.00	110.00
80-F-NR-1-006	Wrapping Christmas Presents	90.00	110.00
80-F-NR-1-007	The Student	110.00	140.00
80-F-NR-1-008	Birthday Party	110.00	110.00
80-F-NR-1-009	Little Mother	110.00	110.00
80-F-NR-1-010	Washing Our Dog	110.00	110.00
81-F-NR-1-011	Mother's Little Helpers	110.00	110.00
81-F-NR-1-012	Bride And Groom	110.00	120.00
Norman Rockwell Museum, Inc.	Christmas	N. Rockwell	Year of Issue
80-F-NR-2-001	Checking His List	65.00	85.00
81-F-NR-2-002	Ringing In Good Cheer	95.00	95.00
82-F-NR-2-003	Waiting For Santa	95.00	110.00
83-F-NR-2-004	High Hopes	95.00	95.00
Norman Rockwell Museum, Inc.	Classic	N. Rockwell	Open
80-F-NR-3-001	Lighthouse Keeper's Daughter	65.00	92.00
80-F-NR-3-002	The Cobbler	65.00	90.00
80-F-NR-3-003	The Toymaker	65.00	150.00
80-F-NR-3-004	Bedtime	65.00	115.00
80-F-NR-3-005	Memories	65.00	85.00
80-F-NR-3-006	For A Good Boy	65.00	85.00
81-F-NR-3-007	A Dollhouse For Sis	65.00	65.00
81-F-NR-3-008	Music Master	65.00	65.00
81-F-NR-3-009	The Music Lesson	65.00	65.00
81-F-NR-3-010	Puppy Love	65.00	65.00
81-F-NR-3-011	While The Audience Waits	65.00	65.00
81-F-NR-3-012	Of To School	65.00	65.00
82-F-NR-3-013	The Country Doctor	65.00	65.00
82-F-NR-3-014	Spring Fever	65.00	65.00
82-F-NR-3-015	Words Of Wisdom	65.00	65.00
82-F-NR-3-016	The Kite Maker	65.00	65.00
82-F-NR-3-017	Dreams In The Antique Shop	65.00	65.00
83-F-NR-3-018	Winter Fun	65.00	65.00
83-F-NR-3-019	A Special Treat	65.00	65.00
83-F-NR-3-020	High Stepping	65.00	65.00
83-F-NR-3-021	Bored Of Education	65.00	65.00
Norman Rockwell Museum, Inc.	American Family II	N. Rockwell	9,900
81-F-NR-4-001	New Arrival	135.00	135.00
81-F-NR-4-002	Sweet Dreams	150.00	150.00
82-F-NR-4-003	Little Shaver	150.00	150.00
82-F-NR-4-004	We Missed You Daddy	150.00	150.00
82-F-NR-4-005	Home Run Slugger	110.00	110.00
82-F-NR-4-006	Giving Thanks	160.00	160.00
82-F-NR-4-007	Space Pioneers	150.00	150.00
82-F-NR-4-008	Little Salesman	150.00	150.00
82-F-NR-4-009	Almost Grown Up	135.00	135.00
82-F-NR-4-010	Courageous Hero	150.00	150.00
82-F-NR-4-011	At The Circus	160.00	160.00
82-F-NR-4-012	Good Food, Good Friends	175.00	175.00
Norman Rockwell Museum, Inc.	World Of Children	N. Rockwell	15,000
81-F-NR-5-001	Downhill, Racer	85.00	85.00
81-F-NR-5-002	Vacations Over	85.00	85.00
81-F-NR-5-003	Little Patient	85.00	85.00
81-F-NR-5-004	Bicycle Boys	85.00	85.00
82-F-NR-5-005	Helping Mother	85.00	85.00
82-F-NR-5-006	The Drummers Friend	85.00	85.00
82-F-NR-5-007	Summer Fun	85.00	85.00
82-F-NR-5-008	Vacation	85.00	85.00
82-F-NR-5-009	Bobbing For Apples	85.00	85.00
82-F-NR-5-010	Bringing Home The Christmas Tree	85.00	85.00
82-F-NR-5-011	The Circus Comes To Town	85.00	85.00
82-F-NR-5-012	The Pest	85.00	85.00
Norman Rockwell Museum, Inc.	Commemorative Collection	N. Rockwell	5,000
82-F-NR-6-001	Spirit Of America	125.00	125.00
83-F-NR-6-002	Norman Rockwell, America's Artist	125.00	125.00
Norman Rockwell	Musical	N. Rockwell	10,000
82-F-NR-7-001	Birthday Party	125.00	125.00
82-F-NR-7-002	Bride and Groom	125.00	125.00
82-F-NR-7-003	Checking His List	125.00	125.00
Norman Rockwell Museum, Inc.	Four Freedoms	N. Rockwell	5,000
82-F-NR-8-001	Freedom Of Speech	250.00	250.00
82-F-NR-8-002	Freedom Of Worship	250.00	250.00
82-F-NR-8-003	Freedom From Want	250.00	250.00
82-F-NR-8-004	Freedom From Fear	250.00	250.00
Norman Rockwell Museum, Inc.	Celebration	N. Rockwell	9,900
82-F-NR-9-001	Celebration	135.00	135.00
Norman Rockwell Museum, Inc.	Large Classic	N. Rockwell	1,000
82-F-NR-10-001	Lighthouse Keeper's Daughter	175.00	175.00
82-F-NR-10-002	The Cobbler	175.00	175.00
82-F-NR-10-003	The Toymaker	175.00	175.00
82-F-NR-10-004	Bedtime	175.00	175.00
83-F-NR-10-005	Memories	175.00	175.00
83-F-NR-10-006	For A Good Boy	175.00	175.00
Norman Rockwell Museum, Inc.	The Museum Miniatures	N. Rockwell	Open
83-F-NR-11-001	Puppy Love	25.00	25.00
83-F-NR-11-002	Norman Rockwell	25.00	25.00
83-F-NR-11-003	Baby's First Step	25.00	25.00
83-F-NR-11-004	Downhill Racer	25.00	25.00
83-F-NR-11-005	Off To School	25.00	25.00
83-F-NR-11-006	Summer Fun	25.00	25.00
Norman Rockwell Museum, Inc.	Shirley Temple Nostalgia Collectibles		2,500
82-F-NR-12-001	Baby Take A Bow (autographed)	150.00	175.00
83-F-NR-12-002	Curly Top (autographed)	120.00	130.00
83-F-NR-12-003	Stand Up And Cheer	120.00	120.00
Norman Rockwell Museum, Inc.	Shirley Temple Nostalgia Collectibles		22.500
82-F-NR-12-004	Baby Take A Bow	125.00	125.00
83-F-NR-12-005	Curly Top	95.00	95.00
83-F-NR-12-006	Stand Up And Cheer	95.00	95.00
Norman Rockwell Museum, Inc.	The Birds Of America Collection	J. Audubon	Open
82-F-NR-13-001	Bluebird	45.00	45.00
82-F-NR-13-002	Ruby Throated Hummingbird	45.00	45.00
82-F-NR-13-003	Robin	40.00	40.00
82-F-NR-13-004	Goldfinch	45.00	45.00
82-F-NR-13-005	Cardinal	40.00	40.00
82-F-NR-13-006	Richardson's Owl	40.00	40.00
82-F-NR-13-007	Red Headed Woodpecker	40.00	40.00
82-F-NR-13-008	Barred Owl And Squirrel	185.00	185.00
83-F-NR-13-009	Flicker	35.00	35.00
83-F-NR-13-010	Wood Thrush	35.00	35.00
83-F-NR-13-011	Pelican	35.00	35.00
83-F-NR-13-012	Painted Bunting	35.00	35.00
82-F-NR-13-013	John James Audubon Display	135.00	135.00
Opa's Haus	Lore Of Germany	E. Breiden	950
81-F-OH-1-001	The Monk	30.00	30.00
81-F-OH-1-002	The Beer King	30.00	30.00
81-F-OH-1-003	The Ibex	30.00	30.00
81-F-OH-1-004	The Dancing Couple	30.00	30.00
81-F-OH-1-005	The Cherub	30.00	30.00
Opa's Haus	Americal Wildlife	E. Breiden	950
82-F-OH-1-006	Screech Owl	35.00	35.00
82-F-OH-1-007	Mallard Drake	35.00	35.00
Pemberton And Oakes	Zolan's Children	D. Zolan	17,000
82-F-PO-1-001	Erik And Dandelion	48.00	48.00
Pemberton And Oakes	Zolan's Children	D. Zolan	6,800
83-F-PO-1-002	Sabina In The Grass	48.00	48.00
Reco International	The McClellands	J. McClelland	10,000
XX-F-RI-1-001	John	27.00	27.00
XX-F-RI-1-002	Alice	27.00	27.00
XX-F-RI-1-003	Chimney Sweep	32.00	32.00
XX-F-RI-1-004	Dressing Up	35.00	35.00
Reco International	The McClellands	J. McClelland	
XX-F-RI-2-001	Autumn Dreams	25.00	25.00
XX-F-RI-2-002	Tuck-Me-IN	25.00	25.00
XX-F-RI-2-003	Country Lass	25.00	25.00
XX-F-RI-2-004	Sudsie Suzie	29.00	29.00
XX-F-RI-2-005	Smooth Sailing	27.00	27.00
XX-F-RI-2-006	The Clown	32.00	32.00
XX-F-RI-2-007	The Baker	29.00	29.00
XX-F-RI-2-008	Quiet Moments	35.00	35.00
XX-F-RI-2-009	The Farmer	32.00	32.00
XX-F-RI-2-010	The Nurse	28.00	28.00
XX-F-RI-2-011	The Policeman	32.00	32.00
XX-F-RI-2-012	The Fireman	32.00	32.00
XX-F-RI-2-013	Winter Fun	36.00	36.00
XX-F-RI-2-014	Cowgirl	28.00	28.00
XX-F-RI-2-015	Cowboy	30.00	30.00
XX-F-RI-2-016	Doc	30.00	30.00
XX-F-RI-2-017	Lawyer	28.00	28.00
XX-F-RI-2-018	Farmer's Wife	30.00	30.00
XX-F-RI-2-019	First Outing	30.00	30.00
River Shore, Ltd	Loveable-Baby Animals	R. Brown	15,000
78-F-RS-1-001	Akiku-Seal	37.50	175.00
78-F-RS-1-002	Alfred-Raccoon	42.50	75.00
Reco International	Granget Crystal Sculptures	Granget	350
73-F-RI-1-001	Long Earred Owl, Asio Otus	2250.00	2250.00
Reco International	Granget Crystal Sculptures	Granget	150
XX-F-RI-1-002	Ruffed Grouse	1000.00	1000.00
Reco International	King's Porcelain Figurines		200
74-F-RI-4-001	Blue Jay	900.00	Unknown
74-F-RI-4-002	Weasel	325.00	Unknown
Reco International	King's Porcelain Figurines		350
74-F-RI-4-003	Eurpoean Roller	500.00	Unknown
Reco International	King's Porcelain Figurines		300
74-F-RI-1-004	Hummingbird	700.00	Unknown
74-F-RI-1-005	Robins	650.00	Unknown
Reco International	King's Porcelain Figurines		250
74-F-RI-1-006	Titmouse	700.00	Unknown

Company	Series	Artist	Edition limit
Number	Name	Issue Price	Quote
Reco International	King's Porcelain Figurines		100
74-F-RI-1-007	White Or Western Pelican	975.00	Unknown
74-F-RI-1-008	Woodcock	900.00	Unknown
74-F-RI-1-009	Wood Ducks, Pair	1350.00	Unknown
79-F-RS-1-003	Scooter-Chipmunk	45.00	45.00
79-F-RS-1-004	Matilda- Koala	45.00	45.00
River Shore, Ltd	Wildlife Baby Animals	R. Brown	15,000
78-F-RS-2-001	Fanny-Fawn	45.00	75.00
79-F-RS-2-002	Roosevelt- Bear	50.00	50.00
79-F-RS-2-003	Roscoe- Red Fox	50.00	50.00
80-F-RS-2-004	Priscilla- Skunk	50.00	50.00
River Shore, Ltd	Farm Baby Animals	R. Brown	15,000
80-F-RS-3-001	Buddy- Foal	50.00	50.00
80-F-RS-3-002	Clover- Lamb	50.00	50.00
80-F-RS-3-003	Clementine-Calf	50.00	50.00
80-F-RS-3-004	Zeke- Piglet	50.00	50.00
River Shore, Ltd	Safari Baby Animals	R. Brown	15,000
81-F-RS-4-001	BaKuba- Lion Cub	50.00	50.00
81-F-RS-4-002	Kimbundo-Chimp	50.00	50.00
81-F-RS-4-003	Zuela- Elephant	50.00	50.00
81-F-RS-4-004	Kalina -Tiger Cub	50.00	50.00
River Shore, Ltd	Rockwell Single Issues	N. Rockwell	9,500
81-F-RS-5-001	Looking Out To Sea	85.00	130.00
82-F-RS-5-002	Grandpa's Guardian	125.00	125.00
River Shore, Ltd	Grant Wood Figurines	G. Wood	9,500
82-F-RS-6-001	American Gothic	185.00	185.00
River Shore, Ltd	Vignette		9,500
82-F-RS-7-001	Broken Window	150.00	150.00
River Shore Ltd	Christmas After Christmas	B. Timberlake	5,000
82-F-RS-8-001	Kay's Doll	95.00	95.00
Rohn	Rohn Porcelains	Rohn	100
71-F-RH-1-001	American GI	600.00	600.00
71-F-RH-1-002	Coolie	700.00	700.00
71-F-RH-1-003	Crow Indian	800.00	800.00
71-F-RH-1-004	Riverboat Captain	1000.00	1000.00
71-F-RH-1-005	Trailhand	1200.00	1200.00
74-F-RH-1-006	Hunter	1000.00	1000.00
Rohn	Rohn Porcelains	Rohn	125
72-F-RH-1-007	Gypsy	1450.00	1450.00
72-F-RH-1-008	Jeanine	475.00	475.00
73-F-RH-1-009	Apache	900.00	900.00
76-F-RH-1-010	Chosen One	850.00	850.00
77-F-RH-1-011	Nostalgia, Wally	250.00	250.00
Rohn	Rohn Porcelains	Rohn	175
73-F-RH-1-012	Apprentice	500.00	Unknown
Rohn	Rohn Porcelains	Rohn	150
73-F-RH-1-013	Jazzman	750.00	750.00
73-F-RH-1-014	Sherif	1500.00	1500.00
75-F-RH-1-015	Cougar	700.00	700.00
77-F-RH-1-016	Nostalgia, Flapper	325.00	325.00
Rohn	Rohn Porcelains	Rohn	90
73-R-RH-1-017	Matador	2400.00	2400.00
Rohn	Rohn Porcelains	Rohn	250
74-F-RH-1-018	Missy	250.00	250.00
74-F-RH-1-019	Recruit	250.00	250.00
74-F-RH-1-020	Small World Series, Big Brother	90.00	Unknown
74-F-RH-1-021	Small World Series, Burglars	120.00	Unknown
74-F-RH-1-022	Small World Series, Quackers	75.00	Unknown
75-F-RH-1-023	Small World Series, Field Mushrooms	90.00	Unknown
75-F-RH-1-024	Small World Series, Oyster Mushroom	140.00	Unknown
77-F-RH-1-025	Nostalgia, Sou 'wester	300.00	300.00
Rohn	Rohn Porcelains	Rohn	500
74-F-RH-1-026	Small World Series, Knee Deep	60.00	Unknown
74-F-RH-1-027	Young Confederate Recruit	250.00	250.00
Rohn	Rohn Porcelains	Rohn	300
74-F-RH 1 028	Rhino	600.00	600.00
74-F-RH-1-029	White Rhino	600.00	Unknown
Rohn	Rohn Porcelains	Rohn	25
75-F-RH-1-030	Longhorn	975.00	975.00
Rohn	Rohn Porcelains	Rohn	
75-F-RH-1-031	Monarch Butterflies	850.00	850.00
Rohn	Rohn Porcelains	Rohn	75
76-F-RH-1-032	Truman, Harry	2400.00	2400.00
Rohn	Rohn Porcelains	Rohn	200
76-F-RH-1-033	Indian Woman	850.00	850.00
Rohn	Rohn Porcelains	Rohn	225
77-F-RH-1-034	Nostalgia, Casey	275.00	275.00
Rohn	Rohn Porcelains	Rohn	70
77-F-RH-1-035	Zaide	1950.00	1950.00
78-F-RH-1-036	Sabbath	1825.00	1825.00
Rohn	Rohn Porcelains	Rohn	1500
XX-F-RH-1-037	Small World Series, Johnnie's	90.00	Unknown
Roman Inc.	Fontanini, The Collectible Creche	E. Simonetti	Open
73-F-RO-1-001	10cm 18 piece set	63.00	63.00
73-F-RO-1-002	12cm 19 piece set	83.60	83.60
79-F-RO-1-003	16cm 15 piece set	162.00	162.00
82-F-RO-1-004	17cm 14 piece set	174.00	174.00
73-F-RO-1-005	19cm 18 piece set	186.00	186.00
80-F-RO-1-006	30cm 15 piece set	625.00	625.00

Company	Series	Artist	Edition limit
Number	Name	Issue Price	Quote
Roman Inc.	Ceramica Excelsis		5,000
78-F-RO-2-001	Infant Of Prague	37.50	60.00
78-F-RO-2-002	Christ In The Garden Of Gethsemane	40.00	60.00
78-F-RO-2-003	Flight Into Egypt	59.00	90.00
77-F-RO-2-004	Madonna And Child With Angels	60.00	60.00
77-F-RO-2-005	What Happened To Your Hand ?	60.00	60.00
Roman Inc.	The Masterpiece Collection(1st Edition)	F. Lippe	5,000
79-F-RO-1-001	Adoration (Sculpture)	73.00	73.00
Roman Inc.	The Masterpiece Collection(2nd Edition)	P. Mignard	5,000
80-F-RO-1-002	Madonna With Grapes	85.00	85.00
Roman Inc.	The Masterpiece Collection(3rd Edition)	G. delle Notti	5,000
81-F-RO-1-003	The Holy Family	98.00	98.00
Roman Inc.	The Masterpiece Collection(4th Edition)	R. Ferruzzi	5,000
82-F-RO-1-004	Madonna Of The Streets	65.00	65.00
Roman Inc.	A Child's World (1st Edition)	F. Hook	15,000
80-F-RO-2-001	Nighttime Thoughts	25.00	25.00
80-F-RO-2-002	Kiss Me Good Night	29.00	29.00
80-F-RO-2-003	Sounds Of The Sea	45.00	45.00
80-F-RO-2-004	Beach Buddies	Closed	Closed
80-F-RO-2-005	My Big Brother	39.00	39.00
80-F-RO-2-006	Helping Hands	45.00	45.00
Roman Inc.	A Child's World (2nd Edition)	F. Hook	15,000
81-F-RO-3-001	Making Friends	42.00	42.00
81-F-RO-3-002	Cat Nap	42.00	42.00
81-F-RO-3-003	The Sea And Me	39.00	39.00
81-F-RO-3-004	Sunday School	39.00	39.00
81-F-RO-3-005	I'll Be Good	36.00	36.00
81-F-RO-3-006	All Dressed Up	36.00	36.00
Roman Inc.	A Child's World (3rd Edition)	F. Hook	15,000
81-F-RO-4-001	Pathway To Dreams	47.00	47.00
81-F-RO-4-002	Road To Adventure	47.00	47.00
81-F-RO-4-003	Sisters	64.00	64.00
81-F-RO-4-004	Bear Hug	42.00	42.00
81-F-RO-4-005	Spring Breeze	37.50	37.50
81-F-RO-4-006	Youth	37.50	37.50
Roman Inc.	A Child's World (4th Edition)	F. Hook	15,000
82-F-RO-5-001	All Bundled Up	37.50	37.50
82-F-RO-5-002	Bedtime	35.00	35.00
82-F-RO-5-003	Birdie	37.50	37.50
82-F-RO-5-004	My Dolly !	39.00	39.00
82-F-RO-5-005	Ring Bearer	39.00	39.00
82-F-RO-5-006	Flower Girl	42.00	42.00
Roman Inc.	Hook	F. Hook	2,000
82-F-RO-6-001	Sailor Mates	290.00	290.00
82-F-RO-6-002	Sun Shy	290.00	290.00
Roman Inc.	Classics Of The Arts (Miniatures/Ornaments)		Open
82-F-RO-7-001	Queen Odette From Swan Lake	15.00	15.00
82-F-RO-7-002	The Sugarplum Fairy From The Nutcracker	15.00	15.00
82-F-RO-7-003	Princess Aurora From Sleeping Beauty	15.00	15.00
82-F-RO-7-004	Giselle	15.00	15.00
Roman Inc.	Classics Of The Arts		Open
83-F-RO-8-001	Basil From Don Quixote	50.00	50.00
83-F-RO-8-002	Kitri From Don Quixote	50.00	50.00
83-F-RO-8-003	The Handsome Prince From The Nutcracker	50.00	50.00
83-F-RO-8-004	Clara From The Nutcracker	50.00	50.00
83-F-RO-8-005	Prince Florimund From Sleeping Beauty	50.00	50.00
83-F-RO-8-006	Princess Aurora From Sleeping Beauty	50.00	50.00
82-F-RO-8-007	Queen Odette From Swan Lake	45.00	45.00
82-F-RO-8-008	The Sugarplum Fairy From The Nutcracker	45.00	45.00
82-F-RO-8-009	Princess Aurora From Sleeping Beauty	45.00	45.00
82-F-RO-8-010	Giselle	45.00	45.00
Roman Inc.	Dance Studio (Figurines Endorsed by The Joffrey Ballet)		Open
82-F-RO-9-001	La Lecon	72.00	72.00
82-F-RO-9-002	Cinquieme Position	45.00	45.00
82-F-RO-9-003	Se Coiffant	45.00	45.00
82-F-RO-9-004	Les De'butantes	90.00	90.00
82-F-RO-9-005	Battement Tendu	45.00	45.00
82-F-RO-9-006	Lacant les Chaussons	40.00	40.00
82-F-RO-9-007	Arabesque	48.00	48.00
Roman Inc.	None(Figurines Endorsed by the Ice Capades)		Open
83-F-RO-10-001	Presenting Freddie Trenkler	65.00	65.00
83-F-RO-10-002	Stag Jump	65.00	65.00
83-F-RO-10-003	Attitude	65.00	65.00
83-F-RO-10-004	Spiral	65.00	65.00
Roman Inc.	Andreoli's Cotillion	C. Andreoli	7,500
83-F-RO-11-001	Dancing Couple	95.00	95.00
83-F-RO-11-002	Singer	45.00	45.00
83-F-RO-11-003	Violinist	40.00	40.00
83-F-RO-11-004	Guitarist	45.00	45.00
83-F-RO-11-005	Pianist At Piano	150.00	150.00
83-F-RO-11-006	Cellist	45.00	45.00
83-F-RO-11-007	Harpist	45.00	45.00
83-F-RO-11-008	Clarinetist	40.00	40.00
Roman Inc.	Cottage Street	F. Weedn	Open
83-F-RO-12-001	The Clown	25.00	25.00
83-F-RO-12-002	The Angel	25.00	25.00

Category: Figurine

Company	Series	Artist	Edition limit
Number	**Name**	**Issue Price**	**Quote**
83-F-RO-12-003	Dream Maker	25.00	25.00
83-F-RO-12-004	Balloon Lady	25.00	25.00
83-F-RO-12-005	The Little Girl	25.00	25.00
83-F-RO-12-006	The Little Boy	25.00	25.00
Roman Inc.	Baby Bear Picnic		19,500
83-F-RO-13-001	Panda	25.00	25.00
83-F-RO-13-002	Polar Bear	25.00	25.00
83-F-RO-13-003	Koala	25.00	25.00
83-F-RO-13-004	Black Bear	25.00	25.00
83-F-RO-13-005	Brown Bear	25.00	25.00
Roman Inc.	None(Balloon Sculptures)	T. Rubel	19,500
83-F-RO-14-001	America	75.00	75.00
83-F-RO-14-002	Rainbow	75.00	75.00
83-F-RO-14-003	Wave Of Color	75.00	75.00
83-F-RO-14-004	Windy Leigh	75.00	75.00
Royal Doulton	Royal Doulton Figurines		500
67-F-RD-1-001	Soldiers, Indian Brave	2500.00	2500.00 to 3000.00
71-F-RD-1-002	The Palio	2500.00	2500.00
Royal Doulton	Royal Doulton Figurines		150
69-F-RD-1-003	Prince Charles Bust	400.00	400.00
74-F-RD-1-004	Jefferson, Black-Throated Loon	1750.00	1750.00
74-F-RD-1-005	Jefferson, King Eider Drake	1400.00	1400.00
74-F-RD-1-006	Jefferson, Snowy Owl, Female	1500.00	1500.00
Royal Doulton	Royal Doulton Figurines		750
71-F-RD-1-007	Lady Musicians, Cello	250.00	350.00
71-F-RD-1-008	Lady Musicians, Virginals	250.00	350.00
72-F-RD-1-009	Lady Musicians, Lute	250.00	350.00
72-F-RD-1-010	Lady Musicians, Violin	250.00	350.00
72-F-RD-1-011	Queen Elizabeth & Duke Of Edinburgh Busts	1000.00	500.00 to 1000.00
73-F-RD-1-012	Lady Musicians, Flute	250.00	350.00
73-F-RD-1-013	Lady Muscians, Harp	275.00	350.00
74-F-RD-1-014	Lady Musicians, Chitarrone	350.00	400.00
74-F-RD-1-015	Lady Musicians, Cymbals	325.00	350.00
75-F-RD-1-016	Lady Musicians, Dulcimer	375.00	350.00
75-F-RD-1-017	Lady Musicians, Hurdy-Gurdy	375.00	350.00
76-F-RD-1-018	Lady Musicians, French Horn	400.00	450.00
76-F-RD-1-019	Lady Musicians, Viola D'amore	400.00	450.00
77-F-RD-1-020	Dancers, Flamenco	400.00	750.00
77-F-RD-1-021	Dancers, Indian Temple	400.00	750.00
77-F-RD-1-022	Soldiers, General Washington AT Prayer	875.00	875.00
78-F-RD-1-023	Dancers Philippine	400.00	400.00
78-F-RD-1-024	Dancers, Scottish	400.00	400.00
Royal Doulton	Royal Doulton Figurines		100
74-F-RD-1-025	Jefferson, Roseate Tern	1850.00	2000.00
Royal Doulton	Royal Doulton Figurines		75
74-F-RD-1-026	Jefferson, Chipmunks	1800.00	1800.00
74-F-RD-1-027	Jefferson, Snowy Owl, Male	1800.00	1800.00
75-F-RD-1-028	Jefferson, Harbor Seal	1200.00	1200.00
75-F-RD-1-029	Jefferson, Snowshoe Hare	2000.00	2000.00
Royal Doulton	Royal Doulton Figurines		250
74-F-RD-1-030	Jefferson, Crossbills, White-winged	1000.00	1000.00
74-F-RD-1-031	Jefferson, Puffins	1200.00	1200.00
76-F-RD-1-032	Jefferson, Fledgling Bluebird	450.00	450.00
Royal Doulton	Royal Doulton Figurines		350
75-F-RD-1-033	Soldiers, Corporal, 1st N. Hampshire Reg, 1778	750.00	1000.00
75-F-RD-1-034	Soldiers, Major 3rd New Jersey Reg. 1776	750.00	1000.00
75-F-RD-1-035	Soldiers, Private, 1st Georgia Reg. 1777	750.00	1000.00
75-F-RD-1-036	Soldiers, Private, 2nd, S. Carolina, Reg. 1781	750.00	1000.00
76-F-RD-1-037	Soldiers, Captain, 2nd New York Reg. 1775	750.00	1000.00
76-F-RD-1-038	Soldiers, Private, 3rd, N. Carolina Reg. 1778	750.00	1000.00
76-F-RD-1-039	Soldiers, Sergeant 10th Maryland Reg. 1777	750.00	1000.00
77-F-RD-1-040	Soldiers, Private, Col. Craft's Mass. Reg.	750.00	1000.00
77-F-RD-1-041	Soldiers, Private, Haslet's Delaware Reg.	750.00	1000.00
77-F-RD-1-042	Soldiers, Private, Rhode Island Reg.	750.00	1000.00
77-F-RD-1-043	Virginia	1200.00	1500.00
Royal Doulton	Royal Doulton Figurines		200
76-F-RD-1-044	Jefferson Chipping Sparrow	750.00	750.00
Royal Doulton	Royal Doulton Figurines		350
78-F-RD-1-045	Soldiers, Private, Penn. Rifle Battalion	750.00	750.00
78-F-RD-1-046	Soldiers, Private, 4th Conn. Reg.	750.00	750.00
78-F-RD-1-046	Soldiers, Sergeant, 1st Continental Dragoons	750.00	750.00
Tay	Tay Porcelains		500
XX-F-TA-1-001	Turtledoves, Group Of Two, 10 Inches		500.00
70-F-TA-1-002	Blue Jay, 13 Inches	375.00	675.00
70-F-TA-1-003	Eagle, 12 Inches x 15 Inches	1000.00	1650.00
70-F-TA-1-004	European Woodcock 10.5 Inches	325.00	550.00
70-F-TA-1-005	Limpkin, 20 Inches	600.00	1100.00
71-F-TA-1-006	Falcon, 13 Inches	500.00	925.00
71-F-TA-1-007	Pheasant, 30 Inches	1500.00	2000.00 to 2750.00

Category: Bells

Company	Series	Artist	Edition limit
Number	**Name**	**Issue Price**	**Quote**
71-F-TA-1-008	Quail Group, 10 Inches	400.00	725.00
71-F-TA-1-009	Roadrunner, 10 x 19 Inches	800.00	950.00 to 1400.00
72-F-TA-1-010	Gray Partridge, 11.5 Inches	800.00	1400.00
74-F-TA-1-011	American Woodcock, 10.5 Inches	625.00	700.00
74-F-TA-1-012	Mallard Duck, 13.5 Inches	900.00	1050.00
74-F-TA-1-013	Mallard Duck, Flying, 15 Inches	550.00	675.00
74-F-TA-1-014	Owl, 10.5 Inches	350.00	450.00
74-F-TA-1-015	Turtledoves On Roof Tile, 9.5 Inches	335.00	375.00
75-F-TA-1-016	Carolina Ducks, Group Of Two, 13 Inches	1350.00	1500.00
75-F-TA-1-017	Smergos Ducks, Group Of Two, 10 Inches	1000.00	1100.00
75-F-TA-1-018	White-Throated Sparrow, 5.5 Inches	360.00	400.00
76-F-TA-1-019	Bluebirds, Group Of Two, 9.5 Inches	500.00	550.00
76-F-TA-1-020	Custer On Horse, 13 x 14.5 Inches	1500.00	1500.00
Tay	Tay Porcelains		100
73-F-TA-1-021	Austrian Officer On Horseback	1200.00	1200.00 to 1500.00
Tay	Tay Porcelains		300
74-F-TA-1-022	Gyrfalcon, 18 inches	1250.00	1500.00
Tay	Tay Porcelains		5000
74-F-TA-1-023	Boreal Chickadee, 7 Inches	275.00	360.00
Tay	Tay Porcelains		1000
74-F-TA-1-024	Great Crested Flycatcher 9 Inches	300.00	360.00
75-F-TA-1-025	Oriole, 9.5 Inches	300.00	325.00
Tay	Tay Porcelains		500
76-F-TA-1-026	Indian on Horse, 13 x 14.5 Inches	1500.00	1500.00
76-F-TA-1-027	Robin, 8 Inches	400.00	450.00
Villeroy & Boch	Flower Fairy	C. Barker	15,000
82-F-VB-1-001	Lavender	89.00	89.00
XX-F-VB-1-002	Sweet Pea	109.00	109.00
XX-F-VB-1-003	Candy Tuft	75.00	75.00
XX-F-VB-1-004	Heliotrope	NA	NA
XX-F-VB-1-005	Blackthorn	NA	NA
XX-F-VB-1-006	Appleblossom	NA	NA

Category: Bells

Company	Series	Artist	Edition limit
Brown & Bigelow, Inc.	Brown & Bigelow Bells	N.Rockwell	9,800
79-B-BB-1-001	The Runaway	30.00	30.00
Brown & Bigelow, Inc.	A Boy and His Dog Silver Bells	N.Rockwell	9,800
80-B-BB-2-001	Mysterious Malady	60.00	60.00
80-B-BB-2-002	Pride of Parenthood	60.00	60.00
The Danbury Mint	Various	N.Rockwell	-----
75-B-DM-1-001	Doctor and Doll	27.50	54.00
76-B-DM-1-002	Grandpa Snowman	27.50	44.00
76-B-DM-1-003	Freedom From Want	27.50	44.00
76-B-DM-1-004	No Swimming	27.50	44.00
76-B-DM-1-005	Saying Grace	27.50	44.00
76-B-DM-1-006	The Discovery	27.50	44.00
77-B-DM-1-007	The Runaway	27.50	40.00
77-B-DM-1-008	Knuckles Down	27.50	40.00
77-B-DM-1-009	Tom Sawyer	27.50	40.00
77-B-DM-1-010	Puppy Love	27.50	40.00
77-B-DM-1-011	Santa's Mail	27.50	40.00
77-B-DM-1-012	The Remedy	27.50	40.00
The Danbury Mint	The Wonderful World of Norman Rockwell	N.Rockwell	-----
79-B-DM-2-001	Grandpa's Girl	27.50	29.50
79-B-DM-2-002	Leapfrog	27.50	29.50
79-B-DM-2-003	Baby-Sitter	27.50	29.50
79-B-DM-2-004	Batter Up	27.50	29.50
79-B-DM-2-005	Back to School	27.50	29.50
79-B-DM-2-006	Gramps at the Reins	27.50	29.50
79-B-DM-2-007	Friend in Need	27.50	29.50
79-B-DM-2-008	Puppy in the Pocket	27.50	29.50
The Danbury Mint	The Norman Rockwell Commemorative Bell	N.Rockwell	
79-B-DM-3-001	Triple Self-Portrait	29.50	35.00
Designers Collection	A Mother's Remembrance Collection-Holly Hobbie Figurine Bells	Hobbie	6,000
77-B-DC-1-001	A Mother's Remembrance 1977	12.00	25.00
Designers Collection	A Mother's Remembrance Collection-Holly Hobbie Figurine Bells	Hobbie	7,500
78-B-DC-1-002	A Mother's Keepsake 1978	12.00	25.00
Designers Collection	A Mother's Remembrance Collection-Holly Hobbie Figurine Bells	Hobbie	10,000
79-B-DC-1-003	A Mother's Momento	8.00	8.00
Designers Collection	A Mother's Remembrance Collection-Holly Hobbie Figurine Bells	Hobbie	12,000
80-B-DC-1-004	A Mother's Keepsake 1980	9.00	18.00
81-B-DC-1-005	A Mother's Remembrance 1981	15.00	15.00
82-B-DC-1-006	A Mother's Sunny Ways	15.00	15.00
83-B-DC-1-007	Mother's Kind Ways	15.00	15.00
Designers Collection	Christmas Keepsakes Collection-Holly Hobbie Figurine Bell Ornaments	Hobbie	12,000
78-B-DC-2-001	Christmas Joy 1978	7.50	7.50

Category: Bells

Company / Number	Series / Name	Artist / Issue Price	Edition limit / Quote
Designers Collection	Christmas Keepsakes Collection-Holly Hobbie Figurine Beel Ornaments	Hobbie	15,000
79-B-DC-2-002	A Christmas Remembrance	8.00	8.00
Designers Collection	Christmas Keepsakes Collection-Holly Hobbie Figurine Bell Ornaments	Hobbie	24,000
80-B-DC-2-003	Music Of Christmas	10.00	20.00
81-B-DC-2-004	Christmas Joy 1981	15.00	15.00
82-B-DC-2-005	The Warmth Of Christmas	15.00	15.00
83-B-DC-2-006	Christmas Belle	15.00	15.00
Designers Collection	Christmas Keepsakes Collection-Ziggy Figurine Handle Bells		12,000
80-B-DC-3-001	Merry Christmas 1980	13.00	13.00
81-B-DC-3-002	Merry Christmas 1981	15.00	15.00
82-B-DC-3-003	Ring Out Glad Tidings	15.00	15.00
83-B-DC-3-004	Merry Christmas To All 1983	15.00	15.00
Designers Collection	Christmas Keepsakes Collection- L.K. Powell Bell		18,000
80-B-DC-4-001	Rabbit, Squirrel And Cardinal	12.00	12.00
Designers Collection	Christmas Keepsakes Collection-Holly Hobbie Figurine Handle Bells	Hobbie	21,000
80-B-DC-5-001	Christmas Blessing	10.00	10.00
Designers Collection	Christmas Keepsakes Collection Traditional Bell		18,000
81-B-DC-6-001	Wreath	12.00	12.00
Designers Collection	Holly Hobbie Figurine Handle Bell Collection	Hobbie	12,000
81-B-DC-7-001	Holly Hobbie	15.00	15.00
81-B-DC-7-002	Robby Hobbie	15.00	15.00
Designers Collection	Christmas Keepsakes Collection-Holly Hobbie Figurine Handle Bells	Hobbie	12,000
81-B-DC-8-001	Joyful Echoes	12.00	12.00
82-B-DC-8-002	Christmas Dreams	12.50	12.50
Designers Collection	Bas-Relief Annuals Holly Hobbie Bells	Hobbie	15,000
81-B-DC-9-001	First	27.50	30.00
82-B-DC-9-002	Second	27.50	30.00
83-B-DC-9-003	Third	30.00	30.00
Designers Collection	Love Collection Holly Hobbie Figurine Bells	Hobbie	20,000
82-B-DC-10-001	Tender Love	15.00	15.00
83-B-DC-10-002	Heart's Melody	17.50	17.50
Designers Collection	Christmas Keepsakes Collection Holly Hobbie Bells	Hobbie	18,000
82-B-DC-11-001	Holiday Fun	12.00	12.00
83-B-DC-11-002	Christmas Greetings	12.00	12.00
Goebel Collectors Club	M. I. Hummel Collectibles Annual Bells	M. Hummel	Year of Issue
78-B-GC-1-001	Let's Sing 700	50.00	150.00
79-B-GC-1-002	Farewell 701	70.00	70.00
80-B-GC-1-003	Thoughtful 702	85.00	85.00
81-B-GC-1-004	In Tune 703	85.00	85.00
82-B-GC-1-005	She Loves Me, She Loves Me Not 704	90.00	90.00
83-B-GC-1-006	Knit One 705	90.00	90.00
Gorham	Various	N.Rockwell	Annual
75-B-GO-1-001	Sweet Song So Young	19.50	30.00
75-B-GO-1-002	Santa's Helpers (Christmas)	19.50	30.00
75-B-GO-1-003	Tavern Sign Painter	19.50	30.00
76-B-GO-1-004	Flowers in Tender Bloom	19.50	30.00
76-B-GO-1-005	Snow Sculpture	19.50	30.00
77-B-GO-1-006	Fondly Do We Remember	19.50	30.00
77-B-GO-1-007	Chilling Chore (Christmas)	19.50	30.00
78-B-GO-1-008	Gaily Sharing Vintage Times	22.50	22.50
78-B-GO-1-009	Gay Blades (Christmas)	22.50	22.50
79-B-GO-1-010	Beguiling Buttercup	24.50	24.50
79-B-GO-1-011	A Boy Meets His Dog (Christmas)	24.50	24.50
80-B-GO-1-012	Flying High	27.50	27.50
80-B-GO-1-013	Chilly Reception (Christmas)	27.50	27.50
81-B-GO-1-014	Sweet Serenade	27.50	27.50
81-B-GO-1-015	Ski Skills(Christmas)	27.50	27.50
82-B-GO-1-016	Young Mans Fancy	29.50	29.50
82-B-GO-1-017	Coal Season's Coming (Chistmas)	29.50	29.50
83-B-GO-1-018	Christmas Medley (Christmas)	29.50	29.50
83-B-GO-1-019	The Milkmaid	29.50	29.50
Gorham	Currier & Ives - Mini Bells		Annual
76-B-GO-2-001	Christmas Sleigh Ride	9.95	25.00
77-B-GO-2-002	American Homestead	9.95	25.00
78-B-GO-2-003	Yule Logs	12.95	20.00
79-B-GO-2-004	Sleigh Ride	14.95	20.00
80-B-GO-2-005	Christmas in the Country	14.95	20.00
81-B-GO-2-006	Christmas Tree	14.95	14.95
82-B-GO-2-007	Christmas Visitation	16.50	16.50
83-B-GO-2-008	Winter Wonderland	16.50	16.50
Gorham	Mini Bells	N.Rockwell	Annual
81-B-GO-3-001	Tiny Tim	19.75	19.75
82-B-GO-3-002	Planning Christmas Visit	20.00	20.00
The Hamilton Mint	Four Seasons Silver Bells	N.Rockwell	9,800
80-B-HM-1-001	Adventurers Between Adventures	57.00	57.00
80-B-HM-1-002	The Mysterious Malady	57.00	57.00
80-B-HM-1-003	Pride of Parenthood	57.00	57.00
80-B-HM-1-004	A Boy Meets His Dog	57.00	57.00

Category: Dolls

Company / Number	Series / Name	Artist / Issue Price	Edition limit / Quote
Lincoln Mint	Lincoln Bells	N.Rockwell	
75-B-LM-1-001	Downhill Daring	25.00	70.00
Norman Rockwell Museum, Inc.	Collectors Bells	N.Rockwell	Open
82-B-NR-1-001	Wedding/Anniversary	45.00	45.00
82-B-NR-1-002	25th Anniversary	45.00	45.00
82-B-NR-1-003	50th Anniversary	45.00	45.00
82-B-NR-1-004	For A Good Boy	45.00	45.00
Reco International	Joyous Moments	McClelland	5,000
80-B-RI-1-001	I Love You	25.00	25.00
81-B-RI-1-002	Sea Echoes	25.00	25.00
82-B-RI-1-003	Talk to Me	25.00	25.00
River Shore,Ltd.	Rockwell Children Series I	N.Rockwell	7,500
77-B-RS-1-001	School Play	30.00	60.00
77-B-RS-1-002	First Day of School	30.00	60.00
77-B-RS-1-003	Football Hero	30.00	75.00
77-B-RS-1-004	Flowers for Mother	30.00	60.00
River Shore,Ltd.	Rockwell Children Series II	N.Rockwell	15,000
78-B-RS-2-001	Dressing Up	35.00	40.00
78-B-RS-2-002	Future All American	35.00	52.00
78-B-RS-2-003	Garden Girl	35.00	40.00
78-B-RS-2-004	Five Cents A Glass	35.00	40.00
River Shore,Ltd.	World of Children Bell Collection		15,000
79-B-RS-3-001	Allison	50.00	50.00
79-B-RS-3-002	Rei-Ling	50.00	50.00
80-B-RS-3-003	Katrina	50.00	50.00
80-B-RS-3-004	Kuluk	50.00	50.00
River Shore,Ltd.	Norman Rockwell Single Issues	N.Rockwell	7,000
81-B-RS-4-001	Looking Out to Sea	45.00	60.00
82-B-RS-4-002	Grandpa's Guardian	45.00	45.00
River Shore,Ltd.	Norman Rockwell Single Issues	N.Rockwell	347
81-B-RS-5-001	Spring Flowers	175.00	175.00
River Shore,Ltd.	Grant Wood	G. Wood	7,000
82-B-RS-6-001	American Gothic	50.00	50.00
Roman Inc.	The Masterpiece Collection	F. Lippe	Open
79-B-RO-1-001	Adoration	20.00	20.00
Roman Inc.	The Masterpiece Collection	P. Mignard	Open
80-B-RO-1-002	Madonna with Grapes	25.00	25.00
Roman Inc.	The Masterpiece Collection	G. Notti	Open
81-B-RO-1-003	The Holy Family	25.00	25.00
Roman Inc.	The Masterpiece Collection	R. Ferruzzi	Open
82-B-RO-1-004	Madonna of the Streets	25.00	25.00
Roman Inc.	Classics of the Arts		Open
82-B-RO-2-001	Queen Odette from Swan Lake	32.00	32.00
82-B-RO-2-002	The Sugarplum Fairy from The Nutcracker	32.00	32.00
82-B-RO-2-003	Princess Aurora from Sleeping Beauty	32.00	32.00
82-B-RO-2-004	Giselle	32.00	32.00
Royal Devon	Royal Devon Bells	N.Rockwell	---
76-B-RO-2-005	Butter Girl	15.00	28.00

Category: Dolls

Company / Number	Series / Name	Artist / Issue Price	Edition limit / Quote
Goebel Collectors Club	M.I. Hummel Collectibles Dolls	M.I. Hummel	Open
01-D-GC-1-001	Gretel 1901	55.00	55.00
02-D-GC-1-002	Hansel 1902	55.00	55.00
04-D-GC-1-003	Rosa-Blue Baby 1904/B	45.00	45.00
04-D-GC-1-004	Rosa-Pink Baby 1904/P	45.00	45.00
05-D-GC-1-005	Little Knitter 1905	55.00	55.00
06-D-GC-1-006	Merry Wanderer 1906	55.00	55.00
08-D-GC-1-007	Chimney Sweep 1908	55.00	55.00
09-D-GC-1-008	School Girl 1909	55.00	55.00
10-D-GC-1-009	School Boy 1910	55.00	55.00
14-D-GC-1-010	Goose Girl 1914	55.00	55.00
17-D-GC-1-011	For Father 1917	55.00	55.00
25-D-GC-1-012	Merry Wanderer 1925	55.00	55.00
26-D-GC-1-013	Lost Stocking 1926	55.00	55.00
27-D-GC-1-014	Visiting an Invalid 1927	55.00	55.00
28-D-GC-1-015	On Secret Path 1928	55.00	55.00
Gorham	Gorham Dolls		N-A
81-D-GO-1-001	Jillian, 16"	200.00	200.00
81-D-GO-1-002	Alexandria, 19"	250.00	250.00
81-D-GO-1-003	Christopher, 19"	250.00	250.00
81-D-GO-1-004	Stephanie, 10"	250.00	250.00
81-D-GO-1-005	Cecile, 16"	200.00	200.00
81-D-GO-1-006	Christina, 16"	200.00	200.00
81-D-GO-1-007	Daniella, 14"	150.00	150.00
81-D-GO-1-008	Melinda, 14"	150.00	150.00
81-D-GO-1-009	Elena, 14"	150.00	150.00
81-D-GO-1-010	Rosemond, 19"	250.00	250.00
82-D-GO-1-011	Mlle. Monique, 12"	125.00	125.00
82-D-GO-1-012	Mlle. Jeanette, 12"	125.00	125.00
82-D-GO-1-013	Mlle. Lucille, 12"	125.00	125.00
82-D-GO-1-014	Benjamin, 18"	200.00	200.00
82-D-GO-1-015	Ellice, 18"	200.00	200.00
82-D-GO-1-016	Corrine, 21"	250.00	250.00
82-D-GO-1-017	Baby in Blue Dress, 12"	150.00	150.00
82-D-GO-1-018	Baby in Apricot Dress,16"	175.00	175.00
82-D-GO-1-019	Baby in White Dress, 18"	250.00	250.00
82-D-GO-1-020	Melanie, 23"	300.00	300.00
82-D-GO-1-021	Jeremy, 23"	300.00	300.00
82-D-GO-1-022	Allison	125.00	125.00
82-D-GO-1-023	Mlle. Yvonne, 12"	125.00	125.00
82-D-GO-1-024	M. Anton, 12"	125.00	125.00
82-D-GO-1-025	Mlle. Marsella, 12"	125.00	125.00
82-D-GO-1-026	Kristen, 23"	300.00	300.00
83-D-GO-1-027	Blue Girl	80.00	80.00

Category: Dolls

Company / Number	Series / Name	Artist / Issue Price	Edition limit / Quote
Company	**Series**	**Artist**	**Edition limit**
Number	**Name**	**Issue Price**	**Quote**
83-D-GO-1-028	Christmas Morning	80.00	80.00
83-D-GO-1-029	Heather, 14"	80.00	80.00
83-D-GO-1-030	Little Amy, 14"	80.00	80.00
83-D-GO-1-031	Robbie, 14"	80.00	80.00
83-D-GO-1-032	Sweet Valentine, 16"	100.00	100.00
83-D-GO-1-033	Yesterday's Memories,18"	125.00	125.00
83-D-GO-1-034	Sunday Best, 18"	115.00	115.00
83-D-GO-1-035	Blue Girl, 18"	115.00	115.00
83-D-GO-1-036	Beth, 16"	225.00	225.00
83-D-GO-1-037	Amy, 16"	225.00	225.00
83-D-GO-1-038	Meg,19"	275.00	275.00
83-D-GO-1-039	Jo, 19"	275.00	275.00
83-D-GO-1-040	Jennifer, 19" Bridal Doll	325.00	325.00
Hamilton Collection	Maidens of the Changing Seasons Hakata Doll Coll.		7,500
81-D-HC-1-001	Peony Maiden	75.00	155.00
81-D-HC-1-002	Maple Leaf Maiden	75.00	85.00
81-D-HC-1-003	Snowflake Maiden	75.00	85.00
81-D-HC-1-004	Cherry Blossom Maiden	75.00	85.00
Hamilton Collection	The Art of Kabuki Hakata Doll Collection	Togo San	9,800
82-D-HC-2-001	Wisteria Maiden	75.00	75.00
82-D-HC-2-002	Male Lion Dancer	75.00	75.00
82-D-HC-2-003	White Heron Dancer	75.00	75.00
82-D-HC-2-004	The Marionette	75.00	75.00
82-D-HC-2-005	Dojo Temple Maiden	75.00	75,00
82-D-HC-2-006	Female Lion Dancer	75.00	75.00
U.S. Historical Society	Living Image Dolls		2,500
82-D-US-1-001	Benjamin Franklin	525.00	625.00
82-D-US-1-002	George Washington	525.00	625.00
83-D-US-1-003	Abigail Adams	525.00	625.00
83-D-US-1-004	Thomas Jefferson	525.00	625.00
83-D-US-1-005	Abraham Lincoln	525.00	525.00
83-D-US-1-006	Mary Todd Lincoln	525.00	525.00

Category: Graphics

Company / Number	Series / Name	Artist / Issue Price	Edition limit / Quote
Allison & Co.	Allison	B. Allison	800
77-G-AC-1-001	Nature's Trinity signed & numbered	60.00	60.00
Allison & Co.	Allison	B. Allison	25
77-G-AC-1-002	Nature's Trinity remarques	120.00	120.00
Allison & Co.	Allison	B. Allison	1,000
78-G-AC-1-003	Grizzly	30.00	30.00
79-G-AC-1-004	Cascades in Shade	40.00	40.00
79-G-AC-1-005	He and His Lady	40.00	40.00
79-G-AC-1-006	China Bear	40.00	40.00
79-G-AC-1-007	Winter's Peace	30.00	30.00
80-G-AC-1-008	Los Ninos	50.00	50.00
80-G-AC-1-009	Winter Serenity	50.00	50.00
81-G-AC-1-010	Proud Horns	55.00	55.00
82-G-AC-1-011	Summers Joy	65.00	65.00
Allison & Co.	Allison	B. Allison	100
79-G-AC-1-012	He and His Lady artist proofs	50.00	50.00
Allison & Co.	Allison	B. Allison	1,500
79-G-AC-1-013	He and His Lady signed only	30.00	30.00
Allison & Co.	Allison	B. Allison	1,100
79-G-AC-1-014	China Bear signed only	30.00	30.00
Allison & Co.	Allison	B. Allison	3,000
80-G-AC-1-015	Roses Forever	25.00	25.00
81-G-AC-1-016	Cardinal	30.00	30.00
Graphic Buying Service Ltd.	Various	G. Barrer	150
76-G-GB-1-001	Evening Song	60.00	60.00
76-G-GB-1-002	Summer Garden	60.00	60.00
76-G-GB-1-003	White Vase	50.00	50.00
John Brindle Fine Arts	Beran	L. Beran	1,000
77-G-JB-1-001	Memories of Pan	45.00	45.00
77-G-JB-1-002	Flutist Dream	45.00	45.00
John Brindle Fine Arts	Beran	L. Beran	100
77-G-JB-1-003	The Call of the Piper	150.00	150.00
78-G-JB-1-004	The Dream	200.00	200.00
John Brindle Fine Arts	Beran	L. Beran	10
77-G-JB-1-005	The Call of the Piper (artist proofs)	150.00	150.00
78-G-JB-1-006	The Dream (artist proofs)	200.00	200.00
John Brindle	Beran	L. Beran	500
78-G-JB-1-007	Circle of Enchantment	50.00	50.00
Lenore Beran Art	Beran	L. Beran	50
80-G-LB-1-001	Sachiko	175.00	175.00
Lenore Beran Art	Beran	L. Beran	5
80-G-LB-1-002	Sachiko(artist proofs)	175.00	175.00
Lenore Beran Art	Beran	L. Beran	99
80-G-LB-1-003	Vision	175.00	175.00
80-G-LB-1-004	The Message of the Eagle	175.00	175.00
82-G-LB-1-005	Unicorn	40.00	40.00
82-G-LB-1-006	Pegasus	40.00	40.00
Lenore Beran Art	Beran	L. Beran	10
80-G-LB-1-007	Vision (artist proofs)	175.00	175.00
80-G-LB-1-008	The Message of the Eagle (artist proofs)	175.00	175.00
Lenore Beran Art	Beran	L. Beran	12
82-G-LB-1-009	Unicorn (artist proofs)	40.00	40.00
82-G-LB-1-010	Pegasus (artist proofs)	40.00	40.00
Lenore Beran Art	Beran	L. Beran	500
80-G-LB-1-011	The Gathering	50.00	50.00
Lenore Beran Art	Beran	L. Beran	50 remarques from the edition
80-G-LB-1-012	The Gathering (remarques)	95.00	95.00
Graphics Buying Service, Ltd.	Beran	L. Beran	150

Category: Graphics

Company / Number	Series / Name	Artist / Issue Price	Edition limit / Quote
Company	**Series**	**Artist**	**Edition limit**
Number	**Name**	**Issue Price**	**Quote**
80-G-GB-2-001	Lessons from the Past	175.00	175.00
80-G-GB-2-002	For the Love of a Maiden	150.00	150.00
80-G-GB-2-003	Preparing for the Pow Wow	150.00	150.00
80-G-GB-2-004	Springwater & the Kachina Doll	95.00	95.00
Graphics Buying Service, Ltd.	Beran	L. Beran	15
80-G-GB-2-005	Lessons from the Past (artist proofs)	175.00	175.00
80-G-GB-2-006	Preparing for the Pow Wow (artist proofs)	175.00	175.00
Lenore Beran Art	Beran	L. Beran	315
81-G-LB-1-013	Up, Up and Away	60.00	60.00
Lenore Beran Art	Beran	L. Beran	42
81-G-LB-1-014	Fusion	95.00	95.00
81-G-LB-1-015	Jam Session	95.00	95.00
Lenore Beran Art	Beran	L. Beran	44
82-G-LB-1-016	Dance in my Fantasies	195.00	195.00
Lenore Beran Art	Beran	L. Beran	6
81-G-LB-1-017	Fusion (artist proofs)	95.00	95.00
81-G-LB-1-018	Jam Session (artist proofs)	95.00	95.00
82-G-LB-1-019	Dance in my Fantasies (artist proofs)	195.00	190.00
Etchings, Etc.	Chapple	D. Chapple	150
78-G-EE-1-001	Blue Winged Teal	90.00	150.00
78-G-EE-1-002	Mallards	90.00	150.00
78-G-EE-1-003	Canvasbacks	90.00	150.00
78-G-Ee-1-004	Pintails	90.00	150.00
78-G-EE-1-005	Black Duck	90.00	150.00
78-G-EE-1-006	Bluebills	90.00	150.00
78-G-EE-1-007	Canada Geese	90.00	200.00
78-G-EE-1-008	Wood Duck	90.00	200.00
78-G-EE-1-009	In To Feed/Canada Geese	90.00	150.00
78-G-EE-1-010	Setting Down/Red Heads	90.00	150.00
78-G-EE-1-011	Over the Marsh/Pintails	90.00	150.00
78-G-EE-1-012	Backwater Mallards	90.00	150.00
78-G-EE-1-013	Night Owls	200.00	300.00
79-G-EE-1-014	Springer Spaniel/Pheasant	200.00	750.00
79-G-EE-1-015	Peregrine Falcon	200.00	750.00
79-G-EE-1-016	Canada Goose	200.00	400.00
80-G-EE-1-017	Mallards - Color	200.00	375.00
80-G-EE-1-018	Pintails	150.00	225.00
81-G-EE-1-019	California Quail	150.00	175.00
81-G-EE-1-020	Wood Duck	150.00	225.00
81-G-EE-1-021	Green Winged Teal	150.00	225.00
81-G-EE-1-022	Pheasant	150.00	175.00
Etchings, Etc.	Chapple	D. Chapple	250
82-G-EE-1-023	Jumping-Woodducks	250.00	250.00
Mill Pond Press	Clymer	J. Clymer	950
76-G-MP-1-001	Hiding Place	100.00	150.00
Wild Wings, Inc.	Clymer	J. Clymer	750
79-G-WW-1-001	By the Tundra Pond	200.00	200.00
World Art Editions, Ltd	DeWinne	L. DeWinne	950
78-G-WA-1-001	Mirelle	125.00	125.00
78-G-WA-1-002	Musicians	125.00	125.00
78-G-WA-1-003	Tom	90.00	90.00
79-G-WA-1-004	Brighter Day	140.00	140.00
79-G-WA-1-005	We Three	140.00	140.00
79-G-WA-1-006	Debra	90.00	90.00
World Art Editions, Ltd.	DeWinne	L. DeWinne	175
78-G-WA-1-007	Village Child	125.00	125.00
78-G-WA-1-008	Gypsy Mother	125.00	125.00
World Art Editions, Ltd.	DeWinne	L. DeWinne	325
79-G-WA-1-009	Scaramouche	100.00	100.00
B & J Art Designs	Hagara	J. Hagara	1,750
77-G-BJ-1-001	Hattie & the Jumeau Doll	20.00	20.00
77-G-BJ-1-002	Jason & the Rabbit	21.00	21.00
77-G-BJ-1-003	Laurie & the Pouty Doll	21.00	21.00
77-G-BJ-1-004	Marc & the Toybox	21.00	21.00
77-G-BJ-1-005	Flowers in the Can	25.00	35.00
77-G-BJ-1-006	Spring & Lance	26.00	40.00
B & J Art Designs	Hagara	J. Hagara	250 signed & numbered
77-G-BJ-1-007	Hattie & the Jumeau Doll	25.00	25.00
77-G-BJ-1-008	Jason & the Rabbit	25.00	25.00
77-G-BJ-1-009	Laurie & the Pouty Doll	25.00	25.00
77-G-BJ-1-010	Marc & the Toybox	25.00	25.00
77-G-BJ-1-011	Flowers in the Can	30.00	30.00
77-G-BJ-1-012	Spring & Lance	30.00	30.00
B & J Art Designs	Hagara	J. Hagara	600
78-G-BJ-1-013	Olivia	55.00	55.00
B & J Art Designs	Hagara	J. Hagara	1,200
78-G-BJ-1-014	Lisa	20.00	20.00
B & J Art Designs	Hagara	J. Hagara	750
79-G-BJ-1-015	Jimmy	45.00	45.00
79-G-BJ-1-016	Betsy & Her Dream Baby	45.00	45.00
B & J Art Designs	Hagara	J. Hagara	450
79-G-BJ-1-017	Adrianne & the Byelo Doll	65.00	65.00
xx-G-BJ-1-018	Storytime	125.00	125.00
Connoisseur's Gallery of Art	Hagara	J. Hagara	900
78-G-CG-1-001	Lisa & the Jumeau Doll	20.00	20.00
Connoisseur's Gallery of Art	Hagara	J. Hagara	1,200
78-G-CG-1-002	Jumeau Doll	20.00	20.00
B & J Art Designs	Hagara	J. Hagara	900
78-G-BJ-1-019	Daisies from Mary Beth	20.00	20.00
xx-G-BJ-1-020	Melanie & the Scarlet O'Hara Doll	85.00	85.00
79-G-BJ-1-021	Daisies from Jimmy	20.00	20.00
80-G-BJ-1-022	Daisies from Meg	20.00	20.00
81-G-BJ-1-023	Daisies from Mommy	20.00	20.00

Company	Series	Artist	Edition limit
Number	**Name**	**Issue Price**	**Quote**
xx-G-BJ-1-024	Cara & the Dream Baby	30.00	30.00
xx-G-BJ-1-025	Natalie	40.00	40.00
B & J Art Designs	Hagara	J. Hagara	650
xx-G-BJ-1-026	Lydia & the Shirley Temple Doll	65.00	65.00
B & J Art Designs	Hagara	J. Hagara	850
xx-G-BJ-1-027	Little Sharice	85.00	85.00
B & J Art Designs	Hagara	J. Hagara	1,000
xx-G-BJ-1-028	Victoria's Easter	50.00	50.00
xx-G-BJ-1-029	Sharice	18.00	18.00
xx-G-BJ-1-030	Parry	18.00	18.00
xx-G-BJ-1-031	Wendy	18.00	18.00
xx-G-BJ-1-032	Julie	18.00	18.00
B & J Art Designs	Hagara	J. Hagara	2,000
xx-G-BJ-1-033	Jody & the Toy Horse	45.00	45.00
xx-G-BJ-1-034	Jenny & the Byelo Doll	45.00	45.00
Roman Inc.	Hook	F. Hook	By Time
81-G-RO-1-001	The Carpenter	100.00	300.00
Roman Inc.	Hook	F. Hook	1,150
82-G-RO-1-002	Frolicking	60.00	60.00
82-G-RO-1-003	Gathering	60.00	60.00
82-G-RO-1-004	Poulets	60.00	60.00
82-G-RO-1-005	Bouquet	70.00	70.00
82-G-RO-1-006	Surprise	50.00	50.00
82-G-RO-1-007	Posing	70.00	70.00
Roman	Hook	F. Hook	open
82-G-RO-1-008	The Carpenter	50.00	50.00
Roman Inc	Hook	F. Hook	50-2,000
82-G-RO-1-009	Little Children, Come To Me	50.00	50.00
Roman Inc.	Hook	F. Hook	open
82-G-RO-1-010	Little Children, Come to Me (framed)	50.00	50.00
Roman Inc.	Hook	F. Hook	1-50
82-G-RO-1-011	Little Children, Come to Me (remarque)	100.00	100.00
Anna-Perenna	Krumeich Hector's Window	T. Krumeich	325
xx-G-AP-1-001	Stoned Lithograph	175.00	175.00
Anna-Perenna	Krumeich	T. Krumeich	995
xx-G-AP-1-002	Hector's Window Art Print	95.00	95.00
World Art Editions Ltd.	Masseria	F. Masseria	300
80-G-WA-2-001	Eduardo	275.00	1,650.00
80-G-WA-2-002	Rosanna	275.00	1,650.00
80-G-WA-2-003	Nina	325.00	800.00
80-G-WA-2-004	First Kiss	375.00	700.00
81-G-WA-2-005	Selene	325.00	750.00
81-G-WA-2-006	First Flower	325.00	800.00
81-G-WA-2-007	Elisa with Flower	325.00	650.00
81-G-WA-2-008	Solange	325.00	700.00
81-G-WA-2-009	Susan Sewing	375.00	1,000.00
81-G-WA-2-010	Jessica	375.00	700.00
81-G-WA-2-011	Eleanor	375.00	500.00
81-G-WA-2-012	Julie	375.00	500.00
82-G-WA-2-013	Robin	425.00	425.00
82-G-WA-2-014	Jodie	425.00	425.00
82-G-WA-2-015	Jill	425.00	425.00
82-G-WA-2-016	Jamie	425.00	425.00
	Masseria	F. Masseria	
82-G-FM-1-001	Yasmin	425.00	425.00
82-G-FM-1-002	Yvette	425.00	425.00
82-G-FM-1-003	Judith	425.00	425.00
82-G-FM-1-004	Amy	425.00	425.00
81-G-FM-1-005	Sipario	325.00	325.00
81-G-FM-1-006	Deposition	325.00	325.00
Reco Internat'l	McClelland	J. McClelland	300
xx-G-RI-001	Olivia	175.00	175.00
xx-G-RI-002	Sweet Dreams	145.00	145.00
xx-G-RI-003	Just for You	155.00	155.00
xx-G-RI-004	Reverie	110.00	110.00
Moss Portfolio	Moss	P. Moss	1,000
xx-G-MS-1-001	Apple Picker	30.00	70.00
xx-G-MS-1-002	Barelimbed Reflections	25.00	40.00
xx-G-MS-1-003	Becky & Tom	10.00	30.00
xx-G-MS-1-004	Canada Geese	60.00	140.00
xx-G-MS-1-005	Family Outing	65.00	150.00
xx-G-MS-1-006	Flag Boy	16.00	30.00
xx-G-MS-1-007	Four Little Girls	30.00	65.00
xx-G-MS-1-008	Frosty Frolic	75.00	300.00
xx-G-MS-1-009	Ginny & Chris with Lambs	35.00	80.00
xx-G-MS-1-010	Golden Winter	150.00	300.00
xx-G-MS-1-011	Gossip	45.00	65.00
xx-G-MS-1-012	Hungry Baby Bird	15.00	30.00
xx-G-MS-1-013	Joy	10.00	30.00
xx-G-MS-1-014	Little Fellow	57.00	90.00
xx-G-MS-1-015	Love	10.00	30.00
xx-G-MS-1-016	Mary's Lamb	75.00	200.00
xx-G-MS-1-017	Moonlit Skater	75.00	150.00
xx-G-MS-1-018	Muffet Boy I	10.00	20.00
xx-G-MS-1-019	Muffet Girl I	10.00	20.00
xx-G-MS-1-020	Orchard Helpers	75.00	200.00
xx-G-MS-1-021	Public Gardens & Beacon Street	50.00	125.00
xx-G-MS-1-022	Quilting Dreams	40.00	40.00
xx-G-MS-1-023	Reluctant Ballerina	15.00	30.00
xx-G-MS-1-024	Shenandoah Silhouette	25.00	40.00
xx-G-MS-1-025	Sisters	20.00	40.00
xx-G-MS-1-026	Skating Lesson	50.00	50.00
xx-G-MS-1-027	Snowy Birches	60.00	120.00
xx-G-MS-1-028	Spirit of Equus	100.00	100.00
xx-G-MS-1-029	Tarry Not	35.00	70.00
xx-G-MS-1-030	Wayside Inn	65.00	200.00
xx-G-MS-1-031	Wedding	80.00	200.00
xx-G-MS-1-032	Winter Cameo	30.00	60.00
xx-G-MS-1-033	Workday's O'er	110.00	180.00

Company	Series	Artist	Edition limit
Number	**Name**	**Issue Price**	**Quote**
Moss Portfolio	Moss	P. Moss	99
xx-G-MS-1-034	Together	450.00	1,000.00
Circle Fine Arts Corporation	Neiman	L.Neiman	350
xx-G-CF-1-001	Pool Room		850.00
Circle Fine Arts Corporation	Neiman	L. Neiman	275
xx-G-CF-1-002	Deuce		1,500.00
xx-G-CF-1-003	Sailing		900.00
xx-G-CF-1-004	Chipping On		900.00
Circle Fine Arts Corporation	Neiman	L. Neiman	250
xx-G-CF-1-005	In the Stretch		600.00
xx-G-CF-1-006	Punchinello		300.00
xx-G-CF-1-007	Pierrot		350.00
xx-G-CF-1-008	Harlequin with Sword		300.00
xx-G-CF-1-009	Ocelot		1,200.00
xx-G-CF-1-010	Sudden Death		1,100.00
xx-G-CF-1-011	Hommage to Boucher		700.00
xx-G-CF-1-012	12 Meter Yacht Race		900.00
Circle Fine Arts Corp.	Neiman	L. Neiman	40
xx-G-CF-1-013	Roulette		3.500.00
Circle Fine Arts Corp.	Neiman	L. Neiman	200
xx-G-CF-1-014	Pierrot the Juggler		350.00
xx-G-CF-1-015	Harlequin		325.00
xx-G-CF-1-016	Punchinello with Text		200.00
xx-G-CF-1-017	Harlequin with Text		250.00
Circle Fine Arts Corp.	Neiman	L. Nieman	300
xx-G-CG-1-018	Matchpoint		2,200.00
xx-G-CF-1-019	Tiger		2,800.00
xx-G-CF-1-020	Tennis Player		900.00
xx-G-CF-1-021	The Race		500.00
xx-G-CF-1-022	Stock Market		4,000.00
xx-G-CF-1-023	Jockey		800.00
xx-G-CF-1-024	Casino		1,000.00
xx-G-CF-1-025	Paddock		800.00
xx-G-CF-1-026	Sliding Home		750.00
xx-G-CF-1-027	Skier		600.00
xx-G-CF-1-028	Four Aces		600.00
xx-G-CF-1-029	Slalom		700.00
xx-G-CF-1-030	Leopard		4,200.00
xx-G-CF-1-031	Al Capone		500.00
xx-G-CF-1-032	Hockey Player		1,800.00
xx-G-CF-1-033	Tee Shot		1,000.00
xx-G-CF-1-034	End Around		750.00
xx-G-CF-1-035	Lion Pride		3,500.00
xx-G-CF-1-036	Marathon		750.00
xx-G-CF-1-037	Scramble		750.00
xx-G-CF-1-038	Downhill		750.00
xx-G-CF-1-039	Innsbruck		750.00
xx-G-CF-1-040	Doubles		1,500.00
xx-G-CF-1-041	Trotters		900.00
xx-G-CF-1-042	Goal		700.00
xx-G-CF-1-043	Backhand		800.00
xx-G-CF-1-044	Slapshot		900.00
xx-G-CF-1-045	Fox Hunt		800.00
xx-G-CF-1-046	Smash		1,000.00
Cirle Fine Arts Corp.	Neiman	L. Neiman	150
xx-G-CF-1-047	Baseball Player Folio:		1,600.00
	Batting Practice		
	Wind Up		
	Awaiting the Decision		
	Warm-Up Swings		
	Next at Bat		
	The Pitch		
	The Argument		
	The Umps		
	Sliding Home		
	The Hit		
xx-G-CF-1-048	Skiing Folio:		1,600.00
	Single Skier		
	Between Trees		
	Top of the Crest		
	Two Racers		
	Break Jump		
	Village in the Valley		
	House on the Slopes		
	Pine Trail		
	Three Skiers		
xx-G-CF-1-049	Hockey Folio:		1,600.00
	Face Off No. 20		
	Score No. 22		
	Fight		
	Fight with Policeman		
	Study of No. 4		
	1 Against 1 (straight shot)		
	1 Against 1 (goalie on ice)		
	Goalie Down		
	Goal No. 5		
	High Stick		
xx-G-CF-1-050	Ali-Frazier Folio:		2,500.00
	Study of Ali		
	Ali Down		
	The Introduction		
	Frazier's Corner		
	Ali's Corner		
	The Winner		
xx-G-CF-1-051	Ali-Frazier Folio:		2.500.00
	After the Fight		
	Study of Frazier & Ali		
	Rounds 1 & 2		
	Rounds 3 & 4		
	Rounds 5 & 6		
	Rounds 7 through 9		
	Rounds 10 & 11		
	Rounds 12 through 14		

Company	Series	Artist	Edition limit
Number	**Name**	**Issue Price**	**Quote**
Vague Shadows Limited	Perillo	G. Perillo	500
77-G-VS-1-001	Madre	125.00	300.00
78-G-VS-1-002	Madonna of the Plains	125.00	250.00
78-G-VS-1-003	Snow Pals	125.00	250.00
78-G-VS-1-004	Sioux Scout & Buffalo Hunt (matched set)	150.00	300.00
Vague Shadows Limited	Perillo	G. Perillo	3,000
79-G-VS-1-005	Babysitter	45.00	45.00
79-G-VS-1-006	Puppies	45.00	45.00
81-G-VS-1-007	Tinker	45.00	45.00
Vague Shadows Limited	Perillo	G. Perillo	950
80-G-VS-1-008	Tender Love	75.00	75.00
80-G-VS-1-009	Lonesome Cowboy	75.00	75.00
81-G-VS-1-010	Peaceable Kingdom	100.00	175.00
81-G-VS-1-011	Chief Pontiac	75.00	75.00
82-G-VS-1-012	Hoofbeats	75.00	75.00
82-G-VS-1-013	Indian Style	75.00	75.00
Vague Shadows Limited	Perillo	G. Perillo	550
81-G-VS-1-014	Maria	150.00	150.00
Vague Shadows Limited	Sauber	R. Sauber	3,000
82-G-VS-1-015	Butterfly	45.00	45.00
Irene Spencer	Spencer	I. Spencer	350
xx-G-IR-1-001	Hug Me	80.00	800.00
xx-G-IR-1-002	Contentment	125.00	175.00
xx-G-IR-1-003	No More Tears	125.00	210.00
Irene Spencer	Spencer	I. Spencer	25 Artist Proof
xx-G-IR-1-004	I Love You	285.00	285.00
xx-G-IR-1-005	First Edition	135.00	550.00
xx-G-IR-1-006	Precious Moment	135.00	250.00
xx-G-IR-1-007	Flower Princess	185.00	185.00
Irene Spencer	Spencer	I. Spencer	500
xx-G-IR-1-008	Storytime	95.00	600.00
xx-G-IR-1-009	Mother's Here	95.00	150.00
xx-G-IR-1-010	L'Envoi	95.00	
xx-G-IR-1-011	I Love Little Kitty	95.00	150.00
xx-G-IR-1-012	Pachamama	95.00	
xx-G-IR-1-013	Sleep Little Baby	95.00	400.00
xx-G-IR-1-014	Miracle	125.00	600.00
xx-G-IR-1-015	Empty Saddles	125.00	150.00
Irene Spencer	Spencer	I. Spencer	50
xx-G-IR-1-016	Danny's Tune	110.00	200.00
xx-G-IR-1-017	This is What It's All About	110.00	400.00
xx-G-IR-1-018	Lonesome Melody	220.00	500.00
	Smoke Dreams	55.00	2,000.00
Irene Spencer	Spencer	I. Spencer	100
xx-G-IR-1-019	Hills of Home	110.00	400.00
xx-G-IR-1-020	Summer Afternoon	110.00	300.00
xx-G-IR-1-021	Long, Long Days	110.00	450.00
xx-G-IR-1-022	Dear Child	110.00	300.00
xx-G-IR-1-023	Carefree	110.00	300.00
xx-G-IR-1-024	Yesterday, Today & Tomorrow	110.00	700.00
xx-G-IR-1-025	Larmette	110.00	700.00
xx-G-IR-1-026	Sleep Little Baby	110.00	700.00
Irene Spencer	Spencer	I. Spencer	175
xx-G-IR-1-027	My Devotion	60.00	1,000.00
Irene Spencer	Spencer	I. Spencer	275
xx-G-IR-1-028	Secrets	60.00	1,000.00
xx-G-IR-1-029	First Kiss	15.00	450.00
Irene Spencer	Spencer	I. Spencer	300
xx-G-IR-1-030	Bittersweet	150.00	500.00
Irene Spencer	Spencer	I. Spencer	400
xx-G-IR-1-031	Beyond the Sun	185.00	400.00
Irene Spencer	Spencer	I. Spencer	550
xx-G-IR-1-032	I Love You	285.00	285.00
xx-G-IR-1-033	First Edition	135.00	550.00
xx-G-IR-1-034	Precious Moment	135.00	250.00
xx-G-IR-1-035	Moon Goddess	185.00	190.00
Graphics Buying Service	Stone	F. Stone	500
79-G-GB-3-001	Mare & Foal	90.00	300.00
Graphics Buying Service	Stone	F. Stone	1,000
79-G-GB-3-004	Patience	90.00	440.00
Graphic Buying Service	Stone	F. Stone	750
79-G-GB-3-002	Affirmed, Steve Cauthen Up	100.00	300.00
Graphics Buying Service	Stone	F. Stone	500
79-G-GB-3-003	The Rivals-Affirmed & Alydar	90.00	275.00
Graphics Buying Service	Stone	F. Stone	500
79-G-GB-3-005	One, Two, Three	100.00	525.00
Graphics Buying Service	Stone	F. Stone	500
79-G-GB-3-006	The Moment After	90.00	120.00
Graphics Buying	Stone	F. Stone	500
80-G-GB-3-007	Genuine Risk	100.00	300.00
Graphic Buying Service	Stone	F. Stone	500
80-G-GB-3-008	The Belmont - Bold Forbes	100.00	150.00
Graphic Buying Service	Stone	F. Stone	750
80-G-GB-3-009	The Kentucky Derby	100.00	500.00
Graphics Buying Service	Stone	F. Stone	500
80-G-GB-3-010	The Pasture Pest	100.00	325.00
Graphic Buying Service	Stone	F. Stone	500

Company	Series	Artist	Edition limit
Number	**Name**	**Issue Price**	**Quote**
80-G-GB-3-011	Exceller - Bill Shoemaker	90.00	500.00
Graphic Buying Service	Stone	F. Stone	500
80-G-GB-3-012	Spectacular Bid	65.00	120.00
Graphic Buying Service	Stone	F. Stone	750
80-G-GB-3-013	Kidnapped Mare - Franfreluche	115.00	230.00
Graphic Buying Service	Stone	F. Stone	395
81-G-GB-3-014	The Shoe - 8,000 Wins	200.00	750.00
Graphic Buying Service	Stone	F. Stone	750
81-G-GB-3-015	The Arabians	115.00	250.00
Graphic Buying Service	Stone	F. Stone	750
81-G-GB-3-016	The Thoroughbreds	115.00	190.00
Graphic Buying Service	Stone	F. Stone	750
81-G-GB-3-017	Contentment	115.00	185.00
Graphic Buying Service	Stone	F. Stone	595
81-G-GB-3-018	John Henry	160.00	590.00
Graphic Buying Service	Stone	F. Stone	750
82-G-GB-3-019	Off and Running	125.00	165.00
Graphic Buying Service	Stone	F. Stone	750
82-G-GB-3-020	The Water Trough	125.00	190.00
Graphic Buying Service	Stone	F. Stone	750
82-G-GB-3-021	The Power Horses	125.00	125.00
Graphic Buying Service	Stone	F. Stone	750
82-G-GB-3-022	Man O' War	175.00	390.00
Graphic Buying Service	Stone	F. Stone	750
83-G-GB-3-023	For Only a Moment - Ruffian	175.00	175.00
Graphic Buying Service	Stone	F. Stone	750
83-G-GB-3-024	The Duel	150.00	150.00
Mill Pond Press	Utz	T. Utz	450
81-G-MP-1-001	Pink Lady	85.00	110.00
81-G-MP-1-002	Melanie	85.00	100.00
Mill Pond Press	Utz	T. Utz	550
81-G-MP-1-003	The Greenhouse Nude	95.00	95.00
81-G-MP-1-004	Picnic	110.00	110.00
Mill Pond Press	Utz	T. Utz	950
81-G-MP-1-005	Lavender Lace	75.00	75.00
81-G-MP-1-006	The Soft Wind	75.00	75.00
Graphics Buying Service	Vickers	M. Vickers	200
70-G-GB-4-001	Age of Innocence	40.00	325.00
70-G-GB-4-002	Brother & Sister	40.00	350.00
71-G-GB-4-003	Face in the Window	35.00	200.00
71-G-GB-4-004	Face to the Wind	40.00	250.00
71-G-GB-4-005	Guitar Sold	40.00	250.00
71-G-GB-4-006	Sharing	40.00	250.00
71-G-GB-4-007	Springtime	40.00	175.00
71-G-GB-4-008	Tender Moment	40.00	225.00
72-G-GB-4-009	Keeping Cool	35.00	125.00
72-G-GB-4-010	Wading	40.00	215.00
72-G-GB-4-011	Water Babies	70.00	350.00
73-G-GB-4-012	Autumn	60.00	225.00
73-G-GB-4-013	Flight of Fancy	50.00	200.00
74-G-GB-4-014	Climbing	50.00	150.00
74-G-GB-4-015	Love in Bloom	50.00	250.00
74-G-GB-4-016	Reflections	50.00	200.00
74-G-GB-4-017	Rocking Chair	50.00	150.00
75-G-GB-4-018	Embrace	60.00	200.00
75-G-GB-4-019	Growing Together	60.00	190.00
75-G-GB-4-020	She Loves Me	60.00	175.00
75-G-GB-4-021	String of Pearls	60.00	200.00
Graphic Buying Service	Vickers	M. Vickers	150
70-G-GB-4-022	Mother & Child	40.00	300.00
70-G-GB-4-023	Seated Child	35.00	175.00
70-G-GB-4-024	Two Children in Field	40.00	150.00
73-G-GB-4-025	Autumn Bouquet	60.00	225.00
73-G-GB-4-026	Janine	70.00	200.00
73-G-GB-4-027	Rainy Day	50.00	175.00
74-G-GB-4-028	Blue Moon	80.00	150.00
74-G-GB-4-029	October	80.00	225.00
74-G-GB-4-030	Waiting for Daddy	50.00	235.00
74-G-GB-4-031	Yesterday's Tomorrow	80.00	250.00
75-G-GB-4-032	Alice	50.00	150.00
75-G-GB-4-033	Cameo	30.00	150.00
75-G-GB-4-034	Caroline	35.00	150.00
75-G-GB-4-035	Engagement	90.00	250.00
75-G-GB-4-036	Grace	30.00	125.00
Graphic Buying Service	Vickers	M. Vickers	25
72-G-GB-4-037	Patience	25.00	125.00
Graphic Buying Service	Vickers	M. Vickers	75
72-G-GB-4-038	Is Lunch Ready Mom?	60.00	200.00
Graphic Buying Service	Vickers	M. Vickers	100
72-G-GB-4-039	Lovers	50.00	150.00
73-G-GB-4-040	Breath of Spring	50.00	250.00
73-G-GB-4-041	June	30.00	125.00
73-G-GB-4-042	April	30.00	125.00
73-G-GB-4-043	May	30.00	125.00
73-G-GB-4-044	Tattered Herd	60.00	235.00
73-G-GB-4-045	Three's a Crowd	50.00	200.00
73-G-GB-4-046	Together We're Stronger	40.00	150.00
Graphic Buying Service	Vickers	M. Vickers	250
73-G-GB-4-047	Piggy Back	60.00	250.00
76-G-GB-4-048	Spring Bonnets	50.00	150.00

Category: Graphics

Company	Series	Artist	Edition limit
Number	**Name**	**Issue Price**	**Quote**
76-G-GB-4-049	Sunshine 'n Sand	60.00	200.00
76-G-GB-4-050	Sweet Nothings	60.00	200.00
76-G-GB-4-051	Tulips	100.00	325.00
77-G-GB-4-052	Patience	70.00	150.00
Graphics Buying	Vickers	M. Vickers	175
75-G-GB-4-053	Hide 'n Seek	75.00	175.00
76-G-GB-4-054	Good Times	90.00	225.00
77-G-GB-4-055	All Mine	40.00	100.00
77-G-GB-4-056	Gay	38.00	125.00
77-G-GB-4-057	Letter from Daddy	70.00	125.00
77-G-GB-4-058	Little Girls are Made Of	65.00	125.00
Graphic Buying Service	Vickers	M. Vickers	275
78-G-GB-4-059	Attic Treasures	200.00	300.00
Graphic Buying Service	Vickers	M. Vickers	350
80-G-GB-4-060	Mary Rose	90.00	425.00
Frame House Gallery	Weighorst	O. Weighorst	1,500
72-G-FH-1-001	Navajo Madonna	40.00	1,000.00
American Legacy	Weighorst	O. Weighorst	500
78-G-AL-1-001	Drifting	125.00	900.00
78-G-AL-1-002	The Lost Trail	125.00	125.00
78-G-AL-1-003	Talking Sign	125.00	125.00
78-G-AL-1-004	Horse Wranglers	125.00	125.00
78-G-AL-1-005	Apache Renegade	125.00	125.00
78-G-AL-1-006	Mogollon Trail	125.00	125.00
79-G-AL-1-007	Indian Trail	125.00	125.00
79-G-AL-1-008	Arizona Range	125.00	125.00
79-G-AL-1-009	Indian Scout	125.00	900.00
79-G-AL-1-010	Water Ahead	125.00	400.00
79-G-AL-1-011	Cow Country	125.00	125.00
79-G-AL-1-012	Pleasant Creek	125.00	250.00
79-G-AL-1-013	Range Ponies	125.00	125.00
79 G AL 1 014	Range Chuck	125.00	250.00
American Legacy Ltd	Weighorst	O. Weighorst	50 artist proof
78-G-AL-1-015	Drifting	125.00	200.00
78-G-AL-1-016	The Lost Trail	125.00	200.00
78-G-AL-1-017	Talking Sign	125.00	200.00
78-G-AL-1-018	Horse Wranglers	125.00	200.00
78-G-AL-1-019	Apache Renegade	125.00	200.00
78-G-AL-1-020	Mogollon Trail	125.00	200.00
79-G-AL-1-021	Indian Trail	125.00	200.00
79-G-AL-1-022	Arizona Range	125.00	200.00
79-G-AL-1-023	Indian Scout	125.00	200.00
79-G-AL-1-024	Water Ahead	125.00	200.00
79-G-AL-1-025	Cow Country	125.00	200.00
79-G-AL-1-026	Pleasant Creek	125.00	300.00
79-G-AL-1-027	Range Ponies	125.00	200.00
79-G-AL-1-028	Range Chuck	125.00	200.00
American Legacy	Weighorst	O. Weighorst	900
80-G-AL-1-029	Dead Cottonwood	150.00	150.00
80-G-AL-1-030	Tired	150.00	150.00
80-G-AL-1-031	Chief Sioux Hump	150.00	150.00
American Legacy	Weighorst	O. Weighorst	999
80-G-AL-1-032	Nighthawk	150.00	150.00
80-G-AL-1-033	Los Charros	150.00	150.00
American Legacy	Weighorst	O. Weighorst	1,000
80-G-AL-1-034	Wagon & Remuda	150.00	150.00
Wooden Bird	Weighorst	O. Weighorst	900
82-G-WB-1-001	Salt River Canyon	150.00	150.00
82-G-WB-1-002	Rocky Mountain Trail	150.00	150.00
82-G-WB-1-003	Navajo at Castle Creek	150.00	150.00
82-G-WB-1-004	Canyon Trail	150.00	150.00
82-G-WB-1-005	Watering the Remuda	150.00	150.00
82-G-WB-1-006	Moonlight & Shadows	150.00	150.00
Wooden Bird	Weighorst	O. Weighorst	90 artist proof
82-G-WB-1-007	Salt River Canyon	150.00	250.00
82-G-WB-1-008	Rocky Mountain Trail	150.00	250.00
82-G-WB-1-009	Navajo at Castle Creek	150.00	250.00
82-G-WB-1-010	Canyon Trail	150.00	250.00
82-G-WB-1-011	Watering the Remuda	150.00	250.00
82-G-WB-1-012	Moonlight & Shadows	150.00	250.00
distributor Armstrong's	Various	O. Weighorst	1,000
xx-G-AR-1-001	Navajo Portrait	75.00	150.00
xx-G-AR-1-002	Buffalo Scout	100.00	350.00
xx-G-AR-1-003	California Wrangler	100.00	200.00
xx-G-AR-1-004	Missing in the Roundup	100.00	200.00
xx-G-AR-1-005	Packing In	100.00	200.00
xx-G-AR-1-006	Corralling the Cavvy	100.00	200.00
xx-G-AR-1-007	Boys in the Bunkhouse	150.00	200.00
U.S. Historical Society	Yorktown Prints	J. Woodson	575
81-G-US-1-001	Battle of Virginia Capes	200.00	275.00
81-G-US-1-002	George Washington Fires the First Round at Yorktown	200.00	275.00
81-G-US-1-003	Historical Map of Yorktown	200.00	275.00
Greenwich Workshop	Wysocki	C. Wysocki	1,000
79-G-GW-1-001	Fox Run	75.00	75.00
79-G-GW-1-002	Butternut Farms	75.00	75.00
79-G-GW-1-003	Shall We?	75.00	75.00
79-G-GW-1-004	Fairhaven by the Sea	75.00	75.00
80-G-GW-1-005	Jolly HIll Arms	75.00	120.00
80-G-GW-1-006	Derby Square	90.00	130.00
80-G-GW-1-007	Caleb's Buggy Barn	80.00	80.00
80-G-GW-1-008	Yankee Wine Hollow	95.00	95.00
81-G-GW-1-009	Page's Bake Shop	115.00	115.00
81-G-GW-1-010	Prairie Wind Flowers	125.00	125.00
81-G-GW-1-011	Carver Coggins	145.00	145.00
82-G-GW-1-012	Sunset Hills Texas Wildcatters	125.00	125.00
82-G-GW-1-013	Nantucket	145.00	145.00

Category:Steins

Company	Series	Artist	Edition limit
Number	**Name**	**Issue Price**	**Quote**
Greenwich Workshop	Wysocki	C. Wysocki	1,500
81-G-GW-1-014	Olde America	125.00	125.00
82-G-GW-1-015	Sleepy Town West	150.00	150.00
Greenwich Workshop	Wysocki	C. Wysocki	2,000
82-G-GW-1-016	The 1982 Greenwich Workshop, Christmas Print	80.00	80.00
Mill Pond Press	Zemsky	J. Zemsky	950
79-G-MP-2-001	When the Then & The Now Hold Hands	65.00	100.00
79-G-MP-2-002	Jordan's Dolly	65.00	65.00
79-G-MP-2-003	Love at First Sight	75.00	75.00
79-G-MP-2-004	Come See the New Colt	65.00	65.00
79-G-MP-2-005	Jordan at the Wedding	65.00	65.00
Pemberton & Oakes	Zolan's Children	D. Zolan	880
82-G-PO-1-001	Erik & Dandelion	98.00	98.00
83-G-PO-1-002	By Myself	98.00	98.00
Graphic Buying Service	D. Zolan	D. Zolan	485
80-G-GB-5-001	Sabina's Delight	135.00	140.00
Graphic Buying Service	D. Zolan	D. Zolan	485
80-G-GB-5-002	Special Moments	135.00	135.00
Graphic Buying Service	D. Zolan	D. Zolan	950
82-G-GB-5-003	Petit Fleur	95.00	95.00
Graphic Buying Service	D. Zolan	D. Zolan	475
82-G-GB-5-004	Flowers for Grandma	135.00	135.00
Graphic Buying Service	R. Zolan	R. Zolan	495
80-G-GB-5-001	The Rehearsal	105.00	115.00
Graphic Buying Service	R. Zolan	R. Zolan	450
81-G-GB-5-002	Cora's Recital	125.00	130.00
Graphic Buying Service	R. Zolan	R. Zolan	450
82-G-GB-5-003	Christi's Kitty	125.00	125.00

Category:Steins

Company / Number	Series / Name	Artist / Issue Price	Edition limit / Quote
Gorham	Various	N. Rockwell	9,800
76-S-GO-1-001	Pride of Parenthood	25.00	25.00
77-S-GO-1-002	Boy Meets His Dog	25.00	25.00
78-S-GO-1-003	The Mysterious Malady	27.50	27.50
79-S-GO-1-004	Adventurers Between Adventures	27.50	27.50
80-S-GO-1-005	Going Fishing	32.50	32.50
81-S-GO-1-006	Day Dreamers	35.00	35.00
82-S-GO-1-007	Pensive Pals	37.50	37.50
83-S-GO-1-008	Gay Blades	37.50	37.50
Norman Rockwell Museum, Inc.	Limited Edition Collector Steins	N. Rockwell	9,900
80-S-NR-1-001	Looking Out to Sea	125.00	125.00
81-S-NR-1-002	For A Good Boy	125.00	125.00
82-S-NR-1-003	The Music Lesson	125.00	125.00
82-S-NR-1-004	Braving the Storm	125.00	125.00
83-S-NR-1-005	Fishin' Pals	125.00	125.00
Opa's Haus	Annual Limited Edition		Year of issue
74-S-OH-1-001	Annual Stein		Sold out
75-S-OH-1-002	Annual Stein		Sold out
76-S-OH-1-003	Annual Stein		Sold out
77-S-OH-1-004	Annual Stein		Sold out
78-S-OH-1-005	Annual Stein		Sold out
79-S-OH-1-006	Annual Stein		Sold out
80-S-OH-1-007	Annual Stein		Sold out
81-S-OH-1-008	Annual Stein		118.00
82-S-OH-1-009	Annual Stein		118.00
83-S-OH-1-010	Annual Stein		118.00
Opa's Haus	Miscellaneous Reproductions		5,000
78-S-OH-2-001	The Jousting Tankard		335.00
82-S-OH-2-002	The Herring Stein		175.00
Opa's Haus	Oldie		5,000
80-S-OH-3-001	Beer Here		75.00
80-S-OH-3-002	Bicycle		110.00
80-S-OH-3-003	Railway		70.00
80-S-OH-3-004	Thewalt Commorative		50.00
80-S-OH-3-005	Physician		120.00
80-S-OH-3-006	Pharmacist		55.00
83-S-OH-3-007	Gymnastics		75.00
Opa's Haus	Master Worker		5,000
81-S-OH-4-001	Creussen Apostle		1060.00
Opa's Haus	Commissioned Reproduction		1,000
82-S-OH-5-001	The Festival Stein	79.00	79.00
Opa's Haus	Prussian Style Regimental Reproductions	Cardinales	5,000
82-S-OH-6-001	10th Field Artillery Scharnhorst		165.00
82-S-OH-6-002	14th cavalry, Cassel		165.00
82-S-OH-6-003	Pioneer Regiment, Schoeneberg		165.00
82-S-OH-6-004	3rd Grenadier, Charlottenburg		165.00
Opa's Haus	American Wildlife	Pat Ford	1,950
83-S-OH-7-001	Night Stalker	110.00	110.00
83-S-OH-7-002	Explosion in the Marsh	110.00	110.00
83-S-OH-7-003	Time to Scatter !	110.00	110.00
Opa's Haus	Master Worker		To Be Announced
83-S-OH-8-001	18th Century Faience		To Be Announced

Company	Series	Artist	Edition limit
Number	Name	Issue Price	Quote
Villeroy & Boch	Fairytale	R. Faure	
82-S-VB-1-001	Peter Pan	195.00	195.00
82-S-VB-1-002	Hansel & Gretel	195.00	195.00
82-S-VB-1-003	Pied Piper of Hamlin	195.00	195.00
82-S-VB-1-004	Pinocchio	195.00	195.00
Villeroy & Boch	Four Seasons	J. Van Zundert	10,000
82-S-VB-2-001	Spring	275.00	275.00
82-S-VB-2-002	Summer	275.00	275.00
82-S-VB-2-003	Fall	275.00	275.00
82-S-VB-2-004	Winter	275.00	275.00
Villeroy & Boch	Famous Sea Battles	J. Van Zundert	Year of Issue
82-S-VB-3-001	Battle of Trafalgar	130.00	130.00
82-S-VB-3-002	Battle of Flamborough Head	130.00	130.00
82-S-VB-3-003	Battle of Lepanto 1571	130.00	130.00

Company	Series	Artist	Edition limit
Number	Name	Issue Price	Quote

Number	Name (# Produced)	Issue Price	Quote
Company	Series	Artist	Edition limit
Boehm		Boehm	
BIRDS			
57-F-BH-9-001	American Eagle, large(31)	225.00	11000.00
57-F-BH-9-002	American Eagle, Small(76)	225.00	9200.00
58-F-BH-9-003	American Redstarts(500)	350.00	2000.00
80-F-BH-9-004	Artic Tern(350)	1400.00	2100.00
69-F-BH-9-005	Black-headed Grosbeak (675)	1250.00	1525.00
56-F-BH-9-006	Black-tailed Bantams, pair (57)	350.00	4700.00
58-F-BH-9-007	Black-throated Blue Warbler (500)	400.00	1875.00
76-F-BH-9-008	Black-throated Blue Warbler (200)	900.00	1100.00
67-F-BH-9-009	Blue Grosbeak (750)	1050.00	1500.00
62-F-BH-9-010	Blue Jays, pair (250)	2000.00	12750.00
64-F-BH-9-011	Bobolink (500)	550.00	1550.00
53-F-BH-9-012	Bob White Quail, pair (750)	400.00	2600.00
72-F-BH-9-013	Brown Pelican (100)	10500.00	14500.00
73-F-BH-9-014	Brown Thrasher (260)	1850.00	1875.00
72-F-BH-9-015	Cactus Wren (225)	3000.00	3300.00
57-F-BH-9-016	California Quail, pair (500)	400.00	2900.00
78-F-BH-9-017	Canada Geese, pair (100)	4200.00	4200.00
77-F-BH-9-018	Cape May Warbler (400)	825.00	950.00
55-F-BH-9-019	Cardinals, pair (500)	550.00	3750.00
77-F-BH-9-020	Cardinals (200)	3500.00	3500.00
57-F-BH-9-021	Carolina Wrens (100)	750.00	5500.00
65-F-BH-9-022	Catbird (500)	900.00	2135.00
56-F-BH-9-023	Cedar Waxwings, pair (100)	600.00	7750.00
57-F-BH-9-024	Cerulean Warblers (100)	800.00	4335.00
68-F-BH-9-025	Common Tern (500)	1400.00	6200.00
67-F-BH-9-026	Crested Flycatcher (500)	1650.00	2925.00
57-F-BH-9-027	Downy Woodpeckers (500)	450.00	1775.00
76-F-BH-9-028	Eagle of Freedom I (15)	35000.00	53000.00
59-F-BH-9-029	Eastern Bluebirds, pair (100)	1800.00	12000.00
75-F-BH-9-030	Eastern Kingbird (100)	3500.00	3900.00
73-F-BH-9-031	Everglade Kites (50)	5800.00	7000.00
77-F-BH-9-032	Fledgling Brown Thrashers (400)	500.00	655.00
67-F-BH-9-033	Fledgling Canada Warbler (750)	550.00	2275.00
65-F-BH-9-034	Fledgling Great Horned Owl (750)	350.00	1475.00
71-F-BH-9-035	Flicker (250)	2400.00	2950.00
56-F-BH-9-036	Golden-crowned Kinglets (500)	400.00	2400.00
54-F-BH-9-037	Golden Pheasant, decorated (7)	350.00	19000.00
54-F-BH-9-038	Golden Pheasant, bisque (7)	200.00	11250.00
61-F-BH-9-039	Goldfinches (500)	400.00	1800.00
66-F-BH-9-040	Green Jays, pair (400)	1850.00	4200.00
74-F-BH-9-041	Hooded Warbler (100)	2400.00	3150.00
73-F-BH-9-042	Horned Larks (200)	3800.00	4200.00
68-F-BH-9-043	Kestrels, pair (460)	2300.00	3000.00
64-F-BH-9-044	Killdeer, pair (300)	1750.00	4500.00
74-F-BH-9-045	Lark Sparrow (150)	2100.00	2200.00
73-F-BH-9-046	Lazuli Buntings (250)	1800.00	2300.00
79-F-BH-9-047	Least Tern (350)	1275.00	2950.00
62-F-BH-9-048	Lesser Prairie Chickens pair (300)	1200.00	2400.00
52-F-BH-9-049	Mallards, pair (500)	650.00	1700.00
57-F-BH-9-050	Meadowlark (750)	350.00	3100.00
63-F-BH-9-051	Mearns' Quail, pair(350)	950.00	3450.00
68-F-BH-9-052	Mergansers, pair (440)	2200.00	2825.00
61-F-BH-9-053	Mockingbirds, pair (500)	650.00	3800.00
78-F-BH-9-054	Mockingbirds	2200.00	2800.00
63-F-BH-9-055	Mountain Bluebirds(300)	1900.00	5850.00
58-F-BH-9-056	Mourning Doves (500)	550.00	1250.00
71-F-BH-9-057	Mute Swans, Life-size, pair (3)	Unknown	Unknown
71-F-BH-9-058	Mute Swans, small size, pair (400)	4000.00	7900.00
74-F-BH-9-059	Myrtle Warblers (210)	1850.00	2075.00
58-F-BH-9-060	Nonpareil Buntings (750)	250.00	1075.00
67-F-BH-9-061	Northern Water Thrush (500)	800.00	1400.00
70-F-BH-9-062	Orchard Orioles (550)	1750.00	2200.00
70-F-BH-9-063	Oven-bird (450)	1400.00	1800.00
65-F-BH-9-064	Parula Warblers (400)	1500.00	3150.00
75-F-BH-9-065	Pekin Robins (100)	7000.00	8550.00
62-F-BH-9-066	Ptarmigan, pair (350)	800.00	3575.00
74-F-BH-9-067	Purple Martins (50)	6700.00	8450.00
75-F-BH-9-068	Red-billed Blue Magpie (100)	4600.00	5950.00
57-F-BH-9-069	Red-winged Blackbirds, pair (100)	700.00	5250.00
54-F-BH-9-070	Ringed-necked Pheasants, pair (500)	650.00	1825.00
68-F-BH-9-071	Roadrunner (500)	2600.00	3700.00
64-F-BH-9-072	Robin (Daffodils)(500)	600.00	5700.00
77-F-BH-9-073	Robin (nest) (350)	1650.00	1840.00
60-F-BH-9-074	Ruffed Grouse, pair (250)	950.00	4950.00
66-F-BH-9-075	Rufous Hummingbirds(500)	850.00	1900.00
77-F-BH-9-076	Scarlet Tanager(4)	1800.00	4000.00
77-F-BH-9-077	Scissor-tailed Flycatcher (100)	3200.00	3200.00
79-F-BH-9-078	Scops Owl (300)	975.00	1135.00
80-F-BH-9-079	Screech Owl (350)	2100.00	2825.00
70-F-BH-9-080	Slate-colored Junco	1600.00	2000.00
81-F-BH-9-081	Snow Buntings (350)	2400.00	2640.00
56-F-BH-9-082	Song Sparrows, pair (50)	2000.00	38000.00
61-F-BH-9-083	Sugarbirds (100)	2500.00	13250.00
63-F-BH-9-084	Towhee (500)	350.00	2600.00
65-F-BH-9-085	Tufted Titmice (500)	600.00	2000.00
65-F-BH-9-086	Varied Buntings (300)	2200.00	4500.00
74-F-BH-9-087	Varied Thrush	2500.00	3000.00
69-F-BH-9-088	Verdins (575)	1150.00	1525.00
69-F-BH-9-089	Western Bluebirds(300)	5500.00	6600.00
71-F-BH-9-090	Western Meadowlark(350)	1425.00	1675.00
54-F-BH-9-091	Woodcock (500)	300.00	1950.00
51-F-BH-9-092	Wood Thrush (2)	375.00	-
66-F-BH-9-093	Wood Thrushes, pair(400)	4200.00	8400.00
72-F-BH-9-094	Yellow-bellied sapsucker	2700.00	3200.00
74-F-BH-9-095	Yellow-bellied Cuckoo	2800.00	3000.00
74-F-BH-9-096	Yellow-headed Blackbird (75)	3200.00	3600.00
73-F-BH-9-097	Young American Eagle, Inaugural (100)	1500.00	2100.00
69-F-BH-9-098	Young American Eagle (850)	700.00	1400.00
75-F-BH-9-099	"Young & Spirited 1976" (1121)	950.00	1550.00
79-F-BH-9-100	Avocet (175)	1200.00	1200.00
72-F-BH-9-101	Barn Owl (350)	3600.00	5450.00
73-F-BH-9-102	Blackbirds, pair(75)	5400.00	6300.00
72-F-BH-9-103	Black Grouse (175)	2800.00	3025.00
73-F-BH-9-104	Blue Tits (300)	3000.00	3000.00
74-F-BH-9-105	Chaffinch (125)	2000.00	2200.00
74-F-BH-9-106	Crested Tit (400)	1150.00	1250.00
75-F-BH-9-107	Eurpoean Goldfinch(225)	1150.00	1300.00
72-F-BH-9-108	Goldcrest (500)	650.00	1200.00
73-F-BH-9-109	Green Woodpeckers (50)	4200.00	4800.00
79-F-BH-9-110	Grey Wagtail (150)	1050.00	1260.00
76-F-BH-9-111	Kingfishers (200)	1900.00	2220.00
73-F-BH-9-112	Lapwing (100)	2600.00	2975.00
71-F-BH-9-113	Little Owl (350)	700.00	1325.00
73-F-BH-9-114	Long Tail Tits(200)	2600.00	2900.00
71-F-BH-9-115	Nuthatch (350)	650.00	1100.00
73-F-BH-9-116	Peregrine Falcon(350)	4400.00	5450.00
76-F-BH-9-117	Rivoli's Hummingbird (350)	950.00	1425.00
74-F-BH-9-118	Ruby-throated Hummingbird (200)	1900.00	2650.00
73-F-BH-9-119	Screech Owl (500)	850.00	1425.00
74-F-BH-9-120	Song Thrushes (100)	2800.00	3350.00
74-F-BH-9-121	Stonechats (150)	2200.00	2400.00
74-F-BH-9-122	Swallows (125)	3400.00	4100.00
72-F-BH-9-123	Tree Creepers (200)	3200.00	3875.00
71-F-BH-9-124	Winter Robin (225)	1150.00	1440.00
73-F-BH-9-125	Yellowhammers (350)	3300.00	4100.00
ANIMALS			
69-F-BH-9-126	Adios (130)	1500.00	1800.00
52-F-BH-9-127	Hunter (250)	600.00	1300.00
57-F-BH-9-128	Polo Player (100)	850.00	4450.00
78-F-BH-9-129	Thoroughbred with Jockey (25)	2600.00	2800.00
77-F-BH-9-130	African Elephant(50)	9500.00	14400.00
76-F-BH-9-131	American Mustangs(75)	3700.00	5700.00
80-F-BH-9-132	Asian Lion (100)	1500.00	1500.00
78-F-BH-9-133	Black Rhinoceros (50)	9500.00	9500.00
71-F-BH-9-134	Bobcats (200)	1600.00	2000.00
78-F-BH-9-135	Camel & Calf (50)	3500.00	3700.00
80-F-BH-9-136	Cheetah (100)	2700.00	2700.00
79-F-BH-9-137	Fallow Deer (30)	7500.00	7500.00
71-F-BH-9-138	Foxes (200)	1800.00	2550.00
75-F-BH-9-139	Giant Panda (100)	3800.00	6350.00
78-F-BH-9-140	Gorilla (50)	3800.00	4400.00
79-F-BH-9-141	Hunter Chase (20)	4000.00	4000.00
73-F-BH-9-142	Nyala Antelope (100)	4700.00	6300.00
76-F-BH-9-143	Otter (75)	1100.00	1450.00
75-F-BH-9-144	Puma (50)	5700.00	6800.00
71-F-BH-9-145	Raccoons (200)	1600.00	2250.00
72-F-BH-9-146	Red Squirrels (100)	2600.00	2800.00
78-F-BH-9-147	Snow Leopard (75)	3500.00	4690.00
79-F-BH-9-148	Young & Free Fawns(160)	1875.00	1875.00
FLOWERS			
79-F-BH-9-149	Cactus Dahlia (300)	800.00	960.00
72-F-BH-9-150	Chrysanthemums (350)	1100.00	1950.00
71-F-BH-9-151	Daisies (350)	600.00	975.00
74-F-BH-9-152	Debutante Camellia(500)	625.00	800.00
73-F-BH-9-153	Dogwood (250)	625.00	975.00
78-F-BH-9-154	Double Clematis Centerpiece (150)	1500.00	1750.00
74-F-BH-9-155	Double Peony (275)	575.00	975.00
75-F-BH-9-156	Emmett Barnes Camellia (425)	550.00	780.00
74-F-BH-9-157	Gentians (350)	425.00	725.00
79-F-BH-9-158	Grand Floral Centerpiece (15)	7500.00	8700.00
78-F-BH-9-159	Helen Boehm Camellia (500)	600.00	1050.00
78-F-BH-9-160	Helen Boehm Daylily(175)	975.00	1160.00
78-F-BH-9-161	Helen Boehm Iris (175)	975.00	1175.00
79-F-BH-9-162	Honeysuckle (200)	900.00	1080.00
75-F-BH-9-163	Magnolia Grandiflora (750)	650.00	1350.00
76-F-BH-9-164	Orchid Cactus (100)	650.00	975.00
76-F-BH-9-165	Queen of the Night Cactus (125)	650.00	850.00
78-F-BH-9-166	Rhododendron Centerpiece (350)	1150.00	1750.00
80-F-BH-9-167	Rose, Alec's Red (500)	1050.00	1300.00
78-F-BH-9-168	Rose, Blue Moon (500)	650.00	835.00
78-F-BH-9-169	Rose, Pascali (500)	950.00	1375.00
76-F-BH-9-170	Rose, Supreme Peace(250)	850.00	1575.00
76-F-BH-9-171	Rose, Supreme Yellow (250)	850.00	1575.00
78-F-BH-9-172	Rose, Tropicana (500)	475.00	1085.00
78-F-BH-9-173	Spanish Iris (500)	600.00	600.00
73-F-BH-9-174	Streptocalyx Poeppigii (50)	3400.00	4300.00
71-F-BH-9-175	Swan Centerpiece (135)	1950.00	2725.00
76-F-BH-9-176	Swan Lake Camellia (750)	825.00	1725.00
71-F-BH-9-177	Sweet Viburnum (35)	650.00	1425.00
74-F-BH-9-178	Waterlily (350)	400.00	660.00
78-F-BH-9-179	Watsonii Magnolia(250)	575.00	690.00
OTHER			
77-F-BH-9-180	Beverly Sills (100)	950.00	1050.00
77-F-BH-9-181	Jerome Hines (12)	825.00	1000.00